Family Life and Family Policies in Europe

Volume I

Family Life and Family Policies in Europe

Volume I

Structures and Trends in the 1980s

Edited by

FRANZ-XAVER KAUFMANN

ANTON KUIJSTEN

HANS-JOACHIM SCHULZE

KLAUS PETER STROHMEIER

CLARENDON PRESS · OXFORD

1997

Oxford University Press, Great Clarendon Street, Oxford OX2 6DP

Oxford New York
Athens Auckland Bangkok Bogota Bombay
Buenos Aires Calcutta Cape Town Dar es Salaam
Delhi Florence Hong Kong Istanbul Karachi
Kuala Lumpur Madras Madrid Melbourne
Mexico City Nairobi Paris Singapore
Taipei Tokyo Toronto Warsaw
and associated companies in
Berlin Ibadan

Oxford is a trade mark of Oxford University Press

Published in the United States by
Oxford University Press Inc., New York

© Franz-Xaver Kaufmann, Anton Kuijsten,
Hans-Joachim Schulze, and Klaus Peter Strohmeier 1997

The moral rights of the authors have been asserted

British Library Cataloguing in Publication Data
Data available

Library of Congress Cataloging in Publication Data
Data available
ISBN 0-19-823327-2

1 3 5 7 9 10 8 6 4 2

Typeset by the authors
Printed in Great Britain
on acid-free paper by
Bookcraft Ltd, Midsomer Norton

Preface

International comparative social scientific research is a challenging endeavour, especially in Europe, where the long-standing diversity of nations and countries has created a kind of natural laboratory situation for comparative analysis. The results may be particularly rewarding when such comparative research deals with a topic such as the family, in which policy is at stake. At a time when Europe is striving for economic and political unification, policy harmonization has become a hot issue on political agendas. But to what extent is the existing between-country variation in structural features of families and everyday family life compatible with harmonization of policies with respect to, or with relevance for, families and living arrangements?

This is the underlying question addressed in this book and in its forthcoming companion volume. The attempt to answer the question will be made by an international team of experts, which has worked with a model of cross-national or cross-cultural research that, back in the early 1970s, Stein Rokkan identified as the strongest possible model,[1] and that was also used in the 1980s by the Vienna Centre in its research project on changing patterns of European family life: the model of co-operative cross-national study. This involves international co-operation at each step of the research process, the conception of the problem and the construction of the research instruments being the result of the discussions of the several national researchers involved, the data collection and analysis being done by the national researchers in their own countries using one common research instrument, and interpretation and analysis being done nationally as well as internationally.[2]

The initiative for this research project was taken by Klaus Peter Strohmeier and Franz-Xaver Kaufmann, at the University of Bielefeld, Germany, in the early 1990s. The 'personnel infrastructure' (with only a few extensions)

[1] S. Rokkan, 'Cross-cultural, Cross-societal and Cross-national Research', in *Main Trends of Research in the Social and Human Sciences*, Part I, Paris, UNESCO, 1970: 645–89. Rokkan's typology of models of gathering information and analysis of data across a number of distinct cultures, societies or nations was based on a cross-classification according to two major organizational dimensions: the number of nations from which or about which data are gathered, and the number of countries from which participants in the research are recruited.

[2] See M. Bak, 'Methodological and Organisational Considerations', in K. Boh *et al.* (eds.), *Changing Patterns of European Family Life: a Comparative Analysis of 14 European Countries*, London and New York, Routledge, 1989: 299–314, esp. 304–5.

of the research has been derived from the 'Demography and Social Change' research network initiated and directed by Dirk van de Kaa and Hans-Joachim Hoffmann-Nowotny, on behalf of the European Science Foundation. Participants' reports cover the following countries in Europe: Denmark, France, the Federal Republic of Germany, the former German Democratic Republic, Great Britain, Ireland, Italy, the Netherlands, Sweden, and Switzerland. Eastern Europe appears systematically underrepresented. Because of the war in the former Yugoslavia, co-operation with institutes in that country could not be continued, and co-operation with a Polish institute ceased because of insufficient data. Apart from that, the international research team as it was formed in 1991 remained more or less intact over the years, with only two people (Jaap Visser from the Netherlands and Kathleen Kiernan from Great Britain) having to withdraw, for various reasons.

This first volume contains chapters on the ten countries mentioned, with the 'late' Federal Republic of Germany and the former German Democratic Republic (as the only 'Eastern' country) counted as two. It is based on the country reports delivered by the members of the international research group. Subsequent drafts of these country reports were discussed intensively at a series of four workshops in Lemgo and Werther (both close to Bielefeld) and in Bonn-Bad Godesberg, which were made possible through funding by the Federal Ministry of the Family and the Elderly in Bonn, and by the Institute for Population Research and Social Policy at Bielefeld University. We are deeply indebted to all the authors for the patience and helpfulness with which they tried to meet all our demands in the final editing phase. Thanks to their efforts, we managed to achieve the common layout of all country chapters that was envisaged at the start of the research project. Some of these authors will also contribute to the forthcoming second volume of this book, which will focus on *comparative analyses and integrating perspectives*.

Most of the editing of this volume was done in Amsterdam. We are most grateful to Evelien van der Ploeg and Ingrid van Zelm (University of Amsterdam) for their skilful assistance with the preparation of the manuscript and to Regina van Groningen (Free University of Amsterdam) for preparing the graphs. The editing work on this volume was finalized by Anton Kuijsten while he was a Fellow-in-residence at the Netherlands Institute for Advanced Study in the Humanities and Social Sciences (NIAS) in Wassenaar.

F-X. Kaufmann, A. Kuijsten,
H-J. Schulze, K.P. Strohmeier

Contents

List of Figures

List of Tables

List of Contributors

Lynda Clarke	London School of Hygiene and Tropical Medicine and Family Policy Studies Centre, London
Gero Federkeil	Wissenschaftsrat, Cologne
Beat Fux	University of Zürich
Melanie Henwood	Independent Social Policy Analyst, Northamptonshire, UK
Franz-Xaver Kaufmann	Bielefeld University, Germany
Finola Kennedy	Institute of Public Administration, Dublin
Lisbeth B. Knudsen	Danmarks Statistik, Copenhagen
Anton Kuijsten	University of Amsterdam
Kevin McCormack	Central Statistics Office, Dublin
Tuija Meisaari-Polsa	Statistiska Centralbyrån, Stockholm
Adele Menniti	Institute for Population Research (IRP), Rome
Béatrice Muller-Escoda	Université d'Evry, Val d'Essonne, France
Rossella Palomba	Institute for Population Research (IRP), Rome
Linda Laura Sabbadini	National Statistical Institute, Rome
Hans-Joachim Schulze	Free University of Amsterdam
Klaus Peter Strohmeier	Ruhr-Universität, Bochum, Germany
Ulla Vogt	Northrhine-Westfalia Research Group Public Health, Bielefeld University, Germany
Hartmut Wendt	Bundesamt für die Anerkennung ausländischer Flüchtlinge, Nuremburg, Germany

1 Family Life and Family Policies in Europe: an Introduction

KLAUS PETER STROHMEIER and ANTON KUIJSTEN

Ruhr-Universität, Bochum, Germany, and University of Amsterdam, Amsterdam, the Netherlands

1.1. Introduction

'Individualization' is a term commonly used in the current sociological literature to denote the new 'horizontal' inequalities in modern society, i.e. differentiations in terms of the organization of private life and of 'life-style'. In a stricter scientific use of the concept, it means the emancipation of the individual life course from traditional determining influences of factors such as gender or social and regional origin. It implies an increasing possibility for everyone to lead his or her 'own life'. Individualization in that sense has reached women only after some delay, and it operates along cohort lines, with stronger effects on the younger generations. In this process there is an observable increase in the variation of significant life events over the life course, e.g. marriage or the birth of the first child, with respect to both their timing and their incidence. The resulting increase of the individual's degrees of freedom to choose between distinct biographic options has, on the whole, transformed the status of the family from a self-evident institution in a 'normal' adult's life to a matter of (more or less rational) individual choice. Consequently, in all ten of the countries of Europe on which this volume reports, we have observed a 'pluralization' of life-styles and of the structural forms of private life as an aggregation of such individualized lives. In most of the countries in Europe, the traditional forms of family life have begun to lose out to other family types and in particular to the non-family forms of private life, temporarily or even permanently excluding children.

These trends are a challenge to family policies which, in a broader European framework, are having to take into consideration the need to support an increasing variety of family forms. The international comparative study on *Familiale Lebensformen, Lebenslagen und Familienalltag im internationalen Vergleich* (Family Life and Family Policies in Europe) has studied change and diversity of family life in Europe under varying external conditions in different countries, in order to determine European commonalities and country-specific peculiarities. Our interest is in the sociological background of the actual European demographic trends and variations.

Demographic explanations of the population process assume that there is a unidimensional and unilinear trend interpreted as 'Europe's second demographic transition'. However, the indicators commonly analysed, such as declining fertility and nuptiality and increasing divorce and cohabitation, illuminate only surface phenomena. The question relating to the underlying sociological shifts would be whether, although somehow lagged in time, they are more or less the same everywhere, 'from the golden age of marriage to the dawn of cohabitation', and 'from uniform to pluralistic families and households', to quote only a few of the shifts assumed by Van de Kaa (1987), or whether we find substantial differences between countries or clusters of countries. Transition theorists believe that within the European framework the existing demographic diversity indicates only that countries are unequally far ahead on a unitary transitional path. In our study, much in contrast to these beliefs, we have observed differential structures and processes of family development which, on the contrary, demonstrate the prevalence of national and regional patterns. On the one hand, the sample of ten countries under study contains the variation range of the existing national 'family patterns' (Gauthier, 1991) in Europe. On the other, it also represents the existing differentiations of the actual national, political and socio-economic contexts of family life in Europe. The period under study is the decade of the 1980s.

The existing international variations in the representation of different family types, the differentiations in the life situation of comparable family types in different countries, eventual correlations of material aspects of life situations with different structural forms of private life, as well as the related characteristic spatial, temporal and social structures of families' everyday lives define the social reality into which a European family policy would have to intervene. At the time being there is, of course, no such policy. If it were to be implemented, however, a precondition of its implementation would be to identify the modes in which the actual reality and diversity of private life in general and of family life in particular is affected by the actually existing national family policies. Here it should be noted that, in all probability, the existing structural properties of family life in Europe are not primarily the direct effect of political intervention, but rather the result of broader socio-economic and socio-cultural trends and, most important, of individualized biographic selections of individual persons and couples, taken under different external conditions.

1.2. How the Research was Organized

Experts from the ten participating countries have determined the cross-national diversity and the temporal processes of change of family forms by means of secondary analyses of existing data sets from sources varying from census statistics to micro-analytic surveys. Where there was evidence in the data, they have related differentiations in household and family structure to certain dimensions of the material life situation and the organization of everyday life in families, such as family income, housing, supply with and utilization of day-care facilities, and the internal division of labour between women and men. Different representations of certain family types in different countries can be explained under the hypothesis of differential advantages or disadvantages existing for them in different countries. This leads us to the guiding hypotheses on which all contributions in this volume elaborate.

Differences in the representation of family and non-family forms of private life, as well as differentiations within the family sectors of the societies compared (such as the proportions of 'traditional' and 'modern' families), can be understood as expressing differing degrees and modes of 'structural negligence' (Kaufmann's term *strukturelle Rücksichtslosigkeit*: cf. Kaufmann, 1990) of the family, mainly from the side of state and economy in modern societies. Thus, the question asked here is plainly not how much correlation there is between policies and family structures, but rather what *constraints* are imposed on the options of individual actors by the existing policy profiles.

Furthermore, the question is not only *whether* policy matters, regarding the variation and change of family structures and family life, but *how* such impacts should be understood if there is empirical evidence that they exist. These questions imply a two-step strategy of research. The first step, the results of which are documented in this volume, has been dedicated to the establishment of plausible substantial relationships between family policies and family life in the countries under study, in order to substantiate hypothetical impacts of national policies. The authors have been asked to make explicit their hypotheses as *theoretical impact models* in order to reconstruct how policy matters. In a second research phase, which is to follow, we are planning comparative micro-analytic reconstructions of the modes in which, under the conditions of different national policy profiles, socio-economic, political and cultural variables of the everyday environment of young couples (as parents and prospective parents) translate into typical patterns of household structure and of management of everyday life.

The 'personnel infrastructure' (with only a few extensions) of both the research completed and documented in this volume and that still in the planning stages has been derived from the 'Demography and Social Change' research network initiated and directed by Dirk van de Kaa and Hans-Joachim Hoffmann-Nowotny, on behalf of the European Science Foundation. Participants' reports cover the following countries in Europe: Denmark, France, the Federal Republic of Germany, the former German Democratic Republic, Great Britain, Ireland, Italy, the Netherlands, Sweden, and Switzerland. This volume contains country reports from these countries, with the former Federal Republic of Germany and the former German Democratic Republic (as the only Eastern country) counted as two. Selection of data sources was a matter of decision of our country reporters who were asked to utilize the most 'suitable' and feasible data. Their selections contain population register data and census data, as well as social scientific survey materials. The common feature of all empirical analyses, however, is that they permit disaggregation down to the level of the individual respondent. All country reports follow, as far as possible, a commonly elaborated standard set of tables and research questions.

Aggregate demographic figures such as birth rates or marriage and divorce rates are only very superficial indications of changes in the structure of family life. It has been one of the main features of this project to investigate these structures as such. For that purpose a multidimensional typology of *Lebensformen* (translated here as 'forms of life'), developed and first applied by Zapf *et al.* (1987), was adopted and used in a comparative way. The 'forms of life' are the situational properties of stable patterns of management of everyday life. This typology combines the following variables: marital status of adult household members, number of generations in the household, number of children, and labour-force participation of adult members. The latter indicator marks the difference in the concept from the traditional classifications of household demography. In sociological terms, labour-force participation is the main connection between the family and the 'outside world'.

To ensure that the observed international differences in the distribution of such life forms will not merely reflect unobserved heterogeneity in the composition of the samples compared (e.g. in terms of variations of individuals' position in the family life cycle), we have compared the life forms of special age groups of women in comparable phases of the life course and of the family development process, marked by critical transitions between biographic stages. The first cohort analysed and compared are young women in the phase of early family formation – or, to be precise, at that age at which family formation occurs if it occurs, defined here by the median age at first birth surrounded by an interval of five years. This is often the first time in a young woman's life, and in the course of her relationship with a partner, when the existing balance of gainful employment outside the house and of household and family obligations has to be essentially reorganized. The second cohort under investigation are women at the beginning of the post-parental phase; again, this has been defined by a five-year interval, this time around the median age of the mother when the youngest child gains independence. In this stage of life, the problem of (re)organizing private life and job activities is again at stake, though with different opportunities and under different constraints.

1.3. The Ten Country Reports

In an approach such as ours, it has to be understood that there is no perfect harmonization of definitions and classifications of household and family statistics. In that respect, international comparative research is not an easy task, and it is no wonder that not every author has succeeded in obtaining the required data in precisely the desired format needed for an unambiguous comparison. That is one of the reasons why the structure of the country chapters that follow, though highly similar, is not completely identical.

But there were other reasons why not every chapter meets the standard format decided upon during one of the preparatory meetings. Sometimes people originally involved in the project changed jobs or had to withdraw for other reasons, and their successors did not always have easy access to the same data sets. So, although the ten chapters still have a basic structure in common, more than was originally intended remains hidden behind the influences of national peculiarities, specificities of available data sets, and personal interests. What has been retained in this series of chapters, however, are the basic elements of that common structure: an overview of the main demographic trends in the 1980s that shape family structures; an analysis of the influences of women's labour-market position, trends in education and housing developments as decisive forces in shaping women's everyday family lives; a discussion of the national situation with respect to family policy; and the formulation of hypotheses on the way in which family policy, or the lack of it, has an impact on the everyday life of women in different 'family life forms'.

The country chapters in this book have been ordered alphabetically. The authors of the chapters were each asked to give a short subtitle, in an attempt to provide the reader with a clue to what they thought was the most salient characteristic of (changing) family circumstances in their country during the 1980s. On the basis of the resulting set of ten subtitles, an attempt can be made to arrive at some preliminary qualitative clustering.

The authors of seven out of ten chapters stress some aspect of these processes of individualization and concomitant pluralization that were mentioned in the introductory sections.

In the most embracing way that can be imagined, *Béatrice Muller-Escoda* and *Ulla Vogt* do so when calling their chapter 'France: the Institutionalization of Plurality'. They stipulate that in France, as in other Western European countries, family structures are changing inasmuch as the number of families that no longer fit the 'normal family' model has become significant over the past twenty years. Examples are the decreasing number of marriages, and the increasing number of divorces, of lone-parent families, and of couples living together outside marriage. Alongside the Scandinavian countries, France today is one of the countries with the highest proportion of children born to unmarried parents. Another development these authors mention is the rapid and continuous rise in labour-market participation of French women, even when they have (young) children. As they demonstrate, both trends have an impact on family policy, which plays an important role in France. The changes that can be observed and the 'reactions' of French government are also presented in this chapter.

The decreasing number of marriages is the aspect that is emphasized by *Finola Kennedy* and *Kevin McCormack* in their title (chapter 7): 'Ireland: Marriage Loses Popularity'. They mention that the 1980s was a decade in which marriage lost the popularity it enjoyed in the 1960s and early 1970s. This happened against a background of economic uncertainty and rising unemployment, particularly among young Irish women, who at the same time experienced a rise in educational participation, an increase in cohabitation and an increase in marriage breakdown. Young women, particularly better-educated women, increasingly remained in the workforce after marriage, and in the late 1980s 'newer' life-style dual-earner households were found most frequently among the young, better-educated women. Lone-parent households were more prone to poverty than the average household. Largely owing to the rise in unemployment in the 1980s, households with children faced a greater risk of poverty than in the 1970s. Child care remained largely the task of mothers. Policy changes in Ireland – notably, equal rights legislation, which facilitated women's access to the labour market in the 1970s, the legalization of contraception in 1979 and alterations in the tax code, combined with the pattern of child income support – have accompanied the behavioural changes. But despite these changes in behaviour, values and attitudes of Irish men and women have remained rather traditional.

In the title of her chapter, 'Denmark: the Land of the Vanishing House-wife', *Lisbeth Knudsen* emphasizes the quite different situation of young Danish women. They too experienced a pluralization of family forms during the 1980s. Here the popularity of cohabitation, still most frequent among women in higher socio-economic categories, has increased, and the formation of a family with children has been postponed, most strongly among women with more education. For each cohort, women's rate of full-time employment does not vary much with age, and a high rate is maintained throughout adulthood. The traditional housewife has almost disappeared in Denmark, but can still be found more frequently among women in their fifties than among younger women. The employment rate is highest among women living with a partner, irrespective of their number of children. But employment is not uniformly high among all categories of women. A part of the single-mother category has poor access to the labour market; among single women in particular, unemployment was higher in 1988 than in 1981. Some lone parents seem to have difficulties keeping their employment. Families with children, one-parent families in particular, have less income at their disposal, though the income distribution has changed for the better during the last decade.

It is the latter factor that is particularly emphasized in the title of chapter 4, 'The Federal Republic of Germany: Polarization of Family Structure', by *Gero Federkeil*. Demographic data reveal West Germany among the European countries having the lowest birth rates. Furthermore, it has one of the highest proportions of couples remaining childless. The author shows that the dynamics in family life forms that result from these basic demographic trends, often referred to in terms of a 'pluralization of family life forms' and, as its biographical counterpart, an 'individualization of the life course', during the 1980s were confined to the younger cohorts of women entering the typical parenting age during the 1980s. In contrast, among women in the older cohorts, family life remained rather traditional. According to the author, among the younger cohorts a pattern of family trends has emerged during the 1980s that is particular to (West) German society. This leads him to a revision of the pluralization thesis, to the extent that he suggests a polarization thesis instead, emphasizing the growing discrepancy between, on the one hand, an increasing sector of non-family households, in which a high degree of pluralization can indeed be found, and, on the other, a shrinking proportion of young women who decide in favour of a family but do so in rather traditional ways, i.e. where the 'married-housewife-family' remains largely predominant.

In chapter 6, 'Great Britain: the Lone Parent as the New Norm?', *Lynda*

Clarke and *Melanie Henwood* emphasize that the 1980s in Britain were a decade that saw the most major changes in family and household composition that have taken place this century. Marriage was postponed as more couples established cohabiting unions, and a trend towards the separation of child-bearing and marriage became apparent with a trebling in the proportion of babies born outside marriage. Marital breakdown and divorce were other distinguishing features of the decade. Divorce rates doubled during the 1970s, following legislation that allowed easier divorce. Women have come to be less likely to be living as part of a married couple with children, and more likely to be either a lone parent, living alone, or living as part of a childless couple. There has been a marked shift for women from the role of spouse to that of household head. These demographic developments have been accompanied by social and economic trends which have seen increased economic activity of women. However, the 1980s were also notable for the impact of economic recession and the rise of mass unemployment. These developments had a particular impact on families (particularly lone-parent families), and led to a threefold increase in the numbers of children living in poverty. Unfortunately, in the absence of a clear and comprehensive model of family policy in Britain, response to this demographic and social change has been incremental and at times inconsistent. The family has increasingly become the focus of political and public debate and controversy. But attempts to satisfy at times incompatible objectives make any intervention in the area of family policy extremely difficult. Therefore, there remains a lack of certainty as to the preferred balance between the worlds of family life and paid employment; between equity of treatment for individuals on the one hand, and support for the traditional two-parent family on the other. The authors conclude that many of the trends evident in the British family have their own momentum which is driving them onward in spite of, rather than because of, deliberate policy intervention.

In chapter 9, 'The Netherlands: the Latent Family', *Anton Kuijsten* and *Hans-Joachim Schulze* take the position that, though millions of people live in families or family-like situations, the most characteristic feature of the contemporary Dutch family is its latency, in three different senses: political, public and private. Political latency is expressed by the fact that there is no explicit family policy, family seldom being an issue on the political agenda. Public latency refers to the fact that it is not done to talk or write about the family in public, in order not to be regarded as old-fashioned. Private latency is communicated in everyday casual language. The effect of this national consensus about this family latency on political measures which have an impact on families is that it leads them to be contradictory.

One of the consequences of the fact that the family is no longer a manifest point of reference is that in times of structural unemployment individualized social security makes the unemployed family head vulnerable and easily pushes families of the unemployed towards the poverty line.

Adele Menniti, Rossella Palomba and *Linda Laura Sabbadini* chose 'Italy: Changing the Family from Within' as a title for their chapter. They demonstrate that the Italian family shows signs of continuity of traditions, and that there is not much statistical evidence of new family behaviour. Hence, pluralization of living arrangements and the polarization between marriage and alternatives to marriage are concepts that are inadequate to describe the changes that have taken place in Italian family patterns. In addition, family patterns in Italy show an increasing tendency towards simplification of structure. Their analysis shows that during the 1980s many changes took place, but all within the framework of a unique life choice: to get married and to have children. Changes in family patterns and living arrangements of women in Italy depend mainly on changes in the timing of marriage and childbirth.

The titles of the three remaining chapters refer to the policy situation with respect to the family. Social rights in Sweden, including those related to families, are based on the two guiding ideas which are referred to in the title of the chapter by *Tuija Meisaari-Polsa*: 'Sweden: a Case of Solidarity and Equality'. Therefore, the aim of the complex system of Swedish family policy measures is, firstly, to maintain a reasonable standard of living for all family forms and, secondly, to increase possibilities for both women and men to choose their own way of life and to combine family life and work. Meisaari-Polsa's chapter shows that the solidarity- and equality-based social policy in Sweden is at the same time modern and family-friendly. After describing family policy, family forms, the family life situation and the everyday life of families, she summarizes policy effects on family forms in Sweden, demonstrating that, in some respect, Swedish family policy is relevant with respect to demographic trends, but also that the relationship between family policy and demographic trends is complicated.

Beat Fux connects with the aforementioned concept of structural negligence by calling his chapter 'Switzerland: the Family Neglected by the State'. Some of the trends in family structure that he describes might be influenced by certain deficiencies in family-related policies that clearly favour marital life forms. As in other European countries, traditional living arrangements have retained their importance in Switzerland, especially during the early family formation phase. The increase of new life forms (pluralization) seems a phenomenon that occurs most of all in earlier stages (e.g. unmarried cohabitation) or in later biographical phases (e.g. monoparental families). Furthermore, there is little evidence of changes in the intrafamilial division of labour between spouses. However, low extra-marital fertility, a comparatively late first marriage age of men and women, a rapid increase of voluntary childlessness and a rather high rate of part-time employed women are peculiarities of the Swiss case, which appears to be rather traditional when compared with other countries.

When it comes to traditionality in family matters, however, it curiously seems to be the former GDR that is the champion, as is demonstrated in the chapter 'The Former German Democratic Republic: the Standardized Family' by *Hartmut Wendt*. Rather than withering away, as the founding fathers of Marxist ideology believed, the family – or, to be more precise, its dual-earner modality – became stronger than ever. The one-party system of the former German Democratic Republic propagated high women's employment as the prerequisite of equal rights for women, but the truth was that a second income was simply indispensable to ensure even a modest standard of living for a family. A dense network of day care thus encouraged and facilitated the non-domestic paid work of women. Accordingly, the upbringing of children was entrusted to the state, and conventional family life was redefined. At the same time, the early founding of a family established the couple's right to their own flat. New forms of family living, such as married-like partnerships, at no point questioned the traditional co-resident nuclear family and, therefore, gave no indication of a process of pluralization or a decrease of pressure on family norms, as was the case in the former West Germany. Rather, in East Germany it was the standardized family that was the outcome of a trend towards greater individualization, and remained prevalent until the fall of the Berlin Wall.

References

Gauthier, A. (1991), 'The western European governments' attitudes and responses to the demographic and family question'. Paper presented at the European Science Foundation Conference 'From European Societies to European Society? The National Welfare States and European Integration', St Martin (Pfalz), Germany.

Kaufmann, F.-X. (1990), *Zukunft der Familie: Stabilität, Stabilitätsrisiken und Wandel der familialen Lebensformen sowie ihre gesellschaftlichen und politischen Bedingungen* (The Future of the Family: Stability, Risks to Stability, Changes in Family Forms and their Social and Political Conditions), Verlag C.H. Beck, Munich; 2nd rev. edn. as *Zukunft der Familie im vereinten Deutschland: Gesell-*

schaftliche und politische Bedingungen (The Future of the Family in Reunited Germany: Social and Political Conditions), Verlag C.H. Beck, Munich, 1995.

Van de Kaa, D.J. (1987), 'Europe's Second Demographic Transition', *Population Bulletin*, 42, Population Reference Bureau, Washington DC.

Zapf, W. *et al.* (1987), *Individualisierung und Sicherheit: Untersuchungen zur Lebensqualität in der Bundesrepublik Deutschland* (Individualization and Security: Studies on the Quality of Life in the Federal Republic of Germany), Verlag C.H. Beck, Munich.

2 Denmark: the Land of the Vanishing House-wife

LISBETH B. KNUDSEN

Danmarks Statistik, Copenhagen, Denmark

During the 1980s a pluralization of family forms can be observed in Denmark. The popularity of cohabitation, still most frequent among women in higher socio-economic categories, has increased. The formation of a family with children has been postponed. Age at first birth increased by approximately two years in the 1980s, most strongly among women with more education. Average cohort completed fertility has decreased, and the highest number of children can be observed among women in the lower socio-economic positions. For each cohort, women's rate of full-time employment does not vary much with age, and a high rate is maintained throughout adulthood. The traditional housewife has almost disappeared in Denmark, but can be found more frequently among women in their fifties than among younger women. The employment rate is highest among women living with a partner, irrespective of number of children. Those in the single mother category tend to have poor access to the labour market; among single women in particular, unemployment was higher in 1988 than in 1981. Some lone parents seem to have difficulties keeping their employment.

Household composition varies according to women's socio-economic position. Both among young women and among women in their 'empty-nest' phase, the proportions of married women among unskilled working women are higher than those proportions among salaried employees at senior levels. Families with children, one-parent families in particular, have less income at their disposal, though the income distribution has changed for the better during the last decade.

2.1. Introduction

Since the late 1960s family forms have changed in Denmark. One remarkable sign of this change is the increased proportion of children born to single (never-married or divorced) women. Twenty years ago, in 1970, this proportion was only 11 per cent of all live-born children. By 1980 it had grown to 33.2 per cent, and in 1990 almost half of all births (46.4 per cent) took place outside marriage (Danmarks Statistik, 1992).

However, this increase in extra-marital fertility results from substantial changes in family forms over the past 20 years, rather than from an increase in the proportion of women being lone mothers at the time of birth of their child. Most mothers having a child outside marriage live in a consensual union with a man by whom they may have had another child. Studies have shown that only about 5 per cent of delivering women are really living alone (Christoffersen, 1993).

These changes in family forms have been so fundamental that traditional demographic statistics based on marital status are no longer relevant in Denmark. New statistical classifications have been developed to replace statistics on marital status.

2.1.1. *Changing Family Structures: Pluralization or Polarization?*

The Danish family at the end of the 1980s was not the same as ten or twenty years before. In order to understand or explain what happened during the 1980s, it is necessary to describe how the family changed – what characterizes it and which form(s) are the predominant ones nowadays. It is also important to keep the historical background in mind. The trends in marital behaviour, cohabitation, childbearing and household composition, observed throughout the 1980s, must be looked upon as prolongations of patterns that emerged during the late 1960s and the early 1970s.

There has been a strong increase in cohabitation, which has become a legally accepted family form, even with children. In consequence, extra-marital fertility is reasonably high. However, among women under 30, fertility within marriage is still much higher than that outside marriage. At younger ages, a smaller proportion of women were married in 1988 compared with 1980: among women aged 25 and 35, the proportion married declined from 52 resp. 82 per cent in 1980 to 31 resp. 70 per cent in 1988.[1]

Since most birth statistics used for international comparison are based on marital status, the increasing proportion of babies born to unwed mothers in Denmark has often been misinterpreted as indicating a society where the family nucleus is disappearing and where most children are born into and

---

[1] Data from the Fertility Database.

will grow up in a one-parent family. This is not the case. However, the traditional family has changed, formally as well as structurally.

The prolonged education of women and the higher proportions of females who are economically active through their childbearing years have been mentioned as important reasons for the observed delay of childbearing, of first births in particular, and for the shrinking family size observed in Denmark (Bertelsen, 1981). Compared with survey findings in the 1970s, observed completed cohort fertility in the late 1980s shows that women have not had as many children as they said they wished to have ten years earlier. Together with the finding (from the European Values Study) that in 1990 a larger proportion expressed positive attitudes towards the family than did so in 1980, this indicates a situation in which women (and men) have planned their children in time, space, and number (Knudsen 1993).

But the emerging 'new' patterns are not spread equally through society. The observed social variation in size as well as structure of the family indicates a polarization, at the same time as a plurality in legal forms is becoming more and more accepted.

2.1.2. *Demographic Trends in the 1980s*

This section will focus on main demographic trends in Denmark, with special emphasis on family-related characteristics.

POPULATION. The population of Denmark has been almost unchanged, with an average growth rate below 1 per cent and with natural increase lowest, negative even, in the mid-1980s. In 1980, the mid-year population amounted to 2,528,639 men and 2,594,388 women, totalling 5,123,027. In 1990, the total population number was only slightly higher: 5,139,943.

Owing to a decreasing rate of fertility up until 1983, the age structure of the population has changed. The proportion of population below age 15 has decreased by around one-fifth over the 1980s, but the proportion of old people has increased very little. Because of the low numbers in the cohort 1920–1930 who are now reaching retirement age, the number of old (67–79-year-old) people in Denmark will not increase until the year 2010. The number of very old people (over 80) will increase by 31 per cent between 1993 and 2030 (Danmarks Statistik, 1993).

FERTILITY. From the mid-1960s up until 1983, Denmark experienced an almost constant decline in the annual number of live births: from a peak of 88,332 in 1966 to a low of 50,822 in 1983. After 1983, the number of live births increased to 63,433 in 1990, an increase of approximately 25 per cent. The number of live births in 1992 was 67,726; in 1993 it decreased slightly to 67,442.

In the 1970s, total fertility declined to below 2.0 per woman for the first time. The fertility level continued to decline gradually up until 1983. This decline can be attributed to a continued fertility decline for women aged 25 and older, and to a sharp decline for women aged 20–24 at the end of the 1960s in particular. Period total fertility reached a low of 1.377 per woman in 1983, followed by an increase to 1.668 in 1990, 1.762 in 1992 and 1.748 in 1993. Total fertility is still below 2.1 per woman, the approximate level needed for maintaining population size in the long term. Present low fertility levels are thus attributable to the secular fertility decline that became predominant at the end of the nineteenth century.

From the mid-1960s until 1980, fertility decline could be observed in all age groups, being strongest among women under 25 (Figure 2.1). In the 10-year period from 1970 to 1980, fertility of women aged 20–24 declined by 22 per cent. Among women under 20, who had experienced steadily increasing fertility levels in the 1950s and 1960s, fertility was halved from 32.4 to 16.8 per 1,000 women between 1970 and 1980. In 1990, the level was even lower: 9.1.

Age-specific fertility rates for women over 25 began to increase shortly after 1981, and the increasing fertility among these women accounts for the

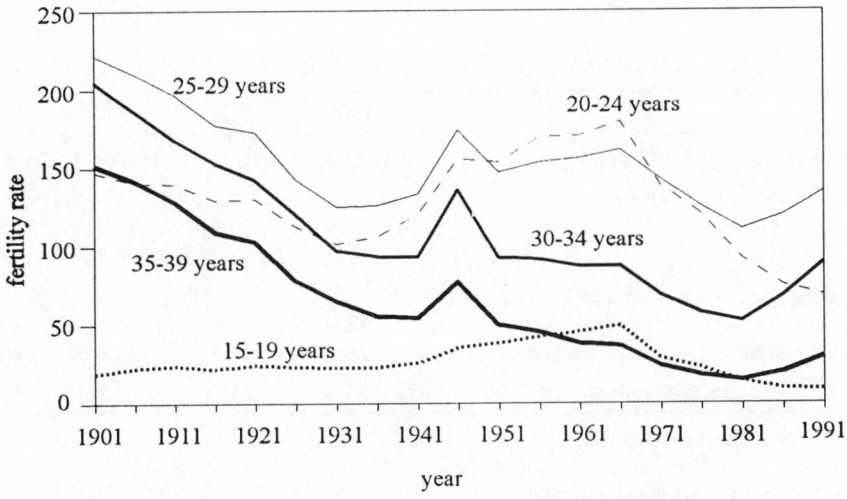

Figure 2.1. Age-specific fertility rates in Denmark, 1901-1992

increase in total fertility throughout the 1980s. These women belong to the first generation that consciously postponed having their first child when they were young in the 1970s. Throughout the 1980s, age-specific fertility increased among women in their late twenties and in their thirties. Women's average age at first birth increased by less than one year between 1970 and 1980, but by almost two years in the next decade: from 24.6 in 1980 to 26.4 in 1990. Men are, on average, about two years older than women when they have their first child. The increase in mean age at first birth among men is somewhat smaller than that among women (Knudsen, 1993).

MARRIAGE. Throughout the 1980s, the never-married proportion among the young age groups, both men and women, has increased. Proportions married more than halved among both women and men in their early twenties, and decreased by one-third among persons aged 25–29 years. Approximately 40 per cent of women aged 25–29 were married in 1989, compared to 25 per cent of men of the same age.

Table 2.1 provides key statistics on marriage in Denmark. For both sexes average age at first marriage has increased by approximately 3 years between 1980 and 1990, when it was 27.6 for women and 30.2 for men. In accordance with this, the number of 20–24-year-old women and men marrying in 1990, expressed per 1,000 never-marrieds of the same age, was almost half of its 1980 level. In the age groups over 25, the decrease in the marriage rate was due particularly to decreasing rates of remarriage. The decrease in marriage propensity reflects both the fact that many people never marry

Table 2.1. *Key statistics on marriage in Denmark, 1965–1990*

	1965	1970	1980	1990
Number of marriages contracted	41,693	36,376	26,448	31,513
Rate of marriage (%)[a]				
Women	59.9	50.5	28.7	27.6
Men	81.4	67.2	36.7	33.3
Average age at 1st marriage				
Women	22.9 [b]	24.6	24.8	27.6
Men	26.0 [b]	27.3	27.5	30.2
% of marriages between bachelor and spinster	83.3	75.7 [c]	62.3	62.3

[a] per 1,000 non-married.
[b] 1960.
[c] 1971; no data available for 1970.

Source: Vital Statistics, 1971, 1972, 1982, 1992.

Table 2.2. *Fertility rates per 1,000 women by age and marital status, Denmark, 1980 and 1990*

Ages	1980		1990	
	Married	Non-married	Married	Non-married
–19	390.7	13.5	259.0	6.6
20–24	232.5	63.9	254.8	54.3
25–29	147.1	76.2	198.1	94.7
30–34	57.7	44.6	97.0	72.1
35–39	15.7	15.5	27.7	26.5
40–44	2.5	2.4	6.4	4.7
45–49	0.1	0.1	0.1	0.2

Source: Danmarks Statistik (1992).

because they live in consensual unions, and the fact that the average age at marriage has increased. But even with fewer people getting married, married couples had a higher risk of divorce in the late 1980s compared to the early 1980s.

It has already been mentioned that increasing fertility out of wedlock was observed, especially among women over 30. Only a very small number of teenagers give birth, and there are hardly any births outside marriage among teenage women in Denmark; in the late 1980s only 6–7 per 1,000 unmarried teenagers gave birth to a child – a proportion that has steadily been declining (Table 2.2).

Marital fertility has been almost constant among the youngest age group. This may reflect a preference for marriage among couples who choose to have a child rather early. In 1980, women under age 20 accounted for 15 per cent of the extra-marital births, compared with less than 5 per cent in the late 1980s. In contrast, in 1990 women aged 25–29 accounted for 41 per cent of the extra-marital births, compared with 28 per cent in 1980. Approximately one in three non-married women who gave birth at age 30–39 in 1985 and 1989 was cohabiting with a man by whom she had at least one other child. Another one in three – roughly speaking – lived together with a man, but had had no children before. Less than one in five was registered as living alone at the beginning of the year in which she gave birth.[2]

FAMILY FORMS. Three major trends in family forms can be observed: (1) living in consensual unions has become more frequent; (2) the average family size has declined; and (3) more families consist of partners who might (also)

[2] Data from the Fertility Database.

have had children with a previous partner.

Since 1976, Censuses in Denmark have been based solely on data from national registers, and more and more routine statistics are based on data in registers (Danmarks Statistik, 1994). As long as a family unit could be defined by legal matrimony, these statistics were sufficient. But there was a need to follow empirical developments, and proportions of people living in consensual unions could only be estimated from surveys. In order to monitor developments more closely, new definitions have been established in recent years, enabling data on cohabiting couples to be retrieved from the registers.

Table 2.3 shows that, from the beginning of the 1970s, cohabitation was predominant mainly among younger people. As these men and women grew older some continued to live in consensual unions, but among those aged 30–34 the proportion of cohabiting couples was not as large as when these same cohorts of men and women were ten years younger.

The earliest classifications in register-based vital statistics of a non-married family nucleus covered only cohabiting couples with at least one child in common. The use of this definition gave figures comparable with data from the various surveys referred to above. The operational definition of a family in use since 1 January 1991 also includes a man and a woman living together at the same address without being legally married, given that the age difference is less than 15 years and that there is no biological relationship between them.[3] These statistical definitions of a family unit, where the partners are not legally married, will be used in some of the sections below.

Social change with respect to legislation and attitudes has tended towards legalizing cohabitation. In 1990, cohabiting couples had almost the same legal status as married couples regarding the right of inheritance, for example, whereas in the 1970s it was still necessary in many municipalities to be married in order to be entitled to a flat. However, legal acknowledgement of paternity still has to be effected with respect to cohabiting couples, so that the man can be registered as the father of a child.

The proportion of people living alone, i.e. without spouse or cohabitee, has been almost unchanged in the total population above age 16 (34 per cent) and shows a small increase from 44 per cent in 1980 to 48 per cent in 1990–1 in the age group 16–39. Among 20–29-year-old men and women, however, a strong trend can be observed, since the proportion living without an adult partner has increased from 27 per cent in 1980 to 38 per cent in 1990–1.

---

[3] As this new definition has only been used from 1 January 1991, it is not possible to describe the development in the 1980s as detailed.

Table 2.3. *Men and women cohabiting as a proportion of all couples living together (married as well as cohabiting), Denmark, 1976–1988 (%, by age group)*

	Men			Women		
	20–24	24–29	30–34	20–24	24–29	30–34
1976–77	69	30	10	49	19	10
1978–79	73	38	15	56	26	12
1980–81	73	48	22	64	32	13
1982–83	79	54	24	68	38	18
1984–85	83	56	34	72	44	21
1986–88	85	81	34	77	44	21

Source: Omnibus surveys referred to in Danmarks Statistik (1992).

The increase is even stronger among the 20–24-year-olds, 49 per cent of whom lived without spouse or cohabitee in 1990–1. This trend might be due to an ongoing postponement of establishing a common household, as well as to the observed postponement of first birth (Christoffersen, 1993).

In 1992, 75 per cent of all children below 18 lived with both their biological parents and 8 per cent with one parent who had a new partner. Only 1 per cent was not living with either parent and 16 per cent lived with a single parent (Knudsen, 1993).

MORTALITY. The crude death rate (per 1,000) increased gradually from 10.9 in 1980 to 11.9 in 1990, when the number of deaths amounted to 60,926. At all ages women can expect to live longer than men. Life expectancy at birth increased only slightly from 71.2 in 1979–80 to 72.0 in 1989–90 for men and from 77.3 to 77.7 for women. The strong increase in life expectancy up until 1980 has, for both sexes, been replaced by a stagnation. This trend is different from the continued increase in life expectancy which can be observed in the other Scandinavian countries (Norway and Sweden). Neither is the trend in Denmark favourable when compared with the other OECD countries. In 1990, life expectancy in Denmark ranked 17th for men and 21st for women among the 23 OECD countries, whereas in the 1970s Denmark had the fifth-longest life expectancy (Bjerregaard and Juel, 1993).

The excess mortality during the 1980s among Danish men was highest among the middle-aged (35–64 years) in comparison with the rest of Scandinavia. However, the excess in mortality was much greater for women aged 35–64, both when compared with the southern and the northern part of the EU, and when compared with the other Scandinavian countries (Bjerregaard and Juel, 1993).

Trends in infant mortality too are less favourable in Denmark than in neighbouring countries. Perinatal mortality changed from 8.9 per 1,000 births in 1980 to 8.2 in 1990, while the infant mortality decreased from 8.5 per 1,000 live births in 1980 to 7.5 in 1990. The gap between the level of perinatal mortality in Denmark (and Norway) and that in Sweden, Finland and Iceland increased during the late 1980s, a development that has initiated several studies (NOMESCO, 1993).

MIGRATION. The proportion of foreign citizens in Denmark is still relatively low compared with a number of other countries. However, Denmark seems to be approaching the status of a multi-ethnic society. Many of the most recent immigrants come from Turkey or Pakistan. On 1 January 1991, more than 95 per cent of the population were both Danish citizens and born in Denmark: only 3.7 per cent were considered immigrants. This group consisted of 190,700 people – an increase from 134,700 in 1980. Among these, 104,500 came originally from more developed countries, such as EU countries (41,000) or Nordic countries (30,250) (Pedersen, 1991). The current low level of fertility in Denmark means that an increase in population will depend on positive net migration.

Some key statistics on demographic trends in Denmark during the 1980s are presented in Table 2.4.

2.1.3. *Recent Research*

This section presents selected recent research in Denmark on issues relevant to family trends.

Fertility patterns in Denmark are rather well described in the 'Vital Statistics' series of Danmarks Statistik as far as demographic variables are concerned, whereas socio-economic factors have been highlighted in special survey-based studies. In the mid-1960s and 1970s surveys on fertility related to women's family situation, and occupational activities were carried out by the National Institute of Social Research as part of comparative international studies of fertility.[4] The earliest study (1965) must be evaluated in connection with a then-existing fear of a diminishing labour force and an interest in knowing under which conditions (married) women would join

---

[4] These were co-ordinated by United Nations and later studies were part of World Fertility Survey. However, Denmark has not participated in the latest WFS.

Table 2.4. *Key statistics on demographic trends in Denmark, 1980–1990*

	1980	1985	1990
Population			
Mid-year population	5123,027	5113,691	5139,943
Population increase (%)	0.03	0.10	0.21
Natural increase (%)	0.03	−0.09	0.05
Net migration rate	0.01	0.19	0.16
Foreign citizens (%)	1.9	2.1	3.1
Asylum seekers[a]	N.A.	8,698	4,668
Age structure (%)			
Below age 15	24.8	18.4	17.1
15–44	43.4	45.2	45.0
45–64	21.3	21.3	22.3
Over 65	14.4	15.1	15.7
Fertility			
Crude birth rate (per 1,000)	11.2	10.5	12.3
Total fertility rate (per 1,000)	1,546	1,447	1,668
Extra-marital births (per 100)	33.2	43.0	46.4
Age at first birth			
Women	24.6	25.5	26.4
Men[b]	26.9	27.4	28.3
Mortality			
Crude death rate	10.9	11.4	11.9
Infant mortality	8.4	7.9	7.5
Life expectancy (women, age 0)[c]	77.2	77.5	77.7
Life expectancy (men, age 0)[c]	71.1	71.6	72.0

[a] Only applications within Denmark, 1985 and 1989.
[b] Based on the Fertility Database, 1980, 1985 and 1988.
[c] Life expectancy is based on 1980–1, 1984–5, 1989–90.

Sources: Vital Statistics, various years, and Knudsen (1993).

the labour market (Noordhoek, 1969; Noordhoek and Smith, 1972). Later studies took the increasing female employment rate into account when analysing family composition and actual and desired number of children, in relation to women's education (basic as well as vocational) and occupational activity (Bertelsen, 1980, 1981). In these studies, interest was in the fertility level as an effect of employment, rather than as an obstacle to it.

Information in earlier studies on family composition and attitudes towards the family and child-rearing was collected from interviews with women, sometimes married women only. The family was described from the woman's perspective, and the drive in the changes was attributed to women. In these studies, the changing role of women as relating to their educational, occupational and economic situation was considered very important, in an attempt to grasp the changing family, particularly the new emerging forms of stable relationships. About the time when the free right to abortion on request had been established (1 October 1973), the research focus shifted towards (married) women's number of children, pregnancies and use of contraceptives, without including any information on female occupation (Ussing and Bruun-Schmidt, 1972).

Throughout the 1980s, fertility patterns were further described in their demographic-medical aspects. An initially rather high rate of induced abortions decreased gradually after 1975, irrespective of the trend in live births (Knudsen and Jensen, 1989). When fertility increased from 1983, the level of induced abortions remained fairly constant. The increasing fertility among women in their thirties, and the high proportions of nulliparous women among women who had had an abortion, pointed to a continuous process of postponing family formation and childbearing (Christoffersen, 1993; Knudsen, 1993).

During the 1980s, the focus shifted somewhat from a pure women's perspective to a description and analysis of the consequences of family disruption, e.g. through divorces, children's experiences of family disruption, and the economic situation of lone parents (Koch-Nielsen, 1985; Nissen, 1980). As part of a European joint study on childhood (Qvortrup and Christoffersen, 1989) there was a growing concern about the child's perspective. The changing family forms initiated studies of family functioning and of the gender division of labour. Even if the traditional family changed with respect to structural features, a family unit still existed (Christoffersen, 1987, 1993; Hjort Andersen, 1991).

In general, the family seemed to be highly respected in Denmark. From the European Values Study, it became clear that young people in Denmark still esteem the family as an institution, even when hesitant about starting their own families (Gundelach and Riis, 1993). This observed postponement behaviour could be explained by high expectations of family life combined with anticipated difficulties in actually realizing them. Concern with family functioning has become more apparent in recent years in studies on time structure, gender division of labour, men's involvement in care activities, and attitudes towards paternity (Avnbirk, 1993; Carlsen and Elm Larsen, 1993; *Fathers in Families of Tomorrow*, 1993).

In short, the trend in Danish family research has moved from women's labour-market perspectives to the family unit and its functioning, to the acceptance of variety in its form and, most recently, to concern about time budget problems. The interest in men's domestic responsibilities can be viewed as a necessity for women's employment.

2.1.4. *Data Sources*

Denmark has a large number of national population-based registers containing the personal identification ('Person Number') of each individual having permanent residence in Denmark. Most data in these registers are based on routine registration for administrative purposes and cover all of the resident population. These registers are increasingly being used for both national statistics and research projects.

For this chapter, information from various sources has been used. Whenever possible, the national figures that are presented are taken from vital statistics, published annually by Danmarks Statistik, and based on the Register on Population Statistics in Danmarks Statistik. Specific data on fertility have been retrieved from the newly established database on fertility (the Fertility Database) in Danmarks Statistik. It contains information on all women and men in the reproductive age groups (12–49, resp. 12–64 years) resident in Denmark in any year during the 1980s, the number of children they have, and an annual classification of their socio-demographic characteristics. The Fertility Database is based solely on national registers; a more detailed description of it can be found in Knudsen (1993).

The description of family forms and household composition is based partly on data published from the Register on Population Statistics, partly on the Fertility Database. Families might be defined by other variables than marriage (cf. above). Data relating family composition and employment of mothers have been retrieved from the IDA database (Integrated Database for Labour Market Research) established by Danmarks Statistik, containing information on the entire population's labour-market status in November of each year (Leth-Sørensen and Rohwer, 1993*a*).

The sections on the dynamics of families, the description of everyday life, economy, day-care provisions and the division of labour in the household are based on various reports, mostly surveys using personal or postal interviews. Many of these investigations have been carried out by the Danish National Institute of Social Research. These surveys cover different time periods and populations. In each case it will be specified from which survey data are used.

2.2. Family Policy in Denmark

In contrast to the strong family orientation – so-called 'familism' – in the southern part of Europe, current laws and regulations in Denmark are directed towards the individual *person*, not the *family*, as a unit. Indirectly, familism was present in certain laws up until 1973, for instance in laws stipulating that a woman's retirement pension should be paid to her husband. Since then, rights (and obligations) have been attached to the individual (Borchorst, 1993). Partly as a consequence of this, Denmark has no separate 'Ministry of the Family'. Rules and regulations that influence family conditions are issued by various ministries, first of all by the Ministry of Social Affairs, e.g. child allowance, day-care provisions, and maternity leave (or rather parental leave – see below). However, other rules too can be seen as part of a family policy, e.g. tax regulations, in which each person is regarded primarily as an individual, and household support, which is provided only on the basis of number of adults and amount of income, irrespective of gender of the adult(s) entitled.

Much of the family policy in Denmark has an influence on the living conditions of children. In fact, the rationale behind many family policy initiatives has been a concern for children's well-being. Very often these initiatives have an impact on gender equality within the family (Christoffersen, 1989). Some of the most recent initiatives deal with joint custody after divorce and with paternal leave.

2.2.1. *Family Policy with Respect to the Relationship between Family and Employment*

Women in Denmark who were in the age group for family formation and childbearing throughout the 1980s were brought up with the basic conviction that they would get some kind of education, preparing them for a working life that they would maintain throughout their adult life, even when (or if) they had children. The high rate of employment was supported by good public provisions of day care for the children. An individual's rights ensure the ability to provide for oneself, and also for one or more children – an option chosen by an increasing number of women throughout the 1980s, when the divorce rate increased.

So, family policy may make it easier to have a one-parent household, but at the same time economic constraints act in favour of families with two breadwinners and a small number of children. There is a law establishing equal payment on the labour market, but, owing to labour-market segregation, women are still, on average, in the lowest income brackets. However, throughout the 1980s, women working as unskilled workers had the lowest average age at birth of a first child, and among the highest average numbers of children at age 35 (Knudsen, 1993).

For couples, as well as for lone parents, the weekday is tightened with 7.5 to 8 hours of work and perhaps 1 to 2 hours of travelling. Even with the shortening of the working week that has taken place, the tendency to live far away from the workplace, combined with the labour participation of both adult household members, have in fact increased the number of hours spent outside the home for the adults in a family (Haslebo, 1982).

CHILD ALLOWANCE. Previously, families with children were entitled to a tax deduction. In 1970 this changed into a child allowance paid by the municipality to all families, irrespective of income and with an extra allowance for single parents. For a few years in the early 1980s a reduction according to taxable income was discussed. Until 1975 this allowance was paid up to the child's nineteenth birthday. For a short period (1975–87) this upper limit was the seventeenth birthday, and afterwards the nineteenth again. The basic child allowance in Denmark (as of 31 December 1991) equalled DKK 570 a month (Dumon, 1993).

The child allowance in Denmark is independent of the number of children in the family. The amount per child does not increase with age, as is the case in several other EU countries. On the contrary, recent changes have increased the allowance for small children. The rationale behind this might be both the rather high costs of day care (crèches are more expensive than kindergarten) and a political wish to increase the families' opportunities to let one parent (the mother) stay at home, e.g. on leave (see below) during the first years. This policy does not favour a large number of children, but might act in favour of shorter age intervals between children. There is an extra allowance for lone-parent families.

DAY-CARE PROVISION. The provision of day care in Denmark is probably the most extended within the European Union as regards coverage and public financing. This system started in the late 1960s and grew quickly during the period in which women entered the labour market. Day care was considered a public responsibility and a necessity for maintaining the high employment rate in Denmark, even of mothers with pre-school children.

For children 0–2 years of age crèches have been established, whereas children aged 3–6 can be enrolled in a kindergarten. Both kinds of institution are financed primarily by the municipality, with an additional payment from the parents; in 1993 parental payment was not allowed to exceed 30 per cent of the running costs. Since the early 1970s, the percentage of children enrolled in day-care institutions has approximately doubled. In 1987, more than half of the children below age 3 were enrolled in crèches or municipal day-care institutions (in private homes). The corresponding figure for children aged 3–5 in kindergarten was 70–74 per cent (*Levevilkår i Danmark*, 1992). Figure 2.2 shows the expansion of coverage between 1973 and 1992.

In order to meet rapidly increasing demand, day care has also been organized in private homes, but still with public support and supervision. In 1989, 18 per cent of 0–2-year-old children were enrolled in crèches while 29 and 12 per cent were in private homes with (resp. without) public supervision (Jensen, 1993).

Both at central and at local levels, the Danish welfare state has established day-care provisions in order to meet the demands from the women (families), at a time when ever-increasing proportions of mothers are needed (and willing) to join the labour market. However, supply cannot keep up with demand, and there are long waiting-lists, especially in some municipalities. The proper level of day care as regards number of employees, economic

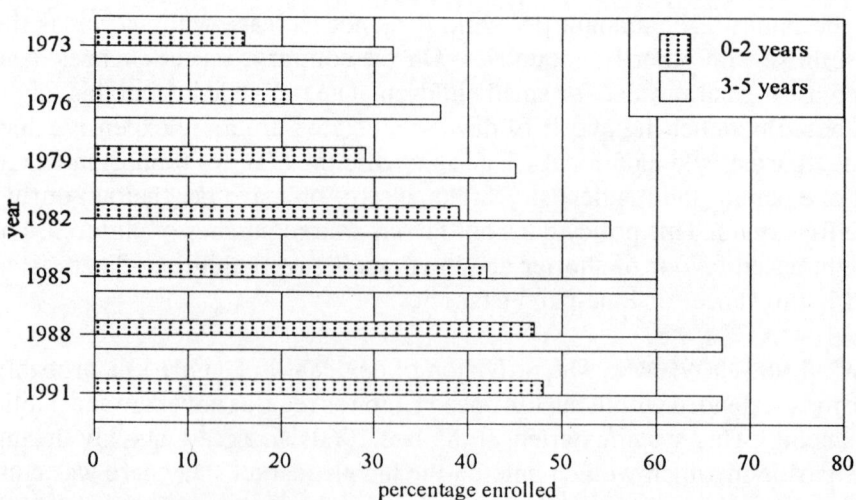

Source: Levevilkår i Danmark, 1992.

Figure 2.2. Percentage of children 0–6 years old enrolled in day-care institutions, Denmark, 1973–1991

possibilities and physical environment has continuously been discussed. Day care tended to be regarded as a supplement to the children's upbringing in the late 1960s and the early 1970s, when young mothers entered the labour market. Later, budget cuts lowered the quality of the institutions and made it more difficult to maintain a high pedagogical level.

In more recent years the value of day-care institutions has been questioned by politicians, following an increase in female unemployment and budget cuts in the municipalities, which are responsible for maintaining the institutions. Unemployed women are urged to keep their children at home, sometimes with a guarantee that the child can return to day care when the mother gets a job. Children of unemployed parents have low priority on the waiting-list. All this indicates that nowadays day care is regarded as a necessary rather than a pedagogical arrangement.

In order to solve the problem of the waiting-lists, which are especially long for children under 3 years of age, there have been some attempts to restructure the organization of day-care facilities. There have been local attempts to introduce a larger element of time-related payments and more daily and hourly flexibility, in order to make greater use of the resources available (Dumon, 1993).

PARENTAL LEAVE AND LEAVE DURING A CHILD'S ILLNESS. In the late 1980s and early 1990s there was a growing concern about the daily time structure of the family. In 1993, the Equal Status Council published a report aimed at analysing the difficulties of combining working life with family commitments (Carlsen and Elm Larsen, 1993). One of the attempts to ease family life was to extend the right of leave.

Till 1 January 1981, the length of maternity leave was 14 weeks; if, e.g. because of illness during pregnancy, a woman was forced to take leave before term, her leave after delivery was reduced accordingly. But in January 1981 the law was changed so that an early start of maternity leave should reduce neither the number of weeks of leave afterwards, nor the economic compensation. Leave after birth was extended on 1 July 1984 from 14 to 20 weeks, and on 1 July 1985 to 24 weeks. The same revision of law gave the father a right to take leave in the last 10 weeks (weeks 15–24), instead of the mother, and to have two weeks of leave immediately after birth together with the mother.

All civil servants, as well as some groups of employees in the private sector, keep their normal salary during parental leave, while some other groups get economic compensation equalling that in case of unemployment (90 per cent of minimum wage at the most). However, if the woman is a housewife or student, the father of the child is not entitled to take leave with compensation.

Having the possibility of parental leave is not the same as using that right. In 1984–89, more than 80 per cent of both mothers and fathers were entitled to take leave, but only 3 per cent of the fathers did so. In 1989, only 586 out of more than 61,000 fathers had at least four weeks of leave. The joint two weeks of leave after delivery was used by approximately half of the fathers (Christoffersen, 1990). Use of joint and/or paternity leave has proved to be dependent on income and on the woman's occupational status. The amount of economic compensation influences whether the mother, the father or both take leave. Because of this, and because the woman's income remains the lower in most families, it is more economical for the woman to take leave. Families where the father took leave were atypical in that the income was more equal between the partners. It was also noted that the general attitude at the workplace towards men's leave needs to change (Christoffersen, 1990). In total, families estimate a loss in monthly income of around DKK 6,000 (appr. 900 ECU) if the father is on leave. Those fathers who took leave often had less vocational training than their partners.

Sick children are not allowed to stay in public day-care institutions. When both parents are working it is often a problem to care for the child when it has to stay at home. Parents can use some of their holidays – in Denmark annual holidays are five weeks, and two to three of these may be split into single days or short periods during the year. In 1990, approximately 76 per cent of occupationally active fathers of small children and more than 83 per cent of the mothers were able to stay at home with full wage compensation on the child's first day of sickness (based on interviews with 598 persons: Christoffersen, 1990). There is no limit to the number of such days per year, but the parents need to find another solution for the second and following days of a child's illness. However, this is only until the child is 10 years old. There is no employment provision – as in Sweden – for a specified number of 'care' days.

2.2.2. *Hypothetical Impact on Family Forms and Life Situations*

Policies in Denmark that influence family life must be regarded as necessary support for individual persons – both women and men – rather than as support for the family's smooth functioning and well-being in case of children.

Nothing in the Danish legislation acts in favour of families with a large number of children. Child allowance does not increase with a child's birth order and there are no tax deductions. There are minor reductions in payment in day-care institutions for siblings – if they are in the same institution, which often means that there is a short age interval between them. The rather high allowances for small children, introduced in the late 1980s, and the more recently improved allowances of parental leave might encourage couples to have children at short intervals. There is easy access to safe contraceptives and to induced abortion – both effectively used in the timing and spacing of births. So, it is easy and accepted to plan and to have a small family – or no children.

Men and women are considered equal, whether they live alone or in families. Family(-relevant) policies consider men and women as equal partners with regard to economic and parental responsibilities. The proportion of women undertaking further vocational education has increased strongly, and in some university studies, e.g. medicine, women comprise more than half of the annual number of freshmen. The law on equal payment for equal work secures – at least formally – women's economic equality, even if many women are in low-salaried jobs or in subordinate positions. This equality, and women's ability to take care of themselves and their children, may put pressure on couples to develop a more equal division of labour at home – i.e. on men to take a bigger share in daily housework and child care. This perspective of equality has become apparent too in the recent law that establishes the possibility of having shared custody after divorce. And legislation concerning cohabitation has made this living arrangement almost equal to marriage.

There is no strong economic encouragement to have a one-breadwinner family. In that case, the economically active partner can have a tax deduction (net effect DKK 6,000) and some money might be 'saved' when the children are not in a day-care institution. *So, support for families is to a large extent a consequence of the high rate of female employment.* Support for families came with increasing levels of employment and education among women. The Danish labour market needed the female work force at the same time that women wished to find employment. During the 1980s, the high cost of living almost forced a dual-earner household. At the beginning of the 1990s there was growing concern about the problematic everyday time structure in families.

2.3. Family Forms in the 1980s

The critical events considered as indicators for the early parental phase and for the beginning of the post-parental phase are the mother's age at birth of first child and the mother's age when children start leaving home. With res-pect to the former, family formation in Denmark is no longer linked solely to getting married, so the birth of the first child might therefore be a better measure of the onset of the parental phase in a family. With respect to the latter, the 'empty nest' should be defined as the period in which the house-hold no longer includes any biological or adopted children of either of the parents. As will be discussed in Section 2.5 below, mothers in Denmark maintain a high rate of employment even through the years when the family includes pre-school children. This means that the 'empty-nest' period does not imply major changes in female employment.

2.3.1. *Timing of Critical Events*

THE EARLY PARENTAL PHASE: AGE AT FIRST BIRTH. The average age of the mother at first birth was 24.6 years in 1980 and 26.8 in 1991, whereas the average age at birth of all children has risen from 26.9 to 28.5 in the same period. In accordance with this, the age groups indicating the early parental phase are 23–27 in 1980–1, 24–28 in 1988 and 25–29 in 1989. These women were born in 1953–7 (1981), resp. 1959–63 (1988). In the Fertility Database, demographic data are available for every year from 1980 to 1989, socio-economic data for 1981–8. This data material gives the best opportunity to illustrate social differences regarding the timing of critical events, so whenever possible data from the Fertility Database will be used.

THE EARLY PARENTAL PHASE: AGE AT FIRST MARRIAGE. As mentioned in Section 2.1.2, average age at first marriage increased by approximately 3 years between 1980 and 1990, when it was 27.6 for women and 30.2 for men. This would point to the use of age groups 22–26 in 1980 and 25–29 in 1990 to indicate the early parental phase. These age groups are almost identical to those indicating mean age at first birth.

THE BEGINNING OF THE POST-PARENTAL PHASE. One of the most important changes in family structure, the increasing probability of having more than one partner through the life course, has caused an increase – though still slight – in the proportion of women who have children from two or more relationships. This may have increased the interval between the first and the last birth and thus the age at which the empty-nest phase is entered. Nevertheless, this has only a minor socio-economic importance, as women are gainfully employed during most of their adult life. Since 1981, fertility rates have increased among women in their late twenties and older. However, in the 1980s a small proportion of women gave birth for the first time only when they were in their late thirties. On 1 January 1988, among 40-year-old women in Denmark, approximately, 1 per cent (400) had given birth for the first time after age 35, and only some 10 per cent of these women had had another child.[5]

A large proportion of young adolescents are enrolled in some kind of education and choose to live with their parents while studying. In 1990, less than 10 per cent of 18-year-olds were not living with their parents. The rather large supply of furnished flats and bed-sitting-rooms, and the possibility of having part of the rent subsidized by the municipality, might signal the onset of a reversal of this trend.

In what follows, the beginning of the empty-nest phase will be indicated by age group 50–54 whenever possible. However, the Fertility Database covers women up to age 50 only, which means that when these data are used women aged 45–49 will be considered. Supplementary data from the IDA database will be used too. An analysis based on IDA data has illustrated a cohort-specific pattern of full-time employment among Danish women. At given ages, each younger cohort has a higher degree of full-time employment compared with previous cohorts. The same analysis shows that the degree of full-time employment for the cohorts relevant here has been increasing throughout the study period for the two young groups and does not begin to decrease until age 52–53 among women belonging to the older groups. There is no sudden increase in employment in the empty-nest phase (Leth-Sørensen and Rohwer, 1993*b*).

THE 'YOUNG' AND THE 'OLD' GROUP OF WOMEN. Women aged 50 in 1980 (born 1930) had their first child when they were 20 – in 1950 – while women aged 50 in 1990 (born 1940) had their first child when they were a little older, in the early 1960s. Levels of education and employment were higher in the latter group than in the former one. The older group comprises women born between the two world wars, who experienced their childhood in the less prosperous 1930s and were in their early teens during the Second World War. More among them became housewives than among the younger group and very few had got a vocational education. When they entered the labour market, they experienced only minor support from the welfare state, in terms of day care and various economic benefits, e.g. in case of unemployment.

---

[5] Data from the Fertility Database.

The largest proportion worked as unskilled workers or salaried employees in low positions – and they typically stayed in their marriages and subordinated their occupational activities to the needs of the family.

The youngest cohorts studied here were born in the 1950s and 1960s, benefiting much more from the then expanding welfare state, and they had their first child at a more advanced age than previous generations. Most of them got a vocational education, and they continued to be employed throughout the years when they had pre-school children.

Table 2.5 shows the cohorts that will be analysed in the sections below, whenever possible.

2.3.2. Structural Characteristics of Family Life

FAMILY SIZE. On 1 January 1990, in 772,342 families in Denmark there was at least one child. In 47 per cent of these families (360,939) there was one child only (Table 2.6). Twenty-five per cent of these families had a woman as a single parent; in 6 per cent the child lived with the father. Even now that cohabitation has become more frequent, married couples have, on average, more children (1.74) than cohabiting ones with children (1.54 – this number includes children from previous relationships as well).

Some minor regional differences can be observed. In the municipality of Copenhagen, 1.7 per cent (5,613) of all families (12 per cent of all families with children) are cohabiting couples with joint children. The corresponding figures of cohabiting couples with children in two counties (Ringkøbing and Sønderjylland) in Jutland (the western part of Denmark) are 8 and 9 per cent of all families with children; these counties are also characterized by a low rate of legally induced abortions, thus indicating different attitudes towards family formation.

NUMBER OF CHILDREN BY MARITAL STATUS AMONG YOUNG WOMEN. The Fertility Database allows calculation of average numbers of live births in any group of women and men living in Denmark in the 1980s. As age at first birth varies strongly with educational level and socio-economic position, the average number of children at a given age of the parents differs too. The overall average number of children for women and men at ages 25 and 27 was 0.80 resp. 0.65 in 1980, and 0.54 resp. 0.44 in 1988. In the latter year, 40-year-old women had on average 1.95 children, compared with 1.72 among 40-year-old men. The number of children as identified in the Fertility Database is considered valid for women born from 1945 onwards. The oldest

Table 2.5. *Age and birth year of the young group and the empty-nest women, Denmark, 1981 and 1988*

	1981		1988	
	Age	Birth years	Age	Birth years
Young group	23–27	1953–7	24–28	1959–63
Empty nest	45–49	1931–5	45–49	1938–42

Table 2.6. *Families with children by number of children and marital status of parent(s), Denmark, 1981 and 1990*

	1981		1990	
	%	No.	%	No.
1 child	41.7	342,188	47.7	360,939
Married	64.4		57.7	
Cohabiting	6.3		10.9	
Single woman	24.4		25.4	
Single man	5.0		6.0	
2 children	42.6	349,575	41.5	320,731
Married	84.5		77.5	
Cohabiting	2.5		8.3	
Single woman	11.6		12.7	
Single man	1.4		1.5	
3+ children	15.7	128,250	10.8	90,672
Married	88.7		83.8	
Cohabiting	1.5		6.1	
Single woman	9.0		9.3	
Single man	0.9		0.8	

Source: Vital Statistics, 1981, table 80; 1989, table 71. No figures are available before 1981.

of these were 35 in 1980 and 43 in 1988, which means that it is not possible from that source to describe in detail all the social conditions of these women at the beginning of the empty-nest phase.

The young groups, which were defined as age group 23–27 in 1981 and 25–29 in 1988, had on average less than one child (Table 2.7). Between 1981 and 1988, the proportion married among these women declined. The average number of children changed only a little; it decreased among married women and increased among never-married ones, thus reflecting the increasing proportion of parents living in a consensual union.

Table 2.7. *Number of children by marital status in the young group, Denmark, 1981 and 1988*

No. of children	Total	Never married	Married	Divorced
1981				
0	40.1	70.6	17.6	23.7
1	31.4	22.5	37.6	40.6
2	24.3	6.2	38.1	28.1
3+	4.2	0.7	6.7	7.6
Average	*0.93*	*0.37*	1.35	*1.21*
No. of women	184,243	77,111	99,003	8,129
1988				
0	46.3	67.6	21.3	25.6
1	28.7	22.5	35.7	36.7
2	21.0	8.8	35.8	28.5
3+	4.1	1.2	7.3	9.2
Average	*0.84*	*0.44*	*1.30*	*1.23*
No. of women	186,158	99,703	78,281	8,174

Note: 'Married' includes separated; 'Divorced' includes widows.

Source: Data from the Fertility Database.

HOUSEHOLD COMPOSITION. Table 2.8 shows the household composition of the young group of women in Denmark on 1 January 1981 and 1988. The numbers in this table are not fully comparable with those in Table 2.7, owing to minor differences in definitions. Apart from the few women living with their parents (only included up to age 26), the other women are head of a family.

During the period considered, there have been shifts in the rank orders of the various family life forms. The most common family life form has changed from 'married, one child' to 'never married, no children, cohabiting'. The category of cohabiting with a man is based on those cases where a man and a woman only – and no other persons – are living at the same address. There have also been increases in the proportions living alone (from rank 4 in 1981 to rank 2 in 1988) and in those 'never married, with children, cohabiting' (from rank 6 to rank 5).

2.4. Aspects of the Family Life Situation

Since September 1989, a full-time job in Denmark entails 37 hours of work a week. Since the 1950s, weekly working hours have diminished from 48

Table 2.8. *Household composition of the young group of women, Denmark, 1981 and 1988*

Household composition	Numbers		Percentages		Ranking	
	1981	1988	1981	1988	1981	1988
Married, one child	31,182	22,631	16.9	11.9	1	3
Never married, no children, cohabiting[a]	28,941	37,267	15.7	19.6	2	1
Married, two or more children	29,432	21,710	15.3	11.4	3	4
Never married, single-living, no children	20,019	24,716	11.2	13.0	4	2
Married, no children	15,083	13,601	9.9	7.1	5	6
Never married, with children, cohabiting	9,142	19,033	5.0	10.0	6	5
Never married, single-living, with children	5,251	6,755	2.9	3.5	7	7
Never married, no children, at parents[b]	4,380	3,556	2.4	1.9	8	9
Never married, flat-sharing community[c]	3,066	4,464	1.7	2.3	9	8
Divorced, single-living mothers	2,270	2,134	1.2	1.1	10	10
Total number of women	184,035	190,307	100	100		

[a] Sharing flat with a man. [b] Only valid for women below 26. [c] Sharing flat with another woman.

Source: Data from the Fertility Database.

to 44 in 1966, to 40 in 1974 and to 37 in 1989. But, in spite of this decline, present-day parents often spend more time outside the family. This is a result of both female participation in the labour force and changing residential patterns around the cities, which have increased commuting time. However, more than 10 per cent of mothers and 30 per cent of fathers in families with children claimed to work more than 39 hours a week in 1989. Compared with families without children, there are only minor differences in the father's weekly working hours, whereas a larger proportion of the mothers with children work fewer than 37 hours (41 per cent, compared with 30 per cent among all women: Hjorth Andersen, 1991).

2.4.1. *Labour-Force Participation and Unemployment*

As already mentioned, women in Denmark stay economically active even when they have children. A survey in 1989 among mothers aged 20–49 showed that only 4 per cent were housewives (Hjorth Andersen, 1991). The

Fertility Database is able to identify women who are 'outside the labour market'. This category consists of women who have deliberately chosen to be at home as housewives, and women who are staying at home because of illness. Unemployed, job-seeking women are not included in this category. In the young age group, 8.4 per cent in 1981 and 6.7 in 1988 are outside the labour market. Among the women entering the empty-nest period a greater change could be observed: for them, the proportion outside the labour force has decreased from 18.8 per cent in 1981 to 8.6 in 1988.

Women outside the labour market live under different conditions. In the empty-nest group approximately 90 per cent are married (92.1 resp. 86.6 in 1981 and 1988) whereas this proportion is much smaller in the young age group (62.6 per cent in 1981, but only 40.6 per cent in 1988). The household composition of the never-married women (selected categories) is illustrated in Figure 2.3. The category of cohabiting women with children includes couples with joint children only. In both age groups there has been an increase in the proportions living alone and cohabiting.

Table 2.9 shows employment rates by family type among women in the early parental and early empty-nest phases in Denmark. For both groups

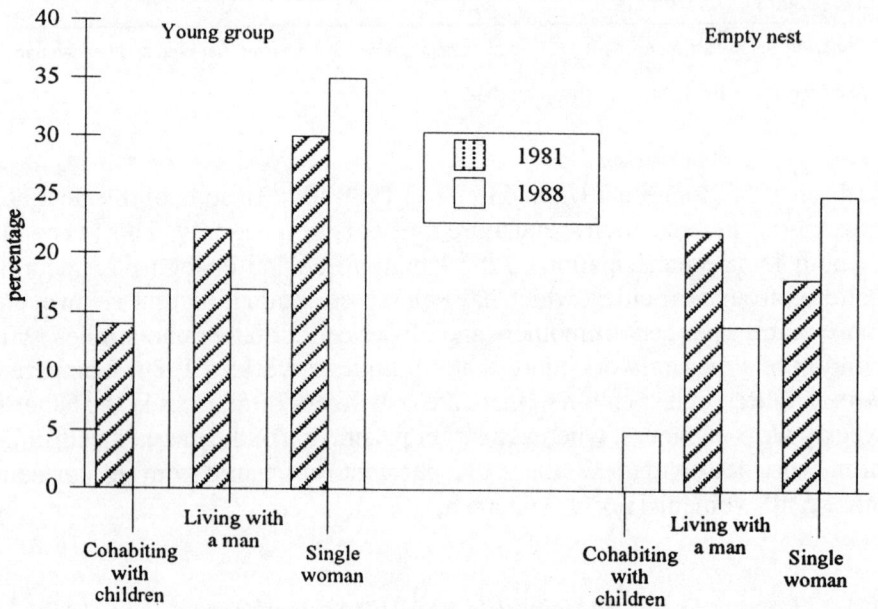

Source: Fertility Database.

Figure 2.3. Distribution by household composition (selected categories) for never-married women outside the labour market, Denmark, 1981 and 1988

Table 2.9. *Employment rate among women by type of family and age of the youngest child, Denmark, 1980 and 1988 (%)*

	Singles		Couples[a]	
	1980	1988	1980	1988
All young women	73.2	70.5	76.0	77.3
Age of youngest child				
No children	77.9	75.7	83.6	85.6
0–6 years	57.3	55.5	72.3	71.3
7–12 years	80.8	46.7	66.7	71.4
13–25 years	.. [b]	..	..	..
All empty-nest women	66.1	63.4	63.1	73.6
Age of youngest child				
No children	64.7	61.0	63.5	71.9
0–6 years	..	..	..	..
7–12 years	55.6	..	56.2	69.3
13–25 years	71.9	73.3	63.5	77.4

[a] 'Couples' includes both married and cohabiting couples with joint children.
[b] '..' means too few observations to make calculations.

Source: Data from the IDA database (sample of approx. 4,500 young women and 3,400 empty-nest women each year).

of women, employment rates are generally highest among women living with a partner. There is an increase in the employment rate with increasing age of the youngest child, indicating slightly increasing labour-force participation when the children grow older. Where comparisons are possible, it can be seen that the rates are higher in the younger generations.

Married or cohabiting mothers with children aged 0–6 years have a higher degree of unemployment than other married women and they are unemployed more often than their husbands (Christoffersen, 1987). What is also typical is that a larger proportion of the women are unemployed for more than six months. Unemployed men have a greater risk of divorce than unemployed women (Hjorth Andersen, 1991). It can be concluded from these figures that the inclination among young men to establish and maintain a family is more closely related to their occupational situation than is the case for women.

For all marital status categories, the percentage unemployed increased between 1981 and 1988. Among all unemployment categories, a smaller proportion have children in 1988 than in 1981. There is no trend of having a greater number of children when unemployed, but a higher proportion of fully employed women have no children (Table 2.10). Table 2.11 shows the degree of unemployment among women at the beginning of the empty-nest phase. As explained before, it is not possible to determine valid numbers of children for these women.

Table 2.10. *Distribution by number of children of young women, by marital status and degree of unemployment, Denmark, 1981 and 1988*

No. of children	Total	Never married	Married	Divorced
1981				
0 %	71.1	71.5	71.5	61.4
0	43.3	27.5	19.1	75.8
1	30.2	41.7	37.9	19.2
2+	26.5	30.9	43.0	5.0
< 50 %	4.5	4.3	4.7	4.5
0	33.8	61.8	14.9	20.4
1	34.0	28.8	37.2	39.8
2+	32.3	9.5	47.9	39.8
50 % +	3.0	3.2	2.8	3.7
0	38.6	64.0	17.3	20.8
1	31.1	26.2	34.7	38.2
2+	30.4	9.8	47.9	41.0
No. of women	184,243	77,111	99,003	8,129
1988				
0 %	59.9	61.2	59.0	51.7
0	53.2	75.3	26.0	31.2
1	26.8	18.4	36.8	37.9
2+	20.1	6.3	37.3	30.9
< 50 %	9.1	8.5	10.2	7.1
0	38.9	61.5	65.7	25.6
1	32.6	26.9	28.7	37.0
2+	28.5	11.6	5.5	37.4
50 % +	3.9	4.0	3.6	3.4
0	43.6	62.6	19.1	27.0
1	29.7	24.9	36.0	33.7
2+	26.6	12.5	44.9	39.3
No. of women	186,158	99,703	78,281	8,174

Source: Fertility Database.

Table 2.11. *Empty-nest women by marital status and degree of unemployment, Denmark, 1981 and 1988*

% of women unemployed	Total	Never married	Married	Divorced
1981				
0	88.8	91.3	89.6	83.1
0–50%	2.1	1.7	2.1	2.9
50+%	1.4	1.2	1.4	1.8
No. unemployed	136,963	7,084	111,002	18,877
1988				
0	83.7	86.4	84.6	78.8
0–50 %	3.8	2.8	3.7	4.2
50+%	1.5	1.0	1.5	1.7
No. unemployed	156,349	7,716	120,910	27,723

Note: The columns do not sum up to 100 because the information is missing for some of the women.

Source: Fertility Database.

Table 2.12. *Distribution by number of children of the young group, for selected socio-economic positions, Denmark, 1981 and 1988*

No. of children	Salaried employees		Unskilled workers	Assisting spouses
	Senior level	Low level		
1981				
0	67.4	41.3	27.4	7.3
1	24.4	35.9	31.3	23.5
2+	8.2	22.7	41.3	69.2
1988				
0	73.5	47.4	30.7	11.1
1	19.6	31.4	29.9	24.5
2+	6.9	21.2	39.4	64.4
Average				
1981	0.41	0.83	1.21	1.79
1988	0.34	0.76	1.17	1.74

Source: Fertility Database.

2.4.2. *Socio-economic Position, Income and Poverty*

The number of children is, on average, higher among women in lower socio-economic positions, e.g. unskilled workers, than among, say, salaried employees at senior levels (Table 2.12). Women outside the labour force have the highest average number of children. The proportion of women having no children increased in all groups between 1981 and 1988. The proportion with no children among salaried employees at senior levels is of the same magnitude as the proportion with two or more children among women who assist their self-employed spouses.

Household composition too varies between socio-economic categories. Drawing on the Fertility Database, this can be demonstrated for the categories

Table 2.13. *Household composition among women belonging to selected socio-economic groups, Denmark, 1981 and 1988 (%)*

Household composition	Young group		Empty nest	
	1981	1988	1981	1988
Salaried employee, senior level				
– Never married, living alone, with or without children	20.4	21.8	15.5	8.9
– Married, with or without children	27.6	24.6	53.6	57.1
– Cohabiting, with joint children	3.4	3.6	–	0.5
– Living with man, no joint children[a]	29.1	32.7	1.5	1.2
Salaried employee, low level				
– Never married, living alone, with or without children	14.1	16.7	4.0	3.3
– Married, with or without children	46.0	34.0	68.4	68.1
– Cohabiting, with joint children	5.0	10.0	–	0.2
– Living with man, no joint children[a]	21.5	24.6	0.4	0.8
Unskilled labourer				
– Never married, living alone, with or without children	10.9	13.1	1.9	1.6
– Married, with or without children	46.4	35.8	71.9	71.1
– Cohabiting, with joint children	6.4	14.9	–	0.2
– Living with man, no joint children[a]	17.7	16.6	1.0	0.7

[a] Only information is that the man and woman have same address.

Source: Fertility Database.

'salaried employee, senior level', 'salaried employee, low level', and 'un-skilled labourer' (Table 2.13). In the young age groups the proportion of never-married women who live alone (with or without a child) is about twice as high among salaried employees in senior levels as among unskilled workers in the young group (20 resp. 11 per cent), whereas the relative difference is much greater among women at the beginning of the empty-nest phase (15 resp. 2 per cent in 1981). In all age groups considered, the proportion of women who are married (with or without children) is highest among unskilled workers and lowest among the salaried employees at senior levels.

INCOME. In 1989 a study of income distribution was conducted by the Danish National Institute of Social Research. A total of 2,656 individuals aged 20–49 were interviewed, and of them 1,865 were living in a family with at least one child aged 0–14. The families in the study were identified from a survey in which data had been collected through questionnaires. Afterwards, the survey data on e.g. income, occupation and unemployment for these families were traced in registers in Danmarks Statistik. The study describes family situations for the years 1982, 1984, 1986 and 1988 (Hansen, 1990).

One important conclusion is that families with children have experienced a strong relative improvement in income, mostly resulting from the increased public support of families. Table 2.14 shows how the increase in real income in families (including single-parent families) has been stronger than that among couples without children. In each group the economic differences have diminished during the period.

For one in three families, expenses related to day care of the children is the third largest part of their annual budget. Many families have no expenses, since they are offered free day care because of their low income. Among lone parents with small children, 10 per cent have no expenses for day care, compared with 5 per cent of couples. About 66 per cent of lone

Table 2.14. *Increase in real disposable income by type of family, Denmark, 1984–1988 (%)*

	Type of family	
	Single parent	Couple
Small children	10	7
Schoolchildren	8	11
No children	3	6

Source: Hansen (1990).

Table 2.15. *Real income by type of family and age of adults, Denmark, selected ages, 1988 (median = 100[a])*

| | Families with | | | |
	Small children	School- children	Grown-up children	No children
Single				
20–29 years	94	97	–	76
40–49 years	125	136	168	100
Couples[b]				
20–29 years	94	94	–	83
40–49 years	118	118	125	94

[a] Income among families of women aged 30–39 without children = 100.
[b] According to age of the women.

Source: Hansen (1990).

parents evaluate their economic situation as unsatisfactory, whereas among families with couples only 12 per cent say that they have an unsatisfactory economic situation.

According to Table 2.15, families with children are better off economically than families without children. However, these figures must be considered in relation to the number of persons in the family. Table 2.16 shows selected data on income per individual in families with children, compared with families without children (women aged 20–49 in both cases). It clearly shows

Table 2.16. *Real income per individual by type of family and occupational activity, Denmark, 1988 (median = 100)*

| | Families[a] with (no. of) | | | | | | |
| | Small children | | | Schoolchildren | | | No |
	1	2	3	1	2	3	children
Single							
Employed	68	59	53	82	76	72	110
Not employed	51	50	–	61	56	–	58
Couples							
Both employed	119	103	90	127	114	107	144
One employed	84	81	75	100	98	93	100
Both not employed	64	65	61	92	92	83	95

[a] Women aged 20–49 years.

Source: Hansen (1990).

that, in spite of the improvements, and irrespective of whether one or both parents are working, disposable income per person is lower in families with children. Looked upon in that way, the economic level of couples with three small children is lower than that of an unemployed childless couple.

2.4.3. *Education*

Throughout the 1980s the gap has widened between women with 'short' (9 years) and 'long' (12 years) general education, respectively, with regard to age at first birth and average number of children at age 40. Fertility patterns among women with 9 years' completed education have changed less: their age at first birth was 23.1 in 1981 and 23.3 in 1988. Among women with 12 years of basic schooling, age at first birth rose from 26.3 to 27.2 (Knudsen, 1993). Among the young women, the average number of children and the proportion without children changed notably among those with the shortest education (Table 2.17). In the other educational categories there was a slight increase in the proportion with no children, but also in that of women with more than two children.

2.4.4. *Housing*

A larger proportion of families with children (80 per cent) than of childless families (50 per cent) own their dwelling. Among parents aged 20–29, 65 per cent own their dwelling; among those 20 years older, this proportion has increased to 90. Single parents have 'poorer' housing: only one in four own their dwelling. But the question of ownership is not a truly valid measure of housing quality, as many rented flats and small houses are similar in quality to those owned.

2.5. Compatibility of Family Life and Employment

2.5.1. *Child-Care Arrangements by Family Type and Employment of Mother/Father*

As mentioned before, the coverage of day care in Denmark is wide. The more children there are in the family, the lower is the proportion of them in day care outside home, probably because more women with many children

Table 2.17. *Number of children, by the number of years of basic schooling received by mothers in the young group, Denmark, 1981 and 1988*

No. of children	No. of years' schooling for mothers			
	8	9	10–11	12+
1981				
0	20.3	24.6	38.7	65.3
1	28.5	34.1	35.5	25.1
2	39.7	35.4	23.3	8.9
3+	11.5	6.0	2.4	0.7
Average	1.45	1.23	0.9	0.45
No. of women	19,174	25,880	79,439	40,902
1988				
0	33.5	26.1	40.2	67.1
1	29.5	30.2	32.2	22.9
2	28.6	34.4	24.2	9.1
3+	8.5	9.3	3.4	0.9
Average	1.13	1.28	0.91	0.44
No. of women	11,586	18,107	93,725	52,827

Source: Fertility Database.

are not working outside the home. Table 2.18 gives the distribution according to children's age, number of children in the family and occupational status of the mother.

2.5.2. *Division of Labour in the Household with Special Reference to Child Care*

The division of labour in families has changed, and fathers take more responsibility for everyday activities, including child care, cleaning and preparation of meals. There is a more equal division of labour in families where the woman has more education. Among women in the labour force, the proportion being responsible for most of the housework decreases in the younger cohorts (Hjorth Andersen, 1991).

Some traditionally male responsibilities such as in- and outdoor repairs are taken over by 4–5 per cent of the women and are regarded as a joint activity in 10–20 per cent of the families. Males are participating in the preparation of meals, dish-washing and cleaning in one-third of the families, and have the sole responsibility for preparing breakfast or cleaning the dishes

Table 2.18. *Percentage of children in public day care, by age, number of children in the family and mother's occupation, Denmark, 1975 and 1989*

| | 0–2 years old | | 3–5 years old | |
	1975	1989	1975	1989
1 child	26	61	65	90
2 children	13	49	38	80
3+ children	13	34	30	53
Salaried employees	24	74	53	89
Workers	12	57	28	78
Self-employed	11	28	25	48

Source: Bertelsen (1991).

in 19 resp. 11 per cent of families with children. Taking care of children aged 0–2 is a joint responsibility in 66 per cent of families, the woman's responsibility only in 30 per cent. The relation between women's amount of weekly hours in the labour market and their responsibility for housework (preparing meals, cleaning, etc.) can be described by a U-shaped curve, since women with jobs of up to 20 hours a week and women working more than 39 hours a week have the heaviest burden at home. Part of this might be explained by the fact that many of the mothers with most working hours are wives assisting their self-employed husbands.

2.6. Summary and Conclusions

During the 1980s a pluralization of family forms could be observed in Denmark – at least formally. Cohabitation is more frequent among higher socio-economic categories of women, while marriage is more common among e.g. unskilled workers, irrespective of the number of children. Whether this can be attributed to the fact that women in higher socio-economic categories are capable of maintaining a family economically in case of break-up of a union remains to be determined.

Family formation has been postponed. Age at first birth increased by approximately two years in the 1980s, most notably for women with more education. Average completed cohort fertility has decreased, and the highest numbers of children are observed among women in lower socio-economic positions.

For every cohort, the rate of full-time employment does not vary much

with the woman's age, and a high rate of employment is maintained throughout adulthood. The housewife category has almost disappeared in Denmark,
but is still more frequent in empty-nest age groups than among younger
women. Employment rates are higher among women living with a partner
than among single women, irrespective of the number of children. The category of single mothers includes a group with poor access to the labour market. This might reflect the fact that unemployment is higher in 1988 than
in 1981, particularly among single women. On the whole, lone parents seem
to experience difficulties in maintaining employment.

Household composition varies among women according to their socio-
economic position. Both among women in the early parental phase and among
those at the beginning of the empty-nest phase, the proportions married are
higher for unskilled workers than for salaried employees at senior levels.

Families with children, lone-parent families in particular, have less income
at their disposal, even though the income distribution has changed over the
past 10 years.

References

Avnbirk, A. (1993), *Forældreskab til forhandling* (Negotiating Parenthood), Forlaget
    Sociologi, Copenhagen.
Bertelsen, O. (1980), *Den unge familie i 70'erne* (The Young Family in the 1970s),
    Danish National Institute of Social Research, Copenhagen.
—— (1981), *Det faldende fødselstal* (The Falling Birth Rate), Danish National
    Institute of Social Research, Copenhagen.
—— (1991), *Offentlig børnepasning* (Public Day Care), Danish National Institute
    of Social Research, Copenhagen.
Bjerregaard, P. and Juel, K. (1993), *Middellevetid og dødelighed* (Life Expectancy
    and Death in Denmark), Danish Institute of Clinical Epidemiology, Copenhagen.
Borchorst, A. (1993), 'Working life and family life in Western Europe', in Carlsen
    and Elm Larsen (1993:167–80).
Carlsen, S. and Elm Larsen, J. (eds.) (1993), *The Equality Dilemma: Reconciling
    Working Life and Family Life, Viewed in an Equality Perspective – the Danish
    Example*, Danish Equal Status Council, Copenhagen.
Christoffersen, M.N. (1987), *Familien under forandring?* (Changing Family?),
    Danish National Institute of Social Research, Copenhagen.
—— (1989), *Børnepolitiske forslag – og deres skæbne: en gennemgang af de sidste
    ti års børnepolitiske arbejde i Folketinget* (Child Policy Initiatives – and their
    Fate: an Overview of Child Policy Related Activities in Parliament in the Past
    Ten Years), Center for Alternative Social Analysis, Copenhagen.
—— (1990), *Barselsorlov* (Paternal Leave), Danish National Institute of Social

Research, Copenhagen.

—— (1993), *Familiens ændring: en statistisk belysning af familieforholdene* (The Changing Family: a Statistical Description of Families), Danish National Institute of Social Research, Copenhagen.

Danmarks Statistik (1992), *Vital Statistics 1990*, Danmarks Statistik, Copenhagen.

—— (1993), Befolkningsprognoser 1993–2020(2030) (Forecast of Population 1993–2020(2030)), *Befolkning og Valg*, 13:1–27.

—— (1994), *Personstatistik i Danmark: et registerbaseret statistiksystem* (Statistics on Persons in Denmark: the Register Based System of Statistics), Danmarks Statistik, Copenhagen.

Dumon, W. (1993), *National Family Policies in EC-countries in 1991*, Commission of the European Communities, European Observatory of National Family Policies, Brussels.

Fathers in Families of Tomorrow (1993), Report from the Conference, Copenhagen, June 1993, Socialministeriet, Copenhagen.

Gundelach, P. and Riis, O. (1993), *Danskernes værdier* (The Values of the Danes), Forlaget Sociologi, Copenhagen.

Hansen, F.K. (1990), *Børnefamiliernes økonomi* (The Economy in Families with Small Children), Danish National Institute of Social Research, Copenhagen.

Haslebo, G. (1982), *Fordeling af tid og arbejde i velfærdsstaten* (Distribution of Time and Work in the Welfare State), Planstyrelsen, Copenhagen.

Hjorth Andersen, B. (1991), *Børnefamiliernes dagligdag* (Everyday Life in Families with Children), Danish National Institute of Social Research, Copenhagen.

Jensen, J.J. (1993), 'Public childcare in an equality perspective', in Carlsen and Elm Larsen (1993:103–16).

Koch-Nielsen, I. (1985), *Divorces*, Danish National Institute of Social Research, Copenhagen.

Knudsen, L.B. (1993), *Fertility Trends in Denmark in the 1980s: a Register-Based Socio-demographic Analysis of Fertility Trends*, Danmarks Statistik, Copenhagen.

—— and Jensen, B. (1989), 'Ændres relationen mellem fødsler og aborter i Danmark?' (Is the relation between births and induced abortions changing in Denmark?), *Nordisk Sexologi*, 7:255-60.

Leth-Sørensen, S. and Rohwer, G. (1993*a*), 'Upward mobility in the Danish labour market', in L. Lund (ed.), *Symposium i anvendt statistik* (Symposium on Applied Statistics), Uni-C, Copenhagen.

—— (1993*b*), 'Aspects of the female life cycle and labour market participation in Denmark', draft paper presented at the Conference on Family Cycle and Growth of Women's Part Time Employment in Europe, Bremen, 17–18 December 1993.

Levevilkår i Danmark: Statistisk oversigt 1992 (Living Conditions in Denmark: Compendium of Statistics 1992), Danmarks Statistik and National Institute of Social Research, Copenhagen.

Nissen, M. (1980), *Skilsmisser og børn* (Children and Divorce), National Institute of Social Research, Copenhagen.

NOMESCO (1993), *Births and Infant Mortality in the Nordic Countries*, Nordic

Medical Statistical Committee, Copenhagen.

Noordhoek, J.A. (1969), *Gifte kvinder i familie og erhverv. I: Deltagelse i erhvervslivet* (Married Women, Family and Work. I: Employment), Danish National Institute of Social Research, Copenhagen.

—— and Smith, Y. (1972), *Gifte kvinder i familie og erhverv. II: Udearbejde og familie* (Married Women, Family and Work. II: Effects on the Family), Danish National Institute of Social Research, Copenhagen.

Pedersen, L. (1991), *Indvandrere og deres efterkommere i Danmark* (Immigrants and their Descendants in Denmark), Danmarks Statistik, Copenhagen (Statistiske Undersøgelser no. 43).

Qvortrup, J. and Christoffersen, M.N. (1989), *Childhood as a Social Phenomenon*, Denmark Project Childhood, SUC, Esbjerg.

Ussing, J. and Bruun-Schmidt, H. (1972), *Nogle resultater fra fertilitetsundersøgelsen* (Preliminary Results from the Danish Fertility Study), Danish National Institute of Social Research, Copenhagen (Study 22).

3 France: the Institutionalization of Plurality

BÉATRICE MULLER-ESCODA and ULLA VOGT

Université d'Evry, Val d'Essonne, France, and Northrhine-Westfalia Research Group Public Health, Bielefeld University, Germany

---

In France, as in other Western European countries, family structures are changing. The number of families that no longer fit the 'normal family' model has become significant in the past twenty years. Signs of these changes include the decreasing number of marriages, and the increasing numbers of divorces, of lone-parent families, and of couples living together outside marriage. Alongside the Scandinavian countries, France today has one of the highest proportions of children born to unmarried parents in Western Europe. Another development that can be observed is the rapid and continuous rise in labour-market participation of French women, even when they have young children. Both trends have an impact on family policy, which has a high profile in France. The changes that can be observed and the 'reactions' of French government are presented in this chapter.

3.1. Introduction

Cécile has her father's name. Her mother is divorced and has changed her surname back to her maiden name. François, the man with whom her mother is now involved in a long-term relationship, his son and Cécile all receive their mail at the same address. Three different surnames are posted on the mailbox of this apparently very 'normal' family made up of an adult couple and two children.

More and more adults are establishing more than one family in the course of a lifetime. In these familial constellations the children tend to come from different families (cf. De Singly, 1991). There are terms to identify the diverse familial configurations in France: stepfamily (*famille recomposée*), uncertain family (*famille incertaine*), one-parent family (*famille mono-parentale*), non-marital long-term relationship (*mariage-compagnonage*), cohabitation (*couple cohabitant*), and consensual union, among others.

Whatever terms may appropriately describe the variation and change in family formation, they clearly characterize a diversification in family forms that developed in the 1960s and continued to establish themselves throughout the 1980s.

One aspect of particular relevance to the transformations in family life and family structure is the increase in labour-market participation of women in the 1980s: in France, two out of every three mothers were gainfully employed, predominantly full-time. According to a study conducted by CERC,[1] the high participation rate of women in France is facilitated mainly by the public child-care system which, in spite of all its shortcomings, makes it easier or at least possible for women to enter employment. In contrast to the situation of women in, e.g., Germany, women in France generally do not have to choose between gainful employment and family obligations, but are much more able to reconcile the two.

3.1.1. *Theoretical Explanations and Empirical Observations*

In France, demographers, psychologists, educationalists and sociologists have for years studied the trends in family life and structure.

Since the beginning of the 1980s, there has been a remarkable increase in the number of studies carried out on the topic of families (Segalen and Zonabend, 1986:498). The focus of the work in this field has shifted from 'the family' to 'new family forms'. These new family forms clearly differ from the traditional father–mother–child family, and there have been various explanations for these transformations. Roussel (1986) argues, for example, that this perception of a plurality of family forms has more to do with appearance than with reality. He considers the married-couple model to have remained prevalent; the other variations of family life (e.g. *'cohabitation juvénile'*, *'mariage association'*) merely precede marriage and therefore are only temporary manifestations. De Singly (1987) also refers to these new forms as being a temporary phase. De Gall and Martin (1988) and Lefaucheur (1985) explain the variations in family households in terms of greater mobility between each phase of married and family life, rather than as a plurality of forms of living. Menahem (1979) points out that, through changes in structure, in composition and in the function and role of the family that have come about, new models of family life have taken their place next to the

---

[1] Centre d'Étude des Revenus et des Coûts (Research Centre on Income and Costs of Living).

traditional model. In his more recent work, Roussel (1991) synthesizes the various explanations of the changes in family forms and life into one formula: the existence of the diverse family forms, and the explanations for it, are mere reflections of the manifold ways in which individuals choose to pursue happiness. He assumes that the 'pursuit of happiness' is the goal pursued by most people. Therefore, there cannot be one single explanation for the choices of family forms.

3.1.2. *Data Sources*

The institution of the family is greatly respected in France, and this is expressed by, *inter alia*, its constitutionally protected rights (Laroque, 1985). Political influence and broad support among the population work to protect this institution. Whereas in Germany most work on family policy is produced by universities or research institutes,[2] in France, as Lenoir (1988) clearly shows, family policy is a public issue, its 'legitimate spokespersons' being agents of the state who use their research findings to develop family policy (INED, INSEE, CNAF and Haut Conseil de la Population). From a demographic perspective, for instance, INED studies the function and the structure of families; INSEE develops statistics and analyses financial burdens and the redistribution of family incomes; CNAF measures the effectiveness of services and transfers for families both specifically and in general; lastly, the General Commissioner of Planning (*Commissariat Général du Plan*) outlines the objectives of family policy years in advance. The bulk of the available literature on family policy and on the changes in family forms and family life represents the results of the work conducted or financed by these institutions.[3]

In this chapter we refer, on the one hand, to the results of the General Censuses (*recensements*) and, on the other, to specific studies such as the Employment Survey (*enquête emploi*), the Household Survey (*enquête ménage*), and the Family Survey (*enquête famille*). Whereas the General Census takes the total French population as the unit of measurement, all three surveys are based on population samples. The Census results indicate, for example, how many children a family has at the time the Census was

---

[2] With the exception of a government commissioned report, *Familienberichte*, published regularly.

[3] INSEE = Institut National de la Statistique et des Études Économiques (National Institute of Statistics and Economic Studies); INED = Institut National d'Études Démographiques (National Institute of Demographic Studies); CNAF = Caisse Nationale d'Allocations Familiales (National Fund of Family Allowances).

taken; however, the data tell nothing about the ultimate completed number of children per family. In contrast, the Family Survey, which is conducted parallel to the General Census carried out by INSEE, reports on the exact number of children per family (CERC, 1989:14).

3.2. Family Policy

'Family disorder' (Commaille, 1991) – which is assumed to be observed in all West European countries – logically leads to questions regarding, first of all, what makes up society's social and political order and, secondly, how the family fits into this scheme. In the postwar period France experienced a 'golden age' of family policy. At that time, family-related changes can be seen as having been a part of a whole process of societal modernization (Commaille, 1991; Prost, 1984). As is true for most European countries, the development of family policy was characterized by separate phases that progressed within the context of its political, economic and social framework; family policy in France as elsewhere followed its own logic (Schultheis, 1988).

Family policy's foremost aim is to provide for the 'well-being' of the family. The impact of family policy is manifold. It influences the structure as well as the functions of the family: Dumon (1987) describes family policy as an instrument used by the government in an effort to maintain, support or change both the structure of families and family life. He distinguishes three phases of family policy development in Western Europe: (1) a phase of financial assistance for the family; followed by (2) a phase of policy directed at the well-being of the family as a whole as well as at the personal development of each of its members; and lastly (3) a phase characterized by measures that aim at rendering themselves temporarily or partially unnecessary. Dumon's three-phased analytical framework – with a few modifications – can be applied to the development of family policy in France.

3.2.1. *The First Initiatives*

At the beginning of the twentieth century, bonus payments (*sursalaire*) were introduced on the initiative of employers with the aim of improving the standard of living among workers and their families (Ceccaldi, 1957). Such practices were observable in the metalworking industry and in mining. Subsequently, they led in 1919 to the founding of the Metallurgy and Mining

Industries Union (*Union des Industries Métallurgiques et Minières*). One of the Union's accomplishments was to extend the bonus payments to all branch employees. In 1921, industry and trade collaborated to form one central fund that would administer allowances for employees' families, and this became an institution. It was followed by a law passed in 1932 that established legal entitlements to family allowances in industry and trade. With the introduction in 1938 of the statute book of family codes (*Code de la Famille*), the institution of the family became an independent component of French public policy (Lenoir, 1988; CES, 1991[4]).

In this phase three aspects are prominent:

(1) the tendency to emphasize a certain family model: the aforementioned 1938 statute book is based on the model of a family with three children (Prost, 1984);

(2) the tendency for government to address familial and demographic problems with public policy (Ceccaldi, 1957; Talmy, 1962);

(3) under fiscal pressures, the tendency to curtail government expenditures (CES, 1991).

Family policy was geared towards a productive labour force (i.e., the 'working class') and not towards disadvantaged groups in the population at large. The latter were excluded from any assistance under family policy. It was not until the fall of the Vichy government that families were considered in a broader context for policy development. Since then, the making of public policy as an instrument to deal with family problems in society at large has been viewed as legitimate.

3.2.2. *Institutionalization of Family Policy*

Ever since 1946, the degree of political influence of actors or interest groups concerned about family issues has been increasingly institutionalized. The Institution of Family Allowances (*Caisse de compensation*) that had existed until then was superseded by UNCAF (*Union Nationale des Caisses d'Allocations Familiales*), which from then on became a nationwide public institution of family allowances.[5]

What was of prime importance in family policy after the Second World

---

[4] CES = Conseil Économique et Social (Economic and Social Council).

[5] UNCAF was introduced to ensure a just distribution of family allowances among enterprises. They used a current-income financing system in which each enterprise, according to size, contributed to payment of the given expenditures (CES, 1991).

War was to raise the birth rate (Messu, 1992). Young couples were to be encouraged to have children. To secure the well-being of the family as a whole as well as the individual development of each family member, various measures – with an emphasis on pro-natalist programmes – were created: the extension of insurance coverage to all family members; the provision of medical care for infants (*protection maternelle infantile*, PMI); and the passage of a tax reform law on 31 December 1945, which introduced a system in which the total of the combined household income is taxed, based on a family member tax allowance scheme.

3.2.3. *Family Policy as an Expression of Political Action*

French family policy in the 1970s is characterized by both selective measures and measures that superseded one another. Family policy covers a wide range of issues that can be classified into two larger and four smaller categories. The two larger categories cover the socially oriented transfer payments (e.g. child allowances, lone-parent allowances, housing allowances, maternity leave benefits) and public welfare means-related benefits. The four smaller categories are (1) benefits for the care of the elderly and of handicapped family members; (2) benefits that should compensate for temporary income loss; (3) institutional facilities offering care services for children and the elderly; and (4) family legal services (Barbier, 1990).

   The next decade of family policy was distinguished by a far-reaching government neutrality with respect to choices of family models. President Mitterand announced in 1981 that everyone should be able to choose the way of life she or he desires. This position was restated almost ten years later by Permanent Secretary Dorlhac (*Quotidien du médecin*, 1990:18). This is not to say that freedom of choice concerning the way of life one wishes to lead is to be mistaken for government non-intervention in this area of policy. On the contrary, the government continued to take an active part in issues concerning, among others, health care and child abuse. Pro-natalist policies have always had priority. The neutral stance taken by the government towards a chosen way of family life has been formally expressed and under-pinned by the French Supreme Court decision in 1989 that granted to a large extent the same legal rights of a married couple to a couple cohabiting in a long-term consensual union without legal or formal marriage (Rubellin-Devichi, 1991).

3.2.4. *Family Social Policy*

According to Dieuleveut (1990), a dominant feature of family policy in the 1980s was the blend of diverse priorities. Family policy under the Mauroy government (1981–3) was a product of an upturn in the economy. Family benefits, e.g. for families with two children, were raised 25 per cent in 1981 and then again in February 1982, so as to adjust to the cost of living. In 1985, under the Fabius government, two new measures were adopted: a child allowance (APJE: *allocation au jeune enfant*) and a parental allowance (APE: *allocation parentale d'éducation*). The APJE is paid until the child reaches the age of 3. The APE is comparable to the German *Erziehungsgeld*; parents are entitled to benefit payments for the first few months – however, only after the birth or the adoption of a third child. The Chirac government in 1986–8 went further in strengthening family policy by providing either parent with the option of not pursuing gainful employment. Its benefits were directed towards working parents with at least one child under 3 years of age who was cared for by a child-minder owing to the job-related absence of the parents. Since 1988 a new phase in family policy has become apparent. No additional benefits have been created, but one can observe increased support of programmes in other areas, such as public housing, child care outside the home, and child abuse.

3.3. Family Life in the 1980s

Until the 1970s, in France as elsewhere, the dominant form of family life was the one that family sociologists call the 'nuclear' or 'normal family', which typically is composed of a working husband/father, a housewife/mother who is generally not gainfully employed, and three or more children. Of course, many families noticeably deviated from this model, but they were consequently socially stigmatized (Dupâquier *et al.*, 1988:533ff.; CERC, 1989). The situation has fundamentally changed since then. The number of families that no longer fit the 'normal family' model has become quantitatively significant in the last twenty years. Although most parents and children in France today still live in a nuclear family household, alternative ways of familial life have increased, and become socially accepted (Dupâquier *et al.*, 1988:535), and are supported by the government in legal as well as financial terms (Segalen and Zonabend, 1986:504).

In the work done in the field of family sociology, terms used often in describing this process of social change with respect to the family are 'pluralization' and 'individualization' (Roussel, 1986; Kellerhals, 1984; Segalen, 1990). 'Pluralization' is used, on the one hand, in connection with the diversification of family forms and refers to a diminishing social position of the nuclear or normal family. On the other hand, the term signifies a diffusion of alternative ways of family life (e.g. long-term consensual unions, lone parenthood, etc.). In contrast, the term 'individualization' describes the process of change taking place at the level of the individual family; it refers to the diversification of life-course options available to individual members of the family and to the fact that each member can choose an option. The individualization of life-course options has been particularly germane to female life courses which, compared with those of men, have significantly changed. Four social phenomena have strongly contributed to the transformation of the woman's role in French society: (1) improved schooling and vocational education of girls and women; (2) changes within the legal system; (3) different views and practices concerning partnership and sexuality; and (4) above all, since the 1960s, the marked increase in the labour-market participation rate of (married) women with (young and infant) children. Today in France, women tend to possess educational and vocational qualifications which, directly after completion, are followed by continuous gainful employment, i.e. employment that is not interrupted even when their children are young (Segalen and Zonabend 1986:505ff.).

In terms of family formation and way of life, variation rather than conformity of the structure of families is characteristic in France, as it is in other European countries (Villac, 1986; Dupâquier *et al.*, 1988). The developments that are important to the underlying issues being discussed here are elaborated below.[6]

3.3.1. *Patterns of Marriage, Divorce and Consensual Union*

Until well into the 1970s, marriage was the only socially and legally legitimate form in which a couple could live together. It was thus expected that almost every person would marry at some point in his/her life. Since then, the decreasing number of marriages, the high rate of divorce and the increase in consensual unions suggest that the institution of marriage no longer plays the meaningful role it used to play. Between 1972 – the year representing the highest number of marriages (416,521) in France since the Second World

---

[6] Since no detailed data sets were available, we refer to the General Census results and to specific surveys, such as the *Enquête emploi*, the *Enquête ménage*, etc.

War – and 1988, the number of marriages (per 1,000 inhabitants) dropped from 7.8 to 4.8. The number of weddings reached its lowest in 1987 with 265,177. Since then, a slightly increasing tendency has become visible: in 1990, the number of registered marriages (reaching 287,000 that year) rose by 2.6 per cent compared with 1989. Not only was there a decline in the total number of marriages, the number of first marriages also fell. In 1990, 480,431 French women and men entered marriage for the first time (76 per cent of all marriages that year), compared with 766,859 persons celebrating a first marriage in 1972 (INSEE *Première* 1/1990:2).

In comparison, the number of remarriages rose during the same period: in 1990, the percentage of French women and men who entered a new marriage was 15.9 and 16.8 per cent, respectively (1970: 7.5 and 8.0 per cent, respectively). With respect to the total number of marriages, however, the number of remarriages has also decreased (Sullerot, 1984:44ff.). Most of those who remarry are divorced (INSEE *Première* 1/1990).

The data reveal not only that the marriage rate settled at a clearly lower level than was the case in the 1970s, but also that the age of first marriage shifted. In 1990, the average age of first marriage of men and women stood at 27.8 and 25.7 years, respectively (1970: 24.4 and 22.4, respectively) (INSEE *Première* 1/1992). A major factor in this development has been the lengthening of the period needed for completion of education.

Not only has the number of marriages decreased, but marriages have also become more fragile, as mentioned by Roussel (1988), who addresses this development in France which arose parallel to the lessening inclination to marry and which has plainly become more salient since 1972. Interestingly, the evident increase in the divorce rate occurred prior to the reform in the divorce law in 1975, which means that the latter cannot be used to explain that increase. Rather, the 1975 divorce law must be understood as a law that had been adapted to societal changes (Sullerot, 1984).[7] In this period there was an annual increase in the number of divorces. In 1986 the highest number of divorces (108,380) was reached; since then it has levelled off to around 106,000 divorces per year (Population, 1991:1098). Whereas in the early 1970s one in ten marriages ended in divorce, approximately 31 out of every 100 marriages have been ended since 1985. This development is much more pronounced in large cities: in the mid-1980s, one in every

---

[7] As a result of the 1975 divorce law that became effective on 1 January 1976, getting a divorce was made easier. Since then, marriages can be ended not only when a spouse can be proven guilty of faulty behaviour (*divorce par faute*), but also when both spouses express mutual consent to a divorce (*divorce par consentement mutuel*) (Levy, 1988; Munoz-Perez and Rondeau-Rivier, 1990).

two marriages in Paris ended in divorce (Sullerot, 1984:42ff.; 1985:150). In most cases the wife filed for divorce; in 1985 this applied to 75 per cent of the cases (Levy, 1988:69).

The decline in matrimony ties in with an increase in consensual unions. The latter form of cohabitation has markedly spread in France since the beginning of the 1970s. At first, as Roussel and Bourgignon (1978) clearly show, there was wide confusion about what this new form of long-term cohabitation should be called. Leridon and Villeneuve-Gokalp (1988:335) and Dupâquier *et al.* (1988:532) point to numerous terms that are used in an undifferentiated manner to refer to this form of living together ('concubinage', 'cohabitation', 'non-married couple', etc.), though these terms are not synonymous and define forms that sometimes differ significantly.

What can be said about the establishment of this new way of living together in France, and how can it be characterized? Before this question can be answered, it must be noted that unmarried couples that are cohabiting have not been taken into account in the aforementioned statistical inquiries. Special studies are needed to describe this development more accurately (Pressat, 1991:35). Such a study was last conducted in 1985 by Leridon and Villeneuve-Gokalp (1988), who provide an overview of the development in France of unmarried couples (with respect to the 21–44-year-old age group) living together at the beginning of 1986. The data gathered showed that during the survey period 19.3 per cent of the 21–24-year-old women and 16.9 per cent of the 25–29-year-old men were living together but not married, which accounts for one-third and one-quarter, respectively, of the total population of coupled persons in the respective age groups. In relation to the total population aged 21–44, 10 per cent were living together without being married and 66 per cent were married (Table 3.1).

Living together out of wedlock is chiefly a form of cohabitation for young couples, for which Roussel coined the term '*cohabitation juvénile*'. In three out of four cases, two single people live together as a couple. The portion of couples made up solely of single partners varies according to age group: 91.0 per cent of the 21–24-year-olds, 73.8 per cent of those aged 25–29, 31.0 per cent of the 35–39-year-olds, and 28.4 per cent of the 40–44-year-olds (Leridon and Villeneuve-Gokalp, 1988:336).

In France, there was a total of 2.5 million unmarried couples of all age groups at the end of the 1980s. This means that what used to be an exception has grown within twenty years to be the rule. Though only 8 per cent of marriages used to be preceded by living with a partner out of wedlock, the percentage had climbed to 80 per cent by 1988 (Roussel, 1989). Moreover, not only do couples tend to live together before getting married, but, as the

Table 3.1. *Marital status by sex and age, France, 1 January 1986 (%)*

| Age | Couples | | Single | Total | Total sample |
	Married couple	Cons. union			population (*N*)
Men					
21–24	17.1	12.7	70.2	100.00	415
25–29	54.1	16.9	29.0	100.00	409
30–34	70.0	9.5	20.5	100.00	376
35–39	81.2	6.6	12.2	100.00	417
40–44	86.6	3.4	10.0	100.00	270
21–44	62.6	10.0	27.4	100.00	1887
Women					
21–24	34.6	19.3	46.1	100.00	443
25–29	69.2	11.3	19.5	100.00	513
30–34	75.5	8.5	16.0	100.00	429
35–39	81.0	5.2	13.8	100.00	462
40–44	79.6	4.6	15.8	100.00	357
21–44	68.8	9.7	21.5	100.00	2204
Combined					
21–44	65.7	9.9	24.4	100.00	4091

Source: Leridon and Villeneuve-Gokalp (1988:335).

rising number of children born out of wedlock and the growing number of single people (Table 3.2) show, the option of living together outside wedlock is increasingly chosen as a substitute for the institution of marriage (Sullerot, 1985).

3.3.2. Trends in Birth Rates

Compared with all European countries, France has maintained a relatively high birth rate, though this has clearly declined since the mid-1960s (Roussel, 1988). In 1989, 765,000 children were born in France, compared with 874,000 in 1964, which corresponds to a birth rate of 13.6 and 18.01 per cent, respectively (INSEE, *Les femmes*, 1991:35). Whereas the level of societal reproduction was still secured in the mid-1960s, the rate of reproduction in the 1980s was slightly under replacement level: in 1965, 100 women gave birth to 290 children, in 1989 to only 180 children (whereas 210 are needed for the level of population to be reproduced – see Roussel, 1988). The drop in the fertility rate can be explained partially by the decrease in the number

Table 3.2. *Demographics: proportions of single persons by age group and sex, France, 1962-1985*

Age	1962[a]	1982[b]	1985[b]
Single men			
20–24	83.6	83.2	88.4
25–29	38.1	36.6	47.5
30–34	20.2	18.1	22.4
35–39	14.7	10.9	13.0
Single women			
20–24	56.0	63.2	71.6
25–29	19.8	23.4	31.7
30–34	12.3	13.5	15.8
35–39	10.5	8.4	8.9

[a] General Census.
[b] Employment Survey.

Note: The data base of the General Census (*Recensement*) is the total population. The Employment Survey (*Enquête emploi*) is essentially a household survey; it excludes the hidden labour force and imprisoned persons. The proportion of single persons is higher among the total population than in the population of households.

Source: Levy (1988:71).

of children per family. As Desplanques and De Saboulin (1990) show, most French families today have one or two children, while the number of families with more than three children is falling. According to the General Census, in 1989, out of every 100 families, 41 had one child, 38 had two children, 15 had three, and 6 families had four or more (INSEE, *Recensement de la population*, 1990). If the total number of children born per woman is considered, the following picture emerges for 1965 and 1981: of the women 45 years of age in 1965, 16 per cent had no children, 19 per cent had one child, 23 per cent had two children, 17 per cent three, 10 per cent four, and 15 per cent had five or more children; of the same age group of women in 1981, 10.5 per cent had no children, 17 per cent had one child, 28 per cent had two children, 21 per cent had three, 11 per cent had four, and 12.5 per cent had five or more children (*L'Express*, 1986:44).

Whereas up into the 1970s couples that lived together used to marry as soon as they wanted children, the high numbers of children born out of wedlock suggest that the birth of a child is no longer directly related to the parents' marriage. In 1960, the proportion of children born out of wedlock was 6.1 per cent, but by 1989 it had climbed to 28.2 per cent. Compared with all European countries, France ranks, alongside the Scandinavian countries, as one of the nations with the highest proportion of children born out of wedlock. Almost every third child is born to unmarried parents. Sullerot (1985) assumes that having children has become a matter of choice, since the legalization of contraceptives and abortion has led to a decrease in the number of unwanted pregnancies (Leridon and Toulemon, 1990). Furthermore, the high numbers of children born outside marriage who have been legally recognized afterwards by both parents suggest that it is a matter of a choice not to marry (Rabin, 1992). In 1982, seven out of ten children born out of wedlock were formally recognized by both parents, compared with two out of ten in the 1960s (Sullerot, 1985:151).

3.3.3. *Lone Parents and One-Person Households*

The changes that have taken place in a family's everyday life since the 1960s are reflected in the changes in the structure of families. It is still true that most families are made up of a cohabiting or married couple with or without children (in 1989, 63 per cent of all households; in 1975, 69 per cent). Still, the number of lone-parent and one-person households has increased (INSEE, *Les femmes*, 1991:39).

The term 'lone-parent family', established in the mid-1970s, describes a household type composed of one parent who lives with his or her children who are under the age of 25 (Lefaucheur, 1991:67). According to the results of the 1989 *Enquête emploi*, 1.09 million lone-parent households were counted, up from only 655,000 in 1968. This is equal to a 60 per cent rise in a period of almost twenty years. In most cases, the lone parents are women: this was true for 85.7 per cent of the lone-parent families in 1989 (compared with 79.5 per cent in 1968), whereas in that same year the number of fathers heading lone-parent households amounted to only 14.3 per cent. Of those lone-parent mothers, 18.3 per cent were never married, a significant increase from the 9.2 per cent in 1968. In contrast, the number of lone-parent widows in the same period decreased markedly: in 1968, widows made up the largest portion of lone-parent mothers, namely 55.8 per cent, whereas in 1989 only 35 per cent were widows (INSEE, *Recensement de la population*, 1968, 1982 and 1990).

The number of one-person households has also increased in this same period. In 1968, just under 3.2 million persons lived alone, whereas in 1989 there were 5.2 million. This is a 61.5 per cent rise in twenty years. As can be drawn from Table 3.3, female one-person households predominate, although the number of male one-person households showed markedly higher increases over this entire period. Living alone among younger age groups is rather an exception, but for the older age groups, especially of elderly women, it is becoming characteristic of their way of life. Usually these women are widowed. In contrast, men under 55 make up a bigger share of the one-person households.

3.4. The Family Life Situation: Income and Housing

The prime importance of the individual in society, on the one hand, and the autonomy of the individual in partnership and in the family, on the other, are the two prominent aspects that have influenced the changes in family formation, i.e. the structure of families and households. These changes are also reflected in the structure of household incomes. In recent years, there have been two opposing trends in household incomes: one is characterized by a double-income earning family, which is on the way to becoming a normality; the other might be best described by the term 'new poverty'. Both trends can be well described if 'the child' as a cost-factor is used as a point of reference. Whether the family has a child is a central factor.

3.4.1. *Children with Gainfully Employed Parents*

The steep and continuous rise in labour-market participation of women has led to an overall absolute high in the labour-force participation rate: 25.3 million persons were gainfully employed in France in 1990, compared with

Table 3.3. *Share of one-person households by sex and age groups, France, 1982 and 1989*

Age groups	Single men		Single women	
	1982	1989	1982	1989
15–24	180,040	217,440	205,680	249,240
	4.25%	5.03%	4.85%	5.20%
25–54	802,020	1,149,260	641,740	880,960
	7.43%	8.40%	6.10%	6.50%
55+	667,600	691,800	2,303,600	2,537,020
	12.00%	12.90%	30.70%	31.10%

Source: INSEE, *Recensement de la population* (1982, 1990).

Table 3.4. *Activity rate[a] by age group and sex, France, 1968–1990*

Age	Men				Women			
	1968	1975	1982	1990	1968	1975	1982	1990
15–19	42.8	27.6	23.8	14.9	31.3	21.2	16.7	9.4
20–24	82.6	81.5	79.1	67.6	62.3	66.0	67.1	59.9
25–29	95.1	94.9	93.3	93.5	50.7	62.7	71.1	80.5
30–34	97.2	97.2	96.4	96.8	42.2	54.6	67.1	76.7
35–39	97.2	97.3	96.8	97.2	41.2	50.6	65.4	75.9
40–44	96.6	96.8	96.2	97.0	43.7	49.4	62.4	75.8
45–49	95.5	95.4	94.9	95.9	45.5	49.9	58.7	71.8
50–54	91.5	92.2	90.8	91.0	45.3	48.1	54.0	63.2
55–59	82.5	91.8	76.8	70.0	42.3	41.9	44.9	46.8
60–64	65.7	54.3	39.1	21.1	32.4	27.8	22.5	16.7

[a] The activity rate with respect to the economically active population (active at work, in the military or in joblessness seeking employment) in relation to the total population of the same age.

Source: INSEE, *Recensement de la population* (1990).

23.8 million in 1982. The employment behaviour of women is increasingly approaching that of men (INSEE *Première*, 1991). As Table 3.4 makes clear, changes in employment behaviour are most prevalent in the 30–44 age group.

In contrast, a declining participation rate was evident for those persons in age groups that were likely to be either entering the job market for the first time, or leaving it. This can be explained by the longer periods of education and by the increased utilization of early-retirement schemes. The most prevalent development, however – which is confirmed by the results of the 1990 General Census – is the rapid and continuous growth of labour-market participation of women, evident in almost every age group (INSEE *Première*, 1991).

If the participation of women in the labour market has become 'normal', what is the situation for women with children? Nowadays, more and more women are often confronted with the problem of having to make gainful employment compatible with family obligations. Since 1962 the activity rate of women aged 25–49 with one child climbed 34 percentage points; of those women with two children it rose 40 percentage points; of those with three children it went up 20 percentage points. Even if two out of three women are gainfully employed these days, whether or not a mother seeks employment is highly dependent on the age and number of children for whom she has to care. The more children, and the younger they are, the less is the likelihood that the mother will work outside the home. Only 27 per cent of mothers with three or more children, of which the youngest is under the age of 3, were gainfully employed; by comparison, of those mothers who had one child under 3 or two children of which one was younger than 3, 69 per cent held jobs (Table 3.5). Mothers who are lone parents have much more difficulty reconciling gainful employment with family responsibilities. Child care alone greatly limits the possibilities of gaining or holding a job.

3.4.2. *The 'Costs' of Children*

In a study conducted by Glaude and Moutardier (1991), it is shown that two children cost less than twice the costs of an only child; that the older the child is, the more costs are incurred; and that even those costs that are directly incurred by children can none the less be calculated only with great difficulty.

The child allowance (*allocation familiale*) is a benefit paid to families in order partially to compensate for the costs incurred by their children. It is paid to every family for every child until completion of compulsory schooling (when the child reaches 16 years of age), but only after the second child is born. Payment is continued for every child under 17 years of age whose training wage does not exceed 55 per cent of the minimum wage determined by law. Benefits also continue for children under 20 years of age whose training wage does not exceed 55 per cent of the legal minimum wage, as well as for those under 20 who study, who have an apprenticeship, who are attending vocational training (*formation professionelle*), or who are entitled to an allowance for handicapped and disabled children (Dupeyroux, 1988). The benefit level is set annually, effective on 1 January. In 1992 it was FRF 621 for two children, FRF 1,416 for three, FRF 2,211 for four, FRF 3,006 for five and FRF 3,801 for six. For every additional child a payment of FRF 795 was made (Table 3.6).

Table 3.5. *Activity rate of women living in long-term partnership, France, 1989*

No. of children	Youngest child <3 years old	Youngest child 3–5 years old	Youngest child 6–17 years old
1	74	80	72
2	63	71	71
3 or more	27	38	50

Source: INSEE, *Enquête emploi* (1989).

Table 3.6. *Family allowances per month, France, 1992 (FRF)*

Allowances	No. of children					
	1	2	3	4	5	6
Child allowance	–	621	1416	2211	3006	3801
Income-related benefits for infants	891	1782	–	–	–	–
Family supplemental allowance (income related)[a]	–	–	808	808	808	808
Allowances for handicapped children	621	–	–	–	–	–
Supplement for loss of one parent	582	1164	1746	2328	2910	3492
Benefits for lone parents	3879	4849	5819	6789	7759	8728
Parental leave payments	–	–	2765	2765	2765	2765
Relocation assistance	–	–	4655	5043	5431	5819

[a] Payments are made for children under 3 years of age, starting with the third child.

Source: Liaisons sociales (1992: No. 6649).

Beyond the allowances listed in Table 3.6, certain expenditures incurred for children can also be reclaimed through tax deductions or allowances.

3.4.3. *Tax Schemes for Child Expenditures*

Tax schemes for married couples (*quotient conjugal*) and for families (*quotient familial*) are characteristic of French government tax strategies to relieve the financial burden of a family budget. Both systems allow for a progressive reduction in taxable income according to a unit scheme that allots units according to family composition: parents are each allotted one unit, and children each receive one half-unit. In lone-parent families the first child is allotted one full unit, then each child after that one-half. Families with three or more children are given an additional one half-unit (Table 3.7). The total of the combined household's incomes is then divided into the total number of allotted units.

The main effects of the tax schemes for families are reductions in taxable income and tax exemptions. These schemes, with a total of FRF 34,000 in 1987, represented 30 per cent of the entire family benefits. If the number of families that do not pay taxes is considered in connection with their actual available incomes, it is evident that family income subject to taxation is reduced starting with the third child. In 1984, 62.2 per cent of families with

Table 3.7. *Allocation of tax units by marital status and number of children, France, 1987*

Marital status	Tax credits (no. of units)
Single person	1
Couple	2
Couple with one child	2.5
Couple with two children	3
Couple with three children	4[a]
Couple with four children	4.5
Lone parents with one child	2
Lone parents with two children	2.5

[a] Since 1980, the third child has been allotted one full unit, i.e. in addition to the two halves for the first and the second child.

Source: Fragonard (1988).

three children in which the father was gainfully employed had an annual income of less than FRF 32,800 that was subject to taxation. In contrast, 31.5 per cent of families with both parents earning incomes had to pay taxes on annual incomes ranging from FRF 32,800 to FRF 43,300 (Table 3.8).

This can be explained mainly by the facts that tax schemes allow families with three or more children to pay less in taxes, and that at the same time they are entitled to benefits that are not subject to taxation.

3.4.4. *Children of Poor Families*

For lack of specific studies, it is not possible at this point to analyse family incomes accurately. What can be noted, however, from the data of the 1986 *Enquête emploi*, is that there are strong indications that poverty is chiefly the result of the unemployment of the head of household or of his or her jobless partner. Children pose a financial burden even for a family with a regular income, and the burden becomes more acute when only a low income or no earned income is available.

There are two public transfer payments, *revenue minimum d'insertion* (RMI) and *allocation de parent isolé* (API), which are intended to assist families that are experiencing financial hardship. RMI is a welfare supplement available to lower-income families and was introduced by law on 1 December

Table 3.8. *Percentage rate of family tax exemptions in France, 1987*

	%
1 child	17
2 children	23
3 children	53
4 children	72
5 children and more	87

Source: Fragonard (1988).

1988. It is comparable to the German '*Sozialhilfe*'. RMI is mainly under the auspices of the Office of Family Assistance (*Caisses d'Allocations Familiales*). It guarantees every person who is a permanent resident in France a minimum monthly income indexed according to family size. For example, on 1 January 1992, a single person received FRF 2,185, while a (married) couple with two children received FRF 4,588. Recipients of RMI are required to accept job offers or advanced training and refresher course placement offers. In most cases (57 per cent), RMI recipients are single persons without children; persons or families with children make up only 36.5 per cent of RMI recipients (Barbier, 1990).

The API is a lone-parent allowance introduced in 1976 to guarantee lone-parent families a minimum monthly income. Single parents are defined as widows, divorcees, a parent separated from his or her spouse, or an unmarried person not living with his or her partner in a marriage-like situation. Benefits are payable when the monthly income does not exceed a given level. Generally, lone-parent families can draw this transfer for one year or at the most until the youngest child reaches 3 years of age. API benefit levels, effective 1 January 1992, amounted to FRF 3,879 for one child, FRF 4,849 for two, and FRF 5,819 for three. For every additional child, the family received FRF 924 (see Table 3.6). A study of poor families in France revealed that 25,000 lone-parent families neither had an earned income nor received unemployment benefits, while 15 per cent of those families were recipients of API benefits. Of the remaining poor families, 30,000 were single persons or couples without children; 13,000 were (married) couples with children who were also without gainful employment or unemployment benefits; and 50,000 were one-person households that were mostly dependent upon unemployment benefits as their sole source of income (Haut Conseil, 1992).

3.4.5. *The Housing Situation*

The major trends in changes in family formation that have been described above have also had effects on the housing situation. As a matter of fact, a changed demand for living space has resulted from the various social developments in the last two decades. For example, taken together, the growing number of elderly persons and the changes in family formation have led to more mobility and a diversification of needs and demands on the housing market (Haumont and Ségnaud, 1989).

According to Aballéa and Benjamin's (1988) study, there is an apparent (though only slightly) increasing tendency for the behaviour of unmarried cohabiting couples to approach that of married couples – in relation to residence ownership, the length of residence, etc. Their findings also suggest that the ever-higher demand for public housing is closely related to the rate of divorce. Spouses who become owners of their own home or flat while married often become tenants after divorce, and then seek less expensive (public) housing. Therefore, the demand for rented housing or private ownership of housing seems to be clearly related to the structure of families, and the type of housing (privately owned flat, home, etc.) is connected to the household type (lone-parent family, one-person household, etc.).

As part of the programme of transfer payments for families mentioned above, there is also financial assistance available for housing and related costs. This area of assistance was expanded in the 1970s, from a general housing allowance (*allocation de logement*) to three benefits: a housing supplement (*aide personalisée au logement*), a relocation allowance (*prime de déménagement*) and a renovation loan (*prêt à l'amélioration de l'habitat*) (CAF, 1990[8]).

3.5. Compatibility of Family Obligations and Employment

How is it, asked Claudia de Weck, a journalist, that women in France are able to make gainful employment and family obligations compatible? (*Die Zeit*, 27 October 1989) She found her answer in the political measures initiated by the French government, which aimed to make a good 'infrastructure' available to working mothers to help make their jobs within and outside the home more reconcilable. All-day school with school cafeterias and fixed opening hours for children of all ages is commonplace in France. Besides

---

[8] CAF = Caisse d'Allocations Familiales.

the many day nurseries, the so-called *garderies* offer day-care facilities for children outside instruction periods in the mornings and afternoons. Whereas in the Federal Republic of Germany in 1990 56.7 per cent of all women between the ages of 25 and 55 were gainfully employed, in France 75 per cent of such women were working. The increase in the number of employed women was particularly noticeable among those in the age group that was more likely to have to care for one or two children. The activity rate of the 25-year-olds was 77 per cent in 1989 compared with 70 per cent of the 49-year-olds. In contrast, the participation rate of 25-year-old women in 1975 was 63 per cent compared with 46 per cent of the 49-year-olds (INSEE, *Données Sociales*, 1990).

However, even if the activity rate of women with one or two children is increasingly approaching that of single women without children, the activity rate of women with three or more children has rather remained low, though it has also risen when observed over a long period: in 1975 it was 26 per cent; by 1989, 37 per cent. Even so, there was a slight decrease in the participation rate of women from 30 to 40 years of age, who tend to be in the primary childbearing and child-rearing phase (INSEE, *Enquête emploi*, 1986–7).

3.5.1. *Division of Labour within the Family*

In France, compared with the Federal Republic of Germany, the availability of child care outside the home seems almost perfectly adequate (*Die Zeit*, 27 October 1989). None the less, it is still difficult to make family obligations and gainful employment compatible in France. As in other countries, child care has remained primarily the mother's responsibility (Villeneuve-Gokalp, 1989; Desplanques and De Saboulin, 1990; De Singly, 1987). A study on time budgeting conducted by INSEE from 1985 to 1986 revealed that the rearing of children had little influence on the employment behaviour and everyday life of fathers. Mothers still tend to take over the housework to a large extent, and they spend three to four times more time with their children than fathers do (INSEE, *Premiers résultats*, 1987).

Problems in many families' everyday lives arise, on the one hand, because a care-taker must be found for the children if both parents are employed, and, on the other, because the housework cannot be done as thoroughly as in a family in which only one parent is employed. Getting the housework done and taking care of the children demands time and requires, particularly in families in which both parents are working, the division of tasks and strict time schedules. Consequently, problems of meeting the demands of both spheres of work arise.

At the same time, however, the rise in the employment rate of women in France has done little to change the understanding of the traditional role of the wife and mother (Desplanques and De Saboulin, 1990). Rather, there appears to be an increase in the orientation towards an occupation among women which has not been accompanied by an increase in the orientation towards the family among men (De Singly, 1987; Roy, 1990).

The problems of making familial obligations and gainful employment compatible have been a salient public issue for a relatively long time. Ever since 1986, compatibility of both life spheres has been a central issue for the social partners (unions, employers, etc.) and has been a topic dealt with on an institutional level as well. In 1989, for example, the *Conseil Supérieur de l'Égalité Professionelle* did a report on the topic of 'Company Management regarding Familial Obligations'. In 1991, the Council for Economic and Social Affairs also took on the issue of compatibility as a part of its report on family policy. The ways in which governmental measures addressed the suggestions made in that report is the subject of the next section.

3.5.2. *Political Measures Related to Compatibility Issues*

Governmental measures to assist families constitute a part of social policy and especially family policy in France. With respect to the issue of compatibility, regulations concerning maternity leave and parental leave and regulations regarding parental time off from work to take care of sick children can both be considered as generally appropriate instruments of social policy that serve to contribute to a better co-ordination of both life spheres. But these legal intervening measures cannot be viewed in isolation from other relevant measures. In Section 3.2, two kinds of policy were distinguished: (1) parental leave allowances, which are to compensate for the loss of income incurred during a temporary interruption of employment arising from the birth of a child (e.g. APE); (2) financial benefits that aim to make gainful employment and family responsibilities more compatible (e.g. AGED). Of primary importance to resolving the problems of compatibility discussed here is the creation of qualitatively good and quantitively adequate (with respect to demand) public child-care facilities (e.g. day care, nurseries, all-day school, pre-school and after-school programmes). Finding satisfactory daytime child care is the main problem faced by families in which both parents are employed and in lone-parent families in which the sole parent is working.

Table 3.9. *Percentage of children in pre-school by age, France, 1976–1986*

Age	1976–7	1979–80	1982–3	1985–6
2	26.1	33.9	33.1	32.1
3	81.6	88.1	91.0	93.7
4	99.3	100.0	100.0	100.0

Source: Norvez (1990:424).

3.5.3. *Child-Care Facilities*

It was calculated that a minimum of 770,000 child-care facility places for children under 3 years of age were needed in 1986 by working parents (Hatchuel, 1989). In 1990 it was estimated that approximately 1 million child-care facility places were needed (Norvez, 1990:323). Only about half of the children under 3 years of age (43 per cent) needing day care can be placed in an institutional facility; 16 per cent are being cared for by publicly licensed nurseries (*assistante maternelle agréée*); the rest are in other privately organized child-care facilities (e.g. *crèches parentales*, which are privately organized for small groups of children) (Haut Conseil, 1992). Although a comprehensive network of child care for children under 3 years exists in France, it falls far short of fulfilling the demand. The conditions of child care for children above that age have markedly improved. All children over 3 attend all-day school and pre-school at no cost to the parents (Table 3.9).

Also, with the introduction of compulsory schooling for children aged 6 and older, the situation regarding the care of children is good compared with that of the Federal Republic of Germany. A sizeable portion (78.8 per cent) of the primary schools that are also all-day schools have their own school cafeterias, so that the afternoon meal is provided. The greatest difficulty is that of co-ordinating the children's school schedules with the parents' work schedules before school begins and directly after school breaks, on Wednesday afternoons when schools are closed and during school holidays. At those times, however, parents can often – though not always – turn to day-care facilities that are organized by local communities (David and Gokalp, 1984).

3.6. Closing Remarks

In the 1960s a change in the structure of families in France began which has continued to the present. This change has come with the decline in the inclination to marry, with the increase in the rate of divorce, with a growing number of unmarried couples cohabiting, and with a high number of children born out of wedlock (see Section 3.3). At the same time, the clear rise in the economic activity rate of women in general, and of mothers with young and infant children in particular, shows that the life course of women has changed significantly in the last decade: continuous employment, even when small children have to be cared for, is characteristic of a woman's life in France. This had an impact on family policy in the 1980s. In 1981, President Mitterrand stressed the state's neutrality with respect to the citizen's choice of family formation, and improving the compatibility of familial obligations and gainful employment became a central goal of family policy in recent years. A pro-natal component has remained a significant aspect of French family policy throughout the years: assistance offered through family policies peaks, as has always been the case, with the third child, even though in recent years financial benefits for families with two children have been significantly increased.

References

Aballéa, F. and Benjamin, I. (1988), 'Nouvelles conjugalités et rapport à l'habitat' (New forms of conjugal life and related housing), *Recherche Sociale*, 105:1–85.

Barbier, J. (1990), *Le revenu minimum d'insertion et politique familiale* (Supplement for Lower Income Families and Family Policy), AISS 18–20/09/1990, Brussels.

CAF (1990), *Le guide des allocations familiales* (Guide to Family Allowances), CAF, Paris.

Ceccaldi, D. (1957), *Histoire des prestations familiales* (History of Family Benefits), CNAF, Paris.

CERC (1985), *Mères de famille: coûts et revenus de l'activité professionelle* (Mothers: Costs and Income of Employment), CERC, Paris.

—— (1989), *Les familles nombreuses* (Large Families), INSEE, Paris.

CES (Conseil Économique et Social) (1991), *La politique familiale française* (French Family Policy), CES, Paris.

Commaille, J. (1991), 'La régulation politique de la famille' (The influence of policy on families), in F. de Singly (ed.), *La famille: l'état des savoirs* (The Family: an Overview), Découverte, Paris: 265–76.

David, M.G. and Gokalp, C. (1984), 'La semaine d'un enfant scolarisé' (The school child's week), *Consommation – Revue de Socio-Économie*, 1:59–88.

De Gall, D. and Martin, C. (1988), *Le réseau de parenté après la désunion* (The Network of Familial Relations after Separation), Université de Caen, Caen.

De Singly, F. (1987), *Fortune et infortune de la femme mariée: Sociologie de la vie conjugale* (Fortune and Misfortune of the Married Woman: the Sociology of Conjugal Life), PUF, Paris.

—— (ed.) (1991), *La famille: l'état des savoirs* (The Family: an Overview), Découverte, Paris.

Desplanques, G. and De Saboulin, M. (1990), 'Les familles aujourd'hui' (Families Today), *Données sociales 1990*:274–84c.

Dieuleveut, T. (1990), 'Quelle cohérence pour la politique familiale' (Suggestions for a coherent family policy), *Problèmes Économiques*, No. 2178:1–4.

Dumon, W. (1987), 'Politique familiale en Europe occidentale' (Family Policy in Western Europe), *L'Année Sociologique*, 37:291–308.

Dupâquier, J. *et al.* (eds.) (1988), *Histoire de la population française: de 1914 à nos jours* (History of the French Population: 1914 to Present), Vol. IV, PUF, Paris.

Dupeyroux, J.J. (1988), *Droit de la sécurité sociale* (Social Security Law), Documentation Française, Paris.

L'Express (1986), 'La famille: une idée moderne' (The family: a modern idea), 6/1986: 42–50.

Fragonard, B. (1988), 'L'aide à la famille: politiques de prestations et politiques fiscales' (Family assistance: benefit policy and fiscal policy), in M.T. Meulders-Klein and J. Eekelaar (eds.), *Famille, état et sécurité économique d'existence* (Family, State and Minimum Income Support), Vol. II, Kluwer, Deventer: 815–28.

Glaude, M. and Moutardier, M. (1991), 'Une évolution du coût direct de l'enfant' (The development of the costs of children), *Économie et Statistiques*, 248:33–49.

Hatchuel, G. (1989), 'Acceuil des jeunes enfants: 'La course à la débrouille'' (Child care: 'coping strategies'), *Consommation et Modes de Vie: Chroniques du Crédoc*, 41:1–4.

Haumont, N. and Ségnaud, M. (1989), *Familles et modes de vie et habitat* (Families, Lifestyles and Housing), L'Harmattan, Paris.

Haut Conseil de la Population et de la Famille (1992), *Mieux concilier la vie professionelle et la vie familiale: Ou en sommes-nous?* (On the Way to Improving Compatibility of Occupational and Family Life: Where Are We Now?), Haut Conseil de la Population et de la Famille, Paris.

Kellerhals, J. (1984), *Microsociologie de la famille* (Microsociology of the Family), PUF, Paris.

Laroque, P. (1985), *La politique familiale en France depuis 1945* (Family Policy in France since 1945), Documentation Française, Paris.

Lefaucheur, N. (1985), 'Familles monoparentales: les mots pour le dire' (Lone-Parent Families: Ways of Referring to Them), in F. Bailleau, N. Lefaucheur and V. Peyre (eds.), *Lecture sociologique du travail social* (Social Work Seen by Sociologists), Édition Ouvrière/Criv, Paris.

—— (1991), 'Les familles dîtes monoparentales' (The So-called Lone-Parent Families), in De Singly (1991:67–74).

Lenoir, R. (1988), 'Politik und Familie' (Policy and family), in K. Lüscher *et al.*

(eds.), *Die 'postmoderne' Familie: Familiale Strategien und Familienpolitik in einer Übergangszeit* (The 'Post-Modern' Family: Family Strategies and Family Policy in an Era of Transition), Universitätsverlag Konstanz GmbH, Konstanz: 364–70.

Leridon, H. and Toulemon, L. (1990), 'La fin des naissances non desirées' (The end of unwanted pregnancies), *Données sociales 1990*: 293–6.

—— and Villeneuve-Gokalp, C. (1988), 'Les nouveaux couples: nombre, caractéristiques et attitudes' (The new couples: Number, characteristics and attitudes), *Population*, 2:331–74.

Levy, H. (1988), 'Familles d'hier et d'aujourd'hui' (Families of the past and the present), *Revue futuribles*, 1:65–73.

Liaisons sociales (1992): 'Emplois familiaux, prestations familiales' (Family work, family benefits), No. 6649.

Menahem, G. (1979), 'Les mutations de la famille et les modes de reproduction de la force de travail' (Changes in the family and the modes of reproduction of the labour force), *L'homme et la société*, No. 51–4: 63ff.

Messu, M. (1992), *Les politiques familiales* (Family Policies), Atelier, Paris.

Munoz-Perez, B. and Rondeau-Rivier, M.C. (1990), 'Une nouvelle phase pour le divorce?' (A new phase for divorce?), *Données sociales 1990*: 297–300.

Norvez, A. (1990): *De la naissance à l'école, santé, modes de garde et préscolarité dans la France contemporaine* (From Birth to School, Health, Modes of Childcare and the Pre-school System in Present-Day France), INED, Paris.

Population (1991), 'Vingtième rapport sur la situation démographique de la France' (Twentieth report on the demographic situation in France), *Population*, 5:1081–1160.

Pressat, R. (1991), 'La famille au travers des chiffres' (The family presented by statistics), *Revue futuribles*, 4:27–40.

Prost, A. (1984), 'L'évolution de la politique familiale en France de 1938 à 1981' (The evolution of French family policy from 1938 to 1981), *Mouvement Social*, 129:7–28.

Quotidien du médecin (1990), 'Politique familiale: le Dr Hélène Dorlhac veut conjuger famille et liberté. Un entretien avec le secrétaire d'Etat à la famille' (Family policy: Dr. Hélène Dorlhac wants to reconcile family and liberty. An interview with the Secretary of State for the family), 4565:18.

Rabin, B. (1992), 'De plus en plus de naissances hors mariage' (Increasing numbers of births out of wedlock), *Économie et Statistiques*, 251:3–13.

Roussel, L. (1986), 'Du pluralisme des modèles familiaux dans les sociétés post-industrielles: quelques problèmes méthodologiques et théoriques' (About the pluralism of family models in post-industrial societies: some methodological and theoretical problems), in Association Internationale des Démographes de Langue Française, *Les familles d'aujourd'hui* (Families of Today), Colloque de Genève (17-20 September 1984), Institut National d'Études Démographiques, Paris: 143–52.

—— (1988), 'Die soziologische Bedeutung der demographischen Erschütterung in den Industrieländern der letzten zwanzig Jahre' (The sociological implication of the demographic changes in industrial nations in the past 20 years), in K. Lüscher, F. Schultheis and M. Wehrspaun (eds.), *Die 'postmoderne' Familie: Familiale Strategien und Familienpolitik in einer Übergangszeit* (The 'Post-Modern' Family: Family Strategies and Family Policy in an Era of Transition), Universitätsverlag Konstanz GmbH, Konstanz: 39–54.

—— (1989), *La famille incertaine* (The Uncertain Family), Éditions Odile Jacob, Paris.

—— (1991), 'Les types de familles' (Family forms), in De Singly (1991:83– 94.

—— and Bourguignon, O. (1978), *Générations nouvelles et mariage traditionnel* (New Generations and Traditional Marriage), PUF, Paris.

Roy, C. (1990), 'Dix ans après, les nouveaux pères existent-ils?' (Ten years later, does the 'New Father' exist?), *École des Parents*, 2:37–42.

Rubellin-Devichi, J. (1991), *Regards sur le droit de la famille dans le monde* (Family Law in International Perspective), PUF, Paris.

Schultheis, F. (1988), *Sozialgeschichte der französischen Familienpolitik* (Social History of the French Family Policy), Campus-Verlag, Frankfurt/Main and New York.

Segalen, M. (1990), *Die Familie: Geschichte, Soziologie, Anthropologie* (The Family: History, Sociology, Anthropology), Campus-Verlag, Frankfurt/Main and New York.

—— and Zonabend, F. (1986), 'Famille en France' (Family in France), in A. Burguière (ed.), *Histoire de la famille française* (History of the French Family), Armand Colin, Paris: 497–527.

Sullerot, E. (1984), *Pour le meilleur et sans le pire* (For the Better and Without the Worse), Fayard, Paris.

—— (1985), 'Des faits...' (Facts...), in P. Kaltenbach (ed.), *La famille contre les pouvoirs: De Louis XIV à Mitterrand* (The Family against the State: From Louis XIV to Mitterrand), Nouvelle Cité, Paris: 147–58.

Talmy, R. (1962), *Histoire du mouvement familial en France 1896-1939* (History of the Family Mouvement in France, 1896-1939), CNAF, Paris.

Villac, M. (1986), 'Parents, enfants... La famille en mouvement' (Parents, children ... The family in progress), *Le groupe familial*, 110:4–10.

Villeneuve-Gokalp, C. (1989), 'Garder son emploi, garder ses enfants: une analyse par catégorie sociale' (Keeping her job, keeping her children: an analysis by social category), *Cahiers Québécois de Démographie*, 18:87–113.

Statistical materials:

CAF (1990), *Statistiques prestations familiales* (Official Statistics of Family Benefits).

CERC (1988), *Protection sociale et pauvreté* (Social Security and Poverty), No. 88.

—— (1988), *Constat de l'évolution récente des revenus en France* (Report on Recent Development of Income in France), No. 89.

CERC–INSEE (1989), *Études sur les familles nombreuses* (Studies on Large Families).

CNDIF–INSEE (1987), *Les femmes en chiffre* (Women in Statistics).[9]

INSEE (1968, 1982, 1990), *Recensement de la population* (General Census of Population).

—— (1989), *Enquête emploi* (Labour Force Survey).

—— (1987), *Premiers résultats* (First Results), Nr. 100, June.

—— (1990), *Annuaire Statistique de la France* (Annual Statistics of France).

—— *Première*, (1990) Nos. 54, 81; (1991) Nos. 116, 125, 146, 147, 149; (1992) No. 152.

—— (1990), *Données sociales* (Social Facts).

—— (1991), *Les femmes: contours et caractères* (Women: Differences and Characteristics).

---

[9] CNDIF = Centre National d'Information sur les Droits des Femmes.

4 The Federal Republic of Germany: Polarization of Family Structure

GERO FEDERKEIL

Wissenschaftsrat, Cologne, Germany

Demographic data reveal that Germany is among the European countries with the lowest birth rates. Furthermore, Germany ranks among those countries with the highest proportions of couples remaining childless. In sociology these trends are often referred to in terms of a 'pluralization of family life forms' and, as its biographical counterpart, an 'individualization of the life course'. On the basis of a multidimensional classification, household structures (including employment) have been analysed for women who were at the average age to begin a family, and for women who had just entered the post-parental phase in their family life course. The results show that the dynamics during the 1980s were confined to the younger cohorts of women entering the typical parenting age. With regard to the older cohorts, family life remained rather traditional. Among the younger cohorts, however, a pattern of family trends has emerged during the 1980s that is particular to (West) German society and that leads to a revision of the pluralization thesis. We found a polarization between, on the one hand, a growing sector of non-family households, in which there was indeed a high degree of pluralization, and, on the other, a shrinking proportion of young women who decide in favour of a family but do so in rather traditional ways, i.e. where the 'married-housewife-family' remains largely predominant. At the same time, those women who did start families, more often than before, went on to have more than one child.

4.1. Introduction

Like most other industrialized countries, Germany witnessed the demographic changes that characterize the 'second demographic transition' (Van de Kaa, 1987). Ever since the end of the 1960s, fertility has been below replacement level. At the end of the last decade, the net reproduction rate in Germany has been among the lowest in the world (1989: 0.67). Within twenty-five years (from 1960 to 1985), the total fertility rate dropped from 2.41 to 1.28 (Birg *et al.*, 1987), while the average age of women at first birth increased from 24.9 years in 1965 to 26.2 years in 1985. Furthermore, between 1960 and 1986, the marriage rate fell from 9.4 to 6.1 per 1,000 inhabitants and this was accompanied by an increase in age at marriage since the mid-1970s, from 25.3 years in 1975 to 27.2 years in 1985 for men, and from 23.7 to 24.6 years for women (Birg *et al.*, 1991).

4.1.1. *Theoretical Background*

In demography the notion of a 'second demographic transition' has become a new paradigm. Central to this concept is the idea that there are common factors responsible for family change operating in a sequence in all European countries. Countries can be grouped by the time they pass through that sequence. The first group of countries, which have already gone through this transition, comprises most countries of Northern and Western Europe, as well as Italy (Van de Kaa, 1987:12). The second group is formed by the countries of Southern Europe, where the birth rate decline has been less marked. The Eastern European countries, marked by their different political development rather than by specific demographic features, form the third group. Finally, Turkey, Albania, Ireland and Iceland form the latecomers of the second demographic transition.

In Germany, family sociologists too usually refer to those demographic changes and, in many cases, to the concept of the second demographic transition. Notwithstanding a variety of interpretations, diagnoses and prognoses, most analyses of family changes have one feature in common: like the notion of the second demographic transition, family change is regarded as a symptom of secular social change (Kaufmann, 1990:9) which is analysed in terms of an ongoing social differentiation (Peuckert, 1991) and as a further step in modernization (Beck, 1986; Beck and Beck-Gernsheim, 1990). As these are ongoing processes in all Western industrial societies, those conceptions imply more or less uniform changes of family life in Europe and the United States – only starting at different times, and being advanced to different degrees.

In Germany the notions of 'individualization' (Beck, 1986) and 'pluralization' (Zapf *et al.*, 1987) gained particular prominence as family-related equivalents of those social changes. However, both terms have often been used as synonyms in describing family change, and hence have lost analytical clarity.[1]

The notion of individualization was made popular in particular by Beck's analysis of the ecological 'risk society'. According to Beck (1986:116), individualization is one aspect of the broader process of modernization, referring to the release from 'traditional class situations and supply networks of the family'. He considers gender conflicts inside and outside the family as expressions of a two-phase process of modernization. At first, with the completion of industrial society and its inherent gender division of labour, the bourgeois breadwinner–housekeeper family became the 'normal' family, as modernization comprised men only. In this context, Beck (1986:179) characterizes modernity as 'divided in half'. The second phase of welfare-state modernization has brought the inclusion of women into the logic of the market economy, through their growing labour-market participation. But, according to Beck, the problem of the completed market economy, that is, the interlocking of two occupational careers, cannot be solved within the institutional structures and living arrangements of a halved market economy: i.e. the breadwinner–housekeeper family (1986:180). Hence, the traditional model of the family is opposed to the necessities of (the second) modernization, as 'the completed market model presupposes a society without marriage and families' (1986:191). While lacking systematic empirical evidence, Beck's analysis implicitly refers to industrial societies as a whole and hence suggests a sequential model of family change.

In its characterization of the causes of observed family changes, this diagnosis is similar to Kaufmann's concept of 'structural neglect' of the family (Kaufmann, 1990:132ff.), which refers to incompatibilities between the logics of the economic and political systems and the assumption of family responsibilities. In this perspective, the main causes of family changes, which are described as a 'loss of plausibility and a biographical disposition towards parenthood', are 'cultural liberalization, growing economic options and – related with both – changes in women's biographies' (1990:9). Again, these are factors characterizing all industrial societies, and are not peculiarities of (Western) Germany alone. The pluralization of family types is conceived of as a 'plausible consequence of growing economic options'. In contrast to Beck's concept, that of Kaufmann does not imply an unstructured individualization in terms of 'the completely normal chaos of love' (Beck and Beck-Gernsheim, 1990) or a post-modern 'anything goes'. He agrees with Zapf

---

[1] In his attempt at conceptual clarification, Strohmeier (1991:187ff.) relates individualization to the loosening of life courses from traditional contexts, whereas pluralization marks a growing variety of living arrangements (and family types) resulting – cross-sectionally, to put it in methodological terms – from the individualization of biographies.

et al. (1987), who point out that in welfare-state societies there is a relationship of 'individualization and security' as a basis of pluralization that leads to an increase in group- and milieu-specific patterns of values. Hence, Kaufmann (1990:398) concludes that 'public discussions about family changes are much more dramatic than are empirical trends'.

With regard to the interpretation of changes, there is a differentiation between marriage and parenthood. The institution of marriage has lost plausibility, and parenthood has become more and more one option among others (Kaufmann, 1990:9). Hence, the process of family formation today is more than ever focused on parenthood. Tyrell (1988) refers to increasing numbers of children not growing up (for at least part of their childhood) within the traditional family, that is, not with both married parents.[2] His conclusion is that of a growing uncoupling of the patterns of traditional family life, that is, an *uncoupling* of the traditional relationship of love, lifelong (monogamous) marriage, living together in the same household and with both biological parents. Recent studies based on large-scale life course data sets for selected birth cohorts found a growing *polarization* of German society into childless women and women with children (and this often means more than one child), and contrasted those findings with the often forecasted trend towards the one-child family (Huinink, 1989).[3]

4.1.2. *Demographic Trends in the 1980s*

MARRIAGE. In Germany, the propensity to marry continuously declined throughout the last decades. Total marriage rates decreased during the 1970s and 1980s (Table 4.1), even if the decline was less dramatic in the 1980s. Looking at different birth cohorts, this trend becomes more evident. Whereas 94 per cent of the women born in 1932, and 95 per cent even of cohort 1938, were married before the age of 50, estimates for the cohorts 1944–50 amount to 91–93 per cent only, and in the cohorts born after 1955 more than 10 per cent of all women will never marry (Lengsfeld and Linke, 1988:347). This decrease in the propensity to marry has been paralleled by a delay in first marriages. After a period of decreasing age at first marriage from 1950 to the mid-1970s (with its nadir in 1975, when the average age at first mar-

---

[2] For Germany, Schwarz (1989) gives an estimation of about 29 per cent of all children not living with both their natural parents during at least part of their childhood.

[3] Applying methods of event history analysis, Huinink could show that the hazard of a second birth, once a woman has become a mother, is higher than the 'risk' of a first birth, even for women belonging to younger cohorts.

Table 4.1. *Summary table of demographic trends in Germany during the 1980s*

	1980	1985	1989
Marriage and divorce			
Crude marriage rate (CMR)	5.9	6.0	6.4
Total first marriage rate (women below age 50)	0.66	0.60	0.57
First marriage age (mean; women)	23.4	24.6	25.7
Crude divorce rate (CDR)	1.6	2.1	2.0
Total divorce rate (TDR)	0.22	0.30	0.30
Fertility			
Crude birth rate (CBR)	10.1	9.6	11.0
Total fertility rate (TFR)	1.45	1.28	1.44
Net reproduction rate (NRR)	0.68	0.60	0.67
Age at first birth (mean; women)	25.2	26.2	26.8
Extra-marital births (percentage of all births)	7.6	9.4	10.2

Sources: Council of Europe (1991); Statistisches Bundesamt (1991).

riage for women was 22.7 years), this figure rose continuously to 25.7 years in 1989.

DIVORCE. At the same time, the number of divorces has steadily increased since 1956 (with a short break after the law reform of 1977). Only after 1984 was there a slight decrease in divorce rates, so that the total divorce rate seems to have remained stable when 1985 is compared with 1989. According to the duration-specific dissolution rates of 1986, about 29 per cent of all marriages end in divorce. At the same time, total remarriage rates dropped from 80 per cent in the 1960s to 64 per cent in the mid-1980s (Lengsfeld and Linke, 1988:351).

COHABITATION. This development was accompanied by a fast growth in the number of cohabiting couples which, according to micro-census data, increased by 504 per cent in the decade between 1975 and 1985.[4] According to these data, the proportion of all such households grew from 0.6 in 1972 to 3.0 per cent in 1990. But most survey studies give a much higher estimate of their number. The Institut für Demoskopie in Allensbach, for example, calculated 3 million adults living in unmarried cohabitation in 1989, which means a proportion of about 5.4 per cent of all households (*Der Spiegel*,

---

[4] The figures on unmarried cohabitation have to rely on estimations based on the micro-censuses, because official German household statistics count cohabiting couples as two households of people living alone. Paradoxically, cohabiting couples with children are registered as a man living alone plus a lone mother.

No. 27, 1989).

The nature of cohabitation has changed too during the last two decades. In 1972, almost half of all cohabiting men and women were over 56, and many of them were divorced or widowed. In 1982, however, almost two-thirds were younger than 35, and most of them had never married. A particularity of unmarried cohabitation in Germany is that the vast majority of cohabiting couples – and even a growing percentage – is childless (in 1990: 88.5 per cent) and most of the few cohabitees who are living with children are stepfamilies (BMJFG, 1985).

FERTILITY. Like most other European countries (see Council of Europe, 1991), Germany witnessed a tremendous decrease in birth rates after the 'baby boom' of the late 1950s and early 1960s. Although recently fertility rates at least partly recovered, German total fertility rates (1.44 in 1989) and net reproduction rates (0.67) are among the lowest in the world (Council of Europe, 1991). These trends are highlighted by completed fertility rates of different birth cohorts of women as shown in Figure 4.1. Up to the women born in 1939, the completed fertility rate was above 2.0; over the next ten cohorts it dropped to 1.71, and then even further to the lowest values of 1.58 resp. 1.59 for cohorts 1954 and 1956. This general decrease hides different trends with regard to parity:

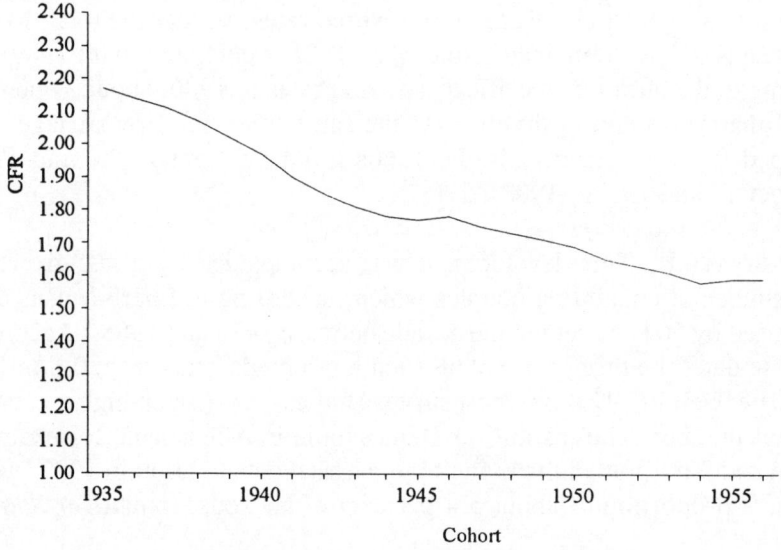

Source: Birg *et al.* (1987); Council of Europe (1991).

Figure 4.1. Average completed fertility, FRG, female birth cohorts 1935–1956

The process of changes in reproductive behaviour started at higher order births and step by step extended to lower order births. In the generation of 1936 the frequency of fourth or higher order births was 8% below the respective frequency in the former generation of 1935. Since the generation of 1939 the decrease in births of third children began to accelerate and since the generation of 1940 those of second children. (Birg *et al.*, 1987:24).

Related to these quantitative trends, there have been changes in the timing of births. Since the mid-1970s, the average age of women giving birth, especially at first birth, has been growing. The mean age of (married) women at the birth of their first child rose from 24.3 in 1971 (the lowest age in the last three decades) to 25.2 in 1980 and 26.8 in 1989. Consequently, mean birth intervals (including those between marriage and first birth) have fallen since the late 1970s. Furthermore, estimates suggest a still-growing percentage of women remaining childless. Unfortunately, these figures, based on micro-census data, refer to children born to married mothers only. Compared with most other European countries (including Catholic Ireland!), the proportion of extra-marital births is still rather low in Germany, although it more than doubled between 1970 and 1992 (from 5.5 to 11.6 per cent).

To sum up, there has been a continuous decline in the propensity to marry, going hand in hand with a rapid growth in cohabitation, which more and more has become the living arrangement of young adults, either premaritally or as an alternative to marriage.[5] But, as most cohabiting couples are childless, it obviously is not an alternative family type. At the same time, while demonstrating a long-term decline, the indicators of the birth level at the end of the 1980s were similar to those at the beginning of this decade (with an intermediate downswing). By and large, Germany has undergone demographic changes similar to those in most other European countries. While the levels of many indicators remained quite different, there are some far-reaching temporal similarities, e.g. in the fluctuations of birth rates in the 1980s (Lengsfeld and Linke, 1988:362). In the analysis below we want to explore how these structures and changes in demographic indicators are reflected in actual living arrangements of specific age groups of women.

4.1.3. *Methods and Data Sources*

In Germany official household statistics have little to offer to the study of family structures; published results are highly aggregated and do not allow

---

[5] Most early studies on cohabitation (e.g. BMJFG, 1985) tended to regard cohabitation mainly as pre-marital, but recently some doubts about this interpretation have been raised (Nave–Herz, 1988:67ff.).

us to relate variables to each other. Moreover, for reasons of data protection, access to individual micro-data is strictly limited. The analyses below, therefore, rely on scientific *survey data* which are generally available for scientific re-analysis. Two data sets were used to study family life:

1. The ALLBUS ('General Population Survey of the Social Sciences') is a representative cross-sectional survey carried out every two years (since 1980), focusing on both subjective and objective indicators of welfare. It comprises a constant module including basic information on household demography, and a varying programme covering selected issues of social scientific interest. The single data sets contain independent samples from West Germany (including West Berlin), each of about 3,000 adult German men and women. Because, at the given sample size of 3,000, the number of cases is still quite small in single five-year age groups, and assuming that distributions do not change significantly within two years, neighbouring data sets (1980–2 and 1988–90) were cumulated.[6]

2. In addition to the ALLBUS, a three-wave panel study, 'Reproductive behaviour in Northrhine-Westfalia', was used to study additional aspects of living conditions. The first two waves (1981 and 1983) include 2,620 resp. 1,470 women aged 18–30 years in four selected cities and districts in Northrhine-Westfalia; the third wave (1986) covered 1,054 women. The main topic of this study was processes of family formation, supplemented by information on living conditions and everyday life (e.g. child-care arrangements, division of labour within the household). Owing to regional selectivity, the data set is not representative for Germany. Hence it will be referred to only where there are no similar data from the ALLBUS survey.

4.2. Family Policy in Germany

After this introductory empirical and theoretical overview, I would like to present a short outline of family policies in the Federal Republic of Germany. From this characterization, I will derive some impact models with regard to different impact levels: family forms, living conditions and the everyday life of families.

---

[6] Statistical tests (χ^2-, Mann-Whitney- and t-tests) of the distribution of central variables (marital status, number of children, partner arrangement, household types, educational level and employment) for the neighbouring data sets justify this strategy. With the exception of employment, where the cumulated distribution seems to convey an even better picture of reality (as measured e.g. by official unemployment rates) than the single-year data do, there are no significant differences in the respective distributions.

Any portrayal of German family policy should start with a reference to the German Constitution, which puts 'marriage and family' under the special protection of the State (Article 6). First, this has to be understood as a prohibition from discriminating against married couples and families, relative to unmarried people and non-family households. But it also prevents state intervention into the private sphere of families (Münch, 1990). At the same time, family protection is shaped not only by this negative definition; Article 6 also includes the positive claim to promote the family by 'appropriate measures' (to use an expression of the Constitutional Court). But as a consequence of the vagueness of this term, the first aspect has always drawn the most attention. Moreover, this constitutional regulation has implications concerning the orientation of family policies towards changing family structures (Münch, 1990:21). The link between marriage and family in the wording of the Constitution is one reason why German family policy has always put a 'primacy on marriage' (Kaufmann, 1989), even if today the exact rating of marriage for legal and political consideration of different family forms is disputed among law commentators. For a long time it seemed that only married couples were considered to be a family, but in recent years this has changed at least partly. Nevertheless, the constitutional guarantee of the institutions of marriage and the family implies *a conservative element in family policy which stands in the way of far-reaching changes in private ways of life.*

German *family law* follows the line set by the Constitution, by stressing the principle of not discriminating against families consisting of a married couple with their children, in relation to non-family and non-marital households. The existence of unmarried cohabitation is largely ignored by German legislation (Limbach, 1988:28); when it is mentioned at all it is aimed at preventing them from being given priority over married couples.[7] The legal status of children born out of wedlock is in most aspects adjusted to that of children with married parents, but there are still some relevant differences left (e.g. with regard to succession law).

The most important difference between married and unmarried parents is the absence of joint custody for unmarried parents. In such families the mother has sole custody, even if both parents had been living together and both want joint custody. The ideology of German custody law perceives lone-parent and cohabiting families as somehow 'deviant' families. In sum,

[7] Those instances all concern means-tested benefits (social assistance, housing allowance and unemployment assistance) where the cohabiting partner's income is taken into account as well as in the case of married couples.

marrying for reasons of childbirth is rational in the context of German family law so that *we should, on the one hand, expect most people with children to be married, and, on the other hand, expect cohabiting couples to be mostly childless and those with children to be rare*. This has already been confirmed by previous research on cohabitation, which shows that only about one-quarter of all cohabiting couples have children, most of them being step-families (BMJFG, 1985).

A detailed description of all measures that may affect families would go beyond the scope of this chapter. It would entail the inclusion of local measures for large families, such as reductions in the price of public transport or vouchers for free entrance to public swimming-pools (Oberhauser, 1989), which differ from town to town. Rather, we take into account some selected measures which we suppose to have an impact on family types, living conditions and the everyday life of families. Three policy fields will be included: measures affecting the income of families, housing benefits, and measures aiming at the relationship between family and employment. The description will be limited to federal measures and regulations, and will not take into account additional measures at the *Land* or local level.

In 1989 about 12 per cent of social expenditure was devoted to marriage and family (Kaufmann, 1989:554), but the share of family measures in the total social budget has been decreasing since the early 1970s.[8] Nevertheless, the focus of German family policy is on *financial benefits* for families.[9] Two kinds of measure can be distinguished: direct transfers to families, and tax allowances, which account for more than half of all expenditures.[10] In the tax system there are two central family-related benefits. The first is the 'tax-splitting' between married partners; that is, their incomes are first added, and then split into two and taxed separately. In terms of expenditures this is the greatest single family benefit (with a share of almost one-third: Kaufmann, 1989). With regard to the possible impact on family structure, two distributional aspects can be stressed. First, this system favours the in-

[8] According to the EU classification of social expenditure, the share of family expenditures in all social expenditures was 8.0 per cent, compared with 10.2 per cent in France, 4.8 in Italy, 11.1 in Great Britain and 5.5 in the Netherlands (Eurostat, 1991).

[9] Below, we refer only to benefits generally available to all families. Besides, there are some extensive benefits for public-sector employees and civil servants including elements of a family wage (Oberhauser, 1989; Willeke and Onken, 1990).

[10] A detailed inventory of transfers to families was compiled by Oberhauser (1989). He made a list of more than 80 different transfers to households, a list containing many that do not relate to the number of children.

stitution of marriage irrespective of children.[11] Second, it privileges those married couples with only one income (traditional breadwinner–homemaker couples and, to a smaller degree, couples with one income from full-time and a smaller income from part-time employment), as their progressive tax rate is lowered by the splitting procedure.

Table 4.2. *Selected monetary transfers to families, FRG*

Universal benefits	Means-tested benefits
(a) Child benefit (monthly)	*(a) Additional child benefit*
DEM 50 for the 1st child	Max. DEM 48 per child if child tax- DEM
130 for the 2nd child	free allowance cannot be exhausted
DEM 220 for the 3rd child	
DEM 240 for further children	*(b) Educational grants*
	Max. DEM 785/month given as an
(b) Child tax-free allowances (per year)	allowance to pupils resp. half
DEM 3024 per child and year in general and	allowance half interest-free loan
DEM 5616 for single parents in addition	to students
(c) Tax-free allowances for children	*(c) Housing subsidy*
in vocational training (per year)	Dependent on income, family size
DEM 1800 for minor children not living in	and housing costs
parental home;	
DEM 2400 for children of age and	
DEM 4200 for children of age not living with	
parents	

With regard to child benefits, there is now a *dual system* of tax-free allowances and direct child benefits (Table 4.2): in 1983, the conservative–liberal government reintroduced tax-free child allowances (annually DEM 3,024 per child in 1992), which had been abolished in the 1970s and replaced by a flat-rate child benefit by the social-democrat–liberal coalition.[12] In addition, there are some tax allowances for specific situations and groups of families, e.g. a household tax-free allowance for lone parents (DEM 5,616), a lone parents' tax deduction for costs of child care, a tax-free

[11] According to the government, one-third of the splitting benefits in the year 1988 (which totalled DEM 24.6 billion) were given to married couples without children (Bundestag-Drucksache 11/5106 of 30 August 1989:20).

[12] In 1992, the Constitutional Court declared the existing tax-free child allowances to be unconstitutional, since they did not exempt the subsistence level from taxation. Legislation was obliged to create a new system of family taxation in 1996 at the latest.

allowance for children enrolled in education, and a special deduction for the costs of domestic servants looking after the children.[13] Child benefit now is the second pillar of the dual system of *Familienlastenausgleich*; it varies (July 1990) from DEM 50 per month for the first child to DEM 240 for the fourth and further children. Families that cannot fully exhaust the child allowance are paid a supplement to the child benefit of DEM 48 per child at most.

In general, the level of benefits has improved for most kinds of family over the last few decades. With some exceptions, the percentage of family transfers in available income has been rising from 1956 to 1986 (with intermediate fluctuations; cf. Willeke and Onken, 1990[14]). Nevertheless, *family policy could compensate only to a small degree for the families' arrears in income compared with childless households*. In particular, the tax-free allowances are much lower than the social subsistence minimum which should be excluded from taxation. An additional problem is that the different benefits are not co-ordinated in a coherent way (Oberhauser, 1989:54): there is a huge variety of possible combinations. As a result, different types of households and families benefit in quite different ways. As Willeke and Onken (1990) showed, there are great differences in the efficiency of the German *Familienlastenausgleich* according to different types of family.

An important aspect of the living conditions of families is *housing*, even if housing policies are not always directed specifically towards families but towards private households in general.[15] With regard to families, the general aim of housing policy is formulated in the 2. *Wohnungsbaugesetz* (Second Housing Act). It is stated that a quality of housing should be supported 'that guarantees a healthy family life, especially for large families' (§1) – an aim that, according to the Deutsches Jugendinstitut (German Youth Institute) (1988:333), was only partly fulfilled. Besides a means-tested housing subsidy (*Wohngeld*) that is related to family size, the focus of German housing policy is more on the support of property of accommodation than on social housing, which was almost completely abandoned in the early 1980s and was revived

---

[13] This last-mentioned benefit in particular has been criticized for its favouring of upper-class families.

[14] Willeke and Onken (1990) analysed the development of child allowances and child-tax-free allowances from 1954 to 1986 by using model calculations for different types of family (distinguished by number of children, income groups, public *v.* private-sector employees and married couples *v.* lone parents) using several indicators of the efficiency of the transfer system, such as the percentage of transfers in total available household income, their distributional effects and the resulting augmentation of the weighed per-capita income of families compared with the income without transfers, i.e. in comparison with childless couples.

[15] For a short overview of housing policies in Germany from a social policy perspective, see Lampert (1991:312ff.).

only in the context of the housing shortage at the end of the 1980s.[16] Another family-related housing benefit is the 'housing child benefit' (*Baukindergeld*): during the first eight years after buying or building a dwelling, families are granted an additional annual tax allowance of DEM 750 per child.

With respect to the *compatibility of family obligations and gainful employment*, two policy models can be distinguished, although in reality, of course, they overlap in various ways (Lampert, 1991:335). Policies aiming at a *successive* compatibility focus on enabling parents to interrupt or reduce employment for some period in order to look after the child without losing too much income. On the other hand, the model of *simultaneous* compatibility focuses on measures that enable parents to be gainfully employed (perhaps with reduced working hours) and to carry out family obligations at the same time. German family policy can clearly be assigned to the first model, the most important measure in this context being parental leave (*Erziehungsurlaub*), which in its existing form was introduced in 1986.[17] Originally it covered a period of ten months; it has since been extended to 24 months for children born after 1992. Parental leave pay (*Erziehungsgeld*) amounts to a flat rate of DEM 600 granted to all (i.e. not only to working) mothers or fathers for a period of six months; after this period, for an additional six months, parental leave pay is (rather strictly) means-tested. The federal government expected the *Länder* to introduce parental leave benefits of their own, in order to fill the gap between the end of (federal) parental leave pay (12 months) and the end of parental leave (24 months). But so far, only Baden-Württemberg has introduced an additional parental leave pay. Undoubtedly, the income situation of low-income families and lone mothers has improved significantly by parental leave. However, it seems questionable whether dual-income families have been relieved to a degree that makes the renunciation of one income possible for them. *In sum, the shift to the Parental Leave Act meant an improvement in the situation of low-income and lone mothers, but also a redistribution in favour of non-working women* (for whom it is a kind a 'birth-bonus'). In comparison with countries where parental leave benefits are earnings-related, the level of benefits is too low to compensate for the loss of income of working women, and the flat-rate principle discourages fathers from taking parental leave.

---

[16] The housing shortage itself is partly the result of demographic and family changes. First, the baby-boom generation entered the housing market at a time when demand was increasing anyway because of decreasing household sizes and the increase in the number of one-person households. The influx of the large number of immigrants after 1987 was only an additional factor.

[17] Parental leave replaced maternity leave for employed women, which had a duration of six months (with protection against dismissal) and for which they were paid DEM 750 per month.

A policy model promoting simultaneous compatibility presupposes a good supply of child-care facilities. In Germany, however, *public child care is more or less limited to morning care for pre-school children above the age of 3*. Kindergarten is almost the only form of public child care available; and, despite a mainly good supply, there are still deficits in some, particularly urban, regions.[18] Moreover, most kindergartens offer morning care only (i.e. from 8.00 am to 12.00 pm), so that the opening hours are fairly incompatible even with part-time work, let alone full-time employment. The supply of whole-day care for children is completely insufficient in Germany: there are only a few day nurseries, almost no all-day (primary or secondary) schools, and very few after-school care centres. Influenced by strong beliefs that children, particularly children under the age of 3, should be looked after by their mothers, young mothers who want to work after the duration of parental leave are heavily dependent on private child-care arrangements. In a comparative perspective, and following from this orientation of family policy, *it seems plausible to expect a relatively low participation of young mothers in the labour market and an enduring predominance of the traditional breadwinner–homemaker family.*

To sum up, the substitution of the costs of children is far from being 'cost-covering', and, moreover, the system of marital tax-splitting and child tax-free allowances favours childless couples and families with higher incomes (at least in absolute terms), so that a young couple's decision to start a family is a decision to live at a lower standard. The description showed that the married-couple family with the mother staying at home looking after her child(ren) still is the 'normal' family of German family policy. Family law, especially by refusing custody to unmarried fathers, makes non-marital forms of parenting anything but attractive. The legislation on parental leave certainly improved the situation of some groups of women, but its impact is more on enabling mothers to stay at home with their babies during the first months after birth, and the (flat-rate) level of parental leave pay far from covers the loss of income for working mothers, not to mention for fathers. At the same time, public day care is quite underdeveloped so that it is very difficult, especially for mothers with pre-school children, to combine family obligations with gainful employment. *Taking into account the growing orientation of women toward employment, this may result in an increasing abstention from*

---

[18] In June 1992, the government introduced a legal right to a place in a kindergarten for all children above the age of three from 1999 onwards. But the impulse for this initiative was not to improve the compatibility of work and family: rather, it is situated in the context of the reform of abortion legislation in order to reduce the number of abortions.

family roles; i.e., more young men and women may stay childless or live alone (Höpflinger *et al.*, 1991). In the empirical analysis of changes in family life, to which we will now turn, we will see how these hypotheses about the impacts of family policy hold true on different levels of impact: family forms, living conditions and everyday life.

4.3. Family Structures in the 1980s

Our analysis of changes in family structure will start with the timing of those family events that are relevant here, i.e. the early parental phase and the beginning of the post-parental phase. With regard to both groups, the evolution of some indicators of household and family structures will be monitored through the 1980s, before we turn to female education and employment. A multidimensional analysis of household types will conclude this section.

4.3.1. *The Timing of Family Phases*

With respect to the problem of compatibility of family and employment, two phases of the family biography are of particular importance, phases in which families are particularly exposed to stress and in which they have to reshape their relationship to the labour market and to their whole environment. First, in the phase of family formation (i.e. at the beginning of the parental 'career'), the problem of fitting in employment and child-rearing becomes critical. Second, problems of labour-market participation are again of particular relevance at the beginning of the post-parental phase, i.e. when children are starting to leave the parental home (usually called the 'empty-nest phase').

FAMILY FORMATION. The criterion for selecting this age group (of women) is the median age of giving birth to the first child plus/minus two years (in order to obtain a five-year interval). Based on ALLBUS data (in 1980–2), *women aged 25–29 years* fulfilled this criterion (54.9 per cent had at least one child). In 1988–90, slightly less than half of the women in this age group already had children. In order to have the same age groups in both years, this slight difference is acceptable and can be interpreted as a first finding which may yet reflect a delay in first births, as well as an increase in childlessness. According to the micro-census, the *mean* age at birth of a first child increased from 25.2 years in 1980 to 26.8 in 1989.

Table 4.3. *'Empty-nest' women, FRG, age 45–49, 1980–1982 and 1988 (%)*

	1980–1982	1988[a]
No children at all	12.3	14.2
All children still at home	44.4	37.8
At least one child left home	25.5	20.5
All children left home	17.7	27.6
Number of cases	243	127

[a] only data for 1988.

Source: ALLBUS.

BEGINNING OF THE POST-PARENTAL PHASE. The criterion in defining this phase is the median age of women when at least one child has left the parental home. We selected the age range 45–49 years as the age group in which the number of women with all children still living at home roughly equals that of women with at least one child living away from home (Table 4.3). The exact median age was met only in 1988–90, but in the next age group (50–54) the problem of employment already begins to turn into that of retirement. Comparing the beginning and the end of the 1980s, we see an earlier emptying of a nest that has grown smaller, as indicated by the drop in the completed fertility rate from 2,175 births per 1,000 women of birth cohort 1935 (which forms the middle of our age group in 1980–2) to 1,854 per 1,000 women born in 1942 (Birg *et al.*, 1987:203).

4.3.2. *Changing Family Structures*

FAMILY DEMOGRAPHY: MARITAL STATUS, CHILDREN, PARTNER ARRANGE-MENTS. Whereas, from 1980–2 to 1988–90, in the younger age group (25–29) the share of married women decreased noticeably and the proportion of never-married women correspondingly increased from 28 to 45 per cent, the proportion of married women even increased slightly in the age group 45–49. The women who were at this age in 1988–90 probably married in the early 1960s, which was the 'golden age' of marriage and the family. With our cross-sectional data we cannot distinguish between delay and rejection of marriage in the younger group of women, but according to life-course research both effects have played a role (Huinink, 1989).

Looking at empirical partner arrangements, which is more informative than the judicial term 'marital status', the often-discussed crisis of partnership

Table 4.4. *Partner arrangements of women, by age group, FRG, 1980–1982 and 1988–1990 (%)*

	25–29 years		45–49 years	
	1980–82	1988–90	1980–82	1988–90
Married, living together	65.6	47.6	75.7	79.2
Cohabiting	1.4	11.1	0.4	3.6
Partner but not living together	32.9	12.2	23.9	2.4
No partner	–	29.2	–	14.8
Number of cases	283	370	243	250

Source: ALLBUS.

and family actually turns out to be a *crisis of the institution of marriage.* The decline in the percentage of married young women is at least partly levelled out by the increase in the proportion of cohabiting women, which rose dramatically during the 1980s (from 1.4 to 11.1 per cent).[19] But, taken together, in 1988–90 fewer women were living with their partners (married or not) than in 1980–2, and having a partner but living apart became more frequent than cohabitation, while almost one-third of the younger women were not living in a stable partnership (Table 4.4). At the same time, we see that both kinds of 'new' partner arrangements still are forms chosen mainly by younger women, as only 3.6 per cent of the women aged 45–49 are cohabiting and 2.4 per cent are counted as having a partner but living apart in 1988–90.

Parallel to the findings on marriage, an increasing proportion of young women remain childless (Table 4.5): in 1980–2, 45 per cent of all women aged 25–29 did not have children; in 1988–90 this proportion had risen to 54.9. However, when using cross-sectional data, effects of birth delay and of growing childlessness cannot be separated. For those women who were 25–29 years old in 1988–90, i.e. for birth cohorts 1959–65, no completed fertility rates are available yet as their fertility biography is not yet concluded. But for the cohorts 1951–7, i.e. for the cohorts in our early-family phase in 1980–2, estimates amount to an average of 1.59 children (Schwarz,

---

[19] Changes in answering questions on 'wild' marriage may have some, yet little, effect on these figures. In 1980–2 only a few women said they were living with their partner but many said they were living with 'non-relatives' and subsequently were counted as flat-sharing communities. In 1988–90 their percentage has shrunk almost to zero. Because of negative social attitudes towards 'living in sin', it seems plausible that a certain portion of those 'non-relatives' in fact are women's partners, so that the real increase in cohabitation may be overestimated by these numbers.

Table 4.5. *Number of children by marital status, women aged 25–29 (per 100 of marital status group), FRG, 1980–1982 and 1988–1990*

No. of children	1980–1982				1988–1990			
	Total	Never married	Married	Separated/ divorced	Total	Never married	Married	Separated/ divorced
0	45.2	96.3	23.1	(53.3)	54.9	92.3	22.2	(34.6)
1	29.7	3.8	40.3	(33.3)	23.0	5.4	35.8	(50.0)
2	20.5	-	29.6	(13.3)	17.3	1.8	33.5	(8.7)
3 or more	4.6	-	7.0	-	4.9	0.6	8.5	(8.7)
No. of cases	283	80	186	15	370	168	176	26

Source: ALLBUS.

1991*b*), which is a further decline compared with earlier cohorts (Schwarz, 1991*a*). According to Birg *et al.* (1991:157ff.), the cumulated age-specific fertility rate until age 29 dropped from 1.53 for cohort 1940 to 1.24 for women born in 1950 and to 1.01 for cohort 1958.

In the older group of women entering the post-parental phase, there is a combined effect of changing patterns of children's leaving home and the fact that the 'average nest' has become smaller. The proportion of women who do not have children at all increased only slightly (from 12.2 to 14.2 per cent), but at the end of the 1980s the proportion of cases where all children of women aged 45–49 have already left home was much higher than at the beginning of the decade.

As Table 4.5 also shows, the increase in the number of childless young women should be seen in relation to the increase in the number of never-married women. Even if there are slightly more unmarried women with children in 1988–90, more than 90 per cent of all unmarried women were childless. In contrast, the vast majority and a slightly growing percentage of married women do have children. Furthermore, demographic findings of a shift from first to higher-order births are confirmed by our data. *The widespread belief in a trend towards the one-child family is clearly disproved with these findings,*[20] *and the thesis of a significant uncoupling of marriage and parenthood has to be questioned as well on this empirical level.*

EDUCATION AND EMPLOYMENT. Several studies using the life-course data of successive birth cohorts showed that the 'educational expansion' of the

---

[20] Cf. also Huinink (1989) on the basis of life-course data for female birth cohorts 1929–31, 1939–41 and 1949–51.

1960s and 1970s primarily resulted in an improvement in the educational level of *women* (Blossfeld and Huinink, 1989; Klein, 1989). Some characteristic changes can be illustrated as well with cross-sectional data. Both in 1980–2 and in 1988–90, the women in the older age group belong to birth cohorts that entered the educational system before its rapid expansion. Nevertheless, an improvement in educational attainment had already taken place between these generations of women (Table 4.6). The proportion of women who had only completed secondary modern school, which used to be the most frequent educational attainment for women, dropped from three-quarters to about one-half, but remained predominant. The women who were 25–29 in 1980–2, i.e. birth cohorts 1951–6, passed through the higher sectors of the educational system during 1965–73, which were the formative years of the educational expansion. The women aged 25–29 in 1988–90, i.e. birth cohorts 1959–65, reached that stage in the second half of the 1970s, during the heyday of the education boom. For this cohort, the proportion of lower secondary school degrees dramatically fell, while A-levels became one of three rather evenly distributed degrees.

According to life-course research, the educational expansion proved to be a decisive factor in explaining changes in family formation (Blossfeld and Huinink, 1989; Klein, 1989). It is the longer educational enrolment, more than the degree obtained, that has led to a postponement of family formation from birth cohorts 1929–31 to cohorts 1949–51 and, to a lesser degree, also to a growing abstention from founding a family.

The ALLBUS data on women aged 25–29 reveal great differences in the number of children according to educational level. Among women with lower educational level, i.e. secondary modern school, the percentage of childless

Table 4.6. *Women's educational attainment, per 100 of age group, FRG, 1980–1982 and 1988–1990*

	25–29		45–49	
	1980–82	1988–90	1980–82	1988–90
No qualification	1.1	2.2	1.2	1.7
Secondary modern school	51.2	27.3	74.1	51.9
Intermediate certificate	27.2	37.3	18.1	29.6
'Fachhochschulreife'	4.9	7.3	2.1	3.1
A–level	15.5	25.1	4.5	13.2
Other	–	0.8	–	0.3
No. of cases	283	370	243	287

Source: ALLBUS.

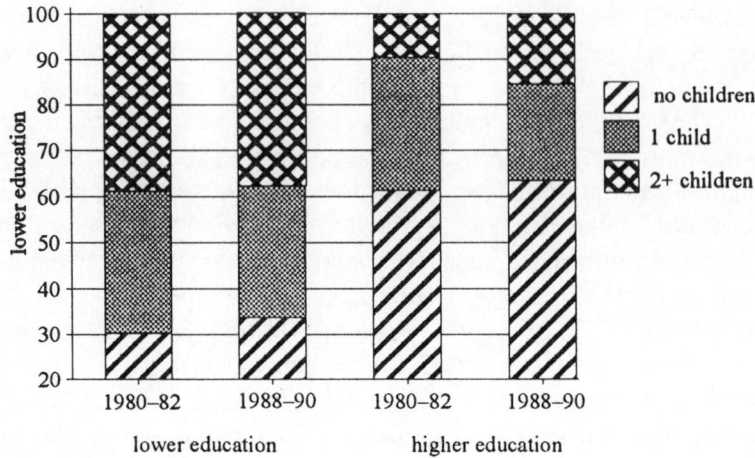

Figure 4.2. Number of children by educational level, women 25–29 years, FRG, 1980–1982 and 1988–1990

women is only half of that among women with higher degrees (Figure 4.2) – although it increased in both groups of women. Whereas the changes in the lower educational group are only small, there is an interesting shift in the group with higher attainments, lending support to the polarization thesis: *among better-educated women, the proportion with only one child diminished during the 1980s while that with two or more children rose from 10 to 16 per cent.*[21]

A central issue in all studies on family trends is women's growing labour-market participation. From a comparative perspective, the total female labour-force participation rate is rather low in Germany and has not grown significantly in recent years: during the 1970s it oscillated around 49 per cent, in 1980 it was exactly 50 per cent and by 1986 it had grown slightly to 51.6 per cent (OECD, 1987). For the 1980s the ALLBUS data reveal a moderate increase in young women's orientation towards the labour market, which is reflected by a rising participation rate (from 47 to 51 per cent). The vast majority of gainfully employed women are working full-time; the proportion of women working part-time (i.e. more than 10 and less than 35 hours per

---

[21] With regard to effects of the educational attainment of partners, our data show findings contradictory to life-course research, which reports positive correlations between the number of children and the educational level of husbands/partners. The ALLBUS data reveal a positive but weak relation between partners' educational attainment and the number of children.

Table 4.7. *Female employment by age group, FRG, 1980–1982 and 1988–1990 (% by category)*

	25–29 years		45–49 years	
	1980–2	1988–90	1980–2	1988–90
Total	47.3	51.4	46.9	48.4
Never-married	75.0	65.5	( )[a]	( )[a]
Married	34.9	36.9	40.2	38.9
Full-time	69.0	72.8	54.3	48.7
Part-time	20.0	13.4	35.4	32.0
Irregularly (< 10h/week)	11.0	13.8	10.2	19.3
No children	71.9	70.0	67.6	58.1
1 child	35.7	40.0	41.2	46.1
2 or more children	16.9	17.1	35.6	36.2
Both partners employed	30.6	37.9	38.5	41.9
Only partner employed	60.2	49.2	55.2	53.5
Only woman employed	4.3	4.6	3.3	1.9
Both not employed	4.8	7.9	3.3	2.8

[a] number of cases too small.

Source: ALLBUS.

week) has even been declining and was surpassed by the proportion of women in 'irregular' work (including fewer than 10 hours per week) in 1988–90 (Table 4.7).

On closer examination, we see that the increase in employment is confined to *married* women, half of whom nevertheless are not working. There is a clear connection between employment and number of children: whereas childless young women are mostly employed,[22] employment rates are continuously declining with the number of children, down to just 17 per cent for women with two or more children. Looking at the constellations of employment for women living together with their partner, we find an increase in the percentage of dual-income couples while the share of the 'traditional' model went down from 60 to 49 per cent.

With regard to women aged 45–49, we should call to mind the decreasing number of children still living with their parents. Consequently, there was a small increase in the employment rate, but the decline in the percentage of housewives more or less equals the increase in the percentage of women

[22] In 1988–90, there are hardly any housewives in this group. Instead, more women declare themselves unemployed which signals a growing orientation towards employment. The sum of housewives and unemployed roughly remained the same.

working fewer than 10 hours a week, i.e. irregularly. In comparison with younger women, self-assessment as 'unemployed' is far less common. The share of dual-income couples slightly increased in this age group, too, but the traditional model of the breadwinner–homemaker couple still is predominant (53.5 per cent). Fewer women are working full-time; the trend is towards part-time (1988–90: 32 per cent) or irregular employment (19.3 per cent).

4.3.3. *Household and Family Types*

The micro-data sets of the ALLBUS surveys allow a multidimensional reconstruction of household and family types. In addition to the household composition, information on both women's and their partners' labour-market participation are included.[23] The notion of pluralization of living arrangements suggests a growing variety of household types and the disappearance of a predominant type; an increasing number and a growing dispersion of household types would be indicators of such a process.

In the age group representing early family formation, the total number of living arrangements increased between 1980 and 1990 while the number of them that amount to more than 1 per cent remained roughly stable (Table 4.8). This means that there is a growing number of household types accounting for only small percentages. Changes in the rank order of various types confirm our previous findings: the share of married couples with traditional roles is shrinking and traditional roles are very rare in cohabiting couples, the proportion of which is growing fast. Living alone has become the predominant form of living – with almost all of those women being employed. Comparing this classification with the former, which took into account only the composition of the household, we see that the dispersion, or the 'pluralization', has to be attributed mainly to differing constellations of employment.

The findings on the group of women entering the post-parental phase of their family biography are difficult to interpret, as they reflect simultaneously decreasing levels of completed fertility and changing patterns of children leaving home (Table 4.9). These two factors together have led to an increase

---

[23] In order to grasp the household composition we use exclusive categories; i.e. the classification refers to the composition of the entire household. We distinguished between children, grandparents, grandchildren, other relatives and non-relatives; so e.g. the label 'married couple with two children' means that there is only a father, a mother and their two children and no other persons, e.g. grandparents; such extended families are counted separately, but in any case they were not among the six most frequent types.

Table 4.8. *'Life-styles' of women, aged 25–29, FRG, 1980–1982 and 1988–1990*

1980–1982			1988–1990		
Rank	%		%	Rank	Difference
1	18.8	Married, >2 children, housewife, partner employed	16.5	2	–2.3
2	18.0	Never married, living alone, gainfully employed	22.4	1	+4.4
3	16.3	Married, 1 child, housewife, partner employed	10.8	3	–5.5
4	11.3	Married, no children, both employed	8.8	5	–2.5
5	10.1	Married, 1 child, both employed	7.3	6	–2.8
6	4.3	Married, 2 or more children, both employed	(4.2)	–	–0.1
–	(1.4)	Never married, cohabiting, both employed	9.1	4	+6.7
	21.2	Other	25.1		+3.9
	58	Total number of living forms	74		
	16	Living forms > 1%	15		
	283	No. of cases	370		

Source: ALLBUS.

Table 4.9. *'Life-styles' of women, aged 45–49, FRG, 1980–1982 and 1988–1990*

1980–1982			1988–1990		
Rank	%		%	Rank	Difference
1	22.3	Married, >2 children, housewife, partner employed	15.8	1	–6.5
2	11.1	Married, no children, both employed	10.6	5	–0.5
3	10.7	Married, 1 child, housewife, partner employed	12.6	3	+1.9
4	10.3	Married, 2 or more children, both employed	7.7	6	–2.6
5	6.2	Married, 1 child, both employed	11.0	4	+4.8
6	5.7	Married, no children, housewife, partner employed	15.1	2	+9.4
	33.7	Other	27.2		–6.5
	66	Total number of living forms	55		
	16	Living forms > 1%	16.		
	242	No. of cases	246		

Source: ALLBUS.

in the number of households without children. But, whereas in 1980–2 the majority of those childless households consisted of a dual-earner couple, in 1988–90 there were more housewife-families than double-income families. Together with our findings on marriage, we see, quite contrary to the younger age group, a more 'conservative' trend in this age group. In terms of birth cohorts, women aged 45–49 in 1988–90 belong to the cohorts of the 'golden age' of marriage and the family, while the same age group in the 1980–2 sample was still affected by the irregularities in family formation of the post-war period. Numerically, the number of living forms dropped by 11 and the share of the six main types increased, but the cumulated percentage of the four main types remained the same and, moreover, these four types are distributed more evenly in 1988–90.

To sum up, the differences between these two age groups in the development of family structures during the 1980s confirm the view that *an analysis of broadly defined age groups which does not pay attention to heterogeneities in the life course cannot grasp important differentiations. Moreover, the changes often described in terms of pluralization of living forms that are attributed to modernization apply only to the younger generations who entered the typical age of family formation during the 1980s. With regard to the older cohorts, family life remains rather traditional.*

These results can be illustrated by referring to some selected 'life-styles'. The early family phase is characterized by a sharp increase in the proportion of the so-called 'new household types' (Spiegel, 1986), i.e. singles, cohabiting couples and lone parents, from 29.2 to 41.1 per cent, including a dramatic growth in the share of cohabiting women by almost ten percentage points (Table 4.10). The greatest decline related to childless couples, which confirms the hypothesis of a 'functional marriage' (Nave-Herz, 1988), i.e. marriage focused exclusively on parenthood. In the older group of women, the earlier beginning of the postparental phase must be considered. Strongly related to this change is the increase (by 3 per cent) in the proportion of dual-income

Table 4.10. *Household types of women, per 100 of age group, FRG, 1980–1982 and 1988–1990*

	25–29 years		45–49 years	
	1980–82	1988–90	1980–82	1988–90
Living alone	23.3	26.5	7.8	9.6
Still living with parents	2.8	3.5	0.8	0.8
Cohabiting	1.8	11.1	0.4	3.6
Lone mothers	3.9	6.2	13.2	4.4
Married couple, no child	15.2	10.5	19.3	27.3
'Traditional' family[a]	18.7	15.7	23.5	16.4
Double-income family[b]	14.1	10.8	17.7	20.0
Other	20.5	15.7	17.3	18.0
No. of cases	283	370	243	250

[a] Married couple with at least 2 children, housewife, husband employed.
[b] Married couple with children, both spouses employed.

Source: ALLBUS.

couples among them. Contrary to the younger group, the proportion of 'new household types' even diminished (from 20.8 to 17.6 per cent). And, while living alone and cohabitation gained importance, the proportion of lone mothers fell by two-thirds, partly because of an earlier emptying of the (smaller) nest, partly because of the declining percentage of widows.

Finally, we would like to examine the thesis of polarization versus pluralization by differentiating between childless women and women with children (Table 4.11). First, we should point out that the number of women aged 25–29 and living in families declined, compared with those living in non-family households. Within both sectors the number of living forms grew equally (in absolute terms), but there are different trends with regard to the variety. While the (cumulated) percentage of the four main types remained stable for childless women, there is a clear decline for women living in families (by 6.9 percentage points). Yet the dominance of one single type is more marked in the non-family sector, and even increased during the 1980s. Apart from this, there is a colourful mixture of constellations of marital statuses and partner arrangements within the non-family sector, while the six main types of family household are all married couples, differing only by number of children and women's labour-market participation. Last but not least, the family types still concentrate on couples with traditional roles of employment, despite a decrease from 65 to 58 per cent. Nevertheless, the increasing labour-force participation of young married mothers represents the most important change within the family sector.

The variety of household types within the non-family sector already existed at the beginning of the decade, but it underwent some characteristic changes. The first point worth mentioning is the growth in the significance of unmarried cohabitation. Whether this living arrangement should be regarded as an alternative or a preliminary stage to marriage cannot be answered from our survey data. But, although the latter is stressed in German literature (Tyrell, 1985; BMJFG, 1985), it can be assumed that an ever-increasing percentage of women regard cohabitation as an independent form of living together. Within the family sector, the traditional breadwinner–homemaker model is still predominant, notwithstanding the slightly increasing labour-force participation of married mothers, so that the term 'pluralization' holds true above all for the non-family sector. Instead, we prefer to speak of a *polarization between an increasing sector of non-family households, in which we indeed find a high degree of pluralization, and a shrinking percentage of women who decide in favour of a family. Of the latter, most women have (or at least will have) more than one child but still live in a more traditional way; i.e. they are married housewives.*

Table 4.11. *'Life-styles' of women aged 25–29, by presence of children, FRG, 1980–1982 and 1988–1990*

1980–82				1988–90		
Rank	%			%	Rank	Difference
	45.2	*Women without children*		*54.9*		
1	44.6	Never married, living alone, employed		42.1	1	–2.5
2	22.7	Married, employed		15.7	3	–7.4
3	9.4	Never married, living alone, on training/education		8.7	4	–0.7
4	7.8	Married, housewife		3.2	6	–3.6
5	4.7	Separated/divorced, living alone, employed		3.3	5	–1.4
6	3.1	Married, on training/education		–	–	–3.1
–	(1.6)	Never married, cohabiting, employed		17.4	2	+15.8
	7.3	Other		10.0		+2.7
	15	Total number of living forms		21		
	8	Living forms > 1%		13		
	128	No. of cases		183		
	54.8	*Women with children*		*45.2*		
1	29.7	Married, 2 children, housewife		27.5	1	–2.2
2	29.7	Married, 1 child, housewife		22.7	2	–7.0
3	17.4	Married, 1 child, employed		15.9	3	–2.5
4	5.8	Married, 3 or more children, housewife		8.0	5	+2.2
5	5.1	Married, 2 children, employed		8.6	4	+3.5
6	2.6	Married, 3 or more children, employed		(1.2)	–	–1.4
–	(1.9)	Separated/divorced, children, employed		4.3	6	+2.4
	9.7	Other		13.0		+3.3
	21	Total number of living forms		26		
	12	Living forms > 1%		17		
	155	No. of cases		163		

Source: ALLBUS.

4.4. Living Conditions

The material deprivation of large families, especially of those who have only one disposable income, is documented in many studies (Wingen, 1986; Buhr *et al.*, 1987). The income situation of lone mothers in particular[24] has been

---

[24] Taking social assistance as an indicator of poverty, lone mothers have the highest poverty rates in Germany: in 1980, 10 per cent of all lone mothers received regular assistance benefits; in 1986 this percentage has grown to 14; among lone mothers under the age of 25, in 1986 39 per cent were dependent on welfare benefits (Federkeil, 1988).

shown to be difficult. Below, we will look at income as the central indicator of living conditions, and at the housing situation which is of particular relevance for families with children.

4.4.1. Income

To a growing extent, the material status of families depends on the combination of the employment status of both partners and, linked with this, on their level of education. But, while education is hardly affected by the process of family formation, the income of a family heavily depends on the number of children, not to mention the fact that the number of children in a family has become a central aspect of social inequality (Kaufmann, 1990:110). To the extent that employment is more or less universal for young women before they enter parenthood, the double income of two partners becomes normal, too. Giving up employment in favour of family and child-rearing leads to a reduction in the household income that is in no way compensated for by family benefits and welfare state transfers (Kaufmann, 1990:112; Teichert, 1991:207). The share of public transfers in total net household income amounts to 7 per cent only for families with one or two children, and it is only for families with three children that, at 14 per cent, it reaches quantitative significance (Statistisches Landesamt Baden-Württemberg, 1986). The aim of improving the household income of families with lower wages and earnings in particular is not achieved coherently (Willeke and Onken, 1990:126). A study based on the micro-census showed a dramatic decrease in weighted per capita income with growing numbers of children, especially with respect to young families (Figure 4.3). According to these calculations, the weighted per capita income in young families with three or more children amounted to less than 40 per cent of the income of childless couples; and even the net household income of young families is decreasing with the number of children (Statistisches Landesamt Baden-Württemberg, 1986; Kaufmann, 1990). With regard to older families, the differences are not that large, but nevertheless reflect an immense loss of wealth. Moreover, it is not only with regard to income inequalities that (large) families belong to the worst-off, but with respect to poverty as well. Among social assistance beneficiaries, the growth in the number of married couples with children was the biggest of all types of household during the 1980s – by 145 per cent from 1980 to 1986, compared with a general increase of 54 per cent (Federkeil, 1988).

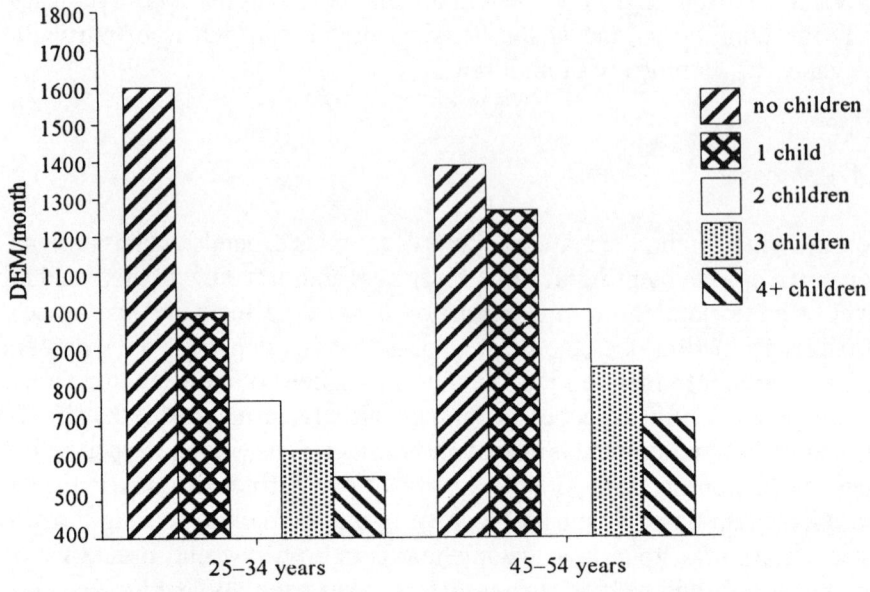

Source: Kaufmann (1990:113).

Figure 4.3. Per-capita income by family size and age of 'head of household', FRG

4.4.2. *Housing*

By and large, the housing situation in Germany has undergone considerable positive changes during the last forty years (Vaskovics, 1988). However, in the face of ongoing class differences and regional disparities, big families (especially lower-class families) have benefited little from that improvement. The three-child family marks the threshold in housing standards: families with four and more children significantly less often live in detached houses than smaller families do. With regard to young women, our data reveal great differences between families with children and households of childless women.[25] While 80 per cent of childless women are living in rented flats or houses, this holds true only for about two-thirds of the families (Table 4.12). On the other hand, women with children live in owner-occupied housing twice as often as childless women do. The decline in the ownership rate can be traced back to compositional effects, as the percentage of married

---

[25] Owing to the small sample size of the ALLBUS data, we cannot discriminate by number of children.

Table 4.12. *Housing, women aged 25–29, by presence of children (per 100 in child presence category), FRG, 1980–1982 and 1988–1990*

	1980–82			1988–90		
	No children	With children	All	No children	With children	All
Sublease	7.0	1.9	5.2	8.9	4.2	6.8
Rented flat/house	74.2	63.6	65.9	74.8	64.2	70.0
Owned flat	3.9	3.2	4.6	2.0	4.8	3.3
Owned house	14.8	31.2	24.3	12.9	26.1	18.8
Other	-	-	-	1.5	0.6	1.1
Owners	18.8	34.6	27.4	15.1	31.1	22.3
among married couples	[a]	[a]	34.2	[a]	[a]	34.3
number of cases	128	154	282	202	165	367

[a] Number of cases too small.

Source: ALLBUS.

women who have higher owner-occupancy rates has decreased during the 1980s. Within this group, the ownership rate remained stable.

Summing up the trends in living conditions, *most large families were able to participate in the general growth in prosperity, but to a smaller degree than childless households and small families* (Kaufmann, 1990:117). Hence, inequalities based on family characteristics did not diminish significantly during the 1980s.

4.5. Organization of Everyday Life

Most aspects of the complexity of the everyday life of families cannot be studied by secondary analysis of large survey data sets that were produced for other purposes. But two features of the organization of everyday life that are particularly important with regard to the compatibility of family and work can be taken up with existing survey data: child-care arrangements of families, and the gender division in housework.

4.5.1. *Child-Care Arrangements*

In Germany, the supply of day care is almost completely restricted to kindergarten. In the German kindergartens, which in the majority of cases offer morning care only (their normal opening hours are from 8.00 am to 12.00

Table 4.13. *Child-care arrangements for children with mothers aged 25–29, FRG, 1981 and 1986*

% of children	Morning		Afternoon	
looked after by ...	1981	1986	1981	1986
Mother	65.2	56.0	85.7	89.0
Father	1.8	1.6	2.8	6.0
Grandparents	5.9	4.1	6.8	1.9
Friends/relatives	0.6	1.5	0.5	–
Child-minder	1.2	–	0.7	–
Day-care centre	1.0	0.6	0.9	–
Day nursery	0.2	–	–	–
Kindergarten	11.1	20.1	1.8	2.5
Primary school	11.2	14.8	–	–
Other schools	1.1	0.9	–	–
Others	0.6	0.3	0.7	0.6
No. of cases (children)	935	318	936	318

Source: IBS Panel Survey.

pm), educational objectives have priority over care aspects. As the German school system is mainly part-time, there is hardly any public child care in the afternoon. Empirical findings on actual child-care arrangements reflect this situation: child care is organized privately by the family – and this means by mothers. In the majority of cases, mothers are caring for their children in the morning, too, even if the proportion has decreased slightly.[26] Kindergartens and – depending upon the age of the child – primary schools are the only forms of child care of quantitative significance, and in particular the proportion of children spending mornings at a kindergarten has increased significantly (Table 4.13). The number of children who are looked after by grandparents is surprisingly low, even declining.

There is some variety in child-care arrangements in the morning hours, but almost none in the afternoons: at that time, the mother is almost the sole person looking after the children. Although there is an increasing number of fathers looking after their children, at least in the afternoon, this seems to be 'at the expense' of grandparents.

Particular stress for families is caused when there are several children who are looked after in different institutions, so that co-ordination efforts,

---

[26] There are some irregularities in the answers to the question about who is looking after the child, as some mothers who at the same time said they were working at that time of the day named themselves as the person looking after the child.

e.g. in transport, are necessary. In the morning 68 per cent of the oldest two children (where there are at least two children[27]) are looked after by the same institution or person, which in 8 out of 10 cases is the mother. This means that in one in three families there are (at least) two children who are looked after by different institutions/persons and who may have to be taken to them. In the afternoons the situation is completely different: owing to the lack of alternative arrangements, we find that in 95 per cent of all families the (oldest two) children spend the afternoon at the same place, which almost exclusively is with their mother. Because of the poor supply of public child care, no more than 8 per cent of all families have their two (oldest) children spending the afternoon outside home. So we see clear obstacles to mothers' employment, especially full-time work but to a lesser extent part-time employment as well.

4.5.2. *Gender Division of Housework*

The sexual division of housework is a central issue of gender relations and significantly shapes the everyday life of families. The persistence of traditional role patterns, which was documented by many studies before and criticized by feminist social scientists (e.g. by Rapin, 1988), is confirmed by our data (Figure 4.4).

Men are still rather reluctant as regards housework, especially with regard to the more 'dirty' kinds of housework. They engage only in the more joyful tasks (shopping) and in those chores that traditionally are their domain (repairs; also insurance affairs, which are not included in the graph). Differences can be found according to the educational level – women with higher educational levels have partners who are more engaged in housework – but even then the division remains far from equal. The same holds true for gainfully employed women, who nevertheless get quite a heavy load of housework. About 60 per cent of them mostly or always prepare the meals and clean the dwelling.

---

[27] The IBS panel survey asks for details of child care with regard to each child (mornings and afternoons). As the analyses of care arrangements for three or more children are very time-consuming with such a data structure, and third and higher-order children are relatively rare in the sample, we take into consideration only first and second children, as this means no real loss of information.

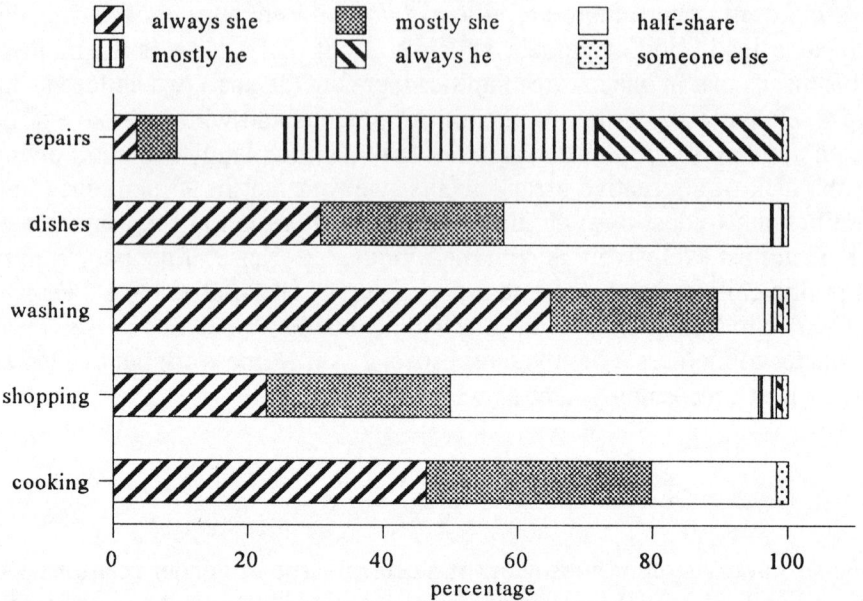

Figure 4.4. Gender division of housework, women aged 25–29, FRG, 1988

4.6. Conclusions

The empirical analysis of family trends, which leaned on the study by Zapf *et al.* (1987), confirmed the necessity of constructing rather narrow age groups that do not conceal heterogeneities of the life course and of different phases of the family biography. The approach followed here was to select groups of women who are at comparable stages in their family biography, who are characterized by critical transitions with regard to living conditions and the compatibility of employment and family. On the one hand, we saw a delay in family formation during the 1980s: in 1988–90 more women aged 25–29 were childless than in 1980–2. On the other hand, at the end of the 1980s the post-parental phase was beginning earlier and the emptying of the nest was proceeding faster, not least because that nest had grown smaller.

In sum, the dynamics of change was restricted to the younger generations of women. In the older age group we could not prove the pluralization thesis. On the contrary, more women aged 45–49 were married at the end of the 1980s than at the beginning of the decade. And even as the educational attainment of this age group improved and their labour-market participation increased slightly, the traditional model of the breadwinner–homemaker couple remained largely intact. With regard to women at the age in which family formation typically starts (i.e. 25–29), the pluralization thesis has to be revised: *we found a polarization between a growing non-family sector on the one hand, which internally is quite heterogeneous or 'pluralized', and a shrinking family sector on the other hand, in which the traditional breadwinner–homemaker model is still dominant, although under some attack.*

The first section of this chapter tried to give an overview of German family policies. Trying to relate the structure of family life and its changes during the 1980s to the policy characteristics (without aiming at a strict impact evaluation, which is impossible on the basis of aggregated cross-sectional data; cf. Kaufmann *et al.*, 1992), there are some findings that are 'in line' with family policy orientation, while other trends seem to be in contradiction of family-related policy measures and regulations. The inventory of family benefits and the analysis of living conditions of families demonstrate that young people's decisions in favour of a family are not supported effectively by policy measures. Hence, in competition with other biographical options, the family has lost some of its attraction for young women (and men).

One characteristic of German family policy is its focus on the institution of marriage (in family law as well as in the transfer system, e.g., the tax-splitting for married couples). Several disadvantages and existing forms of discrimination of unmarried couples and lone parents, implied in family intervention by law, operate in the direction of formalizing the family foundation by marrying. Hence, cohabiting couples with children are very rare in Germany, and most of them are stepfamilies; the number of lone parents (mostly lone mothers) is higher and increasing, but most of them are 'involuntary' lone parents, i.e. separated or divorced. The number of never-married lone mothers is comparatively low. Once a family is founded, German family policy still supports the traditional breadwinner–homemaker family, particularly in the lack of public day care for pre-school children.

Some of our findings on living arrangements can be set in relation to these characteristics of family policies: culturally and normatively, marriage lost some of its attraction for young women, as indicated by the decreasing marriage rates – and the promotion of the institution of marriage through family policy could not alter this trend. Yet, in the context of family formation, i.e. the birth of a first child, most young people do decide to marry – which is quite rational, since any other decision will cause them legal as well as financial disadvantages. Since German family policy does not take many efforts to support the (simultaneous) compatibility of gainful employment and family, we should not be surprised to find that many couples with young children are engaged in traditional patterns of labour-market participation.

The fact that this contradicts the aspirations of young women, who today attain the same educational levels as men and mostly aim at an occupational career of their own – or, to use the expression of the German sociologist Beck-Gernsheim (1983), move from a 'life for others to the claim to "a piece of a life of their own"' – may have led to a *growing abstention from family roles*, as the family may be regarded as an obstacle to this claim. Empirical evidence for this could be found for a growing proportion of women, result-ing in the described polarization between a shrinking family sector and an increasing non-family sector.

In the context of the changes in family life, or more generally, of the pluralization of living forms, the challenge for family policy is to create a frame 'in which an individual biography can be reconciled with taking responsibility as parents without great disadvantages' (Kaufmann, 1990:11). One of the most important issues is the compatibility of family and em-ployment, and at present, German family policy can hardly be said to have answered this challenge adequately.

References

Beck, U. (1986), *Risikogesellschaft* (The Risk Society), Suhrkamp, Frankfurt/Main.
—— and Beck-Gernsheim, E. (1990), *Das ganz normale Chaos der Liebe* (The Com-pletely Normal Chaos of Love), Suhrkamp, Frankfurt/Main.
Beck-Gernsheim, E. (1983), 'Vom "Dasein für andere" zum Anspruch auf ein Stück "eigenes Leben": Individualisierungsprozesse im weiblichen Lebenszusammenhang' (From 'being there for others' to the right of a piece of life 'of one's own': processes of individualization in women's lives), *Soziale Welt*, 34:307–41.
Birg, H., Filip, D. and Flöthmann, E.-J. (1987), *Paritätsspezifische Kohortenanalyse des generativen Verhaltens in der Bundesrepublik Deutschland nach dem 2. Welt-krieg* (Parity-Specific Cohort Analysis of Reproductive Behaviour in the Federal Republic of Germany after the Second World War), IBS, Bielefeld (IBS-Materialien No. 30).
——, Flöthmann, E.-J. and Reiter, I. (1991), *Biographische Theorie der demographi-schen Reproduktion* (Biographic Theory of Demographic Reproduction), Campus Verlag, Frankfurt/Main and New York.
Blossfeld, H.P. and Huinink, J. (1989), 'Die Verbesserung der Bildungs- und Berufschancen der Frauen und ihr Einfluß auf den Prozeß der Familienbildung' (Improvements in the educational and professional opportunities of women and their influence on family formation), *Zeitschrift für Bevölkerungswissenschaft*, 15:383–404.
BMJFG (ed). (1985), *Nicht-eheliche Lebensgemeinschaften in der Bundesrepublik Deutschland* (Unmarried Cohabitation in the Federal Republic of Germany),

Kohlhammer, Stuttgart.

Buhr, P. *et al.* (1987), *Lebenslage und Alltagsorganisation junger Familien in Nord-rhein-Westfalen* (Living Conditions and the Organization of Everyday Life of Young Families in Northrhine-Westfalia), IBS, Bielefeld (IBS-Materialien No. 26).

Council of Europe (1991), *Recent Demographic Trends in Europe*, Council of Europe, Strasbourg.

Deutsches Jugendinstitut (1988): *Kinder unter 3 im Zahlenspiegel* (Children under 3: Numbers and Facts), Deutsches Jugendinstitut, Munich.

Eurostat (1991), *Social Protection Expenditure and Receipts 1980–1989*, Eurostat, Luxemburg.

Federkeil, G. (1988), *Strukturwandel der Sozialhilfe* (Structural Changes in Social Assistance), Universität Bielefeld, Bielefeld.

Höpflinger, F., Charles, M. and Debrunner, A. (1991), *Familienleben und Berufsarbeit: Zum Wechselverhältnis zweier Lebensbereiche* (Family Life and Employment: the Interrelations between Two Areas of Life), Seismo Verlag, Zürich.

Huinink, J. (1989), 'Das zweite Kind: Sind wir auf dem Weg zur Ein-Kind Familie?' (The second child: are we on the way to the one-child family?), *Zeitschrift für Soziologie*, 18:192–207.

Kaufmann, F.X. (1989), 'Familie', in N. Blüm and H. Zacher (eds.), *40 Jahre Sozialstaat Bundesrepublik Deutschland* (Forty Years of Welfare State in the Federal Republic of Germany), Nomos, Baden-Baden.

—— (1990), *Zukunft der Familie: Stabilität, Stabilitätsrisiken und Wandel der famili-alen Lebensformen sowie ihre gesellschaftlichen und politischen Bedingungen* (The Future of the Family: Stability, Risks to Stability, Changes in Family Forms and their Social and Political Conditions), Verlag C.H. Beck, Munich; 2nd rev. edn. as *Zukunft der Familie im vereinten Deutschland: Gesellschaftliche und politische Bedingungen* (The Future of the Family in Reunited Germany: Social and Political Conditions), Verlag C.H. Beck, Munich, 1995.

——, Strohmeier, P. and Federkeil, G. (1992), *Wirkungen politischen Handelns auf den Bevölkerungsprozeß: Ansätze zu methodischen Analysen* (Effects of Political Action on the Population Process), Boldt Verlag, Boppard.

Klein, Th. (1989), 'Bildungsexpansion und Geburtenrückgang: Eine kohorten-bezogene Analyse zum Einfluß veränderter Bildungsbeteiligung auf die Geburt von Kindern im Lebensverlauf' (Educational expansion and birth decline: a cohort analysis of the influence of changing educational participation on the birth of children during the life course), *Kölner Zeitschrift für Soziologie und Sozial-psychologie*, 41:483–503.

Lampert, J. (1991), *Lehrbuch der Sozialpolitik* (Social Policy: a Textbook), Sprin-ger, Berlin.

Lengsfeld, W. and Linke, W. (1988), 'Die demographische Lage in der Bundes-republik Deutschland' (The demographic situation in the Federal Republic of Ger-many), *Zeitschrift für Bevölkerungswissenschaft*, 14:341–433.

Limbach, J. (1988), 'Die Entwicklung des Familienrechts seit 1949' (The evolution of family law since 1949), in R. Nave-Herz (ed.), *Wandel und Kontinuität der Familie in der Bundesrepublik Deutschland*, Enke, Stuttgart: 11–35.

Münch, U. (1990), *Familienpolitik in der Bundesrepublik Deutschland: Maßnahmen, Defizite, Organisation familienpolitischer Staatstätigkeit* (Family Policy in the Federal Republic of Germany: Measures, Deficits, Organization of State Intervention), Lambertus, Freiburg.

Nave-Herz, R. (1988), 'Kontinuität und Wandel in der Bedeutung, in der Struktur und Stabilität von Ehe und Familie in der Bundesrepublik Deutschland' (Continuity and change in importance, structure and stability of marriage and family in the Federal Republic of Germany), in R. Nave-Herz (ed.), *Wandel und Kontinuität der Familie in der Bundesrepublik Deutschland*, Enke, Stuttgart: 61–94.

Oberhauser, A. (1989), *Familie und Haushalt als Transferempfänger: Situation, Mängel und Reformansätze* (Families and Households as Recipients of Transfers: the Situation, Deficits and Possibilities of Reform), Campus Verlag, Frankfurt/-Main and New York.

OECD (1987), *Labour Force Statistics 1967–1987*, OECD, Paris.

Peuckert, R. (1991), *Familienformen im sozialen Wandel* (Family Forms and Social Change), Leske & Budrich, Opladen.

Rapin, H. (ed.) (1988), *Frauenforschung und Hausarbeit* (Women's Studies and Housework), Campus Verlag, Frankfurt/Main and New York.

Schwarz, K. (1989), 'In welchen Familien wachsen unsere Kinder auf?' (In what kinds of families do our children grow up?), *Zeitschrift für Familienforschung*, 3:27–48.

—— (1991a), 'Kinderzahl der Geburtsjahrgänge 1865–1955' (The number of children of the birth cohorts 1865–1955), *Zeitschrift für Bevölkerungswissenschaft*, 17:149–57.

—— (1991b): 'Neuer Babyboom? Zur aktuellen Geburtenentwicklung in der Bundesrepublik Deutschland' (A new baby boom? On recent birth trends in the Federal Republic of Germany), *Zeitschrift für Bevölkerungswissenschaft*, 17:95–103.

Spiegel, E. (1986), *Neue Haushaltstypen* (New Types of Household), Campus Verlag, Frankfurt/Main and New York.

Statistisches Bundesamt (1991), *Statistisches Jahrbuch 1991* (Statistical Yearbook 1991), Statistisches Bundesamt, Wiesbaden.

Statistisches Landesamt Baden-Württemberg (ed.) (1986), *Ökonomische Rahmenbedingungen der Familien* (The Economic Situation of Families), Stuttgart (Materialien und Berichte der familienwissenschaftlichen Forschungsstelle, No. 15).

Strohmeier, K.P. (1991), 'Die Polarisierung der Lebensformen in der Bundesrepublik Deutschland: Neue Probleme der Stadtpolitik' (The polarization of living arrangements in the Federal Republic of Germany: new problems of urban policy), in B. Blanke (ed.), *Staat und Stadt: Systematische, vergleichende und problemorientierte Analysen 'dezentraler' Politik*, Westdeutscher Verlag, Opladen: 177–209.

Teichert, V. (1991), 'Die ökonomischen Rahmenbedingungen junger Familien' (The economic situation of young families), in V. Teichert (ed.), *Junge Familien in der Bundesrepublik*, Leske & Budrich, Opladen: 207–30.

Tyrell, H. (1985), 'Literaturbericht' (Literature review), in BMJFG (1985:93–140).

—— (1988), 'Ehe und Familie: Institutionalisierung und Deinstitutionalisierung' (Marriage and family: institutionalization and de-institutionalization), in K. Lüscher, F. Schultheis and M. Wehrspaun (eds.), *Die 'postmoderne' Familie* (The 'Post-Modern' Family), Universitätsverlag Konstanz GmbH, Konstanz: 145–56.

Van de Kaa, D.J. (1987), 'Europe's Second Demographic Transition', *Population Bulletin*, 42, Population Reference Bureau, Washington, DC.

Vaskovics, L. (1988), 'Veränderungen der Wohn- und Wohnumweltbedingungen in ihren Auswirkungen auf die Sozialisationsleistung der Familie' (Changes in the conditions of housing and housing environment and their impact on family socialization), in R. Nave-Herz (ed.), *Wandel und Kontinuität der Familie in der Bundesrepublik Deutschland*, Enke, Stuttgart: 36–60.

Willeke, F.-K. and Onken, R. (1990), *Allgemeiner Familienlastenausgleich in der Bundesrepublik Deutschland: Eine empirische Analyse zu drei Jahrzehnten monetärer Familienpolitik* (The System of Equalization of Family Burdens in the Federal Republic of Germany: an Empirical Analysis of Three Decades of Family Policy), Campus Verlag, Frankfurt/Main and New York.

Wingen, M. (1986), 'Zur sozialökonomischen Situation von Familien heute: Daten und Probleme' (The socio-economic situation of families today: data and problems), *Zeitschrift für Bevölkerungswissenschaft*, 12:221–37.

Zapf, W. *et al.* (1987), *Individualisierung und Sicherheit: Untersuchungen zur Lebensqualität in der Bundesrepublik Deutschland* (Individualization and Security: Studies on the Quality of Life in the Federal Republic of Germany), Verlag C.H. Beck, Munich.

5 The Former German Democratic Republic: the Standardized Family

HARTMUT WENDT[1]

Bundesamt für die Anerkennung ausländischer Flüchtlinge, Nürnberg, Germany

The one-party system of the former German Democratic Republic propagated a high women's employment rate as the prerequisite of equal rights for women. The truth was that a second income was simply indispensable to ensure even a modest standard of living for a family. A dense network of day care, thus, encouraged and facilitated the non-domestic paid work of women. The upbringing of children was thereby entrusted to the state, and conventional family life was redefined. At the same time, the early founding of a family established the right to one's own flat. New forms of family living, such as married-like partnerships, did at no point contest the traditional co-resident nuclear family, and therefore were no indication of a process of pluralization or of a decrease of pressure on family norms, as was the case in the former West Germany. Rather, in East Germany they were the outcome of a trend towards greater individualization. As a result of all this, standardized motherhood and the standardized family became and remained prevalent until the fall of the Berlin Wall.

5.1. Introduction

5.1.1. *Changes in Family Structure: Pluralization or Polarization?*

In spite of all the similarities in what constitutes the family in both the new eastern and the former western parts of today's Germany, a clear differentiation of characteristics and potentials in family life-styles is bound to be distinguishable, considering the respective social, economic, and cultural as well as political and institutional differences that had existed prior to

---

[1] Translation by Faith Dasko, Zentrum für Sozialpolitik (ZeS), Universität Bremen, Germany.

unification. The question is whether, and to what extent, family structures, family formation, and the everyday life of the family in the former German Democratic Republic (GDR) were influenced by the restrictive external conditions created by the one-party system and by the ideals it propagated. In the process of this development in the former GDR, did the number of family types multiply or decrease? Were tendencies of pluralization discernible, and if so to what degree? Studies show that patterns of development in family formation and everyday family life can be said at the most to have been ambivalent. There were stagnating tendencies in society at large, as well as extensive forms of 'social levelling-out' (Geißler, 1993:583). These tendencies led in diverging directions – to a conservation of traditional family forms and a reinforcement of the normative base of family structures, on the one hand, and to new family forms which took on characteristics particular to the former GDR, on the other (Wendt, 1993:5ff.).

Of particular interest in this chapter is the scope and goals of family policy in the former GDR, and how they influenced family formation and structure. The active, obviously pro-natalist, family policy was definitely able to effect short-term results. In the long term, however, as will be argued in more detail below, it was relatively ineffective. The policy outcome must be understood in the context of the GDR regime which restricted the viable choices of action of its citizens. The effects that family policies can bring about in such a system presumably differ from those of policies implemented in a pluralistic system.

After briefly presenting the more important demographic trends in the 1980s, we shall analyse family policy in the former GDR, family forms and living conditions, patterns of life-styles, problems of compatibility of family and paid work, child care, and the familial division of labour. The 1980s, as the last decade of existence of the GDR, is particularly revealing for questions regarding typical family structures and everyday life. With respect to differentiation in family formation and different problem situations arising in families, the age group that was in the family-building years in the 1980s is of particular interest. These women and men were entirely socialized under the GDR regime and their family background was rooted in the GDR as well. This study not only aims to provide insight into family life in the new *Länder*.[2] It also serves to facilitate understanding of the fundamental changes in family formation and in the institution of the family taking place there

---

[2] Both before and after unification, the Federal Republic of Germany is subdivided into a number of federal states (*Länder*). After unification, the states situated in the former GDR were called 'new *Länder*', as against the 'old *Länder*' that made up the FRG till the end of 1990.

(Wendt, 1993:99–110; Dorbritz, 1993; Winkler, 1992:223–43).

A critical analysis of population policy and of family structure and every-day life in the former GDR, together with a neutralization of the ideological basis of useful former policies, can serve as a basis for an ever more urgently needed discourse on appropriate political measures suiting family needs in a united Germany. The ultimate concern is to dismantle structural disadvantages to families – especially those facing women who are gainfully employed or would wish to be so – by improving the institutional framework that structures the environment influencing their everyday life.

5.1.2. *Demographic Trends in the 1980s*

Many factors had a lasting effect on family formation and family structure in the GDR. Marriage and family were highly valued institutions in a restrictive society. Moreover, there were pressures to follow norms and a decidedly pro-natalist population policy which aimed to increase the birth rate while maintaining labour participation among women and men. Generally, a policy was pursued which sought to alleviate the tensions and burdens that confronted parents who sought to co-ordinate occupational and family life.

Marrying and bearing children at a young age emerged as a characteristic demographic behavioural pattern resulting from state policies (Wendt, 1991; Dorbritz, 1993). In contrast, the 1980s were characterized by a decrease in the marriage rate accompanied by a reduction in the number of children as well as a clear increase in the divorce rate.

MARRIAGE. Couples married for both emotional and pragmatic reasons. In the case of first marriages, the decisive motives for getting married were love, respect and trust, safety and security, the desire to have children and to find fulfilment in a parent–child relationship – but in addition to these and other traditional reasons, the wish thereby to acquire entitlement to a flat (Winkler, 1990a:105; Meyer, 1991:35). Despite a declining marriage rate, the inclination to marry remained high. In 1987 there were 8.5 marriages per 1,000 of population. On the basis of 1987 rates, 74 out of 100 single men and 81 out of 100 single women married, whereas according to the 1980 rates this proportion was 79 men and 81 women, respectively. In 1989, the proportion of single people who married decreased further (Höhn *et al.*, 1990:141).

The decline in marriage propensity was accompanied by an increase in marital dissolution. The proportion of divorced brides and grooms among marrying women and men had clearly increased. In 1987, almost a quarter of all marriages represented second marriages for the bride or groom, or both. As always, however, most of the men and women entering matrimony in a given year were single: 73 and 74 per cent, respectively, in 1987 (Table 5.1).

Both men and women married comparatively young. In 1987, average marrying age was 22.7 for single women and 24.8 for single men. During the decade, however, average age at first marriage began to rise slightly. From 1980 until 1989, it rose by roughly two years, and in 1989 it was already 25 for men and just slightly over 23 for women (Table 5.2).

Table 5.1. *Marrying men and women, by marital status, former GDR, 1970–1989*

| | Marital status as a percentage of all marrying | | | |
| | Men | | Women | |
	Single	Divorced	Single	Divorced
1970	79.1	16.0	82.9	13.5
1975	78.8	17.8	81.4	16.0
1980	78.7	18.8	80.3	17.7
1985	74.5	22.9	75.7	22.3
1987	73.4	24.4	74.1	23.8
1988	72.2	25.4	72.9	24.9
1989	71.3	26.3	71.6	26.1

Source: Die Frau in der DDR (1990:25).

Table 5.2. *Mean age at marriage, by marital status, former GDR, 1970–1989 (%)*

| | Single | | Divorced | | Total | |
	Men	Women	Men	Women	Men	Women
1970	24.0	21.9	35.8	33.6	27.5	24.5
1975	23.2	21.3	35.5	32.7	26.5	23.8
1980	23.4	21.3	35.7	32.8	26.5	23.8
1985	24.3	22.2	36.8	33.6	27.9	25.2
1987	24.8	22.7	36.8	33.4	28.4	25.7
1988	25.0	22.9	37.3	33.9	28.8	26.2
1989	25.3	23.2	37.6	34.0	29.2	26.5

Source: Statistisches Jahrbuch der DDR 1989 (1990:379); *Die Frau in der DDR* (1990:28).

FERTILITY. An international comparative study has shown that low fertility rates (number of children per woman of childbearing age) were common in the former GDR as well as in the FRG prior to unification in October 1990 (Höhn and Schubnell, 1986:187; Wendt, 1991:256).

The 1980s were characterized by a continuous decline in the fertility rate, albeit throughout the former GDR's existence until 1989 it did not reach levels as low as those in the former Federal Republic; this did not occur until 1990 in the new *Länder*. Still, during the 1980s the largest decline in the fertility rate took place. In 1989, 199,000 children were born, 17,000 fewer than in 1988 (–8 per cent; see Figure 5.1). In terms of fertility *rates*, in 1980 the total fertility rate was 1,942 children born per 1,000 women during their childbearing phase; this fell to 1,734 children in 1985, and to 1,557 in 1989.

Since the mid-1960s the drop in the fertility rate has been for the most part attributable to the fall in the number of births per woman. However, though the number of births per woman decreased, the proportion of women

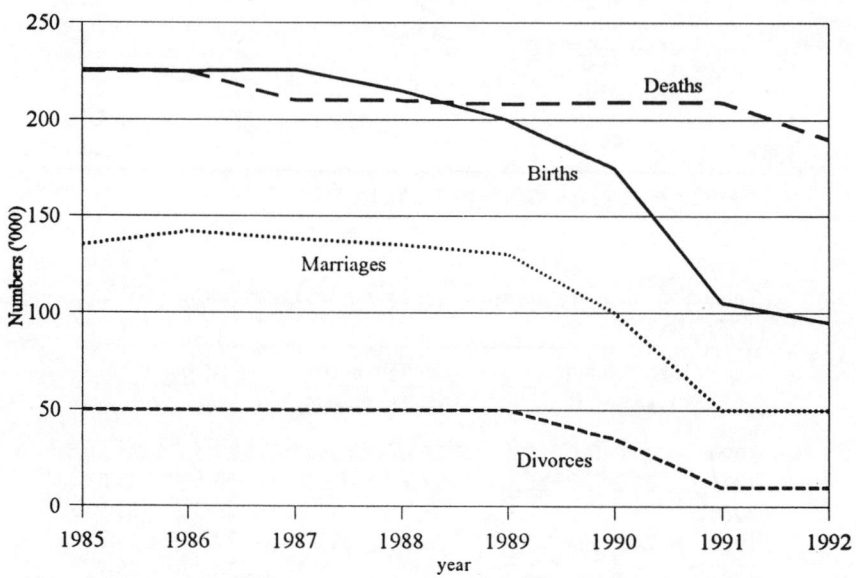

Note: 1992 estimated.

Source: Statistisches Bundesamt FRG.

Figure 5.1. Marriages, births, deaths and divorces in the former GDR and in the new *Länder*, 1985–1992

Table 5.3. *Total fertility rates, numbers of live births, and proportions by birth order in the former GDR, 1950–1991*

	Total fertility rate	Total live births	Birth order as a percentage of all live births		
			First child	Second child	Third child
1950	2374.1	303,866	48.7	29.9	21.4
1955	2346.7	293,280	40.9	29.6	29.4
1960	2328.3	292,985	41.2	27.7	31.1
1965	2483.4	281,058	37.7	29.5	32.8
1970	2192.5	236,929	44.3	29.8	25.9
1975	1541.7	181,798	58.6	30.8	10.6
1980	1941.8	245,132	53.9	35.5	10.6
1981	1853.9	237,543	52.9	36.2	10.9
1982	1858.2	240,102	51.8	36.7	11.5
1983	1789.8	233,756	51.4	36.6	12.1
1984	1735.4	228,135	50.6	36.9	12.5
1985	1734.2	227,648	48.5	37.0	14.5
1986	1699.9	222,269	48.0	37.3	14.6
1987	1739.9	225,959	46.3	38.0	15.7
1988	1670.2	245,734	45.9	38.2	15.9
1989	1572.3	198,922	45.9	37.9	16.2
1990[a]	1517.4	178,446	–	–	–
1991[a]	970	107,769	–	–	–

[a] estimated figures for the new *Länder*, using the Calot method.

Source: 1950–9: *Statistisches Jahrbuch der DDR* (various years); 1990 and 1991: data from the Statistisches Bundesamt FRG.

giving birth in fact increased. For example, only 8 per cent of cohorts 1946 and 1947 were childless, according to the 1981 population census. So, there was an increasing number of women bearing fewer children: every next generation of women was bearing fewer children though the number of mothers per generation was increasing. Childlessness was still seldom desired and thus remained the exception. Families typically had one or two children while larger families became ever more rare.

Although differences in the number of children per family in the former GDR were less pronounced, these were strongly influenced by both regional and social factors. Higher birth rates were registered in agricultural areas (Wendt, 1990:16) as well as among women without completed schooling or occupational training (Meyer and Wendt, 1984:46). The larger percentage of children born in a year were first children (Table 5.3).

The childbearing age for women in the GDR was young compared with

West European countries. In 1986 the average childbearing age of a mother was 24.1 years, and that at birth of the first child 22 years. In contrast to the 1970s, this meant an increase in the average childbearing age.

Fertility was highest among the 22–24-year-olds: 28 per cent of children born in 1989 were born to women in this age group. The age-specific fertility rate was highest among 23-year-olds (159.5 live births per 1,000 women aged 23). In that same year almost 70 per cent of all births were to mothers not older than 25. According to data gathered from a sociological survey seeking information on the number of children desired (*Kinderwunsch '87*), almost 80 per cent of all female respondents between the ages of 18 and 40 had at least one child and almost half of them (45 per cent) had two or more.

The proportion of children born out of wedlock in the former GDR has doubled since the mid-1970s. Since the mid-1980s approximately one-third of all live births were to unmarried women: 33.4 per cent in 1989, compared with 16.1 per cent in 1975. These figures, however, also reflect children born to unmarried couples in a consensual relationship who first married after the birth of a child in common. Accordingly, there was a considerable percentage of couples marrying who had premaritally conceived a child in common: nearly 39 per cent of all marriages in 1987 had a child in common born out of wedlock, and 26.9 per cent in 1989. Thus, in the former GDR marriage did not necessarily precede childbearing, though consensual unions outside of legal marriage were oriented towards a life with children.

Factors explaining the high proportion of children born out of wedlock stem above all from the politico-ideological and socio-economic conditions in the former communist system. They encouraged cohabitation as a 'trial marriage' which consequently became commonplace particularly among younger age groups. Because of their economic independence (i.e. their labour-force participation) women were independently capable of rearing a child. However, the related burdens and economic disadvantages to lone mothers were considerable. Moreover, living under such economic and social constraints posed problems to the children's development.

DIVORCE. A significant part of the change in family forms is due to the high number of divorces. In the former GDR the institution of marriage no longer represented a lifetime commitment or arrangement. Rather, from the start it included the possibility of divorce (Meyer, 1991:33). The number of divorces rose tremendously – in the period 1970–89 from 27,407 to 50,063, i.e. by 82.7 per cent (Table 5.4). In the second half of the 1980s those marriages that broke down had lasted an average of nine years before ending in divorce. The rate of divorce was high, with 30 marriages out of a population of 10,000 (of over-18-year-olds) so ending. In 1987, out of the total population of marrying age, nearly every thirteenth person was divorced.

Young marriages in particular ended disproportionately in divorce. Approximately 50 per cent of divorced marriages lasted a maximum of seven years. Those in the age group 25–30 divorced most frequently, accounting for 25 per cent of all divorces. The second-highest rate of divorce was among the 40-year-olds, by which time the children generally had left the parental home. Since approximately two-thirds of all marriages (in 1987, 69 per cent) that ended in divorce had children, an increasing number of children were affected by divorce. Every year in the latter half of the 1980s, nearly 50,000 children experienced divorce in their families (Table 5.4).

In the former GDR the loss of civic values and social responsibility in society at large led to increased appreciation of 'the family'. But, at the same time, marriages became more susceptible to conflict as the pressure grew for families to compensate for this social vacuum. Consequently, coping with societal problems shifted more and more to the individual level, destabilizing families and increasing the possibility of divorce. Despite increasing social inequalities, a family sociologist observed again in 1989 that 'socialist values' would necessarily produce great expectations on the partner and family (Gysi *et al.*, 1989:13–4).

Table 5.4. *Divorces in the former GDR, 1960–1989*

	Total number of divorces	Per 10,000 of population		Number of children in divorced marriages	Percentages of divorces with minor children
		Total	Over 18 years old		
1960	24,540	14.2	19.0	22,214	59.9
1970	27,407	16.1	22.3	32,647	68.2
1975	41,632	24.7	33.6	47,100	71.0
1980	44,794	26.8	35.8	46,075	70.4
1985	51,240	30.8	40.2	51,433	70.3
1986	52,439	31.5	41.2	52,618	69.5
1987	50,640	30.4	39.6	50,776	69.0
1988	49,380	29.6	38.6	48,911	68.2
1989	50,063	30.1	–	50,194	68.1

Source: Statistisches Amt der DDR, *Bevölkerungsstatistische Übersichten: Ehescheidungen 1989* (Population Statistics: Divorces 1989), Berlin (1990:6); *Die Frau in der DDR* (1990:29).

The conflict potential expressed itself chiefly in differences in interest, in opinion and perspective, not least in relation to questions of child-rearing. This was compounded by issues relating to sexual relations and equality (concerning the division of household labour, family responsibilities, and access to and distribution of monetary resources) which provided for conflict potential in role relationships. If the reasons given for divorce were chiefly attributed to 'incompatible character or opinion' or 'problems in sexual relations', then the real reasons for divorce were more precisely infidelity, alcoholism, and acts of violence (Gysi *et al.*, 1989:17).

The high rate of remarriage was an indication that divorce was not directly related to a general rejection of marriage. Moreover, a second marriage again created a place to retreat into; in a family the individual was seeking a sphere where she or he could have a meaningful life and act freely inside the very restrictive GDR society.

MARITAL STATUS AND NUMBER OF CHILDREN. Among women aged 18–40, nearly 80 per cent had children (Survey *Kinderwunsch '87*), almost every fifth woman being childless. Data broken down by marital status showed that most married women (94.7 per cent) had one or more children; 60 per cent had two or more children (Table 5.5). Thus, married women without children were more an exception. Single women not cohabiting with a male partner had for the most part no children (75.7 per cent); about one in five had one child (22 per cent). Single women with two or more children were

Table 5.5. *Number of children, by marital status, women aged 18–40, former GDR, 1987 (%)*

No. of children	Marital status					
	Never married	Married	Consensual union	Divorced	Widowed	Total
0	75.7	5.3 (8.2)[a]	25.2	6.2	7.7	20.8 (28.2)[a]
1	21.9	34.5 (35.8)[a]	47.0	39.7	38.5	33.7 (33.8)[a]
2 or more	2.4	60.2 (56.0)[a]	27.8	54.1	53.8	45.8 (38.0)[a]
Total	19.0	64.9	10.1	5.5	0.5	100
No. of cases	507	1,728	279	146	13	2,664

[a] Married women 18–40 years old, Population Census 1981, partially own calculations.

Source: Survey *Kinderwunsch '87*; secondary analysis, 1992.

extremely rare. Divorced and widowed women were predominantly (93 per cent) mothers, mostly of two or more children. Very rarely did divorced women not have any children (6 per cent). But divorced women with three or more children were also the exception. It was particularly unusual to find widowed mothers among the 18–40-year-olds.

Cohabiting unmarried women often had children, but in that case one child only. Women in these forms of relationship tended just as often to have no children (25 per cent) as they did to have two or more children (28 per cent). In comparison, married couples (women aged 18–40) tended to have children five times more often. This evidence also supports the argument that consensual unions serve as a trial marriage, especially for the younger generation.

5.1.3. *Data Sources*

More detailed official data on families, such as data on structure and size, or differentiated data on income and household provisions according to family size or social grouping, were largely lacking in the GDR or were not accessible to the public.

Since the GDR family was observed solely as a consumption unit, that which the family provided in terms of (re)production was left ignored and not analysed. Similarly, the role the family played in providing social welfare as well as care and support was hardly given any sort of recognition, though this role essentially constituted the psycho-social nature of the warmth of the family nest and significantly influenced the well-being of the individual family members.

The insufficient official statistical data tended more to obscure than to furnish information on the living situation of families. Existing social inequalities among households (or families) were kept concealed. The last population census in 1981 filled in some of the missing information, though a regular survey and updating of family and household structure did not follow.

The official statistics that were used for this report include several issues of the Statistical Yearbook of the GDR (*Statistisches Jahrbuch der DDR*), detailed information on households, families, and number of children obtained from the Population, Housing, and Buildings Survey of 31 December 1981 (East Berlin), and statistics on income and assets of blue- and white-collar households in 1980–8, published in 1989. It was not until after the political turnabout in the autumn of 1989 that additional sources of information became available (*Die Frau in der DDR*, 1990; Statistisches Bundesamt,

1991; Winkler, 1990*a,b*).

Sociological representative surveys on family life in 1982 and 1987 published by the former Institut für Soziologie und Sozialpolitik der Akademie der Wissenschaften der DDR (Institute of Sociology and Social Policy of the Academy of Sciences of the GDR) remained unpublished, or else their use was largely limited to providing the legitimation of family policy goals and/or to describing the functions of 'the socialist family' and individual value systems. Among the few surveys available was an analysis of the division of labour in the family and studies of partner behaviour. Problems concerning the compatibility of family and occupational life, particular difficulties confronting lone parenthood, and social or regional differences among families were left unmentioned or trivialized. The book entitled *Familienleben in der DDR* (Gysi, 1989), which was published prior to the political changes in 1989, illustrates this practice well.

In order to improve the information base on the situation of the family, a secondary analysis of a sociological survey (*Kinderwunsch 1987*) was conducted by the former Institute of Sociology and Social Policy of the Academy of Sciences of the GDR.[3] This survey consists of a sociological and demographic analysis of the general inclination to have children, and the growth in population and number of births in the GDR in the 1980s. It was conducted between March and October 1987 in the areas Berlin–Lichtenberg, Riesa (Saxony), Frankfurt/Oder (Brandenburg), Friedland (Mecklenburg), and in 16 communities within the district of Bad Freienwalde (Brandenburg). There were a total of 2,710 female respondents between the ages of 18 and 40. The sample was based on a representative random selection within the relevant age group, and a standardized written questionnaire was used.

Although an ample number of studies in the social sciences is available on the former GDR, comprehensive analyses specifically on the family are rare. In addition to a book on this subject by the author himself (Wendt, 1993), Vaskovics *et al.* (1994) have recently published a comparative study on family and household structures of the former GDR and the FRG in the period 1980–9, based on an extensive review of approximately 200 studies. The data gathered produced mainly a cross-sectional comparison of household structures and family forms. Also, a documentary piece of work with an annotated bibliography in multiple volumes was published by the Information Centre for the Social Sciences (IZ) at the GESIS (Gesellschaft Sozialwissen-

---

[3] The secondary analysis was carried out with the assistance of Eberhard Riedel (Zentralarchiv, Cologne). Additional data sets were furnished by J. Dorbritz of the former Academy of Sciences, East Berlin. I would like to take the opportunity here to thank them for their assistance.

schaftlicher Infrastruktureinrichtungen e.V.) Berlin office (GESIS, 1993: chapter 5, on population sociology and demography). The publication by Vascovics and Silbereisen (1993) deserves special mention, because in it an evaluation of family research in the GDR is undertaken. Recent research on the family in the GDR has just been published by colleagues at the Sozial-wissenschaftliche Forschungsstelle of the University of Bamberg, under the direction of Professor L.A. Vaskovics (see e.g. Schneider, 1994).

5.2. Family Policy in the Former GDR

An explicit family policy did not exist in the former GDR. Family policy was part of a comprehensive social policy, which above all was characterized by a pro-natalist population policy. A main thrust of this policy in the 1980s was to support the two-parent family consisting of wedded parents and two or more children and to influence families to be more ideologically oriented (Gysi, 1988:524). With these broader social-policy directions in mind, the political measures were directed towards two main goals: (1) 'to secure the natural reproduction of the population' (Winkler, 1987:39), and (2) to facilit-ate the simultaneous compatibility of gainful employment and motherhood.

Economic issues were central to this policy, i.e. to secure the needs of the labour force in an inefficient economic system:

By working towards this goal society influences the relation between fertility and mortality; the population's size and structure will be determined by the conditions of reproduction and will at the same time correspond to the requirements of production of material goods. (trans. of Speigner, 1982:1489)

This type of pro-natalist population policy was considered essential by the former GDR's state party and government. Specifically, it was developed in reaction to a decline in the number of births per female and to higher divorce rates at the beginning of the 1970s. Both developments were thought to indicate women's reactions to the growing burden of reconciling gainful employment and family responsibilities. Pro-natalist policy also was intended to compensate the coverage of medical costs that were to be included in the planned legalization of abortion (which became law in March 1972). In the interest of the economy, fluctuations in the birth rate were to be avoided. In this sense fluctuations in the fertility rate were considered suboptimal with respect to economic as well as social processes and structures (Büttner, 1981:98). This goal had priority over family policy, and it was hoped that individual demographic behavioural patterns would ultimately lead to the formation of a 'population of socialist reproduction' which was to be characterized by 'homogeneity of, rationality of, and a national consciousness of demographic reproduction' (Büttner, 1981:95). The right to subordinate the interests of the individual to those of the 'socialist society' did not exclude generative behaviour (Wendt, 1991:270–1). The primary aim was the promotion of women bearing a third child (Wirtschaftswissenschaft, 1979:781). This preoccupation with the decline in the number of children per family was well grounded. Whereas in 1970 26 per cent of all live births represented a third or higher-order child in a family, in 1971 this was only 19 per cent, and in 1974 it fell to 11 per cent (Wendt, 1990:15,28).

Despite the clear pro-natalist direction and substantial expenditures for social political programmes, the target of raising the number of children to three or more per family was not achieved (Schwarz, 1992:255,260). In the 1980s reproduction fell below replacement level by 15–20 per cent. The declining trend in the birth rate could be halted only temporarily (Birg, 1993:61; Wendt, 1991:253–4). Pro-natalist measures were able to encourage childbearing in one way. Parents who already desired or planned to have children were influenced to have them earlier rather than later. The policy's impact can be seen at the end of the 1970s in the frequency of periods of high fertility rates (Schwarz, 1992:260–1; Wendt, 1991:255–6).

Cohort analyses confirm the fact that there were no significant increases in birth rates. A temporary halting of a downward trend in the number of births could, however, be observed (Vortmann, 1989:557–8). In fact, it has been argued that a decrease in the cohort fertility rate was warded off (Dinkel, 1984:157). Thus, one can point to temporary achievements of population policy, but state measures were incapable of halting the trend of having no more than two children.

The increasing efforts at indoctrination led to an intensification and expansion of control and surveillance in all spheres of society, to the loss of civic values and social responsibility, and to a lack of space for individual development. In response, there was a stronger need to seek privacy and a sphere where one could speak unregulated and uncontrolled about what one considered important in life. This need became ever more difficult to fulfil outside the private sphere. In particular, the family was able to play an important role here because of the strong emotional bonds and relations of trust. In this sense, family and children were increasingly confronted with fulfilling a compensatory role. For this reason also, family, children, and partnerships, together made up one of the most important areas of life. The process of valuation of this private sphere intensified despite, or perhaps even because of, increasing collectivization, control, and observation in conjunction with the loss of civic values, hopelessness, and constraints to individual development (Speigner, 1987:104–5; Frauen in den neuen Bundes-ländern, 1991:265–6).

The measures implemented as population policy led to even higher expectations of family and children in their compensatory role. Demographic figures showing that almost all women had at least one child, but that the number of women bearing three or more children was steadily decreasing, substantiate this hypothesis.

The pro-natalist social policy stressed that women had the 'natural' responsibility of rearing and minding children (Penrose, 1990:63). Policy was mainly directed at the concerns of women tied down by household duties and child-minding and at the incompatibility of these familial responsibilities with gainful employment. That incompatibility remained, as ever, almost exclusively a woman's problem. With a high percentage of women in the paid labour force and the high value placed upon having children, pro-natalist measures were able to improve the co-ordination of gainful employment and motherhood, though they could hardly resolve all areas of conflict. Families – more specifically, women and children – were entitled to several direct and indirect financial benefits and to privileges at certain times (Cornelius, 1990; Wendt, 1993).

Whereas direct monetary benefits were judged quite favourably, benefits received indirectly (such as health- and education-related in-kind benefits, subsidized children's clothing and staple foods, public transportation fare reductions, etc.) were taken for granted and expected. The relatively low household net monthly income of DME 2,185 for a double-earner, married couple with two children has to be taken into account. Lone-parent households had much lower monthly incomes, totalling an average of DME 1,029 (cf. Section 5.4.1).

The following direct benefits were provided:

1. a maternity benefit amounting to DME 1,000 per child contingent upon receipt of pre- and post-natal medical care; the benefit to be handed over in a series of payments made at special governmental offices for advice on pregnancy and motherhood;

2. a monthly child allowance: DME 50 for the first child, DME 100 for the second child, and DME 150 for each additional child;

3. a supplementary allowance of DME 60 for students and mothers in occupational training;

4. no-interest loans for young married couples (up to 30 years of age) of DME 7,000 for household furnishings and aquisitions, with loan write-offs according to the number of children in the family (DME 1,000 for the first

child, DME 1,500 for the second child, and DME 2,500 for the third child), the loan to be repaid in 11 years;

5. tuition-free schooling and occupational training;

6. educational cash benefits for pupils in the eleventh and twelfth years of school amounting to DME 110 and DME 150, respectively; and a basic grant for university and polytechnical students amounting to DME 200 (Winkler, 1990a:140).

In addition to the monetary benefits there were many privileges connected to specific phases in motherhood:

1. *Paid maternity leave* was offered during pregnancy for a maximum of six weeks prior to giving birth, then to a maximum of twenty weeks following birth, whereby during the entire 26 weeks of maternity leave (prior to and following birth) mothers were entitled to benefits equivalent to their prior average weekly wages. Further, supplementary paid maternity leave existed after the first 20 weeks following birth: until the first child reached his/her first birthday (infant care); until the third child was 18 months old (in the case of twins, until the children reached two years of age; in the case of triplets, until the children reached three years of age). During the supplementary maternal leave, cash benefits were provided in an amount equivalent to sickness insurance benefits after seven weeks of disability. The minimum cash benefit level for mothers who were employed full-time and had one child amounted to DME 250, for those with two children DME 300, and for those with three children DME 350.

2. *Working-time arrangements for mothers and wives* existed for women with two children at home: they had a reduction in working time without a loss in wages from the official working week of 43¾ hours, set by law, to 40 hours. Married women with two or more children as well as lone mothers were entitled to paid sick leave to care for a sick child under the age of 14 for a total of 6 weeks, for mothers of three children 8 weeks, and for mothers of four children 10 weeks. For mothers doing shift work, the annual holiday entitlement was increased to a total of 20 days where two children were present, and up to 21 days where there were three children. Women were given one paid day off from work each month to take care of household tasks if they were married, had children under 18 years of age, or were single and over 40 years old; lone fathers were also given this privilege.

3. Hormonal *contraceptives* were free of charge but required a prescription. They were used by 40 per cent of the women at childbearing age. *Abortion* in the first 12 weeks of pregnancy was legal and covered by sickness insur-

ance funds. There were approximately 40 abortions to every 100 live births in the mid-1980s.

4. Under the *labour protection laws*, pregnant women and mothers with children under one year of age had extensive protection against dismissal, and lone mothers had up to three years' protection. Pregnant women were excused from job tasks that were health hazardous, from night work, and from overtime, and they received other privileges (breaks for breastfeeding, protection against dismissal for one year following birth).

5. *Benefits for families with three or more children* included priority status in the provision of sufficient housing space, in child-care placement, and in the labour union's holiday accommodations. There were cash benefits as well, e.g. children's and school meals, children's clothing, costs incurred when children started school, for a traditional ceremony for 14-year-olds in the GDR, for children's holiday camps. For families with four or more children additional benefits were provided (credit, rental allowance, etc.). Such benefits were intended to keep the standard of living of large families relatively stable.

6. Finally, *lone-parent support* included cash payments to care for a sick child, equivalent to sickness insurance benefits. If there was no place for a child in a day-care centre, a flat cash grant of DME 250–350 was payable.

5.3. Family Forms in the 1980s

Young families were typical, since couples tended to marry and become parents at an early age. It was equally typical that the second generation left their parents' home as young adults (cf. Section 5.4.1).

As part of the changes in family structure, chiefly attributable to high divorce rates and depreciation of the institution of marriage sanctioned by law, non-marital cohabitation as a family form established itself. A relatively high remarriage rate led to a high number of second marriages and frequent step-parenthood.

Since two-parent families – consisting of married/unmarried parents with children – were predominant, there was no 'crisis of the institution of the family' to speak of. However, another trend, related to the high level of labour participation of women and their resulting economic independence in the GDR, that was particularly noticeable was the significant increase in the number of lone mothers.

The decrease in the proportion of the married population (in particular of males) at marriageable age (of 5.1 per cent from 1971 to 1989) was accompanied by an increase in the proportion of single people (4.6 per cent) and divorcees (3.9 per cent). Still, the most typical family form remained a married couple with children: in 1987, 64 per cent of the total population over 18 years of age was married, the majority of which had children; about 18 per cent of the population was single, almost 8 per cent divorced, and nearly 11 per cent widowed (Table 5.6). There was, however, an increasing proportion of the population that was unmarried and cohabiting.

The traditional, and once largely dominant, nuclear family, with dual-earner parents, was still prevalent but there was also a tendency towards a pluralization of life-styles; however, there was still an inclination towards living as a couple and having children. There was a clear orientation towards family forms similar to the traditional one, such as non-marital cohabitation (often with children), second marriages and step-parent families, but also

Table 5.6. *Marital status of the resident population, aged 18 and over, former GDR, 1971–1989 (%)*

Marital status	Year				
	1971	1981	1987[a]	1987[b]	1989
Total single	14.0	16.6	18.2	22.2	18.6
Male	15.7	19.9	21.8	27.0	22.3
Female	12.6	13.9	15.1	19.7	15.3
Total married	68.7	65.5	63.7	63.0	63.6
Male	77.7	71.6	68.5	61.1	67.8
Female	61.7	60.3	59.6	64.0	60.0
Total consensual union	–	(2.3)	–	10.3	(14.8)
Total widowed	13.3	11.7	10.6	0.3	10.0
Male	4.3	3.7	3.5	0.1	3.2
Female	20.4	18.4	16.8	0.5	16.0
Total divorced	3.9	6.1	7.4	7.8	7.8
Male	2.3	4.8	6.2	6.6	6.6
Female	5.3	7.4	8.5	8.8	8.8

Sources: 1971: Population Census 1971, data on household, family, number of children, Berlin: 34–5.
1981: Population Census 1981, ibid.
1987[a]: *Statistisches Jahrbuch der DDR 1987*, own calculations.
1987[b]: Survey *Kinderwunsch '87*; secondary analysis of the data on women aged 18–40 in 1987, 1992.
1989: *Statistisches Jahrbuch der DDR 1990*, own calculations.
1989 Total consensual union: projections based on sociological survey *Leben DDR, '90* (Life in the GDR, 1990), in Häder (1991:574).

lone-parent families, the heads of which, i.e. the mothers, were gainfully employed. Yet the extent of the development of these 'new' family forms was particular to the GDR. Such alternative forms as commuter-marriages, sharing flats, and families with 'double incomes but no kids' remained rare.

Cohabitation became increasingly popular among the younger generations. It gradually became a socially accepted form to live together in partnership. Sociologists conducted a survey and found that in 1987 approximately 10 per cent of the resident population between the ages of 18 and 40 lived in a consensual union (*Kinderwunsch '87*); surveys conducted in 1989 and 1990 showed that the proportion had grown to 14 per cent (Häder, 1991:56–7). Not only single but also divorced and widowed women and men lived in consensual unions, sharing housekeeping responsibilities.

The growing number of unwed cohabiting couples was thought to indicate greater expectations attached to partnership and family life as well as problems in this area of personal relations. Moreover, it was said to be evidence of the depreciation of the institution of marriage (Winkler, 1990*a*:111–2). Most consensual unions were considered 'trial marriages' which preceded the long-term, legally certified form of living together. The consensual unions were therefore concentrated among single adults in their twenties and divorcees in their thirties.

Although consensual unions were widely established as a family form, there was no legal framework protecting its members, including the children. But mothers who lived in consensual unions had certain advantages. They were classified as lone mothers and thus were entitled to priority status in child-care placement and to the more generous paid sick leave when a child fell ill. Many chose to remain unmarried in order to be beneficiaries of these additional privileges and benefits.

The growth in the numbers of divorces and of children born out of wedlock led to a rise in the proportion of lone-parent families. Lone parents were almost exclusively lone mothers. In 1981 (the last population census of the GDR) 18 out of 100 families were lone-parent families, 17 of them female-headed. According to the survey *Kinderwunsch '87*, 22.5 per cent of all female respondents between the ages of 18 and 40 were lone mothers, though 9.6 per cent of these women actually lived in consensual unions. This meant that 23 per cent qualified officially as lone mothers though only 13 per cent truly parented alone. Hence 87 per cent of all women with children lived in a partnership (either married or in consensual union).

Most of the women who were genuinely lone parents had not chosen life without a partner. The lone-parent situation resulted in most cases from failed partnerships rather than from choosing single parenthood as an alternative family form. The majority of lone mothers who were over 30 years old were divorced. The large proportion of divorced lone mothers can also be attributed to the courts' bias in divorce cases when awarding the custody of the children.

With a rise in the remarriage rate, there was a concomitant growth in the number of stepfamilies (especially stepfathers). About one-quarter of all men and women who married in 1989 were entering their second marriage. The average age of divorced women was 34 at the time of remarriage, 37 for divorced men (in 1987). Most remarried shortly after the divorce; it took less than three years for 45 per cent of the divorced women to remarry (Winkler, 1990*a*:108).

5.4. Family Living Arrangements

5.4.1. *Income, Labour-Force Patterns, Education and Housing*

HOUSEHOLD INCOME. The household income was almost exclusively dependent on gainful employment of both men and women. Although women's average income was significantly lower than that of men, the second income was an economic necessity. Women provided 40 per cent of the household income (*Haushaltseinkommen*, 1989:2). At the same time as family income rose, there was a widening gap between nominal income and purchasing power, on the one hand, and rising prices (mainly of consumer durables) and their generally short supply, on the other. This officially denied hidden inflation particularly affected large families' economic situation. In spite of child allowances and other state benefits, the average net monthly household income of a married couple with two children amounted to DME 2,185, which was just slightly above the average net monthly household income of DEM 2,067 of a childless married couple (Table 5.7). Families were thus structurally economically disadvantaged – though not to the extent that they were in the Federal Republic – despite an active population policy.

Compared with two-parent households, lone-parent households were particularly economically disadvantaged. The average net monthly income of a lone-parent household was only half that of a married couple (DME 1,029 and 2,067, respectively). General provision of lone-parent households was thus typically poor. Compared with two-parent families, they were also disadvantaged with respect to their leisure-time activities. Lone parents endured physical and psychological hardship in coping with the workplace, the household and in regard to child-rearing and their social relationships; their opportunities for communication were limited as well.

Women earned less on average. There was a discrepancy between the equal pay for women and men propagated by the state, and what women actually earned. An analysis of women's earned income clearly shows that pay differences were gender-specific. The majority of women worked in sectors and branches of the economy where low-paid jobs are the rule. In branches dominated by the male labour force and in which higher-paying jobs were available, women tended to be underrepresented (*Die Frau in der DDR*, 1990:39; Winkler, 1990*a*:66–7). Thus, one can refer to a gender-specific structural feature of the economy which was indicated by a female-dominated labour force in sectors with low-paid jobs and a male-dominated labour force in the sectors with higher-paying jobs. On average, women earned approximately 20 per cent less than their male co-workers. Even in the sectors offering jobs considered typically female, women were overrepresented among the lowest wage groups (Roloff, 1991:137,144). The gender-specific wage system worked especially to the disadvantage of a significant number of lone mothers (in 1989, approximately 340,000). In particular, low-paying jobs meant economic hardship for lone mothers which rather detracted from the more favourable aspects of economic independence; moreover, the disadvantages were strengthened after retirement. Since the right to a job and the duty to work were determined by law, unemployment was unknown and full-time employment was the norm.

Table 5.7. *Average net household income and net earned income per month, former GDR, 1988*

	Net household income[a]	Net earned income	Net wages/ salary
Total households	1,946	1,695	1,536
Total married couples	2,067	1,803	1,638
Married couples with 2 children	2,185	1,855	1,689
Married couples with 3 children	2,293	1,777	1,623
Lone parents with 1 child	1,029	818	747
Lone parents with 2 children	1,245	819	747
Young married couples (under age 26)	1,798	1,513	1,394

[a] Household net income was calculated on the basis of the net earned income, child allowance, public and company benefits, sickness insurance payments as well as miscellaneous sources of income.

Source: Haushaltseinkommen und Austattung von Arbeitern und Angestellten 1980 bis 1988 (1989).

FEMALE ACTIVITY RATE. The female economic activity rate (employed women as a percentage of the female working-age population) was 78 per cent, or 91.2 if the apprentices and students are included. In 1989, 48.8 per cent of the total employed labour force were continuously employed women. Labour-force activity of married women with one or two children remained high (Kirner *et al.*, 1990:580). Age had a negative effect on the activity rate of women (Wendt, 1993:89). Women's occupational careers were to orient themselves on men's life-course patterns. Women's strong demand for part-time work was seldom met. On the one hand, women's labour participation was initially high because they were needed to replace the lost male labour arising from war casualties and from the massive amount of those of working age who had fled to the Federal Republic. On the other hand, women's activity rates were kept artificially high by an inefficient economic system's demand for labour, an inflated bureaucracy, and an enormous security apparatus.

The economic necessity of a large female labour force was ideologically abused by misrepresenting it as part of the political propaganda of social equality. It was through the integration of female labour into the production process that women were to be socially liberated and women's emancipation was to be achieved (Penrose, 1990:64). However, a high proportion of women in gainful employment (Table 5.8) was not enough to end the social inequality between men and women, although it did contribute to the establishment of more equal rights. Despite inequalities between men and women that continued to exist at the workplace, women's equal rights at work progressed further in the former GDR than in the FRG.

Female labour was dominant in certain branches of the economy: in the postal and communications branch (69 per cent), in trade (72 per cent), and in non-production branches (56 per cent). In the health service branch women held almost 83 per cent of the (mostly health-care) jobs. In the industrial sector 41 per cent of the labour force was female, in farming and forestry 37 per cent. Compared with other European countries, the former GDR had one of the longest working weeks, at 43¾ hours. Only mothers with two or more children were allowed to reduce their working week to 40 hours, without a reduction in pay. Thirty per cent of all employed women worked shifts in the chemical, textile, and foodstuffs industries (Winkler, 1990a:82). For these women the compatibility of family and (paid) work responsibilities was particularly difficult. A rigid working time regime was the rule; flexible working time regimes were largely unknown. In 1989, 27 per cent of the active female labour force were entitled to a reduced working week.

Table 5.8. *Female labour-force participation rates in the former GDR and the FRG, 1989*

Age group	Labour-force participation rate[a]	
	Former GDR	FRG
15–25	92.1	56.3
25–30	82.4	68.3
30–35	87.5	62.9
35–40	88.4	64.4
40–45	91.8	64.8
45–50	87.7	61.8
50–55	83.2	54.4
55–60	73.5	40.9
60–65	28.3	11.2
15–65 total[b]	89.5	55.5

[a] employed persons of one age group in relation to the age group's aggregate in total population.
[b] the ratio of active women to the total population of women at working age.

Sources: Die Frau in der DDR (1990:42); Statistisches Bundesamt, *Bevölkerung und Erwerbstätigkeit* (Population and Employment), Fachserie 1 R.4.1.1, Wiesbaden (1990:122).

WOMEN'S EDUCATIONAL LEVELS. Along with the increased integration of women into the paid labour force, the general and vocational level of education among women rose. It is evident that the education deficit that women traditionally had, compared with men, gradually diminished and that women's chances on the labour market improved. In 1989, approximately 88 per cent of all women employed by the state or in co-operatives were either craftsworkers (with a certificate of completion of apprenticeship) or possessed higher qualifications. Lower levels of education or lack of skills were more of a problem for older cohorts of women. In fact, among the 20–25-year-olds, fewer women (47 per cent) were unskilled than men. In contrast, among those aged 45–50 the majority of the unskilled labour was female (74 per cent).

According to the survey *Kinderwunsch '87*, only 8 per cent of the 18–40-year-old women did not have an occupational qualification (Table 5.9). Every third woman had completed technical training or got a university degree. Among these women, however, a greater proportion had completed technical training (particularly among the medium-level medical personnel: 25.4 per cent) than a university degree (8.1 per cent).

Table 5.9. *Level of qualification and education, women aged 18-40, in the former GDR, 1987*

Level of qualification	%	years of schooling	%
Un-/semi-skilled labour/ semi-skilled craftsworker	8.3	8, or no certificate of completion	14.4
(Master) craftsworker[a]	58.2	10	49.1
Completion of technical training[a]/university degree	33.5	12	36.5

[a] Including medical technicians with a certificate of completion of training.

Source: Survey *Kinderwunsch '87*; secondary analysis, 1992.

Women aged 18-40 without qualifications or with lower qualifications and/or skills had comparatively the most children: two or more children were characteristic of this group (Table 5.10). Craftswomen, the women with the highest rate of employment, usually had one or two children, though 45 per cent had two or more children, and 36 per cent only one child. Interestingly, women with a degree in post-secondary education (e.g. university) tended to have two or more children more frequently (48 per cent). These women typically had two children and tended to work full-time.

Since the mid-1980s the majority of young women (approximately 56 per cent) has been acquiring the *Abitur* (certificate of aptitude for higher education for admission to a university). Women made up approximately half of the student body at the universities and colleges (51 per cent in 1987; 47 per cent in 1989). In fact, at the schools of specialized technical and vocational training, female students (since 1989 at about 70 per cent) clearly outnumbered male students (Winkler, 1990a:40,43). The majority of women between 18 and 40 years of age had completed the compulsory ten years of schooling; only every seventh woman had completed no more than eight years of schooling or had left school without a certificate. In contrast, nearly one-third of women had a certificate of completion of technical or vocational training – including for medical technical-assistance jobs – or a university degree (32 per cent), and at least 4 per cent had completed the *Abitur* (*Kinderwunsch '87*).

Women with the lowest level of schooling (eight years, or without completion of any specific training or educational programme) had the highest number of children. However, this group constituted scarcely 15 per cent of all 15–40-year-old women (Table 5.11). The largest group was composed

Table 5.10. *Number of children by level of qualification, women aged 18–40, in the former GDR, 1987 (%)*[a]

Qualification	Number of children			
	0	1	2+	Total
Un-/semi-skilled	17.8	25.7	56.5	8.3
craftsworker	(38)	(55)	(121)	(214)
(Master) craftsworker	18.9	35.7	45.4	58.2
	(282)	(534)	(679)	(1,495)
Specialized/technical	17.2	34.9	47.9	33.5
college of post-secondary	(148)	(300)	(412)	(860)
education or university				
Total	18.2	34.6	47.2	100
Total no. of cases	(468)	(889)	(1,212)	(2,569)

[a] Numbers of cases are given in parentheses.

Source: Survey *Kinderwunsch '87*; secondary analysis, 1992.

Table 5.11. *Number of children by level of education, women aged 18–40, in the former GDR, 1987 (%)*[a]

Years/level of schooling	Number of children			
	0	1	2+	Total
8: uncompleted	10.3	25.5	64.2	14.6
programme	(40)	(99)	(249)	(388)
10	22.1	36.4	41.5	49.0
	(288)	(476)	(542)	(1,306)
12: university or	23.2	32.1	43.7	36.4
specialized technical/	(225)	(321)	(424)	(970)
vocational college degree				
Total	20.8	33.6	45.6	100
Total no. of cases	(553)	(896)	(1,215)	(2,664)

[a] Numbers of cases are given in parentheses.

Source: Survey *Kinderwunsch '87*; secondary analysis, 1992.

of women with ten years of schooling. Typically, these women (78 per cent) had either one or two children; two children was more common than one child (42 versus 36 per cent). Twenty-two per cent were (still) childless at the time of the survey. Within the group with a higher level of schooling or training (*Abitur* or a degree either from a college of specialized technical or vocational training or from a university) women tended even more frequently to have two or more children: 44 per cent had two or more compared with 32 per cent who had only one child. Twenty-three per cent of the women in this group, presumably mostly the younger ones, had no children.

HOUSING. Housing was a problem chiefly for young families, divorcees, and young adults who wanted to move out of their parents' home. Finding one's own flat was particularly difficult. The 1971 Housing Construction Plan announced that the housing shortage issue was to be resolved by 1990. This goal was unrealistic for economic reasons, however. High subsidies going to housing increased the state deficit. Even housing rental fees were being subsidized, which meant that only 36 per cent of total housing costs were being covered by tenants' payments (Schulz, 1993:589). The Housing Construction Plan was to have mainly very large, multi-storey and multi-unit housing complexes (using the large-panel construction method) built by large industrial combines in housing construction. However, these new blocks of housing led to the destruction of older urban structures and to the creation of new faceless satellite towns on cities' rims, with housing of modest standard, made of poor building materials and with a deficient infrastructure.

Housing was under state control, and the allotting of dwellings was also government-regulated. 'Members of the working class' – in particular, shift-workers, families with three or more children, young married couples, and comrades in the struggle against fascism as well as victims of fascism and their survivors – received preferential treatment (Wohnraumlenkungsverordnung – state housing provision regulation – 1985, §§ 6 and 11).

Housing units were also used as rewards for politically and socially correct behaviour. The number of privately owned dwellings dropped by 20 per cent, down to 42 per cent (Klös, 1990:2,5); these consisted mainly of one- and two-family houses. The Housing Construction Plan failed to resolve the housing shortage. Housing demand had greatly increased as a result of the rise in one-person households. As late as 1989, 24 per cent of all dwellings did not have an inside toilet and 18 per cent had neither a shower nor a bath (Winkler, 1990a:126). Owing to the widespread unsatisfactory housing conditions, newly furnished and sufficiently spacious dwellings were highly valued (Winkler, 1990a:126). In a sociological survey conducted in 1982, findings indicated that 17 per cent of the younger women with one child did not live in their own flat. Lone mothers were in a worse position than married mothers. Women with two or more children often lived in over-crowded conditions: in 1982, 40 per cent of families with three children lived in three-room flats, 5 per cent in two-room flats.[4] Such circumstances usually coincided with a lack of other modern conveniences of a dwelling. In 1982, 12 per cent of all women and children were living in housing units without a bath or shower, 40 per cent did not have a modern heating system, and 14 per cent were without an indoor toilet (Wendt, 1985).

Although the decision to have the first child would be made without consideration of the housing situation, available housing was a larger factor in the decision to have any further children. In the 1982 survey, 61 per cent of all female respondents aged 18-40 claimed that they were not prepared to bear any further children because of their inadequate housing situation.

If one considers the demographic figures, it can be inferred that in families where mothers were 45 or older most of the children had already left home to live on their own. It was also usual that this step was coupled with a career, marriage, and the birth of a child. Evidence of young marriage and childbearing also serves as an indicator of children leaving their parents' home at an early age. Marriage at an early age was further encouraged by a policy giving priority to married couples in the allocation of state housing. As a consequence, only a small proportion (25 per cent) of single women (19.7 per cent of all women aged 18-40) had their own flat.

5.4.2. *Patterns of Life-Style in the 1980s*

Patterns of life-style of family households were ascertained by the inclusion of such characteristics as marital status, number of children and the amount of female economic activity. It becomes apparent that patterns of life-style of GDR families were largely characterized by both the presence of children and gainful employment of the two parents. In 1987 over three-quarters of all women 18–40 years old had children and a job. The social demographic characteristics (Section 5.4.1) showed that the two-earner family was the typical model family life-style of real socialism in the former GDR (62 per cent of all women 18–40 years old; see also Tables 5.12 and 5.13). This was true more often for full-time employed married mothers with two or more children than for those employed full-time with one child or for mothers working part-time.

The so-called 'traditional family' with at least two children and a mother who is not gainfully employed was entirely atypical (1.7 per cent). Women

---

[4] A three-room flat is a rental unit with the same number of separate rooms without any obvious designated function, plus kitchen and bathroom or toilet, if not otherwise indicated.

Table 5.12. *Patterns of 'life-style', women aged 18–40, former GDR, 1987*

Life-styles[a]	No. of cases	%	Ranking
Married, 2 or more children, full-time job	844	33.2	1
Married, 1 child, full-time job	515	20.3	2
Single, childless, full-time job	260	10.2	3
Married, children, part-time job	221	8.7	4
Unmarried cohabiting, children, full-time job	173	6.8	5
Single, 1 child, completing training/schooling	124	4.8	6
Divorced, children, full-time job	118	4.6	7
Single, children, full-time job	113	4.4	8
Married, childless, full-time job	75	3.0	9
Unmarried cohabiting, childless, full-time job	57	2.2	10
Married, children, housewife	43	1.7	11
Total	2,542	100	–

Missing cases: 168 (= 6.2 %) out of 2,710 female respondents

[a] Patterns of life-styles making up less than 1.5 % of the total sample were excluded.

Source: Survey *Kinderwunsch '87*; secondary analysis, 1992.

Table 5.13. *'Life-styles', women aged 18–40 with children, former GDR, 1987*

Life-styles[a]	No. of cases	%	Ranking
Married, 2 or more children, full-time job	844	41.6	1
Married, 1 child, full-time job	515	25.4	2
Married, with children, part-time job	221	10.9	3
Unmarried cohabiting, with children, full-time job	173	8.5	4
Divorced, with children, full-time job	118	5.8	5
Single, no partner, with children, full-time job	113	5.3	6
Married, with children, housewife	43	2.1	7
Total	2,027	102	

Missing cases: 80 (= 3.8 %) out of 2,107 female respondents

[a] Patterns of life-styles constituting less than 2 % of the sample were excluded.

Source: Survey *Kinderwunsch '87*; secondary analysis, 1992.

outside the paid labour force were just as rare as lone fathers. In spite of the dominance of the typical dual-earner family with child(ren), there was an indication of a pluralization of patterns of life-style, in particular in the appearance of unmarried cohabiting couple-households (mostly with a child) and of lone-mother households.

Most women with children were married and gainfully employed (78 per cent of all mothers); 25 per cent of these women had one child, 42 had two or more. A very small proportion was employed part-time. Full-time employment was typical for lone mothers as well as unmarried cohabiting mothers. Two or more children were common among married and divorced women. In contrast, lone mothers and unmarried cohabiting mothers tended to have one child only. Regardless of marital status, nearly all mothers were gainfully employed, for the most part full-time. The absence of children correlated highly with the marital status 'single'. The largest proportion of women without children (71 per cent) were either single and employed full-time (48 per cent) or single and completing training or schooling (23 per cent). The absence of children among married women was atypical (16 per cent); but unmarried cohabiting women were childless just as seldom as divorced women were.

Despite the rise in the numbers of unmarried cohabiting couples and lone mothers, the two-parent family (married parents, both of whom were gainfully employed) remained the dominant normative model of all life-styles.

The shortcomings in the former GDR society that existed at the time of the German unification, as also exemplified in the backwardness of family structures, are currently undergoing fundamental changes. These changes have had a far-reaching impact on family formation. Decisions creating social bonds, as is the case in decisions to marry and to have children, make the necessary social flexibility and spatial mobility more difficult in times of major changes. A considerable decline in the number of births and marriages as well as divorces in the new *Länder* has been attributed to fears concerning future prospects and social security and to a general state of disorientation. The continuing tendency to migrate from the new to the old *Länder* has made it possible at least temporarily to speak of a process of 'demographic erosion' in the new *Länder*. In the long term, however, family formation in the new *Länder* should assimilate to that in the old ones. This process of assimilation depends on the establishing of similar external and internal preconditions (Wendt, 1993).

5.5. Compatibility of Family Life and Gainful Employment

Characteristic of everyday family life was both parents working outside the home (96 per cent of all families, married as well as cohabiting couples). Women's everyday life was therefore typically shaped by the daily co-ordination of gainful employment and child-rearing and minding. Ninety-two per cent of all women aged 18–40 were either engaged in paid work or enrolled in an educational or occupational training programme; 67 per cent of these women were married (Tables 5.14 and 5.15). The majority of the women in paid work (83 per cent) had children. In fact, more women had two or more children (48 per cent) than one child (35 per cent). Most of these mothers had full-time jobs. Mothers who had part-time paid jobs (10 per cent) tended to have two or more children (68 per cent). Higher numbers of children seem to be responsible for the tendency among the mothers to be employed part-time. In the former GDR women who were not in paid

Table 5.14. *Female labour-force participation rate, by marital status and number of children, women aged 18–40, former GDR, 1987*

	No. of cases	%
Working full-time	2,213	81.8
of those:		
Married	1,441	(65.1)
Single	393	(17.8)
Unmarried, cohabiting	238	(10.8)
Divorced	129	(5.8)
Widowed	12	(0.5)
Working part-time	271	10
of those:		
Married	228	(84.1)
Unmarried, cohabiting	21	(7.7)
Divorced	16	(5.9)
Not gainfully employed	47	1.7
of those: Married	44	(93.6)
Enrolled in schooling/training programme	176	6.5
of those:		
Single	134	(76.1)
Married	21	(11.9)
Unmarried, cohabiting	18	(10.2)
Children of working women	2,042	83.3
No children	409	(16.7)
1 child	865	(35.3)
2 or more children	1,177	(48.0)
Both partners in paid work married/unmarried, cohabiting (full-time or part-time)	1,928	95.7
Only 1 partner in paid work married/unmarried, cohabiting	86	4.3

Source: Survey *Kinderwunsch '87*; secondary analysis, 1992.

Table 5.15. *Activity rate, by type of activity and number of children, women aged 18–40, former GDR, 1987 (%)*[a]

Type of activity	No. of children			
	0	1	2+	Total
Full-time employed	18.4	36.0	45.6	81.9
	(402)	(784)	(994)	(2,180)
Part-time employed	2.5	30.0	67.5	10.2
	(7)	(81)	(183)	(271)
Not employed	2.1	23.4	74.5	1.8
	(1)	(11)	(35)	(47)
In education/training	86.1	12.7	1.2	6.2
	(142)	(21)	(2)	(165)
Total	20.7	33.7	45.6	100
Total no. of cases	(552)	(897)	(1,214)	(2,663)

[a] Numbers of cases are given in parentheses.

Source: Survey *Kinderwunsch '87*; secondary analysis, 1992.

employment were as uncommon as women without children. For the most part it was young women who were in an educational or occupational training programme who were (still) single and had not (yet) had any children.

The manifold burdens resulting from reconciling occupational, child/family, and household responsibilities created numerous social, health, and psychological problems as well as conflicts in everyday life for women. Equality between the sexes was established by law, ideologically justified, and by means of great propagandistic efforts considered to have been put into effect. That women were enjoying equal rights could at least be statistically proven: women were shown to have high employment rates and a wide network of functional conditions to facilitate the compatibility of gainful employment and motherhood.

Although social policy measures were seen to be directed towards women's needs, actual social discrimination of women at the workplace and in the family with regard to their traditional role was reinforced rather than stunted. Beside the long weekly working hours (of 43¾ hours, or 40 hours for mothers with two or more children) women had to work a second shift at home to take care of family and household duties. In 1985 married women spent two and a half times as much time on household activities as men (Statistisches Bundesamt, 1991:21). Women spent three times as much time as men caring for children or other persons. Not only did women take over the largest portion of the housework and the minding and rearing of children, the patterns of activities were to a large extent traditional (Wendt, 1993:92).

Existing problems stemming from the incompatibility of occupational and familial life for women were ignored. In 1989 it was announced in a statement that 'the desire to have children was nearly fulfilled, and the compatibility of motherhood/parenthood and occupational life can be achieved without any conflicts' (Speigner, 1989:30).

It was not until after unification that problems relating to the reconciliation of paid work and family responsibilities as well as the social inequality between men and women were pointed out. Although it was common for both women and men to expect to have an occupation, a family, and children, for the sake of the family and in order to care for the children it was the women who sacrificed occupational qualifications, the opportunity for occupational advancement and a higher income.[5] Officially, scholars in the field of women's studies accepted this one-sided point of view, as captured in the following citation:

Socialist conditions of production for the first time made it possible for women to reconcile these functions [as a paid worker, mother, and family member – the author]. (Erhardt and Weichert, 1988:526)

All of this, of course, has nothing to do with emancipation. The social responsibility of men for their families was not a political issue and remained outside the domain of social policy.

5.6. Child Care for Employed Parents

In order to promote a high labour participation rate among women, the state worked to establish conditions that would alleviate the burden of familial responsibilities. Being engaged in paid work while at the same time being a parent was made possible only by a comprehensive system of child care. Day-care centres for children under 3 (*Kinderkrippen*) provided for approximately 80 per cent of demand until the mid-1980s: in 1989 with 353,203 places 80.2 per cent of the demand was met (Winkler, 1990*a*:142–3). If desired, child-care spaces in a kindergarten were available for all children between the ages of 3 and 6 (*Die Frau in der DDR*, 1989:84–5). In fact, owing to the high activity rate among women, 95 per cent of the children in this age

---

[5] According to M. Beyer, official representative responsible for women's affairs of the first elected government of the still-existing GDR, in the preface to Winkler (1990*a*:9).

group were placed in kindergartens (in 1989, 747,140 kindergarten places: Winkler, 1990*a*:142–3).

The child-care facilities were mainly provided by the state but financed at the local or company level. There were also a small number of child-care facilities provided by churches. The Ministry of Health was in charge of the *Kinderkrippen*, whereas the Ministry of Education and the Sciences was in control of the kindergarten facilities. Child care was free of charge in both types of facility. Parents did however have to contribute partially to the costs of meals.

The provision of day-care facilities for the older children (up into their fourth year of primary school) also served the purpose of reconciling gainful employment and child-rearing for mothers: 86 per cent of all schoolchildren ate lunch at school and 76 per cent drank a serving of low-fat pasteurized milk at a break period. None the less, such extensive child-care provision did not solve all conflicts or problems that arose for mothers in paid work. Rather, it may be said that they even produced new problems. The daily separation of mother and child that was endured over many years often led to alienation, problems in family relations, and psychological disturbances. Collectivized child-minding and rearing not only permitted mothers to pursue paid work but also was an opportunity for the state to indoctrinate the children; it was equivalent to instruction in discipline (Maaz, 1990:35ff.; Wingen, 1991:8; Geißler, 1991:19).

Not only the mothers but also the children suffered under these conditions. Children, who were none the less loved and wanted, were subject to the emo-tional and physical state of their mothers, who were being overtaxed on a daily basis. Hence, 'mothers [were] most often overly stressed or hard pressed to teach their children the basic social norms and values' (Maaz, 1990:35).

5.7. Domestic Division of Labour

The gender-specific differences in average income have been mainly responsible for maintaining a traditional domestic division of labour. Economic reasoning provided the justification for keeping the traditional female and male roles. Despite recognizable improvements in equality between the sexes, a gender-specific division of labour in the home continued. Child care and rearing was still regarded as women's work.

In families with two children, approximately 47–49 hours per week were spent on household duties; about another 8 hours were needed to provide for child care and rearing. Despite increasing available services and technical conveniences, the amount of time needed for housework remained quite constant (Statistisches Bundesamt, 1991:21,27). The pattern of household activities and the time allotted for them reveal a traditional division of labour.

Through an analysis of time usage, the extent to which women were burdened more in their everyday family life than men becomes apparent. Routine household chores (cooking, washing dishes, doing the laundry, etc.) were typically women's, whereas men tended to do repair jobs and gardening. Child-rearing and minding were again for the most part women's work: 75 per cent of the time spent on these responsibilities was the mothers' time. In two-parent families with two children the mothers took on about 70 per cent of the total load of household chores (Table 5.16). In fact, women spent 18 times as much time as men doing the so-called typical female chores (e.g. cleaning and mending clothes). Women also spent over twice as much time as men doing the shopping. Owing to the poor available supply of consumer goods, in the former GDR, shopping was synonymous with queuing.

Changes in the traditional division of domestic labour were visible only in families whose members had a higher level of education (Meier, 1991: 181). In contrast, in working-class families household tasks tended to be delegated in a traditional manner.

As it became increasingly difficult to keep up with the costs of living, families were forced to make do by way of private production. Economic opportunities became scarce and providing for oneself or the family became ever more difficult. As a result, in the 1980s domestic 'manufacturing' grew (Winkler, 1990*a*:130). For instance, the shortage of fruits and vegetables

Table 5.16. *Daily time usage for household activities on a weekly average and its distribution between women and men in families with 2 children, former GDR, 1985*

Household activities	Women and men		Husband			Wife
	Hrs:mins	%	Hrs:mins	%	Hrs:mins	%
Total activities	5:52	100	1:46	30.1	4:06	69.9
among those:						
Preparing meals	1:43	100	0:22	21.4	1:21	78.6
Doing laundry	0:59	100	0:03	5.1	0:56	94.9
Installation/making something new	0:21	100	0:03	14.3	0:18	85.7
Housekeeping	0:56	100	0:07	12.5	0:49	87.5
Maintenance/repair	0:29	100	0:27	93.1	0:02	6.9
Repair/care of household goods	0:21	100	0:20	85.2	0:01	4.8
Shopping	0:42	100	0:13	31.0	0:29	69.0

Source: calculated from Statistisches Bundesamt (1991:27).

led families – in particular women – to preserve and bottle these foods to improve their availability. Millions of items of clothing were also home-made in the former GDR (e.g. 60 per cent of all skirts and 58 per cent of all dresses: Koch, 1982). Thus, domestic production consumed an enormous amount of leisure time, particularly for women.

It was evident in the data on the use of free time that there were gender-specific differences. Although men's average working hours were longer, they actually had one hour more of average free time per day than women as a result of the domestic division of labour: 3 hours and 54 minutes of free time daily compared with 3 hours and 1 minute for women (Statistisches Bundesamt, 1991:21). Whereas women would spend more of their free time on family-related activities and would consider many of the household activities as things they could do in their 'spare' time (Winkler, 1990*a*:134), men tended to use more of their spare time for sports, education/qualifications, and social activities.

5.8. Summary and Conclusions

The strong tendency towards standardization and uniformity of social structure in the former GDR (Geißler, 1991:17), the closely meshed social fabric, behavioural conformism, ideologically laden value orientations and a rigid set of norms necessarily tended to lead to uniformity in life-course patterns, and to a normalization or standardization of family structures, family formation, and everyday family life.

Even though changes in forms of family living in the former GDR seemed to lag behind those in the Federal Republic, under conditions of 'real socialism', families consisting of married couples with one or two children, in which both parents were gainfully employed full-time, were predominant: this configuration constituted the typical GDR family. Married couples without children, families with many children, and three-generation families were in contrast infrequent. Sixty-two per cent of all households with women between the ages of 18 and 40 represented families with married parents. Households with children were almost exclusively nuclear families (with only two generations present). Generally speaking, there was characteristically a strong orientation towards partnership and children. A life without a partner and children was almost unimaginable. Childlessness was usually not desired and remained the exception; in fact, it was hardly socially accepted, even though almost all women were in paid work.

Married couples without children and the so-called 'traditional families' with at least two children and in which the mother was not gainfully employed were the exception. The 'breadwinner–homemaker model' was not suited to the economic and ideological constraints in the GDR. Even if it would have been economically feasible for a family to have a woman who was solely a housewife and mother doing exclusively domestic non-paid work, there were strong normative pressures against this; and a deficient social network and poor communication opportunities could easily have led to her isolation and marginalization.

Thus, the family played a vital role in the former GDR society. Little or no purpose was to be found in the work or the public spheres. Furthermore, it was difficult to satisfy consumer needs. As a result of the failure of society to generate values that would orientate and integrate its citizens, compensation was sought in the private sphere, in the family and children. Under the restrictive social circumstances, this family sphere offered a special psycho-social protective shelter (Wendt, 1991:266), but as a result the family became psycho-socially overburdened. The family, and in particular women, were affected in this situation. Women were already burdened with their double function as working mothers, and on account of their ascribed social role they were to a large extent responsible for stability in the family. These developments led in general to higher demands on the partnership and family but in particular to an overburdening of the women. The high divorce rates were only one indicator of the continuous heavy burden. However, this did not lead to a fundamental questioning of the value bestowed on marriage and partnership, as the high remarriage rate and the rising number of stepfamilies and of consensual unions with children indicates. The divorce rate was also a result of the high employment rate among women which gave them economic independence. In that way, the importance of the institution of marriage as a source of psycho-social security for the family was at the same time undermined to some extent.

Partnership and the family (with children) remained highly valued, even though the incompatibility of gainful employment and parenthood was a problem. Almost all women had children, but the number of families with more than two children was declining. There was an increase in the number of women bearing children while the number of children born decreased.

Despite social restrictions and tendencies towards gender equality in the period under review, there were increasing deviations from the predominant standard life course in the youngest generation: in addition to the marriage-based nuclear family, consensual unions, lone-parent families (headed mostly by lone mothers) and stepfamilies (resulting from a second marriage) emerged. Marriage was no longer necessarily a prerequisite for starting a family. Consensual unions were however largely duplicates of the traditional marriage-based two-parent family and lone-parent families resulted for the most part from failed marriages rather than as a chosen alternative family form. The formation of stepfamilies counterbalanced the divorce rate, and consensual unions counterbalanced the declining marriage rate. If economic independence by way of paid work contributed to the increase in lone motherhood, it still left lone-parent families economically disadvantaged compared with two-parent families.

Although these new patterns of family life, in particular consensual unions, structurally corresponded highly to the traditional nuclear family, they also constituted a framework offering – relatively speaking – a certain degree of individualism and flexibility rather than a general decrease in social pressure to comply with norms or than a pluralization of values relating to family. These life-styles allowed for the high rate of gainfully employed women whose income became indispensable. Families provided for an intimate sphere in which one could escape the pressures to conform to norms and where the pluralization of values was possible.

Compared with standards worldwide, women in the former GDR had a high labour-participation rate (91 per cent). This had many consequences. Men's and women's roles in occupational life became similar. Women's independent income increased their self-confidence and independence. And, in comparison with women in the FRG at the time, there were more gains concerning women's equal rights. These achievements were far from constituting social equality between the sexes. Co-ordinating parenthood and an occupational life took up a considerable part of women's everyday life. Female employment fulfilled a prerequisite of the propagated social equality and the demands of an inefficient production process. Moreover, the wage policy had made a second income indispensible in order to maintain a modest standard of living. At the same time, there was a stated 'population and family policy' goal of securing reproduction of the parent generation in order to secure the needed future labour force. Thus, family formation was required to fulfil these societal needs. Accordingly, family policy explicitly supported families with two or more children. The trend towards one-child families was to be warded off. These policies favoured, moreover, *marriage*-based families with children.

Both goals – high female employment and higher birth rates – were consequently met with measures to improve the compatibility of paid work and motherhood. Young couples starting a family were given priority in housing placements. There was a strong connection between motherhood and having one's own dwelling which was a precondition for adulthood and at the same time a symbol of having become independent of one's parents.

In spite of a clearly pro-natalist policy goal and the high material invest-ment that accompanied an ideological campaign to encourage large families, the simple reproduction of the parent generation (2.1 births per woman) was not achieved. What was accomplished, however, was a temporary in-crease in the birth rate and thus a warding off of its observable decline.

Family was highly valued at the individual level: it functioned as an im-portant protective institution in a restrictive society. On the other hand, families became ever more destabilized by their incapacity to cope with all of the demands they were being confronted with. Family as a social institu-tion lost some of its importance by the socialization of some of its respons-ibilities. Among others, extensive child care was provided. State day care also had the function of politically socializing the children. Socialized child care became institutionalized to such an extent that parents were no longer *de facto* responsible for providing it and considered it rather the state's obligation. Non-domestic care institutions were established for cases of sick-ness, disability, and agedness. Non-domestic socialization was oriented to-wards strict norms of behaviour and thus required much discipline. On the one hand, this facilitated integration in the state-defined social structures, producing above all 'an unimaginable pressure to assimilate' (Maaz, 1990: 29). Deviant behaviour was punished from early childhood on. On the other hand, feelings of emotional and psychic emptiness resulted within the domin-ant socialist system of values and norms. This became particularly visible during the general state of disorientation in the region of the former GDR following the turn in the political climate in the autumn of 1989.

The domestic division of labour (housework and child care) continued to follow traditional patterns despite women's high activity rate. A gender-specific assignment of tasks in occupational and family life resulted in occu-pational disadvantages for women. The sectors of economy where female labour was dominant offered mainly low-paid jobs. Although social problems worsened, the surveillance and control of all social areas increased. Living conditions became poorer as well. All the same, in 1989 the two-parent family continued to be propagated as the 'socialist typical family' which was a 'constituent part of the ongoing process of societal formation towards socialism/communism'. This basic type of family would fulfil 'the common needs of family and society, by way of equality between men and women in all areas of society, through the participation of both parents in the production process and in the shaping of public life' (Gysi, 1989:11). Differences in family and societal needs as well as socio-cultural and regional differences were left ignored.

In the long run, family formation and family structure in the new *Länder* will most likely assimilate to West German patterns. At the moment, however, during processes of transformation, differences in these respects have become clearly visible. The present drastic drop in the number of births and marriages is a reflection of this anomic demographic behaviour in reaction to the extensive societal changes in the new *Länder*.

References

Birg, H. (1993), 'Demographische Wirkungen politischen Handelns' (Policy impacts on demographic trends), in H.-U. Klose (ed.), *Altern hat Zukunft: Bevölkerungsentwicklung und dynamische Wirtschaft* (Ageing has a Future: Population Development and Dynamic Economy), Westdeutscher Verlag, Opladen: 52–79.

Büttner, T. (1981), 'Zu einigen Grundzügen der demographischen Reproduktion im Sozialismus' (Basic trends in demographic reproduction under socialism), in *Bevölkerungstheorie und Bevölkerungspolitik* (Population Theory and Population Policy), Akademie-Verlag, Berlin: 87–101.

Cornelius, I. (1990), 'Familien- und Bevölkerungspolitik in der DDR' (Family and population policy in the GDR), *Arbeit und Sozialpolitik*, 8/9:308–16.

Die Frau in der DDR: Statistische Kennziffernsammlung (Women in the GDR: Statistical Key Figures) (1990), Statistisches Amt der DDR, Berlin.

Dinkel, R. (1984), 'Haben die geburtenfördernden Maßnahmen der DDR Erfolg?' (Did pro-natalist measures in the GDR achieve their goals?), *IFO-Studien: Zeitschrift für empirische Wirtschaftsforschung*, 30:139–62.

Dorbritz, J. (1993), 'Sozialer Systemwandel und die Folgen für die Familienbildung' (Changes in a social system and their consequences for family formation), *Berliner Journal für Soziologie*, 3:355–68.

Erhardt, G. and Weichert, B. (1988), 'Einige soziologische Aspekte zur Entwicklung der Frau im gesellschaftlichen Arbeitsprozeß' (Sociological aspects of women's development in the labour force), in *Jahrbuch für Soziologie und Sozialpolitik 1988*, Akademie-Verlag, Berlin.

'Frauen in den neuen Bundesländern im Prozeß der deutschen Einheit' (1991) (Women in the New Länder in the Process of German Unification), in *Materialien zur Frauenpolitik 1991*, 11, BMFuJ, Bonn.

Geißler, R. (1991), 'Soziale Ungleichheit zwischen Frauen und Männern im geteilten und im vereinten Deutschland' (Social inequality between women and men in the divided and in the unified Germany), *Aus Politik und Zeitgeschichte: Beilage zur Wochenzeitung Das Parlement*, 14/15:13–24.

—— (1993), 'Sozialer Wandel' (Social change), in W. Weidenfeld and K.-R. Korte (eds.), *Handbuch zur Deutschen Einheit* (Handbook on German Unification), Campus Verlag, Frankfurt/Main and New York.

GESIS (1993), *Sozialwissenschaften in der DDR* (Social Sciences in the GDR),

GESIS, Bonn.

Gysi, J. (1988), 'Familienformen in der DDR' (Forms of family living in the GDR), in *Jahrbuch für Soziologie und Sozialpolitik 1988*, Akademie-Verlag, Berlin: 508–24.

——(ed.) (1989), *Familienleben in der DDR* (Family Life in the GDR), Akademie-Verlag, Berlin.

——, Dorbritz, J. and Hempel, U. (1989), 'Information über Ehescheidungen in der DDR' (Information on divorce in the GDR), in Wissenschaftlicher Rat für Sozialpolitik und Demographie, *Protokolle und Informationen*, Vol. 1, Institut für Soziologie und Sozialpolitik an der Akademie der Wissenschaften der DDR, Berlin.

Häder, M. (ed.) (1991), *Denken und Handeln in der Krise* (Thought and Action in a Crisis), Akademie-Verlag, Berlin.

Haushaltseinkommen und Ausstattung von Arbeitern und Angestellten 1980 bis 1988 (Household Income and Assets of Blue- and White-Collar Workers 1980–1988) (1989), Staatliche Zentralverwaltung für Statistik, Berlin.

Höhn, Ch. and Schubnell, H. (1986), 'Bevölkerungspolitische Maßnahmen und ihre Wirksamkeit in ausgewählten europäischen Industrieländern (II)' (The impact and effectiveness of population policy in selected European industrialized countries), *Zeitschrift für Bevölkerungswissenschaft*, 12:185–219.

——, Mammey, U. and Wendt, H. (1990), 'Bericht 1990 zur demographischen Lage: Trends in beiden Teilen Deutschlands und Ausländer in der Bundesrepublik Deutschland' (1990 report on the demographic situation: trends in both parts of Germany and foreigners in the FRG), *Zeitschrift für Bevölkerungswissenschaft*, 16:135–205.

Kirner, E., Schulz, E. and Roloff, J. (1990), 'Vereintes Deutschland: geteilte Frauengesellschaft' (Unified Germany: a divided society for women), *Wochenbericht des DIW*, 41:575–82.

Klös, H.-P. (1990), 'Wohnungs- und Städtebau in der DDR' (Housing and urban development in the GDR), *IW-Trends*, 17:1–8.

Koch, H. (1982), 'Zu einigen Aspekten der gesellschaftlichen Bedeutung der Hausarbeit' (Some aspects of the social meaning of housework), *Informationen des Wissenschaftlichen Rates 'Die Frau in der sozialistischen Gesellschaft'*, 5:52–6.

Maaz, H.-J. (1990), *Der Gefühlsstau: Ein Psychogramm der DDR* (Congested Feelings: A Psychological Diagram of the GDR), Argon, Berlin.

Meier, U. (1991), 'Familiale Lebensweise und ökonomische Funktion von Familien in der Ex-DDR' (Family life-styles and the economic function of families in the former GDR), in S. Gräve (ed.), *Der private Haushalt als Wirtschaftsfaktor* (The Private Household as an Economic Factor), Campus Verlag, Frankfurt/Main and New York: 175–85.

Meyer, D. (1991), 'Ehescheidung in der ehemaligen DDR' (Divorce in the former GDR), *Zeitschrift für Bevölkerungswissenschaft*, 17:33–47.

—— and Wendt, H. (1984), 'Zur Geburtenentwicklung und zum Reproduktionsverhalten in der DDR im Gefüge seiner Determinanten – unter besonderer Berücksichtigung der Wertorientierungen' (On determinants of trends in births and reproductive behaviour in the GDR – with special consideration of value orientations), in *Fertilitätstrends* (Fertility Trends), Berlin: 39–62.

Penrose, V. (1990), 'Vierzig Jahre SED-Frauenpolitik: Ziele, Strategien und Ergebnisse' (Forty years of SED's policy on women's issues: goals, strategies and outcomes), *Frauenforschung*, 8:60–77.

Roloff, J. (1991), 'Probleme und Ursachen der Einkommensunterschiede zwischen männlichen und weiblichen Erwerbstätigen in der ehemaligen DDR' (Problems and causes of earnings differences between men and women in the former GDR), *Zeitschrift für Bevölkerungswissenschaft*, 17:135–47.

Schneider, N.F. (1994), *Familie und private Lebensführung in Deutschland Ost und West* (Family and Private Life in Germany East and West), Enke Verlag, Stuttgart.

Schulz, M. (1993), 'Wohnbedingungen und innerstädtische Differenzierung in Ost-Berlin' (Housing conditions and inner-city differences in East Berlin), *Geographische Rundschau*, 45:588–93.

Schwarz, K. (1992), 'Geburtenentwicklung und Familienpolitik in der (früheren) DDR: Beispiel einer pronatalistischen Politik' (Trends in births and family policy in the (former) GDR: an example of a pro-natalist policy), *Zeitschrift für Familienforschung*, 4:248–62.

Speigner, W. (1982), 'Vom kapitalistischen zum sozialistischen Typ der Bevölkerungsreproduktion' (From the capitalist to the socialist type of population reproduction), *Wirtschaftswissenschaft*, 30:1471–90.

—— (ed.) (1987), *Kind und Gesellschaft* (Child and Society), Akademie-Verlag, Berlin.

—— (1989), 'Die geburtenfördernde Bevölkerungspolitik der DDR in den 80er Jahren' (The pro-natalist population policy of the GDR in the 1980s), *Wirtschaftswissenschaft*, 37:19–35.

Statistisches Bundesamt (1991), *Zeitverwendung der Personen in Arbeiter- und Angestelltenhaushalten im Gebiet der ehemaligen DDR 1974, 1980, 1985 und 1990* (Time Budgets of Persons in Blue- and White-Collar Households in the Area of the Former GDR in 1974, 1980, 1985 and 1990), Statistisches Bundesamt, Wiesbaden.

Statistisches Jahrbuch der DDR (Statistical Yearbook of the GDR) (various years), Staatsverlag der Deutschen Demokratischen Republik, Berlin.

Vaskovics, L.A. and Silbereisen, R.K. (1993), *Sozialforschung in der DDR* (Social Research in the GDR), Sonderband Forschungsprojektdokumentation 'Familie und Jugend', Bonn.

——, Garhammer, M., Schneider, N.F. and Kabat vel Job, O. (1994), *Familien- und Haushaltsstrukturen in der ehemaligen DDR und in der Bundesrepublik Deutschland von 1980 bis 1989: ein Vergleich* (Family and Household Structures in the former GDR and in the FRG from 1980 to 1989: a Comparison), Bundesinstitut für Bevölkerungsforschung, Wiesbaden (Materialien zur Bevölkerungswissenschaft, Sonderheft 24).

Vortmann, H. (1989), 'DDR: Stabilisierung der Geburtenrate durch Sozialpolitik' (GDR: Stabilization of birth rates through social policy), in Deutsches Institut für Wirtschaftsforschung, *Wochenbericht 56*, 44:548–58.

Wendt, H. (1985), 'Die Bedeutung der Wohnbedingungen bei der Erfüllung des Kinderwunsches' (The significance of housing conditions for the fulfilment of the desire to have a child), Berlin, unpublished.

—— (1990), 'Bevölkerungsentwicklung und Bevölkerungsstruktur in der DDR' (Population development and structure in the GDR), in *Computer-Atlas Demographie*, Bauakademie, Berlin: 7–42.

—— (1991), 'Geburtenhäufigkeit in beiden deutschen Staaten: zwischen Konvergenz und Divergenz' (Fertility in both German states: between convergence and divergence), *Zeitschrift für Bevölkerungswissenschaft*, 17:251–80.

—— (1993), *Familienbildung und Familienpolitik in der ehemaligen DDR* (Family Formation and Family Policy in the former GDR), Bundesinstitut für Bevölkerungsforschung, Wiesbaden (Materialien zur Bevölkerungswissenschaft, Sonderheft 22).

Wingen, M. (1991), 'Familien im gesellschaftlichen Wandel: Herausforderungen an eine künftige Familienpolitik im geeinten Deutschland' (Families in the midst of social change: challenges for future family policy in a unified Germany), *Aus Politik und Zeitgeschichte: Beilage zur Wochenzeitung Das Parlement*, 14/15: 3–12.

Winkler, G. (1987), 'Soziale Entwicklung – Soziologie – Sozialpolitik' (Social trends – sociology – social policy), in *Jahrbuch für Soziologie und Sozialpolitik 1987*, Berlin, Akademie-Verlag: 26–53.

—— (ed.) (1990a), *Frauenreport '90* (Women's Report 1990), Die Wirtschaft, Berlin.

—— (ed.) (1990b), *Sozialreport '90* (Social Report 1990), Die Wirtschaft, Berlin.

—— (ed.) (1992), *Sozialreport '92* (Social Report 1992), Die Wirtschaft, Berlin.

Wirtschaftswissenschaft (1979), 'Probleme der demographischen Entwicklung bei der weiteren Gestaltung der entwickelten sozialistischen Gesellschaft in der DDR (Thesen)' (Problems of demographic trends in the further development of a socialist society in the GDR (hypotheses)), *Wirtschaftswissenschaft*, 6:780–5.

Wohnraumlenkungsverordnung 1985 (State Housing Provision Regulation 1985), Gesetzblatt I: 301, Berlin.

6 Great Britain: the Lone Parent as the New Norm?

LYNDA CLARKE and MELANIE HENWOOD

London School of Hygiene and Tropical Medicine and Family Policy Studies Centre, London, and Independent Social Policy Analyst, Northamptonshire

The 1980s in Britain were a decade which saw the most major changes in family and household composition that have taken place this century. Marriage was postponed as more couples established cohabiting unions, and a trend towards the separation of childbearing and marriage became apparent with a trebling in the proportion of babies born outside marriage. Marital breakdown and divorce were other distinguishing features of the decade. Divorce rates doubled during the 1970s, following legislation that allowed easier divorce. Throughout the 1980s, the plateau that had been reached in divorce rates was maintained, and more than one-third of new marriages were likely to end in divorce.

The impact of these changes has been apparent for women at both ends of the childbearing years. In both age groups women have become less likely to be living as part of a married couple with children, and more likely to be either a lone parent, living alone, or living as part of a childless couple. There has been a marked shift for women from the role of spouse to the status of household head. These demographic developments have been accompanied by social and economic trends which have seen increased economic activity of women. However, the 1980s were also notable for the impact of economic recession and the rise of mass unemployment. These developments had a particular impact on families (particularly lone-parent families), and led to a threefold increase in the numbers of children living in poverty.

While the 1980s were a decade of major change in families, similarly dramatic developments cannot be mapped in the area of family policy. In the absence of a clear and comprehensive model of family policy in Britain, response to demographic and social change has been incremental and at times inconsistent. The family has increasingly become the focus of political and public debate and controversy. Attempts to satisfy at times incompatible

*objectives make any intervention in the area of family policy extremely diffi-
cult. There remains a lack of certainty as to the preferred balance between
the worlds of family life and paid employment; between equity of treatment
for individuals on the one hand, and support for the traditional two-parent
family on the other. It might be concluded that many of the trends evident
in the British family have their own momentum which is driving them onward
in spite of, rather than because of, deliberate policy intervention.*

6.1. Introduction

6.1.1. *Pluralization or Polarization*

In the 1980s there were marked changes in the structure and dynamics of
the British family. These changes started in the 1970s and look as though
they will continue. Although fertility, the major component of family creation, remained constant over the 1980s, there were dramatic changes in the
nature of families. Such changes are not unique to Britain but have occurred
in most developed Western countries, certainly in much of the rest of Europe.
Revolutionary changes in ideas about birth, marriage, divorce, child-rearing,
gender and death have been so dramatic that they have been termed by some
the 'Second Demographic Transition' (Lesthaeghe, 1991).

None of these changes in British family life had been predicted. The traditional husband-and-wife-based household is not as typical as it was, neither
is the traditional division of labour between the spouses. The changes in
demographic behaviour are a subject of great complexity and heated debate.
Traditionalists believe the family is collapsing, while modernists welcome
the new opportunities and equality for women.

It is worth remembering, before we consider the most recent British changes, that the 'traditional' nuclear family is somewhat of a misnomer. Its ori-
gins are relatively recent and its existence has coincided, to a great extent,
with unusual social circumstances, in the form of world war. The most salient
features of this 'modern' family arose in Britain in the twentieth century
and, for many, not until after the Second World War. Previously, life was
far from certain, stable and predictable. Pre-twentieth-century marriage break-
up rates paralleled modern ones but were due to death rather than divorce
(Anderson, 1983). A child born in 1861 stood a 1 per cent chance of orphan-
hood (both parents dead) by the age of 10 and a 6 per cent chance by the
age of 25. In contrast, only 1 per cent of the cohort born in 1946 had lost
just one parent by the age of 25 (Anderson, 1983).

In the last twenty years, undoubtedly, there have been rapid changes in the structure and dynamics of family life in Britain. While the changes in partnership patterns – notably the rise of cohabitation and the increase in divorce – were mainly initiated in the 1970s, the separation of childbearing and marriage, with the consequent growth in births outside marriage and lone-parent families, is a feature of the 1980s. The term 'pluralization' of family forms, i.e. an increasing diversity of family types alongside the 'traditional' nuclear family, might seem the most appropriate description. While most children still grow up in a family with two parents, it is also the case that a growing minority of dependent children are living with cohabiting rather than married parents, or are living with a lone mother or in a reconstituted family, and the proportion of children experiencing these alternative family forms at some point during their childhood has grown over the 1980s. Young and Wilmott (1973) suggested there would be movement towards the 'symmetrical family': one where values of loyalty, obligation and deference are replaced by sharing of earnings and domestic roles. Whether such symmetry has developed is a matter for debate. However, what is clear is that families in Britain are in transition from adapting to a society in which there was a single norm of what family life should be like to a society in which a plurality of types are apparent. The so-called 'traditional' family observed in the 1950s may be only an intermediate stage in the evolution of the modern family.

While the overriding trend has been towards a pluralization of family forms, in some ways this growing plurality can be seen as a *polarization* between different family types. More women are postponing childbearing, and there is evidence of an increase in childlessness, especially for women born in the 1960s (Babb, 1993). It is these women that are the most economically prosperous, and the advantageous position of the dual-earner family exists also for families with children. The growing dominance of the dual-earner family meant that the average family at the end of the 1980s was a far more affluent one than at the start of the decade. But the return of mass unemployment created much poverty among many families. Moreover, divorce and the rise of the lone-parent family brought new causes of poverty. Inequalities were the result. The increasing diversity in family forms has developed alongside a growing division between the economically advantaged and disadvantaged.

6.1.2. *Recent Research*

The family has been the subject of much research interest throughout the 1980s. While earlier research in the 1960s and 1970s was primarily concerned with developing the sociology of the family, more recent work has concentrated on the demographic changes affecting the family, and on analysing the social and economic circumstances of families of different types.

A number of key themes can be identified. In particular, research has examined: women and employment; marriage and divorce; cohabitation; family care (both for children and for elderly and other dependants); family relationships and obligations; lone-parent families; young people and employment; juvenile delinquency; child poverty; and the impact of family change on children. This list does not describe the totality of research being undertaken on family issues; however, it does outline the major issues that have been the focus of concern over the last decade. In addition to the demographic analysis of changing family trends, other streams of academic research have emerged. In particular, much analysis has taken place of women and social policy, which has considered developments from a feminist perspective.

6.1.3. *Data Sources*

The sources used for the demographic data quoted in this chapter include vital registration statistics and various national surveys, notably the General Household Survey (GHS). The most important of these for providing information on family change is the GHS because of its breadth of subjects covered. It is a continuous, annual sample survey of around 10,000 private households in Great Britain, collecting information on a wide range of socio-economic topics. The GHS information on the family comes from two main sources on the questionnaire. The first is the household section, which contains standard data on age, sex, marital status, family membership and relationship to the head of household. The other source is the family information section, addressed to women aged 18–49, which collects *inter alia* detailed information about current cohabitation and full marital and birth histories.

Other data come from a variety of sources as indicated. A particularly useful, and relatively new, series of data is that on British Social Attitudes, established in 1984 and now conducted annually.

6.1.4. *Overview of Demographic Trends in Partnership and Childbearing*

We begin by providing an overview of the major trends in family formation which have emerged during the 1980s.

MARRIAGE. The creation of a new family has traditionally been inextricably linked to marriage, however, this is an event in family life that has undergone major change. Perhaps it has been the most important change for families because of its implications for the care and welfare of dependants (Clarke, 1992 and 1994).

After the Second World War there was an increasing propensity to marry and for marriages to occur at increasingly younger ages and over a narrower range of ages. This trend continued until the beginning of the 1970s (Kiernan, 1989). Since then, however, marriage has been delayed and, for some couples, apparently forgone. First marriage rates have fallen, at least for those at younger ages (OPCS, 1994*a*), and there has been a sharp fall in marriage for both men and women born after the early 1950s (Haskey, 1993*b*). The proportion ever-married by age 25 for both men and women approximately halved between the 1950 and 1965 birth cohorts. It looks as though there is a combination of both postponement and rejection of marriage. (For detailed analyses of marriage trends since 1950 see Kiernan and Eldridge, 1987, and Eldridge and Kiernan, 1985.) There has been an increase in the proportion of single people in the population. It has been estimated that, if 1991 marriage rates continued, the expected proportions of men and women who will have ever married by age 50 will be 70 per cent for men and 73 per cent for women, compared with estimates of 93 and 96 per cent respectively in 1971 (OPCS, 1992*a*).

The increase in average age at first marriage which began in the early 1970s has continued into the 1990s. For both men and women it rose by about three years, reaching 27.5 and 25.5 respectively in 1991. Marriage at older ages has been associated with young people remaining in the parental home for longer than in the past as well as living on their own or sharing with others. There has also been increased financial dependency of young adults on their parents, which is linked to recent changes in employment, education and training as well as social security legislation, which in 1988 removed the right of 16–18-year-olds to claim 'Income Support' (a social security payment for people not in full-time employment) in their own right (Kiernan and Wicks, 1990).

COHABITATION. The sharp fall in marriage rates since the 1970s has been accompanied by a dramatic rise in the proportions of young people cohabiting without legal marriage. The reduction in marriage rates, however, is not totally accounted for by cohabitation. It is estimated that only around a half of the reduction in the proportions of women ever-married at ages 20–24 and one-third of the decline at ages 25–29 in the 1980s could be accounted for by the increased propensity to cohabit (Kiernan and Wicks, 1990). In 1992, 18 per cent of non-married men and women were cohabiting, and those who had previously been married were much more likely than single people to be cohabiting. For example, 36 and 27 per cent of divorced men and women respectively were cohabiting compared with 18 and 15 per cent of single men and women respectively. Cohabitation is more likely for single women with dependent children than those without, for example raising the proportion of single women cohabiting to over one-third (34 per cent) (OPCS, 1994*a*). It is virtually a majority practice to cohabit before marriage nowadays. Over half (51 per cent) of women and just under half (49 per cent) of men who married for the first time in 1985–9 had lived with their partner before marriage (OPCS, 1993*a*). Certainly cohabiting between marriages is the norm and the length of time that divorced women have been cohabiting has increased.

In general, cohabitation is for relatively short periods and may be regarded as a transitional and child-free phase which then either converts into marriage or breaks up (Kiernan and Estaugh, 1993). Post-marital cohabitants tend to be older and to have been cohabiting for longer. Fifty per cent of post-marital cohabitants had children in 1991 and are in effect reconstituted families with the same complexities entailed by *de jure* stepfamilies. Only a minority of cohabitants to date have children together – 1 in 4 of the never-married cohabiting group – but it is these families that are relatively disadvantaged compared with married-couple families (Kiernan and Estaugh, 1993; McRae, 1993). These families, on average, have significantly lower incomes, are more likely to be in receipt of income support and housing benefit, and the male partner is more likely to be unemployed or in semi- and unskilled work than is the case for married-couple families (Kiernan and Estaugh, 1993).

BIRTHS OUTSIDE MARRIAGE. If cohabitation was a major feature of family change in the 1970s, then the increasing separation of marriage and child-bearing, which is not unrelated to developments in cohabitation, has been an important demographic motor in the 1980s for creating further changes in family structure. The proportion of all babies that are born outside marriage has more than trebled, from 9 per cent in 1976 to nearly 31 per cent in 1992. The growth in extra-marital childbearing is partly a result of the older average age at marriage and the larger cohorts of the 'baby boom', born in the late 1950s and early 1960s, increasing the proportion of single women in the population (Ermisch, 1990). Also, marital childbearing has been postponed and somewhat depressed, which has tended to exaggerate the effect of childbearing outside marriage. Even taking these factors into account, the evidence points to a noticeable and increased propensity for women to have children outside marriage, a tendency that is by no means confined to teenagers (Kiernan and Wicks, 1990).

Table 6.1 shows the extra-marital and marital fertility rates for women of different ages in 1981, 1986 and 1991. It also shows the ratios of these rates (in the bottom rows), which indicate the propensity for women of different ages to have births outside marriage. The ratio is larger for older women, suggesting a greater tendency for them to have births outside marriage than younger women. The ratio is very low for teenage women because of the very high fertility rates of the small minority of married teenagers compared with the fertility of the large majority of single teenagers. The ratio of extra-marital to marital fertility rates increased by about 50 per cent for all ages combined in both the early and late 1980s, with a noticeable increase for women aged 20–24 between 1986 and 1991. Not only has the number of births outside marriage increased dramatically in the 1980s, but the propensity for women to have children outside marriage appears to be

Table 6.1. *Birth rates within and outside marriage by age of mother, England and Wales, 1981, 1986 and 1991*

	Age of mother					
	Under 20	20–24	25–29	30–34	35–39	All ages
Extra-marital rate per 1,000 unmarried women						
1981	13.7	27.8	33.7	26.0	11.9	19.7
1986	21.3	38.2	43.1	35.8	17.2	28.9
1991	28.0	54.4	56.1	48.7	26.0	40.7
Marital rate per 1,000 married women						
1981	324.8	204.3	161.5	76.9	23.3	88.8
1986	360.9	209.8	167.2	90.1	26.2	86.3
1991	264.0	189.2	172.5	102.3	33.9	84.6
Ratio of extra-marital to marital rate						
1981	0.04	0.14	0.21	0.34	0.51	0.22
1986	0.06	0.18	0.26	0.40	0.66	0.66
1991	0.11	0.29	0.33	0.48	0.68	0.48

Source: OPCS (1993c: Table 3.1).

Table 6.2. *Births outside marriage, England and Wales, 1981, 1986 and 1991*

		Age of mother				
	All ages	Under 20	20–24	25–29	30–34	35+
Percentage of births outside marriage						
1981	12.8	46.7	14.8	6.6	6.2	8.0
1986	21.4	69.8	28.2	12.1	10.1	12.6
1991	30.2	82.9	44.9	21.1	15.9	18.8
Jointly registered births as a percentage of all births outside marriage						
1981	58	48	58	67	70	70
1986	66	59	67	70	74	74
1991	74	65	75	78	79	80
Percentage of jointly registered births with parents at same usual address						
1986	70	56	71	79	81	80
1991	73	58	73	79	81	81

Source: OPCS (1993*c*: Tables 3.1 and 3.10).

increasing. It is not merely a function of the larger proportion of single women in the population, as mentioned earlier.

What is interesting is that an increasing majority of these births outside marriage are being registered by two parents and by parents living at the same address (see Table 6.2). The proportion of joint registrations has risen from 58 per cent of all births outside marriage in 1981 to 74 per cent in 1991. Moreover, more than 7 out of 10 of the joint registrations made in 1991 (73 per cent) were made by parents living at the same address. In other words, over a half (54 per cent) of all births outside marriage in 1991 were jointly registered by parents living at the same address, presumably cohabiting. Joint registration tends to be viewed as an indicator of a child being born into a relatively stable – if unmarried – relationship, rather than to an unmarried mother living alone. The older the mother, the more likely the birth is to be jointly registered by co-resident parents. The proportions are increasing for mothers of all ages, however, and in 1991 this was the largest category of extra-marital registration for all mothers. While cohabitation has been considered generally to precede rather than substitute for marriage in this country, there is increasing evidence that a growing proportion of couples are no longer marrying before the birth of their children, which accounts for some of the increase in extra-marital childbearing in recent years.

FERTILITY. It should be remembered that the majority of children still are born to married parents. One major feature of recent fertility behaviour, apart from the increase in childbearing outside marriage, is the postponement of parenthood. Couples marrying since the late 1960s have been delaying starting their families. The relative stability in the overall fertility rate (total period fertility rate, or the average family size predicted by period fertility) in the last decade conceals considerable change in the age distribution of fertility. There has been a decrease in the fertility rates of women in their twenties and an increase in those of women in their thirties and forties, especially for first birth rates. Births to remarried women have contributed to this trend, but the evidence is that more women are delaying childbirth, both in first marriages and outside marriage. Later childbirth and the increases in the fertility rates of the over-thirties are noticeable for women born since 1945 (Jones, 1992). Later childbearing has not compensated for the shortfall at younger ages, at least not for women born between 1935 and 1950 who have completed their childbearing. Further declines in completed family size are projected for more recent cohorts of women; for example, women born in 1955 are projected to have on average 1.99 children compared with the 2.19 already achieved by women born in 1945 and the 2.36 for women born in 1940 (Jones, 1992). There is growing conformity to the two-child family ideal, in terms of both actual family size and expectations about future numbers of children.

These trends reflect the increasing likelihood that recent generations of women nearing the end of their reproductive span will remain childless. A higher proportion of women born since 1945 are childless at each age (Jones, 1992; Babb, 1993). Over one-third of women born in 1960 reached the age of 30 without having at least one child, twice the equivalent proportion for women born in 1945. This delayed childbearing, increased fertility for the over-thirties and increase in childlessness have important ramifications for the future place of children in families and their care, and also for the care of an ageing population.

MARITAL BREAKDOWN. The instability of marriage is the most publicized facet of family life in recent times. Without longitudinal data, we know little about how various cohabiting relationships compare with marriage in terms of stability, but the record on marriage in this country is far from 'Till Death do us part'. We do know that couples who have cohabited prior to marriage are at a higher risk of divorce than those who have not cohabited premaritally, and that people in second or subsequent marriages are at a higher risk of divorce than those in first-time marriages (Haskey, 1992). Britain has one of the highest divorce rates in Western Europe (Haskey, 1993b). Divorce rates doubled in the 1970s after the Divorce Reform Act came into force in 1971, from 6 to 12 per 1,000 marriages and have remained at this high level, around 13 per 1,000 marriages, during the 1980s. It is estimated that almost four in every ten marriages will end in divorce within 20 years of marriage if the divorce rates prevailing in the mid-1980s continue, compared with only 7 per cent of marriages contracted at the beginning of the 1950s (Haskey, 1989). Also, it has been estimated that, if the divorce rates prevailing in 1979–80 were to continue, one in five children will experience the divorce of their parents by the age of 16 (Haskey, 1983).

One effect of the divorce trends is the growth in the number of lone-parent families over the past two decades so that currently about one in five families with dependent children is a lone-parent family (Haskey, 1993*a*; Haskey, 1993*c*; OPCS, 1993*b*). The United Kingdom has the highest proportion of lone-parent families in the European Community (Roll, 1993). Nine out of ten of these families are headed by lone mothers and about two-thirds of them have previously been married. As mortality has declined, so have the numbers of widows with dependent children; it is the increase in marital dissolution that has been mainly responsible for the large increase in lone-parent families during the 1970s. In 1991, 6 per cent of all families with dependent children were headed by a divorced lone mother, 4 per cent by a separated lone mother and 1 per cent by a widowed lone mother (OPCS, 1993*b*). There has been an increase in the proportion of lone-mother families headed by never-married mothers in the 1980s, from around one-fifth in 1980 to over one third (35 per cent) in 1991. These lone mothers are on average younger than other lone mothers as might be expected; in 1991 the median age of never-married lone mothers was 25 years compared with 37 years for divorced lone mothers.

REMARRIAGE. Lone parenthood is not a permanent situation for many women and their children, and is often terminated by the formation of 'reconstituted families' through cohabitation or marriage. An increasing proportion of marriages are remarriages for one or both partners; in 1991, 63 per cent of marriages were first marriages for both partners, 21 per cent were remarriages for one partner only, and 17 per cent remarriages for both partners (OPCS, 1993*a*). Men are more likely to remarry than women and more quickly; in 1991 nearly half (45 per cent) of men divorced during the period 1983–6 had remarried within three years of divorce and nearly two-thirds (60 per cent) of those divorced during 1979–82 had remarried within four years of divorce (OPCS, 1993*b*). Divorced men are also more likely to cohabit than divorced women; in 1991, 38 per cent of all divorced men under 60 were cohabiting compared with 25 per cent of divorced women of these ages (OPCS, 1993*b*). Remarriages are at even greater risk of dissolution than first marriages. Kiernan and Wicks (1990) pointed to evidence from the United States which suggests that the risk of dissolution increases alongside the complexity of reconstituted family forms.

6.2. Family Forms in the 1980s

In Section 6.1 we provided an overview of family trends in the 1980s. We turn now to examine in greater detail the position of women at the beginning and end of their childbearing years, and to consider how this changed over the decade.

6.2.1. *Timing of Critical Events*

In both 1981 and 1991 the average age of married women at first birth within the age group 25–29 fell: to 25.4 years and 27.5 years respectively. Unmarried mothers tend to be younger than married mothers, the average age at all births outside marriage being 23.5 years in 1981 and 24.8 years in 1991. The age group 25–29 will be used in the following section as far as is possible for comparative analysis with the available published data.

There is little evidence on the modal age of the start of the 'empty-nest' phase, or the age at which children leave home or become independent. This can vary, depending on the age of the woman at first birth, family size and the likelihood of birth in second or subsequent marriages or unions. Clearly, socio-economic factors will also influence how long adult children remain living in the parental home. The age group of 45–49 that is used elsewhere in this volume will be taken for comparative purposes as far as possible.

6.2.2. *Structural Characteristics of Family Life*

MARITAL STATUS AND PARTNERSHIPS. There has been a dramatic decline in the proportion of married women aged 25–29 over the 1980s; from over three-quarters (76.3 per cent) to just over one-half (56.6 per cent), as can be seen in Table 6.3*a*. The corresponding increase in the proportion of women of this age remaining single reflects an increasing likelihood of cohabitation as well as of remaining single (Table 6.3*b*).

Table 6.3a. *Legal marital status of women in percentages by age group, England and Wales, 1980 and 1990*

Woman's age group	Marital status			
	Single	Married	Widowed	Divorced
25–29				
1980	18.6	76.3	0.3	4.9
1990	37.4	56.6	0.1	5.9
45–49				
1980	5.9	84.6	3.8	5.8
1990	4.8	80.7	2.8	11.7

Source: OPCS (1994a: Table 1.1).

Table 6.3b. *Marital condition for women, England and Wales, 1980 and 1991, for selected age groups, by age group (%)*

Marital status	Age group			
	25-29 1980	25-34 1991	45-49 1980	45-54 1991
Cohabiting	5	10	–	3
First marriage	72	}63	77	}79
Second or subseq. marriage	4		7	
Single	13	17	5	3
Widowed	–	–	4	4
Divorced	3	6	5	9
Separated	2	3	2	2
Base (= 100%)	989	1,965	813	1,515

Source: OPCS (1993a).

Women at the end of their childbearing lives, on the other hand, have not demonstrated as large a movement towards cohabitation rather than marriage as is evident for younger women. This is to be expected, since most women aged 45–49 will have married prior to the 1980s and only those whose marriages end will have the choice of partnership arrangement. Certainly the increase in the likelihood of being divorced at these ages in 1991 is shown in Tables 6.3a and 6.3b, and these women are more likely to cohabit than never-married women (OPCS, 1993a).

LIVING ARRANGEMENTS. The sharp increase in the proportion of women in their late twenties who are lone parents, more than doubling from 4.7

to 10.5 per cent of women over the 1980s, and the corresponding decrease in the proportion living as a couple family is shown in Table 6.4*a*. This reflects the large increase in births outside marriage in the 1980s, described earlier, as well as the breakdown of two-parent families (Brown, 1993). The decrease in couple families is a reflection, also, of the delayed age at marriage and increasing tendency to live independently at an early age.

Over the last decade there have been increases in the proportion of young adults living outside a family, alone or sharing with others, and corresponding reductions in those living as couples with children (Berrington *et al.*, 1993). This increase in non-family living is demonstrated in Table 6.4*a*. There have been major increases in those women living alone and those sharing with other non-family individuals (multi-solo).

Table 6.4*a*. *Living arrangements of women aged 25–29, Great Britain, 1981 and 1991 (%)*

	1981	1991
Living in parental home	9.3	10.9
Living outside parental home		
as a couple	78.8	67.9
as a lone parent	4.7	10.5
Living outside family		
solo + family(s)	0.6	0.8
multi-solo	3.8	4.0
alone	3.3	6.0

Table 6.4*b*. *Highest educational qualification level of women aged 25–29 according to their living arrangement, Great Britain, 1991 (%)*

Highest educational qualification	Living with parents	Living outside parental home				
		In family		Outside a family		
		Couple	Lone parent	Multi-solo	Solo + family	Alone
Above A level	14	16	5	19	43	38
A level	15	11	4	23	16	8
O level	37	40	32	28	24	30
CSE + other	12	15	17	7	14	7
None	21	17	43	23	4	10
Base (= 100%)	604	3803	598	43	209	347

Source: Derived from Labour Force Survey by Berrington *et al.* (1993).

Young people living outside of a family are a distinct group with favourable socio-economic backgrounds (Table 6.4*b*; see also Berrington and Murphy, 1993). In particular, flat-sharing as multi-solos seems to be associated with privileged educational backgrounds (Berrington *et al.*, 1993). The increase in women in their late twenties living alone is associated with increases in the number of women who are single and the increases in the propensity of both single and divorced women to live alone (Berrington *et al.*, 1993). Such trends result to a large extent from changes in the socio-economic structure of the single population as first marriage rates declined from the early 1970s so that people remaining single became a more mixed group. Interestingly, living alone is not necessarily associated with higher levels of education and income but seems to be a more heterogeneous living arrangement. As can be seen from Table 6.4*b*, a significant minority of those living alone have no educational qualification.

The most striking trend in living arrangements among older working-age adults (30–49) has been the substantial rise in the proportion living alone, doubling from 2.5 per cent of women in 1981 to 5 per cent in 1991 (Berrington *et al.*, 1993). This trend has been seen in many developed countries and is related to the marital histories of the older women. As for younger women, some of the explanation of this rise in independent living results from the increase in separation and divorce. There remains, however, an increased propensity for women to live alone after the changes in marital status are controlled (Berrington *et al.*, 1993).

6.3. The Family Life Situation

6.3.1. *Women's Labour-Force Participation and Education*

ECONOMIC ACTIVITY OF WOMEN: WORKING. Women at both ends of the child-rearing age span were increasingly likely to be in paid work with the passage of the 1980s, but there were notable differences according to marital status, as shown in Tables 6.5*a* and 6.5*b*. Married women in their late twenties were much more likely to be in paid work in 1991 than a decade earlier – 65 per cent compared with 47 per cent. The opposite is true for single and other unmarried women, with an increase in the proportions of economically inactive women for both groups. This may be partly a reflection of the changes in marital status of these women which was documented earlier. As a result of an increase in cohabitation, in births outside marriage and in relationship breakdown, more women were single, divorced or separated

Table 6.5*a*. *Economic activity of women aged 25–34 by marital status, Great Britain, 1981 and 1991 (%)*

Marital status	Economically active			
	Working	Unemployed	Total	Base (= 100%)
1981				
Married	47	4	51	1,832
Single	78	5	83	241
W/D/sep.	53	13	66	159
Total	51	5	56	2,232
1991				
Married	65	6	71	1,425
Single	69	7	76	338
W/D/sep.	49	9	58	182
Total	64	6	70	1,945

Source: General Household Survey Reports 1981 and 1991: Tables 4.8 and 5.20; OPCS (1993*a*).

Table 6.5*b*. *Economic activity of women aged 45–54 by marital status, Great Britain, 1981 and 1991 (%)*

Marital status	Economically active			
	Working	Unemployed	Total	Base (= 100%)
1981				
Married	66	2	69	1,490
Single[a]	75	6	81	158
W/D/sep.	63	7	69	227
Total	66	3	69	1,813
1991				
Married	72	4	75	1,218
Single[a]	62	10	72	81
W/D/sep	70	5	75	224
Total	71	4	76	1,493

[a] Aged 45–59 because of small numbers.

Source: General Household Survey Reports 1981 and 1991: Tables 4.8 and 5.20; OPCS (1993*a*).

lone mothers, who are less likely to be in paid employment (see below).

Older women, in their late forties or early fifties, were more likely to be in paid employment in 1991 than in 1981 if they were married or if they had been married previously (Table 6.5*b*). The absence of dependent children for women of these ages would mean that their participation rates were less likely to be depressed; there were few women of these ages who were single.

ECONOMIC ACTIVITY OF WOMEN: UNEMPLOYED. The proportions of women in both age groups that were unemployed have not shown a major increase over the 1980s. Earlier we noted the trend towards the dual-earner household, but it is also known that the likelihood of unemployment is concentrated in families (Kiernan and Wicks, 1990), and is negatively associated with qualification level.

ECONOMIC ACTIVITY OF WOMEN: PRESENCE OF CHILDREN. The impact of marital status and age of children on mothers' work status from 1979–81 to 1989–91 can be seen in Tables 6.6*a* and 6.6*b*. The decrease in lone mothers' participation rates in the labour force results largely from the decreased likelihood of full-time work for single lone mothers; the proportion of single lone mothers working full-time decreased from nearly one in three (27 per cent) in 1979–81 to only one in ten (11 per cent) a decade later. There was a slight increase only in the proportion of these women working part-time from 11 to 16 per cent. The major change was in the proportion who were economically inactive. Single lone mothers are still much less likely than other lone mothers to work, reflecting the fact that they are more likely to have young children.

Married women with dependent children were more likely at both points in time to work part-time than all categories of lone mothers. As we will examine in Section 6.4, this reflects the barriers and disincentives that confront lone parents seeking to make the transition from dependence on social security to independence via paid employment. The pattern of women's employment and the effect of the presence of children is different in Britain from that in many other European countries. There is higher participation of women working part-time in Britain than is the case elsewhere in Europe. In Britain women have typically left the labour force for the first five years of a child's life, and then returned – usually to part-time employment – once the child has entered full-time education (at 5 years). However, over the 1980s this pattern began to change, and married women with a child under the age of 5 were increasingly likely to be in full-time paid work, an increase from 6 to 14 per cent (Table 6.6*b*). The employment patterns of married

Table 6.6a. *Lone mothers and married women with dependent children: percentages working full-time and part-time by marital status, Great Britain, 1979–1981, 1985–1987 and 1989–1991*

	1979–81	1985–87	1989–91
Lone mothers			
Single			
Working full-time	27	14	11
Working part-time	11	13	16
Base (= 100%)	271	319	350
Widowed			
Working full-time	17	13	24
Working part-time	32	35	31
Base (= 100%)	218	112	104
Divorced			
Working full-time	27	22	24
Working part-time	29	29	30
Base (= 100%)	332	565	577
Separated			
Working full-time	18	16	18
Working part-time	26	23	25
Base (= 100%)	320	258	331
Married women with dependent children			
Working full-time	15	17	21
Working part-time	36	38	40
Base (= 100%)	11,392	8,654	7,627

Source: OPCS (1993a).

women are therefore becoming increasingly similar to those of men. In contrast, lone mothers with a child under the age of 5 were less likely to be employed full-time at the end of the decade than they were at the beginning (from 12 to 8 per cent). This reflects a number of factors, including the younger age of these mothers in 1989–91 compared with a decade earlier, and hence their lack of employment experience and low income prospects.

EDUCATIONAL ATTAINMENT. Women in their late twenties or in their forties at the beginning of the 1990s were more highly qualified than women of the same ages at the beginning of the 1980s (Table 6.7). There was a decrease in the proportion of women who had no qualifications and a corres-

Table 6.6b. *Married women and lone mothers with dependent children: percentages working full-time and part-time by age of youngest dependent child, Great Britain, 1979–1981, 1985–1987 and 1989–1991*

	1979–81	1985–87	1989–91
Married women with dependent children			
Under 5 years			
Working full-time	6	9	14
Working part-time	22	25	32
Base (= 100%)	4,244	3,560	3,263
5 years or over			
Working full-time	21	22	27
Working part-time	45	46	47
Base (= 100%)	7,148	5,094	4,364
Lone mothers with children			
Under 5 years			
Working full-time	12	9	8
Working part-time	12	11	14
Base (= 100%)	397	472	703
5 years or over			
Working full-time	28	23	27
Working part-time	31	32	32
Base (= 100%)	944	782	859

Source: OPCS (1993a).

ponding increase in the proportion of women who had qualifications below higher education.

Women with no qualifications are much less likely to be economically active than women with some qualifications regardless of the presence of children or the age of children if they are present, as shown in Table 6.8. Women with higher education are distinct from those with lesser qualifications by being much more likely to be economically active regardless of the age of dependent children or presence of children. Women with their youngest child over the age of ten show similar patterns of activity to those without children. It should be remembered that the women without children will include the young who have not yet had children as well as those women who are older and whose children are no longer dependent.

Table 6.7. *Highest qualification level attained for selected age groups in 1981 and 1990–1991[a], Great Britain (%)*

	1981	1990–1[a]
Women aged 25–29		
Higher education	17	18
Other qualifications	52	62
No qualifications	32	19
Base (= 100%)	355	1,693
Women aged 40–49		
Higher education	13	17
Other qualifications	30	39
No qualifications	58	44
Base (= 100%)	1,259	3,006

[a] 1990 and 1991 figures combined.

Source: General Household Survey Reports 1981 and 1991: Tables 5.7 and 10.7.

6.3.2. *Family Life-Style*

The effects of the demographic changes that we have described in terms of their implications for living arrangements are documented in Figures 6.1*a* and 6.1*b*. While these figures depict the changes over the decade 1981–91 for women of all ages, the particular experience of the two age groups on which we have focused in this paper can be discerned.

The tendency for women in their late twenties to remain in the parental home is apparent. So, too, is the drop (of about 10 percentage points) in young women living as a partner of the household head (and this includes women cohabiting as if married to the household head). The increase in women in their twenties who are themselves household heads largely offsets this trend (see Figure 6.1*a*). It is worth noting that the changes for young women are much sharper than for young males over the same period (Murphy and Berrington, 1993).

Figure 6.1*b* demonstrates the change in family types over the 1980s. Both age groups of women have become less likely to be living as a two-parent family with children, while young women in their twenties have shown a large increase in the proportions who are lone mothers with dependent children. While the proportions of women in their late twenties living as couples without children increased, this was greatly outweighed by the substantial

Table 6.8. *Economic activity of women of working age (16–59) by selected groups of highest educational qualification and age of youngest dependent child, Great Britain, 1991 (%)*

	Highest education qualification			
	Degree or equivalent	GCE 'A' level or equivalent	GCSE grades DG commercial/ apprenticeship	No qualifi- cations
Women with dependent children				
Youngest child aged 0–4				
Working	62	46	43	26
Unemployed	2	4	6	4
Base (= 100%)	266	310	545	1,015
Youngest child aged 5–9				
Working	80	70	68	57
Unemployed	3	6	4	4
Base (= 100%)	115	147	273	762
Youngest child age 10 or over				
Working	87	82	78	71
Unemployed	1	3	3	3
Base (= 100%)	139	128	376	1,201
Women with no dependent children				
Working	89	78	79	61
Unemployed	4	4	5	5
Base (= 100%)	744	1,128	1,303	4,171

Source: General Household Survey Report 1991: Table 5.17.

fall in those living as couples with children (a fall of almost 15 percentage points for women in their late twenties) (Murphy and Berrington, 1993).

For the older group of women the changes in family type are less substantial, although here too there has been a marked shift from the role of spouse to that of household head and living alone.

The effects of the demographic changes we have described in terms of their implications for women's family lives are illustrated in Tables 6.9*a* and 6.9*b*. These tables, derived from the General Household Surveys of 1981 and 1991, rank the six most common 'life-styles' for women aged 25–29 and 45–49. These 'life-styles' combine information on living arrangements, in terms of marital status and presence of children, and information on employment situation, in terms of whether couples are both working or whether the husband is the sole earner.

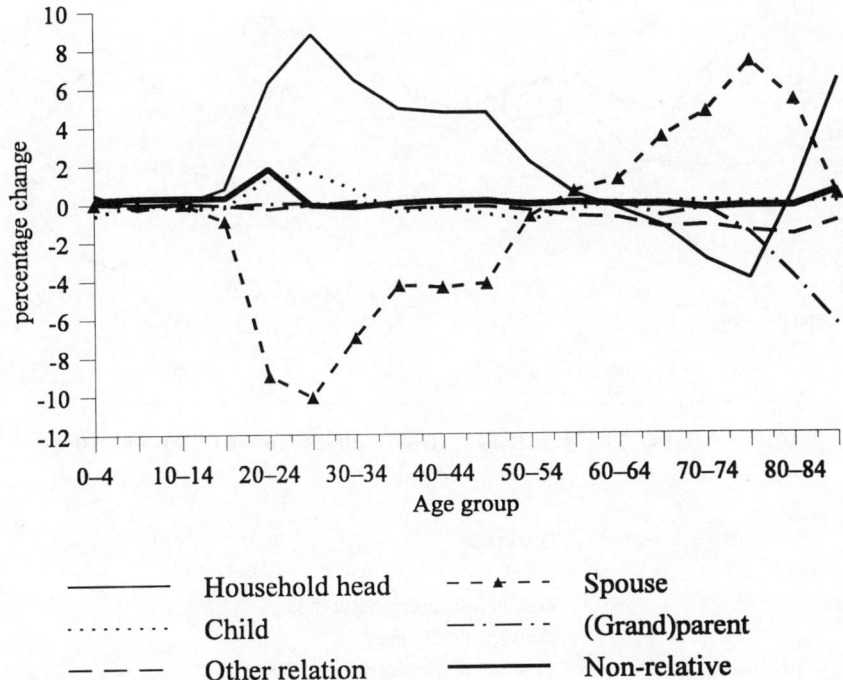

Figure 6.1*a*. Change in relationship to head of household, Great Britain, 1981–1991

There is a clear tendency for women in both age groups to be less likely to be living as a married couple with children and more likely to be living either as a lone parent, or alone or as a childless couple with two incomes. There has been a marked shift for women away from the role of spouse to a more independent living arrangement. Also apparent is evidence of the increased economic activity of married women.

Women in their late twenties at the beginning of the decade were most likely to be in a 'traditional' nuclear family living with a husband, who was the sole breadwinner while her role was looking after two or more children. At the end of the decade, at the beginning of the 1990s, women of these ages were most likely to be either a lone mother or married and working but not having any children – a so-called dual-income, no kids (DINKS) family. The change in the family formation and economic behaviour of young women is clear. The tendency to remain living at home with parents or living

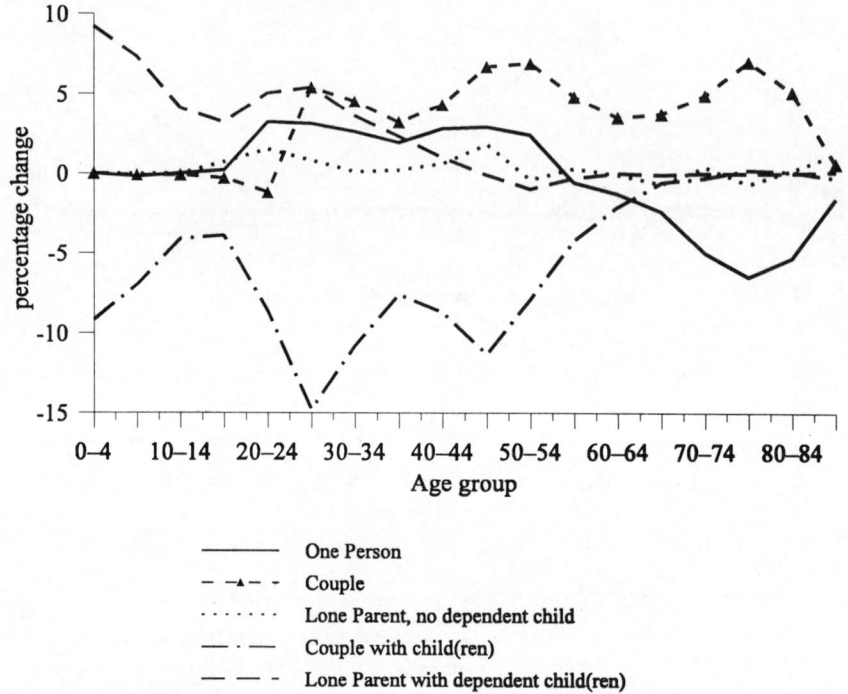

Source: Murphy and Berrington (1993).

Figure 6.1*b***.** Change in family type, Great Britain, 1981–1991

as a single person is also illustrated. Delayed childbearing and increasing childlessness for younger cohorts will account for these results, but also important are the higher proportions of young women who have been students, have pursued a career, or are unemployed.

The results of family fragmentation experienced by these younger women are evident also for women in their late forties. The second most common life-style in the early 1990s is to be living as an ex-married woman alone without children, a category that did not feature in the top-six list in 1981 for women of these ages. Women of these ages are most likely to be living with a husband and to be working and not having children in the household at both dates, but it is much more common in 1991 (32 per cent compared with 25 per cent in 1981). It is not clear whether their children have left home, but it is probable that a higher proportion have never had children in 1991 compared with 1981.

Table 6.9a. *Top-six 'life-styles', women aged 25–29, Great Britain, 1981 and 1991*

1981			1991		Change
Rank	%		%	Rank	in rank
1	22	Married, 2> children, only husband employed	11	2	–
2	14	Married, no children, two incomes	15	1	+
3	12	Married, 1 child, only husband employed	8	4	–
4	10	Married, 2> children, two incomes	8	4	–
5	9	Lone mother (single and widowed)	15	1	+
6	6	Married, 1 child, two incomes	6	–	=
–	(6)	Living with parents	9	3	+
–	(6)	Single (not lone mother or with parents)	9	3	+
		Other			
	1,039	Total (= 100%)	1,017		

Source: Derived from General Household Surveys 1981 and 1991.

Table 6.9b. *Top-six 'life-styles', women aged 45–49, Great Britain, 1981 and 1991*

1981			1991		Change
Rank	%		%	Rank	in rank
1	25	Married, no children, two incomes	32	1	=
2	17	Married, 1 child, two incomes	11	3	–
3	11	Married, 2> children, two incomes	9	4	–
4	9	Married, no children, only husband employed	9	4	=
5	8	Married, 2> children, only husband employed	(2)	–	–
6	7	Married, 1 child, only husband employed	(3)	–	–
–	(6)	Widowed, divorced or separated, no children	12	2	+
–	(6)	Lone mother	5	5	+
	(23)	Other	(22)		
	885	Total (= 100%)	837		

Source: Derived from General Household Surveys 1981 and 1991.

6.3.3. *Family Poverty*

Different approaches can be taken in trying to measure poverty, but the concept itself is a controversial one, and many people reject the idea that absolute poverty exists in Britain today (Roll, 1992). One of the most commonly used approaches in the measurement of poverty is based on an income level of less than half the national average. This standard is also similar to the approach used within the European Union, which defines poverty in terms of half average expenditure. Data provided by the government's figures on households below average income (HBAI) indicate that children are overrepresented among the poor, and that this is especially the case for children in lone-parent families. The number of children living in poverty increased threefold between 1979 and 1990–1, from 10 to over 30 per cent (Kumar, 1993).

The composition of the poorest groups in Britain has changed dramatically. As Table 6.10 indicates, pensioners accounted for a much smaller proportion of the poorest 10 per cent of the population in 1988–9, compared with their situation in 1979. Couples with children and lone parents make up a larger proportion, and single people without children were twice as likely to be among the poorest 10 per cent in 1988–9 as they were ten years previously. This is also indicative of the growing impact of unemployment over the decade (Oppenheim, 1993). The unemployed have the highest risk of being below the bottom decile of income. The latest data published by the government statistical service (Department of Social Security, 1994) confirms that, comparing 1979 with 1991–2, further groups with above-average risk of falling into the lowest income category were 'others' (including long-term sick, disabled and non-working single parents), the self-employed and part-time workers.

The relative poverty of different types of household is also reflected in their housing. Lone-parent families are more likely than married couples to live in rented accommodation, and much less likely to be owner-occupiers. Around half of lone fathers and 70 per cent of lone mothers are tenants, while about a third of lone parents own their home. This is the opposite of the situation for two-parent families, where around one-third live in rented accommodation and seven out of ten are owner-occupiers (Burghes, 1993).

Table 6.10. *The changing composition of the poorest 10 per cent between 1979 and 1988–1989 (income after housing costs), Great Britain (%)*

	1979	1988–9
Pensioner couple	20	6
Single pensioner	11	8
Couple + children	41	44
Couple, no children	9	10
Lone parent	9	10
Single, no children	10	22

Source: Oppenheim (1993: Figure 7).

6.4. Values and Attitudes

How have values and attitudes changed during the 1980s? Has there been an increasing liberalization and tolerance of diversity of family forms? In fact, it is difficult to know to what extent there has been change, because attitudinal data is mostly of very recent origin. However, it is worth looking at recent attitudes to some important areas of family change.

6.4.1. *Cohabitation*

Cohabitation is one development that would appear to have become more accepted by the public, and which no longer carries the stigma it once did. (The same is true of births outside marriage.) However, young people are more likely to be in favour of cohabitation than are people a generation or so older (Kiernan and Estaugh, 1993). The British Social Attitudes Survey of 1989 found that only 18 per cent of people aged under 35 would advise a young couple to marry without first living together. By contrast, only 25 per cent of people aged 55–59 supported pre-marital cohabitation. However, very few people of all ages endorsed cohabitation as a permanent alternative to marriage.

Attitudes to having children out of marriage indicate a sharp gradient with rising age. Thus, while less than half of people aged under 25 believed that people who want children should get married, this rose sharply to 65 per cent of those aged 35–44, and to 80 per cent of those aged 45–54 (Kiernan and Estaugh, 1993). Those people who were currently cohabiting, or who had cohabited previously, were generally more permissive towards the matter of extra-marital childbearing. Such attitudes, and the continued spread of pre-marital cohabitation, might suggest that extramarital births are unlikely to decline in the near future.

6.4.2. *Child Care*

The role of family and friends in providing child care is a central one, and there is a strong preference for such sources of care. A study of women's employment in 1980 found that relatives were the major providers of care for pre-school children. Among women working full-time, 65 per cent of children were cared for by the child's father, grandmother or another relative. Among those women working part-time, 87 per cent of children were cared for by relatives (Martin and Roberts, 1984). Maternal grandmothers are the most frequent providers of child care for women working full-time, while for women working part-time husbands are the most common source of care. The role of fathers in caring for children is an important one which can facilitate both partners going out to work. However, this is likely to be achieved at the cost of reducing the amount of time that couples are able to spend together, particularly when there are pre-school children (Henwood *et al.*, 1987).

Data from the 1991 General Household Survey confirm the central role of relatives in providing care for pre-school-age children, and indicate that there has been little change in the sources of child care over the last decade (Table 6.11). A major study of day-care services for children conducted in 1990 (OPCS, 1994*b*) found substantial differences in the pattern of services used by one-parent and two-parent families. Whether or not lone parents are in employment, their children are more likely to be cared for by grand-parents, other relatives, friends and neighbours than are children in two-parent families. Where lone mothers *are* in employment, their children are less likely to attend either a play group or a nursery school. However, they are more than twice as likely to attend a day nursery.

6.4.3. *Gender Roles within the Household*

While access to good-quality child care is an important factor influencing women's economic activity, the attitudes of men and women to the question of women's – especially mothers' – employment also play a part. Evidence

Table 6.11. *Child care for children under five, 1991, Great Britain*

Type of care	% of families with children aged 0–4
Unpaid family or friends	25
School/nursery school	25
Private/voluntary schemes	17
Paid child-minder/nanny	11
Local authority scheme	7
Workplace facility	1
Total using child care	64

Source: OPCS (1993*a*: Table 7.5).

from the British Social Attitudes Survey (BSAS) that compared Britain with the United States, the Republic of Ireland, the Netherlands and Hungary indicated that in Britain people are the most likely of the five countries to believe that where there is a child under school-age the mother should stay at home to care for it (SCPR, 1990). In part, this may reflect the lack of child-care facilities that are available. It may also partly account for the high use of relatives in providing care for young children where women do go out to work. A more recent comparison made by BSAS substituted West Germany for Hungary, and found the Germans even more likely than the British to see a woman's place as 'in the home' (SCPR, 1993).

Women tend to be more egalitarian in their gender-role attitudes than men. For example, men are less likely than women to believe that women should work part-time when they are mothers of pre-school-age children (23 per cent of men support this view compared with 29 per cent of women). Men are more likely than women to think that a woman should stay at home to care for children, even when those children are of school age. Women who work are also likely to be more egalitarian in outlook than women who do not. (This is also true of men whose wives are in employment.) However, as Table 6.12 indicates, it is age that is the most important predictor of attitudes towards working mothers. Both men and women born between 1950 and 1970 are markedly less concerned that mothers of young children should stay at home than are men and women born earlier.

Attitudes towards women's employment are part of a wider set of attitudes and practices around gender roles within the household. Certainly whether or not women are in paid employment affects their role within the home, and working women are generally less likely to carry the entire responsibility for housework. However, women usually carry the greater responsibility, and for women who work part-time, the demands of the home are similar to those falling on non-working women.

The 1980 survey of women's employment (Martin and Roberts, 1984) examined whether couples were satisfied with the domestic division of labour.

Table 6.12. *Percentage of adults who say a woman should stay at home to care for a child under school-age, Great Britain, 1993*

	Born in:		
	1950–70	1930–49	pre–1930
Men	48	76	86
Women	46	70	79

Source: SCPR (1993).

Table 6.13. *Domestic division of labour and women's employment status, Great Britain, 1988 (%)*

	Not working	Working part-time	Working full-time
Household cleaning			
Mainly man	1	1	4
Mainly woman	86	84	60
Shared equally	11	14	33
Washing and ironing			
Mainly man	2	–	1
Mainly woman	93	94	81
Shared equally	5	5	18
Household shopping			
Mainly man	6	1	8
Mainly woman	62	64	43
Shared equally	31	35	49
Preparation of evening meal			
Mainly man	1	3	1
Mainly woman	89	83	63
Shared equally	15	31	40

Source: SCPR (1990).

Most wives were fairly satisfied with the contributions made by their husbands, although working wives were more likely than non-working wives to think that their husbands did not do enough.

Younger people are more egalitarian in their attitudes than older ones. However, the Social Attitudes Survey has found that it is marital status rather than youth alone that is a major factor influencing more egalitarian attitudes. Young unmarried individuals (especially women) are far more egalitarian in their attitudes towards responsibilities for household tasks than are their married counterparts of the same age. Married couples aged 18–24 in fact show very similar patterns of domestic division of labour to those of married couples of all ages.

The domestic domain remains an unequal one in which women still carry the major responsibility. However, there appears to be a greater equality than was the case in the past, although it is difficult to demonstrate this with any certainty since this is an area of relatively recent research interest in Britain. The symmetrical family concept developed by Young and Willmott (1973) did not claim that the roles of the sexes would be identical, but that there would be 'some role segregation along with a greater degree of equality'. This would appear to be a fairly accurate description of the situation in families in the 1980s.

6.5. Policy Change in the 1980s

6.5.1. *Family Policy Developments*

In this section we will highlight some of the major developments in social policy that have impacted on families of different kinds during the 1980s. The objective is not to describe the totality of social or economic policies that affect families, but to identify the key changes that have taken place, and the impact they have had.

In Britain, unlike many other European countries, the term 'family policy' is not one that is in common currency, nor one that denotes a clear and comprehensive set of policies and commitments in relation to families of different types. Britain does not have an explicit approach to family policy. None the less, the family remains a subject of much public concern, and one that is the focus of political controversy. All political parties have sought to lay claim to the territory of the family, and this has been an especially crowded battlefield since the late 1970s when Margaret Thatcher declared the Conservatives to be 'the party of the family'. Despite such claims, family policy has not developed apace with demographic and social changes, and much of the debate about the relationship between the family and the state has been controversial and reactionary.

In Britain there is no minister for, nor Department of, the family (although in 1994 the Secretary of State for Health was appointed spokesperson on the family). The case for developing a family perspective within the machinery of government is one that has been made by, among others, the Family Policy Studies Centre – a non-partisan research organization which was established in 1983 to provide independent analysis on family trends and the impact of social policy on families. They have argued that there is an apparently poor 'fit' between much social policy, and areas of significant social change, with the result that many of the changes that are taking place in the nature and shape of families are inadequately recognized or acknowledged by policy responses, and that different streams of policy are inconsistent or even contradictory (Henwood and Wicks, 1988).

Certain aspects of family policy, or of social policies that impact on the family, have been influenced by Europe. European directives on the equal treatment of men and women have helped ensure that the social security system, for example, allows equal entitlement. However, in the early 1990s the government resisted full commitment to further implementation of European-led reforms by securing an 'opt-out' from the social protocol of the Maastricht Treaty.

In the absence of clear family policies, it is none the less the case that different social and economic policies *do* have an impact upon families of different kinds, and do make various (often implicit) assumptions about the nature of families. Policies that are not specifically directed towards families may have unforeseen or unintended consequences. Some policies are more explicit. Reform in the income tax system announced in 1988, for example, was intended to cease treating the income of a married woman as if it belonged to her husband, and married women now have the same right to privacy and independence in their tax affairs as men. Such a change was presented as a clear recognition that the old system was 'no longer acceptable' for contemporary society. In the same year, steps were taken to end the tax advantage that cohabiting couples enjoyed on mortgage interest payments by claiming twice the allowance available to their married counterparts. The closure of this loophole explicitly removed a tax penalty on marriage, but implicitly may also have served to underline support for marriage, and to indicate some measure of disapproval of cohabitation trends.

6.5.2. *Cohabitation*

The major area of social policy which is likely to have an impact on cohabiting couples is that of social security. Interestingly, despite the rise in cohabitation throughout the 1980s, the stance of the social security system towards such couples has remained virtually unchanged since 1948. The National Assistance Act of that year included the assumption that, where a man and woman were living together, for social security purposes they would be treated as if they were married – that is, as one benefit unit rather than as two.

One consequence of this situation is that lone parents may face disincentives to establishing new relationships. Moving in to live with a partner also entails the loss of entitlement to one-parent benefit, and to lone-parent premium from income support. The social security system assumes that both partners will provide for any dependent children, even when they are not the children of the non-claimant, who anyway has no legal obligation to maintain them. Unlike husbands and wives, unmarried partners do not face a legal obligation to maintain each other, which is an area of inconsistency with the assumptions made under the rules of social security.

The social security system has further inconsistencies in its treatment of cohabiting couples, particularly in the distinction it makes between means-tested benefits and contributory benefits. Kiernan and Estaugh (1993:43) conclude that 'the system recognises cohabitation where it would restrict entitlement but not where it would give the unmarried partner rights'. For example, widowed individuals who cohabit will lose their entitlement to widow's benefits.

The social security system, taxation and the legal system all operate in a different manner in respect of cohabitation. In general, there is a growing recognition of the status of cohabitants in law, although this still affords them fewer rights than if they were legally married, and cohabitees have no automatic right to their partner's assets (Kiernan and Estaugh, 1993).

6.5.3. *Family Care*

Other important policy developments during the 1980s which have had an impact on families can also be outlined. The changing family trends that we have summarized in earlier sections have concentrated on the beginning and end of the childbearing years. It is important to be aware of other broader changes in the structure of the population itself. In common with all other developed nations, the population in Britain is an ageing one, and the challenges of caring for increasing numbers of very elderly and often frail individuals have been a central concern of social policy throughout the 1980s.

Community care reforms were proposed in 1989 (Secretaries of State, 1989), and subsequently were enacted through the 1990 NHS and Community Care Act, taking effect from April 1993. These reforms continued as in the past to view the role of the family in caring for elderly and other dependants as a central one. However, there also appeared to be a greater recognition of the need to provide practical support to these family carers. Research conducted throughout the 1980s drew attention to these carers, the majority of whom are female and most likely to be caring for elderly parents. Recent evidence from the General Household Survey has indicated that 15 per cent of adults in Britain are carers, with the peak age for caring being between 45 and 64, when 20 per cent of men and 27 per cent of women are carers (OPCS, 1992*b*). These figures cover the entire range of caring responsibilities, from relatively minor involvement to virtual 24-hours-a-day care.

How well the new community care policy is working in practice remains to be seen, although early indications on the experiences of carers are not encouraging, and suggest that they are still being viewed as substitutes for service provision, and are inadequately supported (Warner, 1994). Financial support for carers is limited to a flat rate 'invalid care allowance'. However, the restrictive qualifying criteria for the benefit mean that most carers do not receive it (fewer than one in five). Prior to 1986 married women were specifically excluded from entitlement to the benefit, a situation that was changed only on the eve of an expected ruling by the European Court.

6.5.4. *Children in Families*

Most community care is about the care of an ageing population. At the other end of the life cycle, children also have been the focus of major policy change. The 1987 Family Law Reform Act provided clear acknowledgement of changing social trends by removing the legal distinction between so-called 'legitimate' and 'illegitimate' children, i.e. between those born inside and outside marital unions. The Children Act which followed in 1989 set out the principles underpinning a partnership between parents and statutory social services authorities in the care and protection of children. The Act was in large part a response to a series of child protection tragedies that had occurred throughout the 1970s and 1980s which had seen children murdered by their parents, step-parents or guardians. The Act also established the legal principle of parental responsibility. The rights that accompany such responsibilities are not automatically available to unmarried fathers, although there are legal procedures for allowing joint parental responsibilities. The central principle established by the Children Act is that the welfare of the child is the paramount consideration. This is the principle that should inform any legal judgment that affects children.

Some areas of policy towards families are more explicit than others. The costs incurred in bringing up children are widely recognized in different countries by means of some kind of child support allowance paid by the state. In some countries this support for the family may be complemented through preschool and nursery facilities, while elsewhere the care of young children is regarded primarily as the family's responsibility.

In Britain, 'child benefit' (a weekly allowance payable for all dependent children, and at a higher rate for the oldest or only child) provides the only recognition of the additional costs facing all families bringing up children. (Tax allowances for children used to exist in parallel, but were phased out in 1977 when they were effectively integrated into the new universal Child Benefit system.) However, the long-term future of this universal payment may be in doubt. Proposals to means-test or tax the benefit have been made periodically, but at present the government is committed to honour its 1992 Manifesto pledge to continue to pay child benefit 'to all families, normally to the mother, and in respect of all children' (Conservative Central Office, 1992).

The continuing debate about the future of child benefit highlights an important question about the most effective way of supporting families with children – in particular, whether this can be achieved through a universal system (i.e. in respect of all families with children), or whether a targeted, means-tested approach which directs greater help to the poorest families is the better approach. Lone parents are also entitled to 'one-parent benefit' as a flat rate (and non-means-tested) addition to child benefit, as a recognition of some of the additional costs involved in bringing up a child alone.

Statutory child care in Britain is poorly developed, and the government has viewed this provision as something that can best be developed by the voluntary and independent sectors. As we described in the previous section, the majority of child care continues to be provided by other family members, or through private arrangements. Pre-school educational provision is highly variable across the country, although both the main political parties are beginning to see the development of pre-school education as increasingly important to their electorate, which may force the pace of new provision. Local authority day nursery facilities are primarily for children believed to be 'at risk', or otherwise in need of priority, and lone parents are the most likely to have access to such facilities. As we have already seen, the presence and age of children remains the single most important factor influencing whether or not women (whether single or married) are in paid employment.

Unlike many other European countries, there is no statutory system for parental leave (i.e. a period of time which may be taken by either parent without loss of pay), although mothers who satisfy the employment criteria are able to take a period of maternity leave and then return to their job. Britain objected in 1986 to a proposed European directive on parental leave, arguing that such matters should be negotiated between individuals and their employers, and that statutory regulation would impose rigidity on the labour market and contribute to increased unemployment. Some employers may allow fathers a short period of leave following the birth of a child, but generally speaking this is likely to be taken as part of individuals' ordinary annual holiday entitlement. Similarly, there is no statutory recognition of the caring responsibilities of men and women for older dependent children, or for other dependent family members. Some employers are developing their own career-break arrangements, or other 'family-friendly' practices which can facilitate flexible working, but these remain the exception rather than the rule. Because these arrangements are left to the market-place for resolution, they also form part of the overall remuneration package for employees. Inevitably, this means that such provisions are predominantly found in larger organizations, and are for the benefit of white-collar employees and senior staff only.

6.5.5. *Lone Parents*

In view of the absence of an explicit and comprehensive set of 'family policies', it is perhaps not surprising that different policies towards families are inconsistent and even contradictory. Such tensions can, perhaps, be seen most clearly in respect of policies towards lone parents, where the objectives of helping individuals become self-sufficient are in tension with other concerns about the importance of single parents providing adequate care for their young children. It has been suggested that these tensions in fact 'reflect uncertainty about the position of women generally as mothers and workers' (Burghes, 1993). This uncertainty, or ambivalence, towards women in part reflects the changing role of women in society. In the early days of the welfare state there was no such confusion. The Beveridge report of 1942 provided the basis for the post-war welfare reforms, and set out an explicit view of the role of women:

In the next thirty years housewives as mothers have vital work to do in ensuring the adequate continuance of the British race and of British ideals in the world. (Beveridge, 1942)

Accordingly, the role of social security for married women was a residual one, since Beveridge envisaged that such women had a right to maintenance by their husbands in exchange for 'vital unpaid service'. Today, the role of social policy in supporting women who are balancing the demands of paid employment and of domestic and caring responsibilities is far less clear-cut.

Social security payments are the main source of income for most lone parents, especially for single (i.e. never-married) mothers (Burghes, 1993). This economic dependency also means that single-parent families are likely to experience low living standards. Paid employment offers the main route out of social security dependence, but it is a difficult route to pursue, and policy towards lone parents tries to foster measures to help lone parents enter the labour market, while refraining from actively advocating that lone mothers (or, indeed, any mothers) *should* go out to work. An 'earnings disregard' of £15 a week against social security entitlements provides little incentive for part-time work. For those lone parents who are employed more than 16 hours a week, entitlement to income support is replaced by a means-tested 'family credit'. This benefit is payable to families (one- or two-parent) with dependent children who are in low-paid employment. However, moving off income support and into economic independence carries many disincentives for lone parents. The loss of benefits and entitlements such as free school meals, housing benefit and help with mortgage interest repayments, ensures that many lone parents remain stuck on the 'poverty plateau'. In 1994 measures were introduced which allow the costs of child care to be taken into account when calculating family credit. This may prove to be an important family policy measure which will assist low-income families in moving towards greater financial independence.

The Child Support Act of 1991 was concerned with the financial support of children, and particularly with the financial obligations of parents not living with their children. Although this legislation occurred after the end of the decade with which we are mainly concerned (the 1980s), the issues which it addressed had been on the policy agenda for several years. The child-support arrangements that were introduced were modelled largely on the Australian system which was introduced during the 1980s. The principle that parents should have an ongoing financial responsibility for their dependent children is one which commands widespread popular and political support in Britain. However, the implementation of the legislation has been highly controversial and problematic.

A Child Support Agency was established with effect from April 1993, and was given powers to trace absent and defaulting parents, and to enforce payment of child support. Critics have pointed out that the legislation has failed to benefit most lone mothers and their children because any financial contribution made by the absent parent is deducted from social security payments already being received (apart from a 'maintenance disregard' of just £15 a week). The net beneficiary of the policy, certainly in the short term, is more likely to be the public purse. Other opposition has been based on totally different objections, and has come from a highly organized and vociferous male lobby which has complained about the level of contributions absent fathers have been obliged to make, and the deleterious impact this has had on the income of their second – or subsequent – families. The formula used for calculating the contribution to be made by the absent parent has been criticized particularly for its failure to take account of the costs of a second partner and stepchildren, and for the setting of a 50 per cent deduction rate on assessable income. This raises some central questions about the respective rights and responsibilities of parents and children in different family units. Such issues are far from simple, and policy debate is continuing to develop around these unresolved matters.

Lone-parent families have been the focus of considerable controversy throughout the 1980s. The image of the young, unmarried mother, dependent on the state is one that has been targeted by many politicians and comment-ators. In fact, only about three in ten lone parents come into the category of single (never-married) mothers (although this is a growing group). As we have described earlier, divorce is the major cause of lone parenthood, accounting for around one-third of lone parents. Another fifth of all lone parents are separated from their partners. The struggle between protecting children, while also upholding the institution of marriage, and reinforcing the ideal of the married two-parent family, is one that continues to be waged. The child-support legislation can also be viewed as concerned less with raising the living standards of lone mothers and their children (which it mainly fails to achieve), than with ensuring that absent fathers do not 'get away' from their ongoing responsibilities by simply passing the costs of main-taining their children to the social security system.

6.5.6. *Family Policy Overview*

This brief account of some of the key developments in policies towards famil-ies during the 1980s illustrates some of the inconsistencies and contradictions that result from attempts to protect children, and to create equity between individuals, while also upholding a value system which places the traditional two-parent family at the heart of society. In consequence, the policy changes that have taken place in such a climate have been incremental and uncertain. The respective balance between the worlds of employment and family life, and between individuals' rights and responsibilities, remains unclear. At the end of the 1980s, Britain still lacked a distinct set of objectives that might be defined as 'family policy', or any machinery of government that might facilitate the development of a family perspective within the policy-making process.

6.6. Conclusions

While the 1980s was a decade of relative stability in terms of fertility and mortality in Britain, it did witness some of the most substantial changes in family and household composition this century. The striking rise in cohabitation, childbearing outside marriage, marital breakdown and the move towards independent living has had important consequences for the family situation of women at both the beginning of childbearing and the end of family-rearing. Demographic factors, such as the decline in marriage rates among young adults and the rise in divorce, have played an important role, but there has been a change, also, in the propensity of people to live in different forms of living arrangements (Murphy and Berrington, 1993). It remains to be seen to what extent these changes are influenced by economic, social or attitude change, or by various combinations of all of these factors.

'Family policy' was probably a more familiar term at the end of the decade than it was at the beginning. However, Britain remains a long way from having a clear and comprehensive set of policies which might be grouped under such a heading. None the less, there have been some important policy developments which appear to recognize, or at least to take some account of, the magnitude of social and demographic changes affecting the family. There remain a number of contradictions and tensions in social-policy questions. For example, should policy be following family change, or attempting to lead it? Similarly, does the recognition of diversity in family forms indicate diluted support for the traditional family model? Without greater clarity of purpose, and in the absence of public debate about the role of family policy, Britain is likely to remain in a pattern of slow and incremental policy adjustment which lags behind the rate of change in the demographic, social and economic developments that we have outlined, and does so often to the detriment of many individuals and their families.

Acknowledgement

Figures 6.1*a* and 6.1*b* have been reproduced by kind permission of the authors and the Office for National Statistics.

References

Anderson, M. (1983), 'What is New about the Modern Family: an Historical Perspective', in OPCS, *The Family*, British Society for Population Studies Conference Papers, Occasional Paper 31, Office of Population Censuses and Surveys, London: 1–16.
Babb, P. (1993), 'Birth Statistics 1992', in HMSO, *Population Trends*, 74:8–11.
Berrington, A., and Murphy, M. (1993), 'Leaving Home in the 1980s: Patterns, Determinants and Outcomes', mimeo, London School of Economics and Polit-

ical Science.

——, Lelièvre, E., Kiernan, K. and Murphy, M. (1993), 'Changes in Living Arrangements in Great Britain over the 1980s: a Review', Paper prepared for the session 'The Social and Economic Consequences of Household Structures', IUSSP General Conference, Montreal, August 1993.

Beveridge, Sir W. (1942), *Social Insurance and Allied Services*, Cmd. 6404, HMSO, London.

Brown, M. (1993), 'The Demographic Situation of Single, Never-Married Mothers', mimeo, Family Policy Studies Centre, London.

Burghes, L. (1993), *One Parent Families: Policy Options for the 1990s*, Family Policy Studies Centre/Joseph Rowntree Foundation, London.

Clarke, L. (1992), 'Children's Family Circumstances: Recent Trends in Great Britain', *European Journal of Population*, 8:309–40.

Clarke, L. (1994), 'At the Expense of the Children? Demographic Change and the Family Situation of Children in Britain', paper presented to the International Sociological Association Committee on Family Research XXXIth Seminar, 'Children and Families: Research and Policy', London, 28–30 April 1994.

Conservative Central Office (1992), *The Best Future for Britain: the Conservative Manifesto 1992*, Conservative Central Office, London.

Department of Social Security (1994), *Households below Average Income: a Statistical Analysis 1979–1991/92*, HMSO, London.

Eldridge, S., and Kiernan, K. (1985), 'Declining First Marriage Rates in England and Wales: a Change in Timing or a Rejection of Marriage?', *European Journal of Population*, 1:327–45.

Ermisch, J. (1990), *Fewer Babies, Longer Lives: Policy Implications of Current Demographic Trends*, Joseph Rowntree Foundation, York.

Haskey, J. (1983), 'Children of Divorcing Couples', in HMSO, *Population Trends*, 31:20–6.

—— (1989), 'Current Prospects for the Proportion of Marriages Ending in Divorce', in HMSO, *Population Trends*, 55:34–7.

—— (1992), 'Pre-Marital Cohabitation and the Probability of Subsequent Divorce: Analysis using New Data from the General Household Survey', in HMSO, *Population Trends*, 68:10–9.

—— (1993*a*), 'Trends in the Numbers of One-Parent Families in Great Britain', in HMSO, *Population Trends*, 71:26–33.

—— (1993*b*), 'First Marriage, Divorce, and Remarriage: Birth Cohort Analysis', in HMSO, *Population Trends*, 72:24–33.

—— (1993*c*), 'Lone Parents and Married Parents with Dependent Children in Great Britain: a Comparison of their Occupations and Social Class Profiles', in HMSO, *Population Trends*, 72:34–44.

Henwood, M., and Wicks, M. (1988), *Family Policy: a Position Statement*, Family Policy Studies Centre/Association of County Councils, London.

——, Rimmer, L., and Wicks, M. (1987), *Inside the Family: Changing Roles of*

Men and Women, Family Policy Studies Centre, London.

Jones, C. (1992), 'Fertility of the Over Thirties', in HMSO, *Population Trends*, 67:10–6.

Kiernan, K. (1989), 'The Family: Formation or Fission', in H. Joshi (ed.), *The Changing Population of Britain*, Basil Blackwell, Oxford: 27–41.

—— and Eldridge, S. (1987), 'Inter and Intra Cohort Variation in the Timing of First Marriage', *British Journal of Sociology*, 38:44–65.

—— and Estaugh, V. (1993), *Cohabitation: Extra-Marital Childbearing and Social Policy*, Occasional Paper 17, Family Policy Studies Centre, London.

—— and Wicks, M. (1990), *Family Change and Future Policy*, Family Policy Studies Centre/Joseph Rowntree Memorial Trust, York.

Kumar, V. (1993), *Poverty and Inequality in the UK: the Effects on Children*, National Children's Bureau, London.

Lesthaeghe, R. (1991), *The Second Demographic Transition in Western Countries: an Interpretation*, IPD Working Paper 1991-2, Interuniversity Programme in Demography, Vrije Universiteit, Brussels.

Martin, J., and Roberts, C. (1984), *Women and Employment: a Lifetime Perspective*, Department of Employment, HMSO, London.

McRae, S. (1993), *Cohabiting Mothers: Changing Marriage and Motherhood?* Policy Studies Institute, London.

Murphy, M., and Berrington, A. (1993), 'Household Change in the 1980s: a Review', in HMSO, *Population Trends*, 73:18–27.

OPCS (Office of Population Censuses and Surveys) (1992*a*), *Marriage and Divorce Statistics, England and Wales, 1990*, OPCS Series FM2 No. 18, HMSO, London.

—— (1992*b*), *General Household Survey: Carers in 1990*, OPCS Monitor SS 92/3, HMSO, London.

—— (1993*a*), *General Household Survey 1991*, Series GHS no. 22, HMSO, London.

—— (1993*b*), *Birth Statistics*, OPCS Series FM1 No. 20, HMSO, London.

—— (1993*c*), *Birth Statistics*, OPCS Series FM1 No. 21, HMSO, London.

—— (1994*a*), *Marriage and Divorce Statistics, England and Wales, 1991*, OPCS Series FM2 No. 19, HMSO, London.

—— (1994*b*), *Day Care Services for Children: a Survey Carried out on Behalf of the Department of Health in 1990*, HMSO, London.

Oppenheim, C. (1993), *Poverty: the Facts*, Child Poverty Action Group, London.

Roll, J. (1992), *Understanding Poverty: a Guide to the Concepts and Measures*, Family Policy Studies Centre, London.

—— (1993), *Lone Parent Families in Europe*, Family Policy Studies Centre, London.

SCPR (Social and Community Planning Research) (1990), *British Social Attitudes Survey: Seventh Report*, Dartmouth, Aldershot.

—— (1993), *British Social Attitudes Survey: Tenth Report*, Dartmouth, Aldershot.

Secretaries of State (1989), *Caring for People: Community Care in the Next Decade and Beyond*, Cm. 849, HMSO, London.

Warner, N. (1994), *Community Care: Just a Fairy Tale?* Carers National Association, London.

Young, M., and Willmott, P. (1973), *The Symmetrical Family*, Routledge & Kegan Paul, London.

7 Ireland: Marriage Loses Popularity

FINOLA KENNEDY and KEVIN McCORMACK[1]

Institute of Public Administration, and Central Statistics Office, Dublin, Ireland

The 1980s was a decade in which marriage lost the popularity it enjoyed in the 1960s and early 1970s. Against a background of economic uncertainty and rising unemployment, the proportion of young women who were married in the age group 25–29 years slipped from two-thirds to just over one-half. The decline in the popularity of marriage among the young was accompanied by a rise in educational participation, an increase in cohabitation and an increase in marriage breakdown.

Young women, particularly better-educated women, increasingly remained in the workforce after marriage. Age of children and number of children remained important influences on participation. During the 1980s, first child-birth within marriage was postponed by almost three years, although the age of childbirth outside marriage rose only slightly. The number of births within marriage fell sharply with a rapid rise outside marriage. In the late 1980s 'newer' life-style dual-earner households were found most frequently among the young, better-educated women.

Lone-parent households were more prone to poverty than the average household. Largely because of the rise in unemployment in the 1980s, households with children faced a higher risk of poverty than in the 1970s. Child care remained largely the task of mothers.

Policy changes, notably equality legislation, which facilitated women's access to the labour market in the 1970s, the legalization of contraception in 1979, alterations in the tax code and the pattern of child income support, have accompanied the behavioural changes. Despite changes in behaviour, however, values and attitudes remain rather traditional.

[1] Thanks are due to Damian Hannan, ESRI, for providing material from the 1987 ESRI Survey.

7.1. Introduction

7.1.1. *Pluralization and Polarization*

Since 1980 Ireland has experienced a compressed demographic transition which has resulted in convergence between the Irish demographic pattern and that which is observed in much of the rest of Europe. This follows several decades during which Ireland exhibited features that were unique in Europe (Kennedy, 1989). The focus of this study is that key decade of change – the 1980s.

The facts and analyses in relation to Ireland are presented within the common perspective on which this comparative study of family life and family policy in Europe in the 1980s is based. During the 1980s in Ireland there was evidence of a *pluralization* of family forms, i.e. a growing variety of family types, especially those headed by solo mothers, and also by lone parents, following separation. Ireland is unique among the countries studied in that divorce is not legally available, although foreign divorces are recognized. A fact to be borne in mind, however, is that in earlier decades, too, large numbers of families headed by lone parents were to be found, owing to widowhood and a generally lower life expectancy. It is not, therefore, that one-parent families are novel, but that the nature of the one-parent family has changed. There is also some evidence of *polarization*, arising from an increase in the non-family sector. More young women are at least postponing marriage and childbearing. It is not clear as yet whether this will lead to an increase in permanent childlessness. There is a small increase in childlessness in the age group 45–49.

Following this Introduction, which includes an overview of demographic trends, the chapter is divided into five main parts. Section 7.2 provides a survey of family policy. Section 7.3 deals with family forms in the 1980s, focusing on two age cohorts of women aged 25–29 and 45–49 years. Section 7.4 deals with family life situations. Section 7.5 treats some aspects of values and attitudes. This is followed by the Summary and Conclusions. As a point of departure, the current state of research on family life and family policy is outlined.

7.1.2. *Recent Research*

Among the small, but growing, volume of research on family-related matters, three areas have been dominant in the 1980s. These relate to (1) women and work, (2) family formation and fission, and (3) policies to support families.

In the first area of *women and work* the focus has been twofold. A number of studies have dealt with women in the paid labour force (Callan and Farrell, 1991; Larson Pyle, 1990; Walsh, 1993), while another approach has centred on the household sector identifying two main components of unpaid work – on the family farm and within the household itself (Fahey, 1990). Within the paid labour-force area, different methodologies have been applied. For example, the work of Callan and Farrell is based on a neoclassical labour-supply theory, while the work of Larson Pyle uses a more eclectic methodo-logy, embracing both economic theory and institutional arrangements which include legislative arrangements and state policies governing women's labour-force participation within patriarchal structures.

In the area of *family formation and family fission*, studies have dealt with single mothers (Flanagan and Richardson, 1992; McCashin, 1993) and the elderly (National Council for the Aged, 1988). The number of single mothers has grown substantially during the 1980s as has the number of elderly living alone. Although divorce is not provided under Irish law, increasing attention is being paid to marital breakdown (Office of the Minister of Justice, 1992; Ward, 1993).

The third major strand of family research in the past decade relates to *family policy*. This research has dealt with taxation and social welfare policies (Kennedy, 1989), family law (Binchy, 1984; Shatter, 1986) as well as par-ticular areas such as child care (Gilligan, 1991; McKenna, 1988).

7.1.3. Overview of Demographic Trends

Between 1981 and 1991, the total population of Ireland (26 counties) in-creased from 3.4 million to 3.5 million. Following a twenty-year period between 1961 and 1981 when the number of females per 1,000 males was almost unchanged at 990, the results of the 1986 Census indicated that, for the first time since the foundation of the state in 1921, females outnumbered males, albeit marginally. The preliminary results of the 1991 Census show a continuation of this trend.

MARRIAGE. The highest level of marriages ever recorded was 23,000 in 1974. Since then annual marriages have fallen steadily. During the 1980s total marriages fell by almost one-quarter while the marriage rate fell from 6.4 to 5.0 per 1,000 inhabitants (Table 7.1). Over the decade, the average

Table 7.1. *Some demographic indicators, Ireland, 1980 and 1990 (%)*

	1980	1990
Annual number of marriages	21,792	17,490
Average rate of marriage per 1,000	6.4	5.0
Average age of women at marriage	24.5	26.6
Average age at first birth within marriage	25.5	28.2
Average age at first birth outside marriage	21.0	21.4
Average age at all first births	24.5	25.8

Source: Vital Statistics, Annual Reports, CSO.

age of women at marriage increased by two years, from 24.5 to 26.6 years, while the average age at first birth within marriage increased from 25.5 to 28.2 years.

In the 1980s there was a marked fall in the proportion of females in the younger age groups who were married. There was a sharp decline in the proportion of women aged 20–24 who were married and a significant drop in the age group 25–29. Thus, between 1983 and 1990 the proportion who were married aged 20–24 fell from 24.6 to 14.5 per cent while for the age group 25–29 the decline was from 66.5 to 57.8 per cent. Substantially more young people remained single. The trend towards younger marriages, which was very marked in the 1960s and carried over into the 1970s, has clearly been reversed since 1980. Younger cohorts of Irish women are at least post-poning marriage; for how long, or to what extent permanently, remains to be seen.

COHABITATION. The fall in marriages and in the marriage rate, and the fact that younger cohorts of women are marrying less frequently than a similar cohort a decade earlier, has been accompanied by an increase in cohabitation. In the 1979 partial Census, the first to ask a question on cohabitation, fewer than 500 persons, male and female, either single or widowed, stated they were living together as couples. This figure had just doubled by the Census of 1981. The trend has continued in the 1991 Census and is confirmed by Labour Force Survey data. Further evidence of cohabitation is provided by a survey carried out by the Department of Social Welfare of recipients of rent allowance in 1993. It was found that one in five young people who left home did so to cohabit.

MARRIAGE BREAKDOWN. A referendum in June 1986 on a proposal to remove the constitutional ban on divorce was defeated by 63 to 37 per cent of the votes cast. A second referendum late in 1995 was carried by a slim majority. Accordingly, divorce legislation will be introduced in the near future. The increase in marriage breakdown is evidenced by the acceleration in the pace of marriage cases coming before the courts. In 1989, a major Act, the Judicial Separation and Family Law Reform Act, was passed. The data clearly indicate an upward trend in separation (including those who have obtained foreign divorces). In 1991 there were 55,000 persons classified as separated compared with 37,000 in 1986. Women accounted for 34,000 of the separated in 1991 compared with 23,000 in 1986, an increase of 50 per cent. The much lower numbers of men classified as separated may be explained in part by emigration and by men failing to describe themselves as separated.

BIRTHS AND FERTILITY. The total number of births recorded in Ireland fell by 30 per cent, from a peak of 74,000 to 52,000, between 1980 and 1992. The total period fertility rate (TPFR) fell by just 50 per cent, from 3.23 in 1980 to 2.17 in 1990, having recovered slightly from an all-time low of 2.11 in 1989 (Table 7.2). In 1965 the TPFR was 4.03. The Irish decline is one of the latest, but also one of the most rapid, in recent European demographic experience.

Over the 1960s and 1970s, the fertility rate fell despite rapidly increasing marriage rates, declining ages at marriage, and the increasing number of births because of even more rapid increases in the relevant population 'at risk' (i.e. females aged 15–49). The 1960s and early 1970s, in particular,

Table 7.2. *Total period fertility rate (TPFR),[a] Ireland, 1965–1990*

Year	TPFR
1965	4.03
1970	3.87
1975	3.40
1980	3.23
1985	2.50
1988	2.17
1989	2.11
1990	2.17

[a] The TPFR for a particular year is the average number of live births per woman if throughout her reproductive cycle (ages 15–49) she experienced the age-specific rates of that year.

Source: CSO.

Table 7.3. *Number of births within and outside marriage, Ireland,
1961-1992*

	Average annual no. of births		Total no. of births	% of total outside marriage
	Within marriage	Outside marriage		
1961–70	61,035	1,382	62,417	2.3
1971–80	66,806	2,633	69,439	3.8
1981–90	55,986	5,633	61,619	9.1
1980	70,700	3,700	74,400	5.0
1981	68,244	3,914	72,355	5.4
1990	45,294	7,660	52,954	14.5
1991	44,262	8,766	52,690	16.6
1992	42,258	9,299	51,557	18.0

Source: CSO.

were a time of marital boom with nuclear family households growing rapidly.
In the 1980s, both postponement of marriage and control of fertility *within*
marriage have been important factors in explaining the decline in fertility.
Births outside marriage have risen rapidly throughout the decade. In 1992
non-marital births accounted for almost one in five births compared with
one in twenty in 1980 (Table 7.3).

7.1.4. *Data Sources*

Many sources are used for the tables in this country report. The most important are the Reports on Vital Statistics, Census of Population and Labour
Force Survey from the Irish Central Statistics Office; Reports of the Irish
Revenue Commissioners; and the Survey of Life Styles, Poverty and Uses
of State Services of the Economic and Social Research Institute.

Most use has been made of the Labour Force Survey and the Survey of
Life Styles, Poverty and Uses of State Services. The Labour Force Survey
is a stratified two-stage sample design based on about 4.5 per cent of the
total population of Ireland (sample size of about 45,000 households and
155,000 respondents; this survey has been carried out annually since 1983).
It contains data on age, sex, marital status, employment and unemployment.
The Survey of Life Styles, Poverty and Uses of State Services, carried out
in 1987, is a stratified random sample of households (sample size of 3,320
households and 8,150 respondents). It contains data on household structure,

including marital status and children, and on life-styles, including income and employment.

7.2. Policy Changes Associated with Changing Trends

7.2.1. *Family Policy Related to Family and Employment*

The striking demographic changes delineated in the Introduction to this chapter, including the fall in the marriage rate and in the birth rate accompanied by a sharp rise in extra-marital births, have been associated with legislative and policy change.

CONTRACEPTION. The sharp fall in births in the 1980s would scarcely have been realized without access to contraceptive methods. Until 1973 access to methods of fertility control was limited by the fact that the sale of contraceptives was illegal. The contraceptive pill was available on a limited basis during the 1960s; doctors, however, tended to prescribe it for purposes described as 'cycle regulation'. Following a High Court case it was ruled that, according to the right to marital privacy in the Constitution, individuals had the right to import contraceptives for their own use. In 1979 the Health (Family Planning) Act was passed. This Act provided for the importation, manufacture, sale and advertisement of contraceptives. A further Act, the Health (Family Planning) (Amendment) Act, was passed in 1985. This Act removed the need for a prescription from a doctor for non-medical contraceptives sold to persons aged 18 years and over. The Act also empowered a wider range of outlets to supply contraceptives. In 1992 the range of outlets was increased further and the age at which contraceptives may be purchased was reduced to 17 years.

EMPLOYMENT CONDITIONS. Important legislative changes governing the employment of married women took place following Irish entry to the EC in 1973. On 31 July 1973, the marriage ban in the civil service was abolished following the Civil Service (Employment of Married Women) Act which repealed statutory provisions restricting the employment of married women. In 1974, the Anti-Discrimination (Pay) Act was passed. The Act establishes the right of a woman to equal pay for work of equal value and provides the means by which this right can be enforced. On 1 July 1977, the Employment Equality Act came into operation. This Act makes it unlawful to discriminate on grounds of sex or marital status in recruitment for employment, conditions of employment, training, work experience or opportunities for promotion. Also in 1977 the Unfair Dismissals Act was passed. This Act protects employees, including pregnant employees, from unfair dismissal. Following the implementation of the Equality Directive of the European Community EC/79/7 in 1985, an increase in the number of married women in the labour force took place, despite the lack of jobs, because married women could obtain unemployment payments in their own right for the first time. In Ireland, as throughout the EU, maternity leave is a right for employed women with a period of leave covered by earnings-related payments. The Maternity Allowance Scheme for Women in Employment was introduced in April 1981. For those entitled to leave – in general women in full-time employment – the Act provides a period of 14 weeks' leave. The amount payable is 70 per cent of a woman's earnings, subject to a ceiling. As distinct from maternity leave, there is no parental leave in Ireland, which is the case also in Luxemburg and the United Kingdom.

INCOME SUPPORTS FOR CHILDREN: TAX ALLOWANCES. Child tax allowances existed from the foundation of the Irish Free State in 1921 until 1986. In the tax year 1959/60 the child tax allowance was two-thirds that for a single person; by 1986, when it was abolished, it was only about 7 per cent of the single person's allowance (Table 7.4). However, a reversal of policy was signalled in the 1989 Budget when a child exemption limit of IEP 200 was introduced for low-income families. In the 1991 Budget the exemption limit was set at IEP 300 for the first two children and at IEP 500 for subsequent children in low-income families. From 1980, an important change was made in the tax code to the effect that tax allowances and bands for married couples were double those for single persons.

Table 7.4. *Tax allowances, Ireland, 1972/1973 and 1990/1991, in current and constant 1990 prices*

	Married couples	Widow/ widower	Single person	Child under 11		Child over 11	
	IEP	IEP	IEP	IEP	% of single	IEP	% of single
1972–3 (current)	494	324	299	155	52	177	59
1972–3 (1990 prices)	3,155	2,069	1,909	990	52	1,130	59
1990–1 (current)	4,200	2,600	2,100	0	0	0	0
		4,200 [a]	4,200 [a]				

[a] With children.

Source: Reports of the Revenue Commissioners (various).

Table 7.5. *Child benefit per month in current and constant 1990 prices, Ireland, 1973–1991 (IEP)*

	First child		Second child		Third+ child	
	Current	1990	Current	1990	Current	1990
July 1973	2.00	11.46	3.00	17.19	3.75	21.49
	First–third child				Fourth+ child	
October 1991	15.80	15.38			22.90	22.29

INCOME SUPPORTS FOR CHILDREN: CHILDREN'S ALLOWANCES OR CHILD BENEFIT. When first introduced in 1944, the scheme of children's allowances was confined to the third and each subsequent child aged under 16 years. From July 1952, an allowance was introduced for the second qualified child. The introduction of an allowance for the first child coincided with the introduction of a new Turnover Tax (VAT) in 1963. Following the Social Welfare Act, 1973, the scheme was extended to provide payment in respect of children between the ages of 16 and 18 years who continued in full-time education. Since 1974, children's allowances have been paid to the mother rather than the father. Correcting for inflation, the real value of the allowance for the first child increased over 1973–90, but it declined for the second child and scarcely changed for the third (Table 7.5).

UNMARRIED MOTHERS' ALLOWANCE (LONE-PARENT ALLOWANCE). In 1973 a state allowance was introduced for unmarried mothers who keep their children. The allowance is payable, subject to a means test, until the child is aged 18 years, or 21 years if in full-time education. Since 1990 the allowance has been called 'lone-parent allowance' as fathers may also claim the allowance if they rear a child on their own. Both the number of recipients and their dependants, as well as total expenditure on the allowance, have grown rapidly in line with the rapid increase in births outside marriage. Between 1974 and 1991, the number of unmarried mothers receiving an allowance increased tenfold from 2,200 to 22,000.

FAMILY INCOME SUPPLEMENT. Family income supplement (FIS) was introduced in 1984 to assist families where the head of the household (male or female) is in full-time, but low-paid, employment. Where such workers have several children, they may be little better off than if they were claiming unemployment benefit or assistance. If their wages were low enough, they could actually be better off unemployed. Heads of households with a gross wage below a certain defined standard receive a payment equal to 50 per cent of the difference between their actual gross wage and the defined standard.

CHILD CARE. Although compulsory school does not start until 6 years of age, 100 per cent of five-year-olds and 55 per cent of four-year-olds attend primary school. Most Irish children are, therefore, in early primary education for two years, first as 'junior infants' and then as 'senior infants'. As distinct from the attendance of four—six-year-olds in primary schools, state-funded nursery and pre-school provision is exclusively for children at risk or with health disabilities. Apart from these special categories, children must be catered for privately. Local authorities have powers under the Housing Acts to provide facilities (which may include crèches) in connection with their house-building programmes. These powers have been used to a very limited degree. Sometimes local authorities may provide private individuals with organizational help to launch a play group. In addition, small equipment grants may be made.

The Childcare Act 1991 represents a major update of the law in relation to the care of children, particularly children who have been assaulted, ill-treated, seriously neglected or sexually abused, or who are at risk. It places statutory duty on the Health Boards to promote the welfare of children up to the age of 18 years who are not receiving adequate care and protection. The Childcare Act provides that pre-schools, nurseries and play groups must notify their existence to the Department of Health. The Act enables the Minister for Health, after consultation with the Minister for Education, to make regulations for securing the safety and promoting the development of children attending pre-school services.

According to EU data (Commission of the European Communities, 1990), there were places available in publicly funded child-care services for 2 per cent of children under 3 years in 1988. This compared with 3 per cent in Germany, 20 per cent in France and 48 per cent in Denmark.

During the 1980s a small number of workplace nurseries/crèches were set up in the Dublin area by public-sector employers. Probably the best known of these are the Dublin Airport nursery (DAWN) established in 1984 and the nursery/crèche at the national television and radio studio (RTE) established in 1986. These nurseries are operated by professionals, and payments by parents who avail themselves of the service cover a good deal of the operating costs. In May 1992, the first civil service crèche was opened. At the opening, 15 children were enrolled. The crèche came into existence directly as a result of negotiations between the Irish Congress of Trade Unions and the government. The capital cost is met by the state in its role as employer and the running costs are met by parents. Such a pattern might provide a model for the future.

HOUSING. Each local authority, which is also a housing authority, is required to have schemes of letting priorities for persons whose need for accommodation has been established under the Housing Act, 1988. A number of housing authorities, including Dublin Corporation, base their schemes of letting priorities on a points system. Points can be awarded for reasons such as overcrowding, health circumstances or size of family. A significant feature of the waiting-lists for housing in recent years has been the increase in the number of smaller households, including solo parents, on the lists. These households now have a reasonable chance of obtaining local authority accommodation compared with the past, when the overriding need was to cater for large households and to clear slums, particularly in the larger urban areas. At the end of the 1980s, 80 per cent of those on waiting-lists were in households of three persons or fewer.

Between 1971 and 1990, the average number of persons per household has declined from just 4 to approximately 3.5, while the average number of persons per room has fallen from 0.86 to 0.7. The decline in household size has reflected two elements. Firstly, the average family size has declined. Secondly, there has been a marked increase in 'household fission', associated in particular with more young single people setting up independent households, whereas formerly they would have lived as part of an extended family. One important specific aid towards house purchase is tax relief on mortgage interest. Relief for a married couple (IEP 3,600) is twice that for a single person (IEP 1,800) although there is no additional relief for the presence of children in a household. There are also grants of IEP 3,000 for first-time purchasers.

7.2.2. *Hypothetical Policy Impact Models: Family Forms, Life Situations*

Hypothetical policy-impact models may be formulated on a cross-sectional or longitudinal basis. From a cross-sectional perspective the question to be asked is "How are existing policies related to the variation of family forms and life situations?" From a longitudinal perspective the question to be asked is "How do changes in policy relate to changes in family forms or life situations?" Of course there is not a strict division between the two questions, as the present picture is a result of a continuous sequence of pictures over a period of time.

With the important *caveat* that policy may simply reinforce behavioural patterns and trends whose roots run deeper than policy, and are embedded in the matrix of culture and values, one possible impact model is proposed with regard to the cross-sectional data and one with regard to the longitudinal data. The hypotheses should reflect at least the *direction* of effects of policy, if not the strength of those effects.

CROSS-SECTIONAL. The first hypothesis focuses on two facets of policy related to *children*: child income support and legal status. The hypothesis states that the pattern of child income support, combined with provisions regarding the legal status of children inside and outside marriage, is consonant with the pluralization of family forms. The abolition of child tax allowances and the relatively low and static real level of child benefit provided little, or very modest, economic support for children in general, although family income supplement and child dependant allowances for the recipients of social welfare payments provided support at the lower end of the income distribution scale. In contrast to the child born within marriage, a special allowance exists for children born outside marriage (predominantly to unmarried mothers) on condition that the parents do not cohabit. Furthermore, the abolition of illegitimacy under the Status of Children Act, 1987, has meant that marital and non-marital children are, as far as possible, treated the same, e.g. with regard to inheritance rights. Therefore an increase in out-of-wedlock births is to be expected.

LONGITUDINAL. The hypothesis proposed here relates to the *labour-force participation of married women*. The hypothesis proposes a 'pull' of married women into the labour market owing to the dismantling of legal barriers, greater opportunities associated with wider access to public education, and a 'push' out of the home, resulting from reduced fertility in turn related to the legalization of contraception. Three legislative strands underpin the changing economic realities. These are the equality legislation regarding conditions of employment, the equality legislation providing equal access to social welfare payments, notably unemployment assistance (which has served to draw women into the labour market, notwithstanding the jobs deficit), and the changes in the taxation law regarding married couples. The two first mentioned legal strands were directly influenced by Irish membership of the EU. This hypothesis would be consonant with a shift away from the more traditional male breadwinner–female housekeeper model of family to the 'newer' household types of a married couple, with or without children, with both parents in the workforce. The latter couples, i.e. those without children, are colloquially known as DINKIES (double income, no kids).

7.3. Family Forms in the 1980s

7.3.1. *Timing of Critical Events*

In both 1980 and 1990, the average age of married women at first birth occurred within the age group 25–29. Single mothers tend to be younger, on
average, than married mothers. For example in 1981, 80 per cent of *all* births
to unmarried mothers were to women aged 24 years or less; in 1991 the
average age of all first births – married and non-married – was 25.8 years.
This was just below the average age at marriage. While the start of the
'empty-nest' phase shows greater variability, and can occur in the post-45–49
age group, the latter age group is the one selected here, in line with the
decision taken by the team of researchers participating in the international
project on which this volume reports. The age group 45–54 has been used
for the older age group for the household composition and life-style data
(Tables 7.16 and 7.17), for data availability reasons.

7.3.2. *Structural Characteristics of Family Life*

MARITAL STATUS AND DEPENDENT CHILDREN. There has been a significant
decline in the proportion of married women aged 25–29 over the 1980s while
the proportion rose among 45–49-year-olds because of the surge in marriages
in the 1960s (Table 7.6). On the other hand, there has been a significant
increase in the proportion of young women remaining single.

Table 7.6. *Partner arrangements of women aged 25-29
and 45-49, Ireland, 1983 and 1990 (%)*

	Age 25–29		Age 45–49	
	1983	1990	1983	1990
Married	66.5	57.8	79.3	82.3
Single	32.0	40.3	12.7	10.2
Separated[a]	1.1	1.7	2.1	3.3
Widowed	0.2	0.2	5.9	4.1

[a] Including foreign divorce.

Source: Labour Force Survey, 1983 and 1990.

Table 7.7. *Share of children by marital status of women, aged 25–29, Ireland, 1983 and 1990 (%)*

No. of children	Married		Single		Separated		Widowed		Total	
	1983	1990	1983	1990	1983	1990	1983	1990	1983	1990
0	21.2	27.3	69.8	67.3	22.2	15.0	33.3	50	36.8	43.2
1	25.4	26.4	16.1	20.0	33.3	20.0	33.3	0	22.5	23.6
2	28.8	28.8	7.9	7.6	33.3	35.0	33.3	50	22.2	20.4
3+	24.6	17.6	6.2	4.9	11.1	30.0	0	0	18.5	12.7

Source: Labour Force Survey, 1983 and 1990.

Table 7.8. *Share of children by marital status of women, aged 45–49, Ireland, 1983 and 1990 (%)*

No. of children	Married		Single		Separated		Widowed		Total	
	1983	1990	1983	1990	1983	1990	1983	1990	1983	1990
0	16.7	17.8	87.8	89.0	43.8	29.0	26.7	33.3	25.0	26.1
1	19.3	23.9	9.2	8.8	12.5	32.3	22.2	30.6	17.1	23.0
2	23.9	24.6	2.0	2.2	25.0	19.4	24.4	16.7	19.9	21.7
3+	40.1	33.7	1.0	0.0	18.8	19.4	28.9	19.4	38.0	29.2

Source: Labour Force Survey, 1983 and 1990.

Tables 7.7 and 7.8 show the number of children by marital status for women aged 25–29 and 45–49. The most striking features in the age group 25–29 are (1) the increase in the share of the total with no children, and the decline in the share of the total (by 50 per cent) of those with three and more children; and (2) the rise in the share of single women with one child (by 25 per cent): in 1990 one in every five single women aged 25–29 had just one child, compared with over one in four married women.

The main features in the age group 45–49 are (1) the increase in the proportion who are married with no children or just one child and the decline in the proportion who are married with three or more children; (2) the increase in the proportion of single women with no children and a decline in the proportion of single women with one or more children; and (3) a decline in the proportion who are separated with no children and an increase in the proportion separated with one child.

LABOUR-FORCE PARTICIPATION OF WOMEN. In 1990 women comprised just one-third of the Irish labour force, compared with an EU average of 40 per cent. However, the participation rate of married women has been growing rapidly. Between 1977 and 1990 the participation rate of married women increased from 14 to 25 per cent (Table 7.9). The growth in the participation rate has been from 28 to 47 per cent for married women aged 20–24 and from 17 to 41 per cent for those aged 25–34. There was also a marked jump in the participation rate of women aged 45–54 years, both single (from 60 to 70 per cent) and married (from 14 to 22 per cent). There is a high retirement rate on the birth of a child or children and there is no return peak in

Table 7.9. *Female labour-force participation rates, aged 15 years and over, Ireland, 1977 and 1990 (%)*

	Age groups			
	20–24	25–34	40–54	15+
Total				
1977	66.4	31.4	23.7	29.0
1990	73.3	54.5	27.8	31.2
of which:				
Single				
1977	88.7	86.6	60.0	58.0
1990	77.9	88.2	69.9	50.0
Married				
1977	28.4	16.7	14.4	14.4
1990	46.9	40.5	22.0	25.0

Source: CSO.

Table 7.10. *Participation rates of married women classified by number of dependent children, Ireland, 1987*

No. of children	Age group	
	25-34	45-49
0	81.8	31.1[a]
1	47.6	21.9
2	28.5	20.6
3 or more	13.2	18.7
Total	35.9	21.8

[a] Different sources used.

Source: Blackwell (1989).

Table 7.11. *Participation rates of married women classified by age of youngest child, Ireland, 1987*

Age of youngest child	Age group	
	25–34	45–49
(no children)	89.5	34.9[a]
13+	31.1	24.0
5–12	29.4	20.8
0–4	26.9	19.8

[a] Different sources used.

Source: ESRI (1987).

Table 7.12. *Female employment by marital status, job type and number of dependent children, Ireland, 1983 and 1990 (%)*

	Age 25-29		Age 45-49	
	1983	1990	1983	1990
Married	43.4	45.1	57.3	67.2
Single	56.8	54.2	30.8	24.7
Separated	.5	.7	2.8	4.0
Widowed	.2	.0	9.0	4.0
Full-time	93.0	92.7	76.8	74.9
Part-time	7.0	7.3	23.2	25.1
No children	67.5	64.5	48.3	42.5
1 child	19.4	21.5	15.2	21.5
2 children	9.5	10.3	15.2	19.0
3+ children	3.7	3.9	21.3	17.0

Source: Labour Force Surveys, 1983 and 1990.

the Irish pattern. The extent to which older married women do not return to the labour market on the basis of choice or on the basis of no opportunity because of a lack of jobs, is unknown.

Children have a clear impact on the participation of women in the work-force (Tables 7.10 and 7.11). Women with children under 5 have the lowest participation rate in each group. More sophisticated econometric analysis (Callan and Farrell, 1991) shows an even stronger effect from the presence of small children.

Table 7.12 refers to women who are actually employed. It shows female employment by marital status, job type and number of dependent children for women aged 25–29 and 45–49 in 1983 and 1990. It is in a sense remarkable for being unremarkable, and to an extent illustrates the limitations of a snapshot approach. Among the younger cohort there appears to be little change according to the various indicators. For the older age group, 45–49, there is a more substantial increase in the population married, reflecting the increase in the marriage rate in the 1960s and early 1970s. There is little change as between full-time and part-time employment. For both age groups there is a decline in the proportion who are childless and an increase in the share of those with one and two children. For the younger age group, 25–29, there is a very slight increase in the share of those with three or more children, while there is a definite reduction in the share of older women with three or more children.

UNEMPLOYMENT, POVERTY AND FAMILIES. In 1990 women accounted for just one-third of the total unemployed. Between January 1980 and December 1990 the Live Register unemployment of women rose over three and a half times, from 22,000 to 75,000. Over the same period the unemployment of men rose slightly more than twofold, from 70,000 to 158,000. Throughout Europe, the unemployment of women has been rising more rapidly than the unemployment of men. Nor do official figures give a complete picture of women's unemployment. Many married women who would work if jobs were available may not be registered as unemployed as they may not qualify for a payment. This raises the question of the measurement of employment and unemployment. It has been pointed out by a leading statistician that measures now in use in Europe would tend to give higher levels of labour-force participation for women in Ireland if the exact same measures were used (Garvey, 1988).

In 1990 there were 221,000 recipients of unemployment benefit and assistance, together with 72,000 adult dependants and 237,000 child dependants. Out of a total of 1.2 million children in respect of whom child benefit was paid in 1990, more than one child in every five is in a family that depends on unemployment benefit or assistance. One child in every three lives in a family in receipt of some social welfare payment – widows, unmarried mothers, unemployment, etc. A study by Callan and Nolan (1988) demonstrates the strong impact of unemployment on family poverty. For two-adult households with three or more children, 45 per cent of those below the poverty line – as measured by 50 per cent of the mean household income in 1987 – were headed by an unemployed man. There is some evidence that unemployment tends to be concentrated in families. In households where the head of the household is unemployed, there is a higher incidence of unemployment of spouses than in households where the head of household is employed (Blackwell, 1988).

Households where the head is unemployed face the highest risk of being poor. Unemployment is, in fact, the most important single cause of poverty (Nolan and Callan, 1994). As a consequence of the rise in unemployment during the 1980s, households with children, particularly those with three or more children, face a much higher risk of poverty than in the 1970s.

In a study of poverty based on 1980 data, Roche (1984) shows a relationship between child poverty and the number of children per household. He found that two-thirds of all poor children were in households with four or more children. Households with four or more children were at a greater risk of poverty than households with fewer children. Research published by the Combat Poverty Agency in 1988 found that the risk of poverty for house-holds with children *increased* during the periods 1973–80 and 1980–7. Households with several children as well as one-parent households are at a significantly higher risk of poverty than other households.

Most women in poor households in 1987 were married women and nearly 80 per cent of women in households below half the average income were married – many to unemployed men or to farmers (Nolan and Callan, 1994). The number of lone mothers, a group at high risk of poverty, has grown rapidly during the 1980s. Thus, most women, whether married or not, in poor households have children; i.e., most poor women in Ireland are mothers with dependent children.

EDUCATIONAL ATTAINMENT. Besides age and marital status, educational level has significant effects on the participation rate. Educational participation rates have increased dramatically in Ireland over the past 25 years – from around 30 per cent of girls completing second level in the mid-1960s to over 80 per cent by the beginning of the 1990s. For women aged 25–29, one in five had attained third-level education in 1990 compared with one in eight in 1981. For women aged 45–49, one in eight had attained third level in 1990 compared with one in fifteen in 1981. The contrast between the older and the younger women is particularly marked for those who attended primary school only: in 1990 primary school represented the highest level of educational attainment for 38 per cent of women aged 45–49 compared with less than 13 per cent of women aged 25–29. However, the level of 38 per cent compared with almost 50 per cent of older women in 1981, which in part can be accounted for by the abolition of a compulsory primary

Table 7.13. *Women's educational attainment by age group 25-29 and 45-49, Ireland, 1981 and 1990 (%)*

Level of education	Age 25-29		Age 45-49	
	1981	1990	1981	1990
Primary only (incl. not stated)	21.6	12.7	49.8	38.2
Secondary and vocational only	66.9	66.9	44.2	49.5
of which:				
Inter/group cert.		24.5		26.4
Leaving cert.		42.5		23.2
Third level, non-university and university	11.7	20.3	6.0	12.2

Source: Census 1981; Labour Force Survey, 1990.

Table 7.14. *Number of dependent children by education completed of women, aged 25-29, Ireland, 1990*

No. of children	Primary (incl.not stated)		Inter/ group		Leaving		Third level		Total	
	No.[a]	%	No.[a]	%	No.[a]	%	No.[a]	%	No.[a]	%
0	2.6	17.4	7.4	25.8	24.7	49.8	15.9	66.8	50.6	43.2
1	3.1	20.8	7.7	26.8	12.7	25.6	4.2	17.6	27.6	23.6
2	4.6	30.9	8.2	28.5	8.5	17.1	2.6	10.9	23.9	20.4
3+	4.6	30.9	5.5	19.2	3.7	7.5	1.1	4.6	14.9	12.7
Total	14.9	100	28.7	100	49.6	100	23.8	100	117	100

[a] Number ('000).

Source: Labour Force Survey, 1990.

certificate examination and the introduction of free post-primary education in 1967 (Table 7.13). Tables 7.14 and 7.15 show the number of children by education completed of women aged 25-29 and 45-49 in 1990. As might be expected, a high proportion (72 per cent) of women aged 25-29 who had completed the third level had no children (Table 7.14). It is clear that the factors that influence women's labour-force participation are age, marital status, number and ages of children, and education. There is clear evidence of a rise over time in the participation rate of married women, but the rate is reduced according to the number and ages of children. Also, for married women work participation is highly correlated with level of education.

Table 7.15. *Number of dependent children by education completed of women, aged 45–49, Ireland, 1990*

No. of children	Primary (incl. not stated)		Inter/ group		Leaving		Third level		Total	
	No.ᵃ	%	No.ᵃ	%	No.ᵃ	%	No.ᵃ	%	No.ᵃ	%
0	9.1	26.8	5.3	22.6	4.9	23.8	3.9	36.1	23.2	26.1
1	8.6	25.4	5.7	24.4	4.7	22.8	1.5	13.9	20.4	23.0
2	6.5	19.2	5.8	24.8	4.9	23.8	2.1	19.4	19.2	21.6
3+	9.8	28.9	6.6	28.2	6.1	29.6	3.3	30.6	25.9	29.2
Total	33.9	100	23.4	100	20.6	100	10.8	100	88.8	100

ᵃ Number ('000).

Source: Labour Force Survey, 1990.

7.4. The Family Life Situation

7.4.1. *Household Composition*

Table 7.16 gives a picture of household composition by age of women in 1987. The source is a large national survey of 3,500 households (ESRI, 1987). There were 4,200 women aged 20 years and over in these households. Three main variables were used in its construction: (1) marital status (single, married, widowed/divorced/separated); (2) number of children of respondent in household of respondent; and (3) some basic characteristics of the relationships of people in the households – whether parent–child(ren), whether both spouses were present if married, and whether a multi-generational household existed. Five of the most popular categories accounted for 83 per cent of all women. These categories were : (1) married, with two or more children in household with husband; (2) married, no children, on own with husband; (3) single, no children, in household with parents; (4) married, one child, with husband; and (5) widowed, separated, divorced with others in household.

Twelve relevant household composition categories are given in Table 7.16. Six of these accounted for just 10 per cent of the respondents. The categories of household composition are rank-ordered by their 'popularity'. The two most frequently occurring are married-couple (nuclear family) households with and without children, where there is no three-generation relationship (i.e. the parent(s) of either spouse are not present). Households with two or more children, with both parents present, comprise just under 30 per cent

Table 7.16. *Household composition by age of women, Ireland, 1987 (%)*

Household composition	Age of women		
	25-29	45-54	20+
1. Married + 2 or more children + husband	28.3	31.6	26.0
2. Married, no children, with husband	10.3	25.0	21.3
3. Single, no children, living in household with parents	27.5	2.2	17.1
4. Married, 1 child, with husband	12.3	23.7	9.5
5. Widowed, separated, divorced, + others	2.7	7.7	9.0
6. Single, no children, + 2 or more people not in a family relationship	11.8	2.5	6.8
7. Married, + > 1 child, + parents/in-laws	2.9	4.6	3.2
8. Widow/single/divorced, living on own	–	0.3	2.8
9. Married, no children, + parents	–	0.7	1.3
10. Single, no children, on own	0.2	1.1	1.2
11. Single + children	2.7	–	0.8
12. Residual	1.2	0.6	0.9
Total			
%	100	100	100
No.	407	716	4,173

Source: ESRI (1987).

of households in which women aged 25–29 are present and just over 30 per cent of households in which women aged 45–54 are present. For 25–29-year-olds the most popular household options are marriage with one or two children (41 per cent), single and still living at home (28 per cent), and single living with other/s (12 per cent). For those aged 45–54, over 80 per cent are married, living with their husbands with one, two or more children, or no children.

7.4.2. *Household 'Life-Style' Characteristics*

Categorization by 'life-style' was carried out using a number of variables: marital status; whether or not respondents had children; whether household was one where respondent was in husband–wife or parent–child relationship, or both; and whether respondent and/or spouse was employed. Of all the possible combinations, those in Table 7.17 have frequencies greater than 3 per cent for all women aged 20 and over. Unlike the conventional household composition variables, the 'life-style' categorization also includes the employment status of both the woman and her spouse. We do not have accurate information on 'living together' arrangements or agreements, whether in the same household or apart.

Six 'life-style' arrangements account for 57 per cent of all women over 20: the conventional, larger, nuclear family arrangement – married, two children at least at home, with conventional wife–mother–homemaker/husband–provider roles (15.4 per cent); married, one child, wife at home, husband working or not working (7.3 per cent); single, no children, living at home, working or not working (17.7 per cent, categories 2 and 5 in Table 7.17); and the general older 'empty-nest' arrangement (16.8 per cent, categories 3 and 6 in Table 7.17).

Over 17 per cent of both 25–29 and 45–54-year-olds are in the category married, breadwinner husband, and more than two children. Twenty-one per cent of 25–29-year-olds are single with no children, at work and living at home. Almost one in five of the 45–54-year-olds are in the 'empty-nest' category. For 25–29-year-olds the category single, no children, living in non-family household accounts for 11 per cent; while single, not at work and living at home accounts for over 8 per cent.

Most of the 45–54-year-olds are in conventional (wife in home duties, husband working) situations, with 14 per cent having no children, and 18 per cent having two or more. More than half of 45–54-year-olds are located in widely dispersed household types, depending on presence and number of children and whether or not the husband is employed. Very few of the over-44s are in 'dual-career' households (about 10 per cent at most).

The 'newer' life-style, dual-earner-household arrangements (categories 7 and 12 in Table 7.17 and two other similar categories included in the residual) account for 9 per cent of all women in households and 18 per cent of all women aged 25–29. Such 'new-style' households are much more characteristic of better-educated people, particularly of better-educated young people (Table 7.18).

Table 7.17. *The 'life-style' characteristics of women aged 25–29 and 45–54, Ireland, 1987 (%)*

Life-styles	Age group		
	25-29	45-54	20+
1. Married, > 2 children, home duties, husband working	17.4	17.6	15.4
2. Single, no children, at work, living at home	20.9	0.4	10.6
3. Married, no children, home duties, husband not working	–	4.5	9.8
4. Married, 1 child, home duties, husband working/not working	5.4	20.2	7.3
5. Single, not at work, living at home	8.4	1.8	7.1
6. Married, no children, home duties, husband working	0.7	13.5	7.0
7. Married, 1 or > 1 child, husband and wife working	7.6	6.3	5.6
8. Widowed/separated/divorced, with/without children	2.4	5.7	5.5
9. Married > 1 child, wife not working, husband not working	7.4	7.3	5.4
10. Single, no children, working, non-family household	10.6	1.3	4.6
11. Single, no children, not working, living on own	2.0	1.4	3.4
12. Married, no children, both working	7.9	3.5	3.3
13. Residual	8.3	16.6	15.8
Total			
%	100	100	100
No.	407	716	4,173

Source: ESRI (1987).

Table 7.18 shows that for women aged 30–40 years the proportion who live in 'new' life-style household types rises from under 10 per cent for those with no second-level qualifications to 37 per cent for those with third-level qualifications. For those women who have ever been married, such new household arrangements are most popular among the young third level, or successful second level, graduates: over 50 per cent of 20–30-year-olds live in such households. At the other extreme, it is the older and most poorly qualified who are least likely to live in such 'modern' arrangements.

Table 7.18. *Percentage of women in 'new' life-style household types (married, with/without children, working, husband working or not), by level of education and age, Ireland, 1987*

Age group	Level of education: qualifications				
	No second level	Junior level	Leaving cert. certificate	Third level	Total
All women					
20-30	4.9	6.6	10.4	10.7	8.4
	(225)	(273)	(450)	(150)	(1101)
30-40	9.6	11.6	20.7	36.8	16.1
	(270)	(181)	(179)	(87)	(721)
40-54	8.1	11.9	15.6	39.1	12.5
	(595)	(210)	(160)	(87)	(1052)
55-64	3.2	7.7	7.4	32.4	6.0
	(408)	(65)	(81)	(34)	(558)
65+	0.4	0.0	3.6	3.0	0.8
	(526)	(49)	(56)	(33)	(664)
Total					
%	4.9	8.9	12.6	24.0	9.2
(No.)	(2024)	(778)	(926)	(391)	(4126)
All ever-married women					
20-30	12.8	28.2	50.5	53.3	31.6
	(86)	(82)	(93)	(30)	(291)
30-40	11.0	12.9	22.8	42.1	18.2
	(237)	(163)	(162)	(76)	(639)
40-54	8.7	12.8	16.7	42.5	13.5
	(553)	(195)	(150)	(80)	(978)
55-64	3.4	2.1	8.1	33.3	6.3
	(385)	(62)	(74)	(33)	(554)
65+	0.4	–	4.1	5.0	0.9
	(456)	(47)	(49)	(20)	(572)

Source: ESRI (1987).

7.4.3. *Gender Roles within the Household*

There are few data available on the extent to which husbands, partners or children help with household tasks. Collins (1986) suggests that husbands may help a little with the housework, more so if the wife is working. Fine-Davis (1988) makes a similar finding. However, while today's husbands do more about the house than a generation ago, 'the housework is perceived by everyone in the family as essentially the work of the housewife' (Collins, 1986).

More detailed analysis of the distribution of housework and child care is provided by Fahey in a survey drawn on by the Working Party on Women's Affairs and Family Law Reform (1984). Fahey's findings pointed to the persistence of the 'double burden'. Of the housewives sampled, 82 per cent felt that they did most, or all, of the housework themselves, while only a very small proportion – under 4 per cent – felt that they did less than half. Although a significantly smaller proportion of women with full-time jobs did most, or all, of the housework, 57 per cent of such women did fall into this category, with under 13 per cent with full-time jobs claiming to do less than half the housework. In general, the information suggests that where women, employed or otherwise, get help from within the home in managing housework, it may well be that they depend on their children for that help as much as on their husbands, 'so that patterns of household management, as well as being a women's issue, are both a children's and a men's issue' (Fahey, 1984).

7.5. Values and Attitudes

The 1990 European Values Study provides comparative material with an earlier survey in 1981. 'One of the factors which makes the European Values Study material of particular interest in the Irish case is the distinctive situation in relation to female participation in the labour force' (Whelan, 1992).

The widespread increase in different countries in female labour-force participation rates has been due largely to the growth in married women's participation. There is evidence from many countries that factors which influence women's participation include potential earnings, non-employment income, husband's earnings, the number and age of children, and education levels (Callan and Farrell, 1991). Different factors may have different emphasis in different countries. Callan and Farrell ask the question:

Do trends in Irish women's participation in the labour market simply reflect changes in social attitudes and customs, or are they sensitive to economic influences such as wages and taxes?

Behavioural changes are linked to changes in the economy and society. The author of the Irish Value Study poses the question:

… whether the distinctive pattern of female labour force participation in Ireland has its source in values and attitudes which also mark Ireland out in comparative terms as an exceptional case?

The most striking feature of the Irish Value Study is how close Irish attitudes are to European ones. In the evaluation of career costs, the Irish (men and women) show no evidence of being more traditional than other Europeans.

Just over one-third of Irish respondents do not accept that a working mother can establish just as satisfactory a relationship [with a child] as a mother who does not work. This figure is almost identical to the European average. While just over half of the Irish sample think a pre-school child is likely to suffer if his or her mother works, [the] corresponding European figure is considerably higher – coming close to seven out of ten. Indeed, for Italy, Portugal and West Germany the traditional response exceeds 80 per cent. (Whelan, 1992)

Age and education levels are found to be key factors in explaining variations in attitude. The most substantial differences occur by age groups. Thus, for example, while only one in four of those aged between 18 and 29 think that it is more difficult for a working mother to establish a warm and secure relationship with her children, this figure gradually rises to just one in two for those aged 45–49 and to over one in two for those aged over 60 years. Similarly, while two in five of the younger age group feel that a pre-school child will suffer because of a working mother, the proportion is two out of three for women aged 45–49.

7.5.1. *Fathers*

In the European Values Study 1990, about 90 per cent of persons believed that a child needs a home with both a father and a mother to grow up happy. While the Irish percentage holding this view is actually slightly below the European average in 1990, 'over time the emphasis on the contribution of both parents to a child's prospects of happiness has actually increased' (Whelan, 1992).

Under the Irish Constitution, the father of a child born outside marriage has no special rights or duties. Under the Guardianship of Infants Act, 1964, married parents are recognized as joint guardians of their children; the mother of a child born outside marriage is its sole guardian. An unmarried father may apply to the courts for guardianship rights and the courts will decide on the basis of the welfare of the child. The legal position, combined with the fact that the lone-parent allowance (overwhelmingly paid to unmarried mothers) is paid on condition that the mother and father of the child(ren) are not cohabiting, could contribute to a 'beget and forget' approach which may not be in the best interests of the child.

The legal position of men who father children outside marriage may be about to change as a result of the judgment of the European Court of Human Rights in May 1994. The landmark judgment found that the Irish state violated the rights of an unmarried Dublin man by allowing his child to be placed for adoption without his knowledge or consent. Of crucial importance, the Court found that the notion of 'family' is not confined to marriage-based relationships. The Court ruled that a 'bond amounting to family life exists between the child and its parents, even if at the time of his or her birth the parents are no longer cohabiting or if their relationship has ended'. The Court found that the secret placement of the child in 1988 and subsequent adoption order, without the consent of the unmarried father, 'amounted to an interference with the applicant's right to respect for family life'.

7.6. Summary and Conclusions

During the 1980s, a convergence occurred between the Irish demographic pattern and that which is observed in much of the rest of Europe. Notwithstanding the convergence, however, marked structural differences remain. Relative to the rest of Europe, Ireland has a low employment ratio and a high dependency ratio. The low employment ratio means that in Ireland every ten workers have to support an average of twenty-two dependants; in Denmark, at the other end of the scale, every ten workers have to support only nine dependants (Kennedy, 1992).

During the 1980s both the total number of marriages and the marriage rate fell sharply. The trend towards younger marriages that occurred in the 1960s and 1970s has been reversed in the 1980s with a rise of two years in the average age of women getting married. Over the decade, births declined in total by 30 per cent and within marriage by 36 per cent, as extramarital births increased rapidly. By 1992 extra-marital births accounted for almost one in five births overall (one in three births in the capital city, Dublin) compared with one in twenty births overall in 1980.

Family structures reflect the demographic changes with an increase of almost one-quarter in the proportion of young women aged 25–29 who remained single in 1990. By contrast, there was an increase in the proportion of older married women aged 45–49, reflecting the increase in the marriage rate in the 1960s. Furthermore, there has been a large increase in the share of 25–29-year-old women with no children and a decline of 50 per cent in the share of those with three or more children. Increasingly, when women marry, they are seeking marriage and a career, rather than marriage *as* a career.

During the 1980s there was a marked increase in the participation rate of married women and mothers in the workforce. This increase was strongly correlated with age and education levels. These changes must be seen in the context of a slow-down in economic growth and mounting unemployment, which at present affects 20 per cent of the workforce. Education appears to be linked with postponement of childbirth as 69 per cent of those aged 25–29 with third-level education in 1990 had no children compared with 17 per cent with primary-level education only.

With regard to household arrangements in 1987, the most popular household options for 25–29-year-olds are marriage with one or two children (41 per cent), single and living at home (28 per cent) and single and living with other/s (12 per cent). For those aged 45–54, 80 per cent are married, living with their husbands, with or without children. In 1987 almost one in five women aged 25–29 lived in a household where both husband and wife were in the workforce.

Policy changes, notably the legalization of contraception in 1979 and the alterations in the tax code in 1980, have facilitated behavioural change regarding family size and workforce participation of married women. The decline in child support for those liable to income tax and the introduction of unmarried mothers' (now lone-parent) allowance have also been associated with a decline in marital, and an increase in non-marital, births. One interesting question, as yet unanswered, is why, with the increased availability of contraceptives, all the decline in births has taken place *within* marriage? Another question also awaiting answer relates to the consequences for children of the exclusion of fathers from some households. This occurs in those households where an allowance is paid to mothers with extra-marital children, on condition that they do not cohabit with the fathers.

The changes in conditions governing the employment of married women following Irish entry to the EU clearly had an important influence on the rise in labour-force participation of married women since the early 1970s. Evidence from the 1990 European Values Study related to women, motherhood and workforce participation shows that Irish attitudes approximate to those in the rest of Europe, which is not surprising, given the convergence of behavioural patterns.

To conclude, therefore, it may be said that the data presented in this chapter support the hypothetical impact models proposed. From the cross-section perspective, the pattern of child income support together with legal changes has supported the pluralization of family forms. While over time the economic 'pull' of married women and mothers into the workforce, combined with a 'push' out of the home related to a decline in the fertility, are compatible with some degree of polarization.

References

Becker, G.S. (1988), 'Family Economics and Macro Behaviour', *American Economic Review*, 78:1–13.
—— (1989), Introduction to Kennedy (1989).
—— (1991), *A Treatise on the Family*, 2nd edn., Harvard University Press, Cambridge, Mass.
Binchy, W. (1984), *A Casebook of Irish Family Law*, Professional Books, Abingdon, Oxon.
Blackwell, J. (1986), *Women in the Labour Force: a Statistical Digest*, Employment Equality Agency, Dublin.
—— (1988), 'Family Income Support: Policy Options', in B. Reynolds and S. Healy (eds.), *Poverty and Family Income Policy*, CMRS, Dublin: 109–69.
—— (1989), *Women in the Labour Force*, 2nd edn., Employment Equality Agency, Dublin.
Callan, T. and Farrell, B. (1991), *Women's Participation in the Labour Market*, Paper No. 91, NESC, Dublin.
—— and Nolan, B. (1988), 'Family Poverty in Ireland: a Survey-Based Analysis', in B. Reynolds and S. Healy (eds.), *Poverty and Family Income Policy*, CMRS, Dublin: 51–96.
Central Statistics Office (1980, 1990), *Live Register*, Stationery Office, Dublin.
Coleman, D.A. (1993), 'The Demographic Transition in Ireland in International Context', in J.H. Goldthorpe and C.T. Whelan (eds.), *The Development of Industrial Society in Ireland*, Oxford University Press, Oxford: 53–78.
Collins, L. (1986), *The Irish Housewife: a Portrait*, Irish Consumer Research, Dublin.
Commission of the European Communities (1990), *Childcare in the European Communities 1985–1990*, Women of Europe Supplement No. 31, August 1990, Brussels.
Economic and Social Research Institute (ESRI) (1987), *Survey of Income Distribution, Poverty and Usage of State Services*, ESRI, Dublin.
Fahey, A. (1983), 'Marital Fertility Control in Ireland: Some Evidence Examined', ESRI seminar paper, unpublished.
—— (1984), 'Woman, Work and Family', report prepared for Working Party on Women's Affairs and Family Law Reform, unpublished.
—— (1990), 'Measuring the Female Labour Supply: Conceptual and Procedural Problems in Irish Official Statistics', *Economic and Social Review*, 21: 163–91.
—— (1993), Review Article, *Economic and Social Review*, 24:199–210.
Fine-Davis, M. (1988), *Changing Gender Role Attitudes in Ireland: 1975–1986*, Vol. 1: *Attitudes towards the Role and Status of Women, 1975–1986*, First Report of the Second Joint Oireachtas Committee on Women's Rights, CSO, Dublin.
Flanagan, N. and Richardson, V. (1992), *Unmarried Mothers: a Social Profile*, University College, Dublin.

Garvey, D. (1988), 'What is the Best Measure of Employment and Unemployment in Ireland', *Journal of the Statistical and Social Inquiry Society of Ireland*, 25:185-227.

Gilligan, R. (1991), *Irish Child Care Services*, Institute of Public Administration, Dublin.

Kennedy, F. (1989), *Family, Economy and Government in Ireland*, ESRI, Dublin; reprinted 1991.

Kennedy, K.A. (1992), 'Real Convergence, the European Community and Ireland', *Journal of the Statistical and Social Inquiry Society of Ireland*, 26:213-57.

Larson Pyle, J. (1990), *The State and Women in the Economy: Lessons from Sex Discrimination in the Republic of Ireland*, State University of New York Press, Albany.

Mahon, E. (1991), *Motherhood, Work and Equal Opportunity*, Report of the Joint Oireachtas Committee on Women's Rights, Stationery Office, Dublin.

Millar, J., Keeper, S. and Davis, C. (1992), *Lone Parents, Poverty and Public Policy in Ireland*, Combat Poverty Agency, Dublin.

McCashin, A. (1993), *Lone Parents in the Republic of Ireland*, ESRI, Dublin.

McKenna, A. (1988), *Childcare and Equal Opportunities*, Employment Equality Agency, Dublin.

National Council for the Aged (1988), *Caring for the Elderly*, Part 1: *A Study of Carers at Home and in the Community*, Stationery Office, Dublin.

Nolan, B. and Callan, T. (1994), *Poverty and Policy in Ireland*, Gill & MacMillan, Dublin.

Office of the Minister of Justice (1992), *Marital Breakdown: a Review and Proposed Changes*, White Paper, Stationery Office, Dublin.

Roche, J.D. (1984), *Poverty and Income Maintenance Policies in Ireland, 1973-1980*, Institute of Public Administration, Dublin.

Shatter, A. (1986), *Family Law in the Republic of Ireland*, 3rd edn., Wolfhound Press, Dublin.

Walsh, B. M. (1993), 'Labour Force Participation and the Growth of Women's Employment, Ireland 1971-1991', *Economic and Social Review*, 24:369-400.

Ward, P. (1993), *Divorce in Ireland: Who Should Bear the Cost?* Cork University Press, Cork.

Whelan, C.T. (1992), 'Report to the Commission on the Status of Women', unpublished.

Working Party on Women's Affairs and Family Law Reform (1984), *Irishwomen: Agenda for Practical Action*, Stationery Office, Dublin.

8 Italy: Changing the Family from Within

ADELE MENNITI, ROSSELLA PALOMBA and LINDA LAURA
SABBADINI

*National Institute for Population Research, and National Statistical
Institute, Rome*

*The Italian family shows signs of a continuity of tradition, and there is not
much statistical evidence of new family behaviour. Pluralization of living
arrangements and polarization between marriage and alternatives to marriage
are concepts that are inadequate to describe the changes that have taken
place in Italian family patterns. In addition, family patterns in Italy show
an increasing tendency towards a simplification of structure. Our analysis,
focused on living arrangements of women at the early parental phase and
at the beginning of the post-parental phase, showed that during the 1980s
many changes did take place, but mostly within the framework of a unique
life choice: to get married and to have children. Changes in family patterns
and living arrangements of women in Italy are mainly changes in the timing
of marriage and childbirth.*

8.1. Family, Italian-Style

8.1.1. *Polarization or Pluralization of Living Arrangements?*

What are the characteristics of the Italian demographic situation concerning
the family? One of the major Italian characteristics is a lack of social 'visibil-
ity' of many of the changes in mentality and values that have occurred and
have prompted changes in demographic behaviour, without producing alternative living arrangements and life-styles. The changes in values in the marital
and procreative field have been mediated and translated within a scarcity
of demographic and household models that receive collective approval, instead of in a multiplicity of non-traditional events and life models. This seems
to suggest some specific 'Italian-style' behaviour in the demographic field,
not only in terms of a very low birth rate or an ageing population, but also
in the Italians' capacity to change without breaking with their history and

their convictions, and to adapt to new demands of social life in a very gentle way.

The Italian family model seems more strongly concentrated on the married couple. This does not mean that there have not been changes or that the Italian situation could be dismissed superficially with the label of traditionality. 'Traditional' and 'modern' are terms that have a relative, rather than absolute, meaning, depending on the historical and cultural context in which they are expressed. Certainly, Italy is not Sweden. The two countries do not have the same starting-point, nor are they experiencing the same changes in the family (Sabbadini, 1987). The Italian changes are not superficial or external. There are profound changes in internal family relations, in the meaning of family and marriage, and in everyday life. The change in families and living arrangements is a process of renewal 'from within' the family institution. Even if this change is more difficult to quantify statistically, this does not mean that it is any less relevant or significant.

8.1.2. *Demographic Trends in the 1980s*

Italian fertility began to show a definite fall between the late 1960s and early 1970s, and it has dropped so sharply that Italy now has the lowest fertility rate in the world. Births totalled 923,000 in 1960 and over one million in 1965, but they fell to 561,000 in 1992. The total fertility rate is well under replacement level, at 1.27 children per woman in 1991. Recent estimates show that the cohort fertility rate of women born in the mid-1950s is 1.8, and is probably 1.68 for women born in the late 1950s (ISTAT, 1993*b*).

The considerable fall in the number of marriages (from 7.6 per 1,000 in 1961 to 5.4 in 1992), although occurring later in Italy than in other European countries, seems to be slowing down now without, however, producing a diffusion of life-styles alongside the traditional married couple.

HOUSEHOLD STRUCTURE IN THE 1980S. The Italian family scenario has changed considerably over the past 20–30 years, the changes being characterized by an increasing 'simplification' of family and household structure. Various factors have caused changes in the make-up of the Italian family, factors that are hardly peculiar to the demographic history of Italy, but in fact are shared by most Western countries. General trends in both the structure and the evolution of Italian households include a remarkable decrease in the number of households containing more than one family. In addition, average family size has been reduced (from 3.6 members in 1961 to 2.8 in 1990), and the proportion of families with six or more members fell from 14.4 per cent of all families in 1961 to a mere 2.4 per cent in 1990 (Menniti, 1991; ISTAT, 1993*a*).

Owing to the drop in the birth rate, between 1983 and 1988 the number of families with at least one dependent minor child decreased from 8.117 million to 7.577 million, that is, from 51.8 to 47.5 per cent of the total number of families (ISTAT, 1989). The most common kind of household remains that of the married couple with children. Unmarried cohabitation, singles, LAT (living apart together) relationships, etc., widespread in other European countries, especially in Northern and Central Europe, are not common in Italy. Dynamics in marital status are above all related to the death of a spouse, since the divorce rate is still very low. (In 1991 the divorce rate was 7.8 per cent.)

In 1961 there were 13.7 million households in Italy; by 1990 that number had become 20.3 million. This rise is due to the increase in the number of those who live alone. One-person households made up 20.3 per cent of the total number of households in 1990, as compared with 10.7 per cent in 1961. It is important to note that one-person households are, largely, made up of aged women, who outlive men by ten years. Interestingly, the youngest age groups are underrepresented among those who live alone, because high unemployment rates and the scarcity of accommodation for rent in the big cities have discouraged young Italians from leaving the parental home. In fact, Italy has the lowest number in Europe of young people living alone (Kiernan, 1986; De Sandre, 1988).

ITALIAN WOMEN IN REPRODUCTIVE AGE: MARRIED WITH CHILDREN. The typical Italian woman between the ages of 25 and 44 is married (in over 80 per cent of the cases) and has one or two children. This has not changed over time, though the share of unmarried women increased in the 1980s by 3.4 percentage points, from 12.2 to 15.6 per cent (Table 8.1). With respect to the number of children, the two-child family model has become dominant at the expense of the three-child family. Nowadays, there are also more families with only one child. The percentage of women in the labour force saw the most significant change. In the 1980s, the proportion of housewives fell from 46 to 40 per cent, while that of working women increased to the same extent. In 1988, half of all women aged 25–44 were working. The position of Italian women in society seems to have changed more quickly than their position within the family.

Table 8.1. *Women aged 25–44 by civil status, employment status and number of children, Italy, 1983 and 1988 (%)*

	1983	1988
Civil status		
Unmarried	12.2	15.6
Married	85.0	81.4
Other	2.8	3.0
No. of children[a]		
0	8.4	11.0
1	28.2	29.6
2	41.7	43.6
3 or more	21.7	15.6
Employment status		
Employed	44.5	50.7
Housewife	45.8	40.0
Other	9.7	9.3

[a] Married women.

CHANGES IN THE FAMILY TYPES THAT ARE ALTERNATIVES TO MARRIAGE. Changes in the Italian family do not exhibit the revolutionary aspects shown in other countries. On the contrary, observing the percentages of women married or cohabiting with children, we have the impression that nothing has changed. In reality there have been changes, but only in a minority of households which are particularly difficult to analyse in statistical terms. Nothing has happened with regard to the de-institutionalization of marriage, since the number of women who cohabit without being married has remained the same, though the meaning of marriage seems to have changed, giving less importance to the Catholic requirements of indissolubility and procreative finality (Sabbadini, 1987). The proportion of married couples without children has slightly risen, and lone-parent families have become numerically more important, as shown in Table 8.2. Remaining with the minor household types, we observe that the number of women who live alone has doubled, and that of households containing more than one family has dropped significantly.

The ranking of household types in which women were living in 1983 and 1988 shows in the first three places married couples with children, married couples without children and lone-parent families, with a strengthening of position for the last two over the period. The most significant change is the reversal of ranking between positions 4 and 5: women who live alone moved up to fourth place in the ranking of household types, while women who live

Table 8.2. *Women aged 25–44, ranking by household type, Italy, 1983 and 1988*

	1983		1988	
Rank	%		%	Rank
1	80.1	Married couples with children	79.7	1
2	7.0	Married couples, without children	7.6	2
3	5.4	Lone-parent families[a]	6.6	3
4	4.2	More than 1 family	1.9	5
5	1.7	Singles[b]	2.6	4
6	0.8	Unmarried couples with children	0.7	6
7	0.4	Unmarried couples, without children	0.4	7
8	0.4	Other	0.4	8

[a] Regardless of the age of the children. [b] 'Single' is a person who lives alone.

in multi-family households not only fell in ranking, but also saw their proportional share drop by more than half.

8.1.3. *Family Studies in Italy*

In Italy, the development of family research was late compared with other countries, probably because of the Catholic view of life that considers the family a natural 'entity', a constant and an unchangeable aspect of the social structure (CISP, 1982*a*). Since 1980, however, the family has been the object of growing interest on the part of demographers, sociologists and other social scientists, owing to the significant changes that have taken place in its structure and its functions (CISP, 1982*a* and 1982*b*; ISTAT, 1986; Scabini and Donati, 1988; Menniti, 1991; Donati, 1992). Even research institutes and national bodies have shown a growing interest in studies on the family, by sponsoring and funding research projects on this theme. In particular, the CNR (National Council of Research) financed a three-year interdisciplinary project to investigate changes in Italian families and households in the 1980s from a demographic, juridical, economic and social point of view; and ISTAT (National Statistical Institute) has carried out surveys since 1983 on household and family structure and behaviour (ISTAT, 1993*a*).

8.1.4. *Methods and Data Sources*

Until a few years ago, any research on the family in Italy could refer to census data only, but recently ISTAT carried out sample surveys on families and households. These sample surveys allow researchers to conduct more accurate analyses, both on morphological characteristics of households and on various aspects of familial behaviour. Data coming from censuses and from sample surveys are not completely comparable, because the sample units differ. (It is the families of the Population Register in the census, and the *de facto* households in the surveys.)

In this chapter we make use of two surveys carried out by ISTAT during the 1980s. The first one dealt with 'Structure and Behaviour of the Family' and was carried out in 1983 among a sample of 28,408 households with a total of 91,458 people (ISTAT, 1985). The second survey is the Multi-purpose Survey (II cycle) and was carried out in 1988 among a sample of about 23,000 households with a total of 70,000 people. Both surveys are representative of Italian households.

For purposes of international comparison, it is necessary to define 'household' and 'family' as used in our surveys. In the Italian surveys, 'household' is defined as the group of people who live together, being bound together by relationships of close or distant blood-ties, affection or friendship. The term 'family' means a group of people bound together by a couple bond and/or parent–child ties.

Households are classified according to the number of families that they have, and thus we may have households with no family, with one family, and with more than one family[1]. The families are identified according to the relationships between the members.

8.2. Family Policies in Italy

8.2.1. *A Synthesis of the Main Family-Related Policies in Italy*

The system of Italian family policies is not a monolithic body of measures that favours families. Many policies are implemented at a local or regional level. Furthermore, it is difficult to estimate what political measures might have affected family life and structure. In fact, policies for housing, social services, work or education are all interventions that in some way, directly or indirectly, influence familial behaviour of the citizens. Italian legislation

---

[1] According to the Italian household classification, non-family households include one-person households, a parent plus separated/divorced child(ren), two or more relatives or a group of non-relatives. One-family households include married/unmarried couples with or without children and one-parent families. Households with two or more families have two or more family units. Every type of family or household can include one or more non-family members.

recognizes as family only the 'married couple', though some years ago a proposal of law was presented that extended to cohabitees the same rights and duties that spouses have; this law, however, was not yet passed.

We will describe here, very synthetically, the most significant aspects of Italian family policies, plus those that are particularly lacking. Specifically, we will consider maternity leave, child allowances, part-time job opportunities and the changes that came about with the New Family Law. We also will give some information on local regulations when relevant for better understanding the Italian situation.

COMPULSORY MATERNITY LEAVE. In Italy the law on maternity protection was introduced in 1971 (law 1204/71). Maternity leave is compulsory for two months before the expected date of delivery, for the period between the expected and actual dates of delivery, and for three months after delivery. Maternity benefits depend on the salary of the working woman. For employees working in the public and private sectors during this period, the payments amount to 80 per cent of the last month's salary (excluding benefits). For self-employed professionals, the state pays 80 per cent of the average monthly salary declared by them, but never less than the minimum wage. For other self-employed people (in agriculture, arts, crafts and trade), the state pays 80 per cent of the minimum wage received in the year before delivery. As far as other benefits are concerned (pension rights, holidays), periods of maternity leave are considered equivalent to periods of work for the woman. Female workers may not be dismissed during pregnancy, or until their child has reached its first birthday. If the woman has a job that could be considered too tiring or dangerous for her health during pregnancy, she must be transferred to some more suitable department in the same firm; if this is not possible, she may stay at home. In particular circumstances, such as the death of the mother (law 903/77), the father may take the compulsory maternity leave.

ADDITIONAL MATERNITY LEAVE AND OTHER PROVISIONS. After compulsory maternity leave, the mother who is working in either the public or private sector may stay at home for six months during the first year of the life of her child (additional maternity leave) and may be absent from work for reasons of sickness of the child until its third year. Self-employed mothers cannot benefit from these additional leaves. During the period of optional maternity leave, the salary is reduced by 30 per cent, whereas in periods of leave for illness of the child the salary equals that stipulated for sickness of the worker. Furthermore, the mother's daily work schedule is reduced by two hours until the child's first birthday, without any wage reduction.

CHILD ALLOWANCES. Throughout the years, child allowances in Italy have undergone changes regarding the rules for their payment and their amount. Until a few years ago, family allowances were paid irrespective of income since children were seen as an economic burden, and as such the state felt a duty to contribute. Now child allowance benefits vary according to the total income of the family and the number of family members. Allowances are paid for children under 18 years of age. The amount of the child allowances is fairly small, as shown in Table 8.3*a*, and Italians do not consider this economic policy measure an effective support structure in the raising of children. For particularly needy families or for those in difficulties, such as lone-parent families and families in which there is a disabled child or a grown-up child that for mental or physical reasons is unfit to work, the law stipulates a very modest increase in the child allowance.

Table 8.3*a*. *Italian family allowances by family income and number of members of the family, 1 January 1992 (ECU)*

Family income (ECU)	Family size (no. of children)					
	2	3	4	5	6	7+
Up to 9,273	58	104	175	228	281	334
9,274 – 11,591	46	91	152	213	273	295
11,592 – 13,909	38	84	129	197	266	256
13,910 – 16,226	15	61	91	167	251	289
16,227 – 18,545	–	38	84	152	243	273
18,546 – 20,863	–	15	61	129	228	258
20,864 – 23,180	–	–	39	91	205	235
23,181 – 25,498	–	–	15	46	182	213
25,499 – 27,816	–	–	–	–	159	197
27,817 – 30,134	–	–	–	–	76	175
30,135 – 32,452	–	–	–	–	–	76
Over 32,452	–	–	–	–	–	–

Family allowances are paid by the Institute of Social Welfare by drawing from a specific fund (the Fund for Family Allowances), built up by deducting an income-related percentage of the employees' salaries. This system produces a growing credit balance between the total sum deposited by employees and the 'withdrawals', i.e. the family allowances paid to the families. For example, in 1987 over 13,000 billion lire were deposited in the fund and only 4,200 billion lire were withdrawn. This represents a credit balance of

69.3 per cent. (In 1977 it was 38.6 per cent.) This balance is funnelled by the Institute of Social Welfare into several projects, but none designed for the benefit of families.

PART-TIME JOBS. In Italy, part-time work is not very widespread. Many factors contribute to this Italian particularity. Above all, part-time labour has been introduced only recently by a law (law 863 of 19 December 1984) stipulating its recognition in work contracts.[2] In addition, politicians did not push for a diffusion of part-time contracts, while trade unions, which play a central role in the world of Italian labour, were not particularly supportive of a kind of contract that they considered suitable only for work at a low level of qualification, and difficult to manage (Maruani *et al.*, 1990).

Although part-time jobs are generally considered particularly favourable for mothers with small children, who thus would be able to reconcile family, children and work, it has been noted that part-time work may result in the occupational segregation of women and in discriminating attitudes against them on the job (Hoem, 1992; Palomba and Menniti, 1991). It is also necessary to stress that the work schedule is established by the company with production criteria in mind, and thus, the part-time option often does not ease the burden of family commitments for a working mother. Furthermore, Italian labour unions are pressing for a general reduction of the work schedule: currently, in Italy the average work week does not exceed 40 hours, and it is 36 hours or fewer in the public sector (Table 8.3*b*).

Beyond these contextual considerations, the needs of both employees and employers should be considered. From the employee's point of view, the part-time job is not advantageous since, generally speaking, the demand for part-time workers is concentrated at levels of ability lower than that of skilled workers, on jobs to which the lowest pay levels apply. Furthermore, the part-time job offers limited career promotion and little possibility of an increase in salary (overtime, seniority, other benefits). From the employer's economic point of view, there are several disadvantages in hiring part-time workers. If the salary of part-time workers is a percentage of that of full-time workers, the company is at a disadvantage when distributing the fixed costs

---

[2] In Italy, a part-time job means either a reduced number of daily working hours, or a reduction in the number of days worked per week. With regard to wages, the law does not set precise rules, since in Italy these are included in national employment contracts. Usually the principle of proportionality is applied. Other benefits apply equally to both full-time and part-time workers (weekends, public holidays, annual leave, sick pay, health services, family allowances) as long as there are at least 24 working hours a week. Still other benefits (such as severance payment, unemployment benefits, and pensions) are paid proportional to the length of the period in service.

Table 8.3*b*. *Work schedules in different countries*

Country	Full-time		Part-time	
	hrs/week	weeks/yr	hrs/week	weeks/yr
Australia	35 or more	52	less than 35 or	less than 52
Canada	40 or more	52	less than 40 or	less than 52
Former FRG	40 or more	52	less than 40 or	less than 52
Netherlands	38 or more	52	less than 38 or	less than 52
Sweden	1872 hours per year		1872 hours per year	
Italy	36 on average		about 50% of full-time schedule	
UK	40 or more	52	less than 40 or	less than 52

Source: McLanahan *et al.* (1992).

(administrative, research, selection for hiring, formation) (Ministero del Lavoro e della Previdenza Sociale, 1988). In light of the current economic crisis and unemployment, the availability of part-time jobs is actually being reconsidered.

THE FAMILY LAW: FROM INEQUALITY TO EQUALITY OF THE MARRIED COUPLE. Until the 1950s, the Italian legislation referred to a family model, established in the Civil Code, which defined a hierarchical and authoritarian family structure in which the male played a determining role. In fact, the husband had a duty to protect the wife, keep her close to him and supply her with all that was necessary to live. But the woman was in a position of inferiority, considered incapable of facing some situations and difficulties of life. For example, in the case of his death, the husband had the right to establish, via explicit instructions, how the wife should raise and educate the children. With the new Family Law of 1975, the juridical setting has changed. The wives have acquired the same rights and obligations, and the organization of the family life is decided jointly, keeping in mind the needs of the household's members. The husband as head of the family has disappeared in Italian legislation, and the concept of the 'authority of the father' has been substituted by that of 'authority of both parents' (Vincenzi Amato, 1988).

8.2.2. *Possible Impacts of Existing Family Laws on Household Structures*

Concrete difficulties exist in measuring the degree of influence of political measures on the family structure. No one, not even demographers or politicians, could ever establish with certainty whether a specific change in the trends of fertility or in the family structure was due to a given political action or whether, instead, this change would have shown up anyway, maybe at a different time. Who could confirm with certainty that in Italy such a sharp drop in the birth rate as has occurred recently should be attributed to the low family allowances? And who could confirm that an increase in these allowances would provoke an increase in the number of children per woman? But who could affirm the contrary, i.e. that the absence of economic support for Italian families with children did not have a negative effect on the number of children per woman?

The existence of laws makes for a very limited approximate vision of their effects, and the relationship between the family and the state is very complex. Much depends on the social and personal circumstances of each family and individual. On the other hand, the state itself is not a simple entity: on the contrary, it consists of a variety of institutions, dimensions (local, regional, etc.) and interventions, sometimes self-contradicting and sending conflicting messages to its citizens. All this invites us to use prudence in evaluating the effects of political actions and measures on the familial field, or in reducing them to the demographic environment alone.

In Italy it is very difficult for citizens to obtain or even to be informed about the economic and other benefits to which they are entitled. The institutional pattern has become more and more complicated and increasingly more out of touch with the real needs of families. However, positive exceptions exist, and there are Italian regions or provinces where efforts have been made to simplify the procedures or to make them more easily accessible.

Some household types, such as one-parent families – those headed by unmarried mothers in particular – or very large families, are favoured over others. This could have led to fictitious separations or late marriages in order for couples to benefit from a particular measure, thus producing unwanted demographic effects. Second marriages and reconstituted families are still very rare, and this fact might be attributed to the existing law on divorce, which maintains economic links (reversibility pension, alimonies, etc.) between the divorced spouses until one of them remarries.

In the field of housing, the state intervenes by renting dwellings to needy families at particularly low rates established by the 'social rent ceiling'. The state even lends funds for the purchase of the first house. Large families and families with only one parent are favoured in housing allocation. Other measures, the so-called 'housing rent laws', had the effect of worsening the situation on the housing market. These laws establish a fair rent policy for houses and set rules for tenant eviction, but unwanted effects included stagnation of residential mobility within the rental sector of the housing market, encouraging existing tenants to stay put and creating problems for young people wanting to leave their parents' houses or to marry and find homes of their own.

8.3. Women, Marriage and the Family

8.3.1. *Timing of Critical Events in Italy*

Women are an ideal frame of observation regarding changes within the family, though we often tend to consider them as a 'homogeneous group for social membership, territorial location and age' (Saraceno, 1988:153). Age is of particular importance because, on the one hand, it is related to different phases of individual and family life and, on the other, it situates the female experience in different historical contexts. Two ages are of particular interest in this volume: the age at the early parental phase and the age at the beginning of the post-parental phase.

As age at the early parental phase, we considered the median age of women when their first child is about two years old. In Italy, the two selected cohorts were: 1955–9 for 1983, and 1960–4 for 1988 (women aged 24–28). Concerning the age at the beginning of the post-parental phase, we did not use the median age of women when at least one child had left the parental home (which is around 55–60), because at that age all women will have left the labour market. Since working mothers are a very interesting category to analyse both on the national and on the international level, we decided to take the 1930–4 cohorts for 1983 and the 1935–9 cohorts for 1988, that is women 49–53 years old, as indicating the beginning of the post-parental phase. At this age, more than 40 per cent of married women with children had entered the post-parental phase, but were still far away from retirement age.

8.3.2. *The Four Cohorts: The Italian Context*

THE GENERATIONS OF THE 'FIRST BIG CHANGES'. Women born in the 1930s, who at the two moments of observation were between 49 and 53 years old, faced the big transformations of Italian society, and they represent a fairly homogeneous group. Born during the Fascist period and raised in wartime, they were, when compared with their parents' generation and with their mothers in particular, the first ones to benefit from increasing educational levels and to experience the new prosperity and Italian consumerism in daily and family life. In fact, these generations are old enough to have seen the arrival of household appliances and the diffusion of private transportation and the mass media. Refrigerators, washing-machines, televisions and private cars, to list just a few examples, became common goods on the Italian market in the 1960s when these women were already grown up and probably married. Furthermore, this cohort witnessed the most significant changes of our legislation in terms of the family: divorce, abortion, new family laws.

Concerning the participation of these women on the labour market, on the one hand, thanks to the greater level of well-being in the country and to the increasing urbanization that came about during their youth, middle-class women aspired to the model of the 'full-time housewife' as they never had done before. On the other hand, other women of the same cohort entered the world of labour and created the first core of the future army of women committed to clerical and teaching careers.

THE 'LAST FEMINISTS' AND THE 'GENERATION OF ACQUIRED RIGHTS'. The political–cultural context in which the younger women, who were 24–28 years old, were raised and have lived in the two periods of observation is completely different, so that they make up two notably not-homogeneous groups concerning expectations, values and family life. The generation born near the end of the 1950s was entering adulthood in the 1970s when feminism, the women's liberation movement, and the debates on 'gender', equality between the sexes and maternity as a choice all blossomed. All this influenced their decisions in the fields of marriage, children and work. These 'last feminists' were the first to experience the contradiction of an increase in female employment and, at the same time, female unemployment, because their entrance into the labour force coincided with a phase of economic recession.

The youngest women, born in the mid-1960s, may be defined as the generation of 'acquired rights'. For them, many of the victories of the generations of women from preceding cohorts are a 'natural' part of social and family life. Mass education, social services, birth control and policies for youth were a 'normal' part of their cultural context (Saraceno, 1991). Work was for many of them an obvious next step after their educational career, even if they were aware of the fact that the employment crisis would make their participation in the labour force difficult.

Finally, we note that among the delineated cohorts there can exist a bond of descent, in the sense that the mothers of some of the younger women may belong to the cohorts of the post-parental phase.

Table 8.4. *Women at early parental and post-parental phases,*
by civil status and number of children, Italy, 1983 and 1988 (%)

	49–53 years		24–28 years	
	1983	1988	1983	1988
Civil status				
Unmarried	7.3	5.9	31.3	40.9
Married	83.3	84.6	67.4	58.6
Divorced, separated	1.5	2.4	1.0	0.4
Widows	7.9	7.1	0.2	0.1
Number of children[a]				
0	6.8	7.2	21.7	26.8
1	17.4	15.5	44.8	45.9
2	34.3	40.2	27.7	24.2
3 and more	41.5	34.7	5.8	3.1

[a] Married women.

8.3.3. Choices in the Field of Marriage and Children: from the Strengthening of the Two-Child Model to its Crisis

Women aged 49–53 are to a large extent married (83.3 and 84.6 per cent respectively in the two years of observation), but the effects of the increase in marriage instability had begun to emerge: in 1988, 2.4 per cent of this age group were separated or divorced (Table 8.4).

The most significant difference between the two cohorts has to do with the number of children. Whereas in the first cohort (those born between 1930 and 1934) 41.5 per cent of married women had three or more children and 34.3 per cent had two children, in the second cohort (born 1935–9) the percentages are literally reversed: 34.7 per cent had three or more children and 40.2 per cent had two (Table 8.4). Basically, passing from one generation to the other we notice a strengthening of the two-child model.

The process in the younger generations is even more disruptive. Differences emerge both in the propensity to get married and in that to give birth. Between 1983 and 1988, the proportion of unmarried women rose from 31.3 to 40.9 per cent, almost completely at the cost of the proportion of married women (dropping from 67.4 to 58.6 per cent). Women who were 24–28 years old got married less, but on top of that they also had fewer children. In 1988, 26.8 per cent of younger married women did not have any children, against 21.7 per cent in 1983. The proportion of women with a child showed a small increase too. The rank order changed in the five years under observation: in 1988 we find women with one child in first place, followed by women without children, women with two children coming on in third place only.

Thus, the tendency towards a reduction in the number of children has increased: whereas mothers born in 1935–9 contributed to the passage from the three-and-more-child model to the two-child model, it is their daughters who are now postponing marriage and childbirth and are putting the two-child model into crisis.

8.4. Women and Household Arrangements at the Parental and Post-parental Phases

Changes in the Italian family and household arrangements seem to involve changes in the timing of demographic events like births and marriages. This could be due to other factors of increasing importance for women, above all in the fields of education and work. It is thus important to consider these two aspects when examining the family life of women.[3]

8.4.1. *The Increase in Levels of Education*

Notably large differences in education level between the younger and older cohorts are shown in Table 8.5. Most 49–53-year-old women finished elementary school only, but even for women born in the late 1930s the level of education had risen somewhat compared with women born in the early 1930s. Most of the younger women in this age group fulfilled at least minimum educational requirements (junior high school). Furthermore, we notice that between the two groups of the younger generations a further increase in the level of education took place: between 1983 and 1988 there was a 6 percentage point rise in the completion of junior high school and a 5 percentage point increase in the completion of high school education.

Mass schooling involved the younger generations of women, who experienced a completely new situation compared with that of their mothers. Analysis of the level of education attained by mothers by their number of children shows that in the younger generation the percentage of women

---

[3] In order to identify two-income families, we limited ourselves to considering the employment status of women. In fact, female labour-force participation introduced the necessity of considering those families in which both spouses work as a separate category. Married men have high rates of employment, whereas families in which only the wife works are a small minority. We have thus hypothesized that when the woman works, we can speak of a two-income family.

Table 8.5. *Women at early parental and postparental phases,*
by level of education, Italy, 1983 and 1988 (%)

| Educational | 49–53 years | | 24–28 years | |
level attained	1983	1988	1983	1988
No qualification	21.5	12.0	1.9	0.8
Elementary	56.0	55.9	18.4	8.4
Junior high school	13.3	19.6	42.5	48.6
High school	7.1	9.4	32.4	37.8
University	2.1	3.1	4.8	4.3

Table 8.6. *Women at early parental and postparental phases, by level of education*
and number of children, Italy, 1983-1988 (%)

No. of children	University		High school		Junior high school		Elementary		No qualification	
	1983	1988	1983	1988	1983	1988	1983	1988	1983	1988
Women at early parental phase										
0	89.1	88.6	64.1	71.0	37.2	47.2	22.6	31.5	37.4	37.8
1	9.6	10.3	25.4	20.2	38.3	34.5	32.1	27.6	22.0	10.8
2	1.2	1.1	10.0	8.5	21.8	16.6	32.2	31.6	24.3	31.3
3 or more	0.0	–	0.6	0.1	3.2	1.7	13.1	9.2	16.4	20.1
Women at postparental phase										
0	28.6	15.2	19.1	19.7	17.6	16.4	11.9	8.7	9.8	14.6
1	10.9	17.1	13.2	17.5	17.2	18.3	18.3	18.3	13.3	12.6
2	26.5	47.7	40.9	41.5	37.5	38.4	33.1	39.4	24.6	27.0
3 or more	25.2	19.9	26.8	21.3	27.7	26.9	36.7	33.6	52.3	45.8

without children increases at all levels of education. This happens particularly
for women who have completed high school (from 64.1 to 71.0 per cent)
and junior high school (from 37.2 to 47.2 per cent). Among women aged
49–53, the two-child model is particularly frequent among better-educated
women, while the three-child model is more widespread among women with
only elementary-school education (Table 8.6).

8.4.2. *The Increase in Labour-Force Participation*

Housewives have diminished in number and the numbers of working women
and women looking for work have increased: this is the situation among
the two youngest generations analysed. The percentage of employed women
among 24–28-year-olds is greater than that among 49–53-year-olds, and

Table 8.7. *Women at early parental and post-parental phases,*
by occupational and vocational status, Italy, 1983 and 1988 (%)

Status	24–28 years		49–53 years	
	1983	1988	1983	1988
Occupational				
Employed	44.5	47.7	32.2	32.9
Unemployed	12.3	14.6	1.3	1.1
Housewife	34.5	30.3	58.6	57.9
Other	8.7	7.4	7.9	8.1
Vocational				
Manager	3.6	4.2	3.8	5.3
White collar	48.2	49.6	18.7	27.9
Blue collar	28.6	27.4	29.4	22.6
Other	19.6	18.8	48.1	44.2

even more interesting is the fact that half of the employed young women
are white-collar workers (although few of them are yet managers), whereas
among older women there is a larger proportion employed in 'other activities'
(Table 8.7).

Among employed women of the younger generation, the majority are without children. The opposite is the case for housewives (Table 8.8), but it is
interesting to note how, even for housewives, over a time span of five years
the proportion of women without children has increased (from 17.1 to 21.7
per cent) at the cost of those with two or three children. The choice of the

Table 8.8. *Employed and housewife: married women at early*
parental and post-parental phases, by number of children, Italy,
1983 and 1988 (%)

No. of children	Employed		Housewife	
	1983	1988	1983	1988
Women at early parental phase				
0	54.7	65.8	17.1	21.7
1	32.1	24.4	39.9	40.1
2	11.6	6.4	35.0	33.3
3 or more	1.7	0.6	8.0	4.8
Women at post-parental phase				
0	18.4	17.7	9.0	7.5
1	17.8	17.4	15.3	16.8
2	32.5	38.9	32.8	39.2
3 or more	31.4	26.0	42.8	36.6

two-child model by the generation born in 1935–9 is more evident for working women than for housewives.

8.4.3. *Household Arrangements in the 1980s*

As shown in Table 8.9, between 1983 and 1988 in the ranking of living arrangements of women in the post-parental phase the first two places have remained unchanged, but starting from the third place the situation has been turned upside down. The most interesting fact that emerges from the analysis of the family structure of 49–53-year-old women in 1983 and 1988 is that married women without children at home who do not work moved from third to fifth place. In third and fourth place in 1988 we find married women with one or with two children.

These rank-order changes can easily be explained by the increasing lengthening of stay of children in the parental home, which pushed upward the mother's age at the beginning of the empty-nest phase even during this five-year time span. It is also interesting how the proportion of women in households with more than one family (not shown in our ranking) has more than halved (from 5.9 per cent in 1983 to 1.4 per cent in 1988), showing the decline of this type of household and confirming that the nuclear family has definitely prevailed over the extended family.

Table 8.9. *Household arrangement rank order:[a] women at post-parental phase, Italy, 1983 and 1988*

1983				1988
Rank	%		%	Rank
1	23	Married, more than 3 children, not employed	22	1
2	17	Married, 2 children, not employed	20	2
3	9	Married, without children, not employed	8	5
4	8	Married, more than 3 children, employed	7	7
4	8	Lone mothers	8	5
6	7	Married, 2 children, employed	10	3
6	7	Married, 1 child not employed	9	4
8	5	Married, without children, employed	4	8
9	3	Married, 1 child, employed	3	10
9	3	Living alone	4	8
10	1	Cohabiting	1	9

[a] Household arrangements with less than 1% are not included.

Table 8.10. *Household arrangement rank order:ᵃ women at early parental phase, Italy, 1983 and 1988*

1983			1988	
Rank	%		%	Rank
1	15	Married, 1 child, not employed	15	2
2	13	Married, 2 children, not employed	11	4
3	12	Married, 1 child, employed	11	4
3	12	Still living with parents, not employed	14	3
5	11	Still living with parents, employed	17	1
6	8	Married, without children, employed	9	6
7	6	Married, without children, not employed	5	7
8	5	Still living with one parent	5	7
9	4	Married, 2 children, employed	3	9
10	3	Married, more than 3 children, not employed	2	11
11	1	Single	3	9
11	1	Married, more than 3 children, employed	–	14
11	1	Cohabiting	1	12
11	1	Lone mother	1	12

ᵃ Household arrangements with less than 1% are not included.

On the other hand, when analysing the situation of the younger generations, we notice some aspects that mirror the situation of the older ones. During these five years, the proportion of women living in couples with children has increased, but this increase is the net result of a decrease in the proportion of women living in couples with children as 'mothers' and an increase in the proportion living in families as 'daughters' (from 23 to 31 per cent; Table 8.10). The most interesting change in the rank order is the new position of women who are still living with their parents and are employed, a category that in 1988 was in first place, up from only fifth in 1983!

The increasing length of stay in the parental home for women born in 1960–4 cannot be attributed to economic difficulties alone, since most 'daughters' do work, contrary to the 1955–9 cohort. In addition, among women born in 1960–4 who are mothers with children, the proportion of those who have two or more children has decreased. The two situations mirror each other: during these five years, the age at the beginning of the empty nest increases for mothers because the children remain in the family for a longer time, just as the age when the daughters leave the family increases.

But what happens if we examine the participation of women in the labour market? The younger cohorts show higher employment rates than the older ones; however, in the five-year span of observation, only the employment

Table 8.11. *Female employment rates by age, Italy, 1983 and 1988*

No. of children	24–28 years		49–53 years	
	1983	1988	1983	1988
0	53.5	57.7	45.4	48.0
1	45.9	42.7	34.6	32.9
2	27.2	21.5	32.3	33.6
3 or more	19.0	15.7	26.5	26.6
Total	44.5	47.7	32.2	32.9

rate among younger women without children has increased (Table 8.11). Is there just a change in timing hidden beneath these facts, or does it indicate the emergence of quite new female life strategies?

8.4.4. *Older and Younger Cohorts: Two Situations that Mirror Each Other?*

In the space of five years, profound modifications have occurred for both women 49–53 years old and for those 24–28 years old. But it is interesting to examine the problem of the crossed dialectics between the behaviour of the mothers and that of their daughters. We also must ask ourselves, to what extent do such transformations depend on the behaviour of the specific cohorts of women, and to what extent might they be induced by the behaviour of other individuals, for example their children? In particular, the generation born in 1935–9 looks like the one in which the two aspects are most synthesized. On the one hand, we have noted an increasing age at entering the empty-nest phase, as a consequence of the behaviour of the children, who remain longer at home and thus create family life situations different from those of previous generations. On the other hand, there emerges a strengthening of the two-child model among working mothers that is due mainly to women born in 1935–9. The everyday life of these women is the synthesis of innovative decisions in the field of maternity and work taken by themselves, and of changes caused by the behaviour of their children.

Looking at family types from the point of view of the younger generations, we notice that their life choices can be viewed as the continuation of a process started by their mothers: their level of education has increased, as has their participation in the labour market; they continued to reduce fertility, but alternative family forms do not emerge strongly. Are these changes in timing, or are they changes in strategies for women born in 1960–4? How much might all this be tied to economic difficulties, such as the housing shortage or unemployment, and thus will have period effects only on reproductive and familial behaviour? How much does the increasing participation in the labour market contribute to a further reduction in fertility? It is difficult to say. But one thing is certain: the Italian welfare society has 'soothed to sleep' the young within the family, taking away their challenges. Youth autonomy does not necessarily imply leaving the home: rather, it comes with work. This change of mentality had an enormous influence on the behaviour of the younger cohorts, not only in relation to family structure but, above all, in family relationships. How deep a mark it makes on future family life models is difficult to say.

In the light of these results, we cannot but confirm that we face changes that are typically Italian. Changes in the phases of the family life cycle that have been identified in some countries are not meaningful for or applicable to Italy. It is one thing to enter the empty-nest phase at 40 years of age, and another to enter it at retirement age or even later. The lives of women are affected by other changes, too: in values, in cultural determinants, and in the types of relationship within the nuclear family and in the wider kin network. New categories and new instruments, therefore, are necessary to analyse demographic and social trends in the Italian family.

8.5. Organization of Everyday Life

Today, people have fuller lives than they had in the past. Work, study and leisure time are all likely to occupy part of their time – if only briefly. A fuller life means greater complexity in managing and planning the daily life of oneself and one's family, requiring a series of choices and adjustments related to time management. Services for the care of children can be an important help for families and in particular for women, and thus they deserve particular attention. We will describe the situation of child-care services both for pre-school children (3–5 years old) and for infants (0–3 years old). We also will describe some characteristics of the Italian family network and its functioning in supporting young couples with children.

8.5.1. *Child-Care Centres and Kindergartens*

In Italy, there is a fairly diffused system of kindergartens for pre-school children, but care centres for children aged 0–3 are scarce, above all in the central and southern parts of the country. The child-care centres all operate on a local level (municipalities) while 49 per cent of the kindergartens are funded by the state, 15 per cent by the municipality and the rest are run by religious institutes or are privately owned and operated. Access to child-care services and kindergartens is established according to family income and family type. Lone mothers are in general favoured over other families, and families with disabled children are similarly privileged. Different additional priorities may be set by local authorities.

Kindergartens for 3–5-year-old children are free and are open eight hours a day when there is a meal service in the school;[4] 87 per cent of children attend kindergarten, and of these, about 70 per cent remain there for more than seven hours a day. This high attendance at kindergarten is due to an Italian school tradition.

The situation for children aged 0–3 is different. Based on the latest available data, only 5 per cent of children under 3 years of age attend child-care centres. Parents pay up to an average of 36 per cent of the cost, depending on the family income; in some areas, the fees paid by the parents are lower since local authorities pay most of the cost. Child-care centres are open in general ten hours a day, and it is easier to obtain access to this service the younger the children are.

Research carried out among mothers who use these services shows that a consistent part of parental child care continues to be given by mothers. The mothers of very small children (0–3 years old), who work from five to eight hours a day outside the home, tend to devote between one and eight hours a day to their children. A heavy work load indeed, to which is added or – better yet – overlapped three to eight hours spent daily on housework (Bimbi, 1990). Infant services are thus a help, but certainly they do not relieve, nor are they intended to relieve, the woman completely from this task. Certainly, by co-ordinating the morning opening time of the infant services with the work schedule and by offering services for a longer period, better results could be obtained. Experiments along these lines have been conducted in several areas in Italy. The results were satisfactory and the additional expenses, contrary to what was expected, were low, because the experiment concentrated on the improvement of already existing centres.

---

[4] The primary school is open from four to six hours a day, depending on the existence of school cafeterias.

8.5.2. *Family Network*

Many scholars debate the importance of the family network for the functioning and the organization of the family, in particular regarding child care and other forms of support, above all economic support. Working mothers with small children who can count on the family network have at least partially resolved their problem. For the state, the presence of this family solidarity means less economic pressure on the welfare system. In Italy the family network seems to be alive and working. This is due, on the one hand, to a chronic political neglect in the social field and, on the other, to a persistent lack of confidence in some public structures which are considered inefficient and/or inadequate (nurseries, homes for the aged, etc.).

Particularly in the care of small children, grandparents (particularly grandmothers) and aunts are among the principal care-givers when the children are not at school (Table 8.12). It should be noted that a sizeable proportion of children remain alone, without adult surveillance, when their parents are at work.

The amount of help given seems to depend partly on the structure of the receiving family. There are differences in the support received by married couples with children and by lone mothers. Lone mothers seem to depend more on a network of friends and acquaintances or other relatives as opposed to parents or in-laws than a married couple would (Golini *et al.*, 1987). Probably the interruption of marriage implies a breakdown of some ties in the family network, for example that of the ex-in-laws. The number of family members willing to help the one-parent family is thus reduced and the lone mothers must look in other directions for help. Economic support that is given in 75 per cent of cases by parents/parents-in-law decreases to 44 per

Table 8.12. *Care of children under 10 years, by persons who take care of them when parents are working, Italy, 1983 (%)*

Care-givers	Age of children			
	0–2	3–5	6–10	Total
Grandparents	45.5	46.1	35.9	41.2
Other relatives	9.1	8.9	9.7	9.3
Non-relatives	3.2	3.1	4.3	3.7
Paid help	4.5	3.5	2.6	3.3
Nobody	30.2	32.8	39.6	35.4
No need of care	7.6	5.5	7.9	7.1

Source: ISTAT (1985).

cent for one-parent families. Parents/parents-in-law help in housework and child care, but here again, the help is strongly reduced for lone mothers, for whom non-relatives become more important. Regarding financial support, non-relatives account for 6 per cent of this in the case of married couples and for 27 per cent in that of one-parent families; 12 per cent of married couples and 37 per cent of one-parent families receive non-monetary help from non-relatives in running the house.

We are not able to determine the relationship between the type and amount of help received and the occupational status of women. Other studies have pointed out that there seems to be no direct relation between the degree of help in caring for children by the family network and the working activity of the mother. The most important factor is the physical distance between those giving and those receiving help. This distance, despite modern means of communication and transportation, continues to inhibit partly the possibility of giving/receiving help.

8.5.3. *Gender Roles within the Household*

It has been noted that 'the family of the man differs from that of the woman' because returning home from the job, or staying home and taking care of the children, has different meanings for men and women. In every family there is someone who prepares meals for the others, washes and irons clothes, cleans the house and takes care of the children. That 'someone' has traditionally been a female. Many elements, e.g. women with (paid) jobs, higher education for women, equality on the juridical level between spouses and equal expectations in the division of the roles within the couple, make us think that something is causing changes in the organization of family life in Italy.

When we analyse the use of time of men and women, however, we see that everyday behaviour falls short of opinions and expectations (Palomba and Sabbadini, 1992). Generally speaking, the participation of Italian men in housework is very limited and is independent of the working activity of the wife. Even the number of children has little influence on getting the man to make a greater contribution to domestic activities. The domestic participation of fathers remains constant at about two hours a day even with an increase in the number of children, while that of women grows proportionately with an increase in the number of children, rising from a little more than four hours a day devoted to the family if there are no children to eight hours a day if there are three or more children (Palomba and Sabbadini, 1992).

Parents dedicate one and a half hours a day to caring for each child under the age of 14, but, while 65 per cent of the women who have children are daily involved in this activity (the percentage rises notably in the case of small children), the percentage for fathers is only about 33 per cent.

Furthermore, all women spend between four and seven hours a day on housework, while very few men take part in domestic work (about 30 per cent) and for very limited periods of time: from a minimum of 30 minutes a day up to a maximum of one hour. In conclusion, activities (washing, ironing, cooking, etc.) related to the organization and well-being of the family are mostly done by the woman; furthermore, caring for dependent members of the family (children, elderly or other disabled members of the family) is exclusively the responsibility of the woman.

8.6. A Few Notes for the Social Agenda of Italian Policy-Makers

Different interventions could be imagined that could affect family structure, and above all would respond to principles of equality, social justice and clarity. On the level of clarity, the state should make its bureaucracy and its workings understandable to all. The complexity of our system of social assistance and the excessive bureaucracy that regulates access to services makes it difficult for people to obtain their entitlements. Many possibilities for social assistance remain unknown to its potential users.

Furthermore, the different levels of intervention in the family field (local, regional, governmental) could be simplified. The development of an efficient social and family policy requires a global approach to the problems and an economic commitment of the state. On the level of equality, men should be encouraged to participate more actively in everyday family life and organization. In many ways, Italian society and existing social policies support the stereotype of men as unable to take care of children (Palomba and Menniti, 1991). National laws have a 'pedagogical' effect too, and the introduction of compulsory paternity leave, along with campaigns aimed at educating men about the true value of paternity, could produce cultural changes that are by now indispensable for family well-being. The existing family policies are related mainly to caring activities that women carry out (for children, the elderly, the disabled, etc.), and no attempt has been made even to imagine a society in which the state intervenes in all those other activities that women carry out for the well-being of the family and its members and which take up such a large portion of their time (Palomba and Sabbadini, 1992). It is necessary to formulate new political measures that abandon the idea of 'compromising', or of women consenting to maintain the double role at home and at work, and which aim at establishing true equality between the sexes.

A developed country is one in which citizens' rights are watched over and guaranteed, and the level of development depends on the degree to which these rights are protected (Bobbio, 1989). Today, the Italian welfare state seems oriented towards ensuring rights and guarantees for the individual as a member of a family, rather than for the family as an entity. In Italy, mothers, children and, to a lesser extent, fathers are objects of political actions that protect and support them in various ways. It is more difficult to find actions directed towards the *family*, even though particular types of family, i.e. those considered at risk of poverty or in difficulty, are helped by the state. Some kinds of household do not have recognized rights: the unmarried cohabitation household does not exist in Italian law. Stepfamilies and second marriages are penalized in comparison with the time-honoured married couple. The principle of fairness that exists on an individual level does not seem to apply to the family level and, while individuals have equal rights before the state, not all families are protected in the same way. This inequality should be corrected, and in law any form of family in which individuals freely choose to live should have the same rights guaranteed.

References

Bimbi, F. (1990), *Madri e padri* (Mothers and Fathers), Franco Angeli, Milan.

Bobbio, N. (1989), 'Diritti dell'uomo e società' (Rights of man and society), *Sociologia e Diritto*, 1:15–27.

CISP (1982*a*), *La famiglia nell'approccio storico* (The family from a historical approach), Proceedings of the Seminar on 'Evoluzione della famiglia in Italia', Vol. I, CISP, Rome.

—— (1982*b*), *Caratteristiche attuali della famiglia* (Characteristics of the family of today), Proceedings of the Seminar on 'Evoluzione della famiglia in Italia', Vol. II, CISP, Rome.

De Sandre, P. (1988), 'Quando i figli lasciano la famiglia' (When the children leave the family), in Scabini and Donati (1988:15–30).

Donati, P. (1992), *Secondo rapporto sulla famiglia* (Second Report on the Family), CISF, Milan.

Golini, A., Menniti, A. and Palomba, R. (1987), 'Social Needs and Use of Services made by One-parent Families', in L. Shamgar-Handelman and R. Palomba (eds.), *Alternative Patterns of Family Life in Modern Societies*, IRP/CNR, Rome: 433–48.

Kiernan, K. (1986), 'Leaving home: living arrangements of young people in six West-European countries', *European Journal of Population*, 2:177–84.

Hoem, B. (1992), 'Women's Way to the Gender Segregated Swedish Labor Market', paper presented to the IUSSP Seminar on 'Gender and Family Change in the Industrialized Countries', Rome, 27–30 January 1992.

ISTAT (1985), *Indagine sulle strutture ed i comportamenti familiari* (Survey on structure and behaviour of the household), ISTAT, Rome.

—— (1986), 'Atti del convegno La famiglia in Italia' (Proceedings of the Conference on 'The Family in Italy'), *Annali di Statistica*, 115, IX, 6, ISTAT, Rome.

—— (1989), 'Indagine Multiscopo sulle famiglie: primo ciclo, primi risultati' (Multipurpose Survey on the Family: first cycle, first results), *Notiziario*, 4:41.

—— (1993*a*), *Indagine Multiscopo sulle famiglie: anni 1987-91* (Multipurpose Survey on the Family: the years 1987–91), ISTAT, Rome.

—— (1993*b*), 'L'evoluzione della fecondità nelle regioni italiane: indicatori di periodo e di generazione' (The evolution of fertility in the regions of Italy: period and cohort indicators), *Notiziario*, 4, 41, XIV: 1.

Maruani, M., Reynaud, E. and Romeni, C. (eds.) (1990), *La flessibilità del lavoro in Italia* (The flexibility of labour in Italy), Franco Angeli, Milan.

McLanahan, S., Soresen, A. and Casper, L. (1992), 'Women's Status in Family and Work Roles in Eight Industrialized Countries', paper presented to the IUSSP Seminar on 'Gender and Family Change in the Industrialized Countries', Rome, 27–30 January 1992.

Menniti, A. (ed.) (1991), *Le famiglie italiane degli anni 80* (The Italian Family in the 1980s), IRP/CNR, Rome.

Ministero del Lavoro e della Previdenza Sociale (1988), *La sicurezza sociale ed il suo finanziamento* (Social Security and its Financing), Rome.

Palomba, R. and Menniti, A. (1991), 'Social Policies from a Gender Perspective', paper presented to EAPS European Demographic Conference, Paris, 21–25 October 1991.

—— and Sabbadini, L.L. (1992), 'Fertility, Family Structure and Time Use in Italy', paper presented to the IUSSP Seminar on 'Gender and Family Change in the Industrialized Countries', Rome, 27–30 January 1992.

Sabbadini, L.L. (1987), 'Un'ipotesi interpretativa generale' (A general interpretative hypothesis), in R. Palomba, *Vita di coppia e figli* (Family Life and Children), La Nuova Italia, Florence: 135–8.

—— (1991), 'Le libere unioni' (The free unions), in Menniti (1991: 243–78.

Saraceno, C. (1988), *Sociologia della famiglia* (Sociology of the family), Il Mulino, Bologna.

—— (1991), 'Fecondità, famiglie e lavoro' (Fertility, family and work), paper presented to the Seminar on 'Popolazione, tendenze demografiche e mercato del lavoro', Rome, 3–5 June 1991.

Scabini, E. and Donati, P. (1988), *La famiglia 'lunga' del giovane adulto: verso nuovi compiti evolutivi* (The prolonged stay of young adults in the parental house: towards new developments), Studi interdisciplinari sulla famiglia, 7, Vita e Pensiero, Milan.

Vincenzi Amato, D. (1988), 'La famiglia e il diritto' (Family and rights), in P.

Melograni (ed.), *La famiglia italiana dall'ottocento ad oggi* (The Italian Family from the Nineteenth Century till Today), Laterza, Bari.

9 The Netherlands: the Latent Family

ANTON KUIJSTEN and HANS-JOACHIM SCHULZE[1]

University of Amsterdam and Free University of Amsterdam, Amsterdam, the Netherlands

There can be no doubt that millions of people in the Netherlands live in families or family-like situations. At present, however, the most characteristic feature of the Dutch family is its latency, in three different senses: political, public and private. Political latency is indicated by the fact that there is no explicit family policy, family seldom being an issue on the political agenda. Public latency refers to the fact that it is not considered acceptable to talk or write in public about 'het gezin' (the family) as this would be regarded as old-fashioned. Private latency in everyday life is illustrated by the tendency to refer to a spouse or partner as 'life companion', 'relation', 'boy friend' or 'girl friend' even, and for children to be introduced casually just by their first names, instead of by saying 'This is my son/daughter'. The national consensus about this family latency gives rise to political measures that have conflicting impacts on families. One of the consequences of the fact that family is no longer a manifest point of reference is that, in times of structural unemployment, individualized social security makes the unemployed family head vulnerable and easily pushes families of the unemployed towards the poverty line.

9.1. Introduction

9.1.1. *Changing Family Structures in the Netherlands: Pluralization or Polarization?*

The *bourgeois type of family*, denoted as the legally defined affiliation of a woman and a man and their offspring, living together and sharing their

[1] Thanks to Evelien van der Ploeg and Helma Verkleij for their valuable assistance in the preparation of this chapter.

everyday life, with the man/father/husband doing paid work and the woman/ mother/wife doing the housework and taking care of the children (Schulze *et al.*, 1989), grew quantitatively in the Netherlands in the nineteenth century and became the dominant type in the first six decades of the twentieth century. From the 1960s onwards, however, there were new developments, and change is still ongoing. After decades of growing importance and of numerical dominance of the bourgeois type of family, a phase of quantitative reduction and structural change has set in (De Hoog, 1989).

In this chapter we concentrate on this post-war period of social change within the realm of intimate and long-lasting relationships. Our first observation is that these changes in family structure have been gradual: there is no question of a rapid breakdown. Here we will just mention some indices; they will be discussed in more detail below.

Until the mid-1960s, the average age at marriage continued to fall. The proportion of people ever marrying reached its peak in the mid-1960s, and the number of children was relatively high: in the period 1960–4 the birth rate was 20.9 per 1,000 inhabitants, while in 1990 it was only 13.2. Families with four or more children have almost vanished: whereas in 1960–4 the birth-order-specific birth rate for birth orders four and higher was 4.9 per 1,000 inhabitants, this figure plummeted to 0.9 per 1,000 in 1987. During the 1970s the divorce rate became double that of the 1960s, and in the 1980s it rose to three times the 1960s level. At the same time, average age at marriage (first and non-first marriages taken together) rose considerably and reached almost 30 years (29.8) for men and 27 years for women in 1989. Another prominent signal of change is the fact that the proportion of children born outside marriage was about 2 per cent in the 1960s, whereas in 1990, 11.4 per cent of all live-born children were born out of wedlock. In the same period more and more unmarried partners started living together.

How must these developments be summarized – as pluralization or as polarization? Given the former dominance of the bourgeois family, one could interpret 'polarization' as a development that leads to only a few markedly differentiated forms of long-lasting intimate relationships, with outstanding and very different demographic characteristics: some types of family forms would gradually disappear, e.g. that of woman/mother/wife or female partner and man/father/husband or male partner with three or more children, and other types gain importance, e.g. the two-income married couple with one child. 'Pluralization', on the other hand, presupposes an interpretation of developments that stresses the emergence of quite new family types alongside the existing family forms.

There can be no doubt that developments over the past decades should be summarized under the label of pluralization. But it is not so much that the family forms differ, as that the bourgeois family is no longer the only legitimate form: rather, different kinds of living arrangements have become equally accepted, both legally and culturally (see Kronjee, 1989). The bourgeois family from the 1960s on has experienced a phase of *de-institutionalization* (Tyrell, 1989), giving people a choice between basically equivalent living arrangements that can be changed over the life span by the individual members. Alongside the family forms that could be observed during the decades following the Second World War, one now can observe more families in which the parents are living together unmarried, without being regarded (or without regarding themselves) as deviant. Moreover, family forms without permanent co-residence (the so-called LAT relationship), mothers who did not marry or prefer not to live together with the father of their child – all these and other family forms co-exist side by side in real life *and*, so to speak, in public opinion. From a biographical point of view, one can suppose that the ability to make a conscious choice of living arrangement[2] and of changes in relational structures during one's life course is the new normal everyday reality. Moreover, the living arrangement that a person will establish often has to be negotiated and to be decided upon by the eventual partner(s) (Van der Avort, 1987).

But pluralization might be the right keyword only as far as an increasing variation of life forms according to demographic compositional indicators is concerned. As we will demonstrate in Section 9.4, as soon as economic variables are attached to these demographic variables, a picture of *polarization* in the socio-economic dimension of family life emerges, with single-income families in a clearly deprived position, particularly when children are involved.

9.1.2. *Demographic Trends in the 1980s*

From the point of view of basic demographic trends that may have affected changes in family structures and living arrangements, the 1980s do not seem to have been a very exciting decade. The greater part of the developments that have been mentioned briefly in Section 9.1.1 and that can be summarized under the label 'Second Demographic Transition' (Van de Kaa, 1987) occurred during the late 1960s and the 1970s. So, compared with the previous two decades, the 1980s show a picture of relative stability with respect to

---

[2] For a discussion of the topic of conscious choice with respect to childbearing, see Frinking (1990).

the major demographic indicators. Nevertheless, some interesting developments did occur during that decade. Reference tables with basic demographic indicators for the Netherlands in the 1980s are included in Chapter 12.

The total annual number of live births, which still amounted to more than 235,000 in the late 1960s, was 181,000 in 1980 and dropped to a historical post-war low of 170,000 in 1983. Beginning in 1984, the annual number of live births began to rise again and reached almost 198,000 in 1990. Since fluctuations in period total fertility rates (TFR) and net reproduction rates (NRR) (two fertility indicators that also show the lowest values in 1983) have been quite moderate, this 16 per cent rise in natality since 1983 cannot be explained simply by an equally substantial rise in period fertility. Although a significant catch-up of births postponed during the 1970s and early 1980s seems to have taken place, the main part of the explanation is in the changing numbers of women of reproductive age caused by the post-war baby boom.

The parity distribution of the live-born children shows only minor changes over the 1980s. At the beginning of the decade, about 43 per cent were first-born children, and this proportion rises slowly to about 45 per cent in 1990. The proportion of second-born children shows a trend of gradual decline, from about 37 per cent at the beginning to less than 35 per cent at the end of the decade. The proportion of children of birth order 3 is quite stable at the level of about 14 per cent, and that of children of birth orders 4 and higher is in every year but one between 6.5 and 7 per cent. The phenomenon of non-marital fertility continues to gain importance: the proportion of non-marital births among all live births increased from 4.1 per cent in 1980 to 11.4 per cent in 1990, and that among first-borns from 5.2 per cent in 1980 to 15.1 per cent in 1989.

As in many other European countries, the age of the mother at first birth reached a post-war low somewhere in the 1970s and increased afterwards. In the Netherlands, during the 1980s this increase continued without interruption, from 25.6 years in 1980 to 27.6 years in 1990. This two-year shift in the mean age at first birth over just one decade indicates that the Netherlands has passed the threshold between the postponement phase and the catch-up phase in the process of delayed childbearing: the contribution of age-specific fertility rates for ages 30 and above to the period TFR, which rose from 27.5 per cent in 1980 to 43.6 per cent in 1990, is currently one of the highest in Europe (Bosveld *et al.*, 1991).

A similar ongoing increase, after a low in the mid-1970s, can be observed for the female mean age at first marriage: this rose from slightly over 23 years in 1980 to almost 26 years in 1990, reflecting the general tendency to postpone legal marriage and to start intimate relationships with a period of cohabitation. The period total first-marriage rate, which was over 1.0 till the early 1970s as a reflection of ever-younger marrying in the 1960s, fell to 0.683 in 1980, reached its lowest point in 1983 (0.562) and from then on rose to 0.657 in 1990 (Sardon, 1991). According to NCBS marriage dissolution tables by duration of marriage, the proportion of marriages concluded that would end in divorce showed a dramatic increase in the 1970s, from 12.1 per cent in 1971 to 23.9 per cent in 1980. It continued increasing in the first half of the 1980s, reaching a peak of 32.2 per cent in 1985. Then, in the second half of the 1980s, it declined and stabilized at a level of 27–28 per cent. This might be a consequence of a more selective marriage behaviour, in the sense that cohabiting people who wish to remain childless are, relatively less often than before, opting for legal marriage (Tas, 1992).

9.1.3. *An Outline of Recently Published Theoretical and Empirical Literature*

The abundance of family and family-relevant research in the Netherlands means that any selection of relevant literature will inevitably suffer from some arbitrariness.[3] Those interested in fully fledged bibliographic information on current family research should consult the annually published *Gezinswetenschappelijke documentatie* (for the latest edition, see Dumon and Deneffe, 1992).

Research on the history of marriage and the family is oriented towards the last five centuries (Kooy, 1985; Peeters *et al.*, 1988) and has a time-bound focus with respect to the 'Golden Age' of the Netherlands (the seventeenth century) and the eighteenth century (Haks, 1982; Dekker and Groenendijk, 1991; Schellekens, 1991). At the Agricultural University of Wageningen, historical demographers have dealt extensively with the development of household structures (e.g., Van der Woude, 1972), and sociologists have studied regional patterns in nineteenth-century fertility decline, in a way that for decades has aroused substantive debate on the topic of economic versus ideational determinants of fertility decline in the Netherlands (Hofstee, 1972; Van Heek, 1956; Buissink, 1971; Engelen and Hillebrand, 1986).

Demography has a well-established tradition in the Netherlands, its importance stretching well beyond the national frontiers: the very concept of the Second Demographic Transition has been cradled in the Low Countries (Van

---

[3] A more detailed overview of Dutch literature, though still suffering from arbitrariness, is given in our original Country Report to one of the Project Conferences (Kuijsten and Schulze, 1992). A free copy of that report can be provided by the authors.

de Kaa, 1987). Van Nimwegen (1991) provides an overview of population research during the 1980s. Current academic research programmes focus on longitudinal and intercohort comparative research on behaviour in the fields of relationships and fertility (University of Amsterdam; e.g. Manting, 1994; Manting *et al.*, 1992) and on decision-making with respect to fertility and how this is affected by e.g. educational level and by the man's viewpoint (University of Amsterdam, e.g. Wijsen, 1993; Catholic University of Brabant, e.g. Frinking, 1990; Frinking and Nelissen, 1988). A third cluster, currently co-operating within the framework of the Research Programme for Population Studies of the Netherlands Organization for Scientific Research (NWO), focuses on the demography of family and household, a field in which the Netherlands recently has played a leading role (De Vos and Palloni, 1989). In addition, every other year the Social and Cultural Planning Agency publishes a so-called 'Social and Cultural Report' which contains a lot of information relevant for demographers and family sociologists.

Up to 1971, quantitative analysis of household and family trends could be based on census results. (For the results of the 1971 Census, see Corver *et al.*, 1979.) For later periods, analyses must be based upon large-scale surveys such as the Housing Demand Survey (Baanders *et al.*, 1989), or on in-depth surveys such as the 1984 ORIN Life-style Survey (*Relatievormen*, 1989; Kuijsten and Klijzing, 1990). Many special studies by demographers and family sociologists have been devoted to (the problems of) specific household types or to people having experienced specific family or household changes, such as unwed mothers, divorced people, one-parent families, alternative living arrangements and cohabitants. This focus on 'problematic categories' has meant that there is a relative lack of research on the normal family (De Hoog, 1989). At the Agricultural University of Wageningen, demographic and household economic research deals with the assessment of the economic situation of households and their contribution to the economy (e.g. De Hoog and Van Ophem, 1990), and with the structural development of private households (Baanders *et al.*, 1989).

The vast majority of research in family sociology is empirically oriented (e.g. Douma, 1975; Langeveld, 1985). The Dutch Family Council observes, stimulates and informs on family research and forms a lobby for the funding of empirical family projects. Focal points in current research are: socialization, role negotiation and parenthood (e.g. Van den Akker and Van der Avort, 1986), life course and private living arrangements (e.g. Van Leeuwen, 1990; Liefbroer, 1991); family development and the family cycle (e.g. Jonker, 1984; Langeveld, 1985); the family as a group (e.g. Gerris and Van Acker, 1990; Stalpers and Tilborghs, 1981); and multi-level family research (e.g. Jansweijer, 1987).

Currently, women's emancipation is one of the central themes of social research in the Netherlands and penetrates all disciplines relevant for family research. In this field historical perspectives play one part (Kloek, 1989; Grunell, 1985), while other subfields deal with the distribution of repetitive home duties (Havinga, 1983) and with the compatibility of labour-force participation and child care (e.g. De Graaf and Ultee, 1991; Van Stolk and Wouters, 1983).

With regard to the closely connected question of day care for children, one can observe that the emancipation discourse has not led to a strong improvement in day-care facilities. The traditional image of the housewife has not undergone substantial change; one can hypothesize that this situation is due to the number, quality and price of day-care services in the Netherlands. Relevant items discussed recently in the literature are: the historical development of day care (e.g. Clerkx and Van IJzendoorn, 1992), the European context (Moss, 1990), the national situation (e.g. Van Dam and Van IJzendoorn, 1990; Goossens, 1986) and day care as an actual political hot issue (*Kinderopvang*, 1989; Singer and Tijdens, 1991; Zwier and Mostert, 1989).

Whether or not the Netherlands has a population(-oriented) policy is, at least in a functional sense, a question of much debate (e.g. Brands-Bottema, 1989; Frinking, 1986; Heeren, 1985; Leeuw, 1984). In this respect, the decline of the welfare state after the second oil crisis is still a topic of great interest (Idenburg *et al.*, 1983; De Swaan, 1989). Issues concerning the rights of the family and of children (Rood-De Boer, 1990; Sevenhuysen, 1987) and the right to abortion (Outshoorn, 1986) are also hotly debated. Attitudes towards issues of population and family policies in general and of child-care facilities in particular have been the target of repeated NIDI surveys (e.g., Moors *et al.*, 1989). The highly related field of changing values and orientations relevant to family structure and living arrangements has been studied by Halman *et al.* (1987), Kapteyn (1980) and, more specifically with respect to private relationships, by De Feijter (1991), Frinking and Nelissen (1988), Moors *et al.* (1989), Veenhoven and Van der Wolk (1977), and Weeda (1982, 1989). A detailed overview of policy measures relevant for family formation is given by Esveldt and Van Nimwegen (1992).

In summary, in comparison with other countries, one cannot say that the Netherlands has a very strong tradition of family research as such. As mentioned earlier, family research is currently carried out under various different headings. Predominantly, family research has been and still is funded under the headings of minorities, welfare state problems or emancipation (see

Bronsema and Van der Erf, 1992), an assessment that was confirmed by Qvortrup (1992:103):

Most research is applied research and revolves around problem areas. The Social and Cultural Planbureau is among the more important places, but generally one must conclude that research is rather scattered in the areas under review.

It was not until 1992 that official funding policy began to change and to stimulate research on the average Dutch family. From a European viewpoint, Dutch family research can offer a lot in the field of factual knowledge, including modelling of demographic change, provided it can profit from theoretical and conceptual developments that currently take place abroad.

9.1.4. *Data Sources*

The current data situation in the Netherlands is somewhat problematic. It is a well-known fact that there have been no population censuses in the Netherlands since 1971. Although a lot of large-scale surveys and other data sources have been introduced, and can be regarded as substitutes for the missing census data, data from these different sources cannot always easily be linked; moreover, the data have safety constraints for reasons of privacy protection, and access to them is often costly. So the combination of data into the predefined format specified for our comparative research project often requires a lot of scientific jigsawing with results that are not always too satisfactory. Nevertheless, it often is the only way to generate a more or less consistent set of tabulations.

In composing our set of tables presented below, we used a large variety of materials, from both secondary and primary sources. The most important in the latter category are the Current Statistics and the Register Counts of the Netherlands Central Bureau of Statistics, the Netherlands Fertility Surveys 1982 and 1988, the Labour Force Surveys 1981 and 1989, and the Housing Demand Surveys 1981–2 and 1989–90. Of these, we have made most use of the Housing Demand Surveys. The Housing Demand Survey is a repeated (every fourth year) cross-sectional survey based on a 0.65 per cent sample of the total population of the Netherlands aged 18 and over (sample size about 60,000 respondents). It contains data on size and composition of the household and, since 1985, limited retrospective data on household changes (NCBS, 1991*b*).

9.2. Family Policy in the Netherlands

9.2.1. *Main Directions of Policy Related to Family and Employment*

De Swaan (1989) has compared the welfare policies of England, France, Germany, the Netherlands and the United States. Two results of his comparison are relevant here. First, the system of welfare in the Netherlands was established relatively late, and reached its climax in the 1970s. Second, the system of welfare policy is primarily *work oriented*. Family policy has no prominent position within the national welfare policy; or, to be more precise, there is no – at least no explicit – family policy in the Netherlands (see also Dumon, 1991).

In so far as one circumscribes family policy as a set of policies that can be related, on the grounds of plausibility, to the life chances and conditions of families, one can say that the *implicit* family policy in the Netherlands is oriented towards a family in which the man and the woman are married, with the man doing paid work and the woman doing domestic tasks and looking after the children. Given this orientation, one can say that it is far from surprising that there has been no explicit policy directed towards the relation between paid work and family, at least for the better part of the post-war period. Yet, this general picture has to be shaded. The mentioned overall implicit policy towards the family should not lead us to overlook the fact that there are some political perspectives and measures that are directly relevant for family and for work.

EMANCIPATION POLICY. Nowadays 'emancipation' policy takes pride of place, primarily playing its role at the symbolic level[4] and with respect to measures to improve the position of women in the labour market. The perspective of emancipation as a general political goal brought about some changes at the beginning of the 1980s. By the end of that decade, emancipation formed the basis of legitimation for taking political action in favour of day-care institutions[5] and the creation of conditions (legal, monetary) to bring about

---

[4] On 18 May 1981 the so-called Emancipation Council (*Emancipatieraad*) was introduced. Its task is to advise government on emancipation policy matters, i.e. measures that are related to paid work of women, the development of day-care organizations (*Kinderopvang*, 1984) and matters that concern the division of labour between men and women.

[5] While day-care services in the 1960s were legitimated with reasons of 'equal opportunities for children from deprived groups' or with the slogan 'improving the chances for social contacts of single children or children in regions where only a few children are living', one can observe that, within the political discourse of 1988–9, improvement of the number of day-care facilities came to be based now on 'emancipation' and 'general interest' (see Elle, 1991:35; Singer, 1989).

more day-care services. The impact of the Emancipation Council on the field of family policy here must be assessed only hypothetically; the perspectives of organized women have been integrated into the process of policy discussion, but without strong consequences so far. The structural weakness of the political system with respect to formulating clear-cut policy lines is based on the differentiated landscape of political parties and the financial means for implementing new measures: the work and economy-related welfare policy has attracted, and still does attract, the greater part of a budget that is used more and more to pay for expenses that were legally defined in the past (Van Imhoff, 1990).

FINANCIAL MEASURES IN FAVOUR OF FAMILIES. The present tax system takes into account the fact that an adult woman or man is cohabiting with or married to a partner; it used to take into account whether or not someone was the breadwinner of a family.[6] By simplifying the tax system, the family-related rules were almost totally abolished in the 1980s in favour of measures aimed at specific family forms or needs. In the same period, cohabiting and married couples obtained equal status within the tax system.

The most common of all financial transfers for the family is the *child allowance*. This has undergone a lot of changes and at the moment is a measure that is not income-tested but is related primarily to the number and age of the children (Table 9.1). Next to the child benefits, there are some subsidies related to costs that are tied to the participation of children or adolescents in general schooling or vocational training.

One of the central questions with respect to welfare states is whether the different welfare measures lead to secondary class effects, i.e. to *transfer-classes* or to a situation in which different measures add up to zero so that the only effect lies in the fact that a lot of people in the welfare bureaucracy have jobs. The Social and Cultural Planning Agency (SCP) has carried out research on the relations between income, taxes and different transfers, i.e. on the cumulated effects of income and different kinds of allowances (health insurance, child allowances, housing allowances, grants, allowances for students, day care, care for families, legal support). Its most important result is that such cumulations generally do not lead to massive inequality, despite the fact that each of the introduced measures was designed to compensate

---

[6] To a certain extent, one can say that the tax system stimulated participation in work for parents during the 1980s. Income tax for families with children younger than 12 years was such that parents got a supplementary allowance on work (up till 31 December 1989). A single parent could get a single-parent bonus. According to Pelzer (1991:81), this measure was taken in order to register an interest in improving the general provision with day-care facilities that was demanded by the Dutch women's movement.

Table 9.1. *Child benefits, quarterly payments per child, the Netherlands, 1 January 1991 (Dfl.)*

Families with children (no. of children)	Ages of children		
	0–5	6–11 and 18–24	12–17
1	253.62	362.32	471.02
2	311.21	444.58	577.95
3	327.88	468.40	608.92
4	355.13	507.33	659.53
5	371.47	530.67	689.87
6	389.85	556.93	724.01

Source: Sociale Verzekeringsbank, 1 July 1991.

for inequalities. But, with respect to our aims, it should be mentioned that people with a low income and single-parent families in these SCP simulations do indeed experience relatively negative consequences that can be related to the new taxation rules (Van Herwaarden *et al.*, 1990).

LEGAL MEASURES WITH RESPECT TO CHILDBEARING CONCERNING PARENTING AND PAID WORK.

1. Pregnancy leave. Before and after delivery of a child, women receive 100 per cent of their wages. Whereas the old law gave women a leave of at least 10 and at most 12 weeks before and after delivery,[7] a new law (since 2 March 1990) gives women a 4–6-week leave before the expected date of childbearing and another 10–12 weeks (depending on the time that was used before giving birth) after the birth of the child (*Emancipatie in arbeidsorganisaties*, 1991:93).

2. Parental leave. Parental leave was regulated only recently (1 January 1991) by law. Up to 520 hours for a full-time employee of unpaid parental leave is possible for each parent. There is a restriction that one should have a work contract for at least 20 hours a week. Parents can take turns, which would lead to 1,040 hours of parental leave in case of full-time employment of both. These minimum demands in the regulations on parental leave have led to a lot of variations in collective wage agreements.

THE POSITION OF THE POLITICAL SYSTEM WITH RESPECT TO FAMILY IMAGES AND PRO-NATALISM. Observers agree that the Dutch political system has

[7] For an international comparison, see Moors and Koesoebjono (1990).

no well-defined stance with respect to pro- or anti-natalist matters (Beets, 1991[8]). An analysis of programmatic contributions within the political realm to the image of or the view of the family has led to the following conclusion (Brands-Bottema, 1989):

It is not possible to give a description of the image of the family that parties stick to. The arguments they use are very vague. Often parties don't give a motivation at all. Very few parties systematically give their opinion about important notions as parental authority and legal rights for children. Alternative forms of parenthood are accepted by most of the parties as a fact. The legislator has to take them into consideration. Parties formally don't make a choice to force people to raise children in a certain family type.

DAY CARE. The system of day care in the Netherlands during the 1980s and before was based on the principle of 'maximum private responsibility' (OECD, 1990; Clerkx and Van IJzendoorn, 1992), stimulated by tax concessions. It was not until 1989 that the Dutch government defined day-care organizations principally as service organizations for *every* family with children. Since 1990, money raised through a reformed taxation law has been used to stimulate the growth of day-care places.[9] Observers suppose that this measure has been taken because of the expected labour shortage in the national economy, so that the conditions for women to take part in paid work had to be improved (Pelzer, 1991). If these observations are valid, one might say that the Dutch political system does in fact have specific aims relating indirectly to families, but the means to implement these aims are rather small and the family-related consequences are not properly taken into account. (Further data concerning supply and demand of day-care places will be given in Section 9.5.)

COHORT-SPECIFIC POLICY MEASURES. At the beginning of the 1990s a fundamental change with respect to the normal biography of women and men was introduced in the Netherlands. The country's political system was more or less chosen for something one could call 'the Swedish way' of integrating women into the labour market and the welfare system, by introducing the so-called '1990 initiative' (1990 *maatregel*). The contents of this cohort-

---

[8] A modified position has been brought forward in Hoogmoed (1989).

[9] There was a measure '*Stimuleringsmaatregel Kinderopvang*' to encourage child-care arrangements in order to reduce shortages, in force from 1 January 1990 to 31 December 1993. As far as we can see, its influence has been restricted and the shortage problem has been far from solved by it. Critical positions with respect to this measure are given by Pelzer (1991) and in an article in Elle (1991); the relationship with biographical options and choices of cohabiting or married couples is worked out by Frinking (1990).

specific law can be summarized as follows: Adult women and men who are 18 and older have to look for paid work in the first place, in order to secure rights to benefits from the welfare system. If one of the (young) cohabiting or married partners is unemployed, (s)he cannot rely on allowances tied to the status of breadwinner unless (s)he has to care for a child younger than 12 years. Some observers call the measure a kind of *general duty to do paid work* for the new generations (Den Hertog, 1989; Frinking, 1990).

Independent from, but probably stimulated by, the '1990 initiative', the demand for day-care provisions has been rising. As a consequence of the '1990 initiative', one can suppose that in the year 2000 day care will need to provide 25 times as many places as today (Den Hertog, 1989), because of the demand of the new cohorts who will be in their reproductive ages then, and because of the impact the law will have on previous cohorts who are confronted earlier in life with the decision of having or not having children.

The fact that the Netherlands has a very pronounced system of welfare with respect to minimum wages, transfer payments for the unemployed and people who are partly or completely unable to work imposes a factual constraint on a financially directed family policy. The fact that the political system in the Netherlands is built upon small and ideologically different parties that have to co-operate, in a way makes it structurally improbable to launch a profiled family policy. The development of a new family structure has not led to special family policy measures, but the political system has had some influence on the emancipation movement. The decline of family norms that were valid up to the mid-1960s has led to the situation where 'deviant' families are more often making use of transfer measures that originally were designed to help the really deviant families (for example one-parent families) to live at a minimum level. (This is where two different principles, i.e. the social-democratic principle of solidarity and the catholic principle of subsidiarity, come into conflict.) Family policy is now characterized by contradictions and ambiguities between symbolic politics (the introduction of an Emancipation Council; stimulating the establishment of day-care institutions; and enforcing the purely legal right to take a parental leave without getting subsidies) on the one hand and the introduction, on the other, of a forced-choice approach (*either* paid work *or* care for one's children as a precondition for a fully-fledged membership in the welfare state) for the cohorts born from 1972 onwards.

The implicit orientation of the political system towards a bourgeois family type is being reduced, and at the same time general pressure is put on new generations to decide on either work or children if they want to be included completely in the welfare system. With this development in mind, one can expect that women especially will be forced to integrate different roles, and that once more the continuity of family life will be tied primarily to the role of adult women (who have lost almost completely their privileges from a bourgeois family perspective) – a role that might become more demanding than ever before if the role of men does not change significantly.[10] Given the stimulation of every adult to take care of him- or herself in the economic and welfare sense, and given the fact that cohabitational bonds are looked upon as being far from eternal, one can hypothesize that family formation will be put on a second level in the structure of personal preferences of many a young man or woman in the Netherlands, if there are no rules to be established that allow mothers or fathers to take parental leave from paid work during the child's first year(s) on a financially acceptable basis. Such a measure would mean, however, an extension of the existing ones, which seems incompatible with the existing ideological and budgetary landscape of the Netherlands.

9.2.2. Hypothetical Impact Models: Family Forms, Life Situations, Everyday Life

MODEL 1. The de-institutionalization of the bourgeois family in the Netherlands from the mid-1960s onwards has given every adult access to a lot of – more or less reversible – living arrangements. Many possibilities that were regarded as deviant and morally unacceptable in earlier decades are now acceptable options. But it is difficult to generalize. On the one hand, in principle every bourgeois family is a unique group with its own culture, and in this way both before and after the de-institutionalization of the bourgeois family it was relatively *autonomous* (Schulze, 1985; Wallerstein and Smith, 1990). On the other hand, universal norms concerning formation and realization of a family life within normal biographies are fading so that, despite the expected *uniqueness* of modern families as autonomous social units, one observes a lot of different family types in the same cohorts. Some families just seem to ignore the erosion of the bourgeois family (Van der

---

[10] For the relative position of the Netherlands with respect to family policy measures, see the comparative article of Jouko Hulko (1990) discussing measures in almost all countries in Western Europe, and the article (in Dutch) by Moors and Koesoebjono (1990) on paid work and running a family, with respect to Belgium, the Federal Republic of Germany, France, Italy, the Netherlands, and Great Britain.

Avort, 1987), some might decide in favour of a bourgeois arrangement and evangelistically praise its blessings, possibly on the basis of a specific religious orientation.[11] Still others might devote their adult life as far as possible to child(ren) (see Schülein, 1990) – either as long as possible, or for a specific period only. Moreover, it seems quite plausible that families should be oriented towards the most positive combinations of family life (including partnership and housework), paid work (including double-career) and participation in leisure activities, to suit their individual sets of priorities.

Within this 'pluralistic trajectory', one may discern one type of family that commands adequate cultural and financial resources and another type that has not (yet) succeeded in combining the two. The 'combination category' has – at least at the level of preferences – grown substantially in the past decades. The demand for paid work and the growing experience of women with it may have strengthened the orientation of the 'economic family' (instead of the Homo economicus), which is capable of taking into account the benefits or hindrances that are brought about by political decisions which might make it easier or more difficult to realize a group's idea about a family life of its own (De Hoog, 1989; Wallerstein and Smith, 1990). Crucial in this respect is the influence of policies on the degree of *openness* of options, the degree to which parenthood does not destroy the possibilities of choosing other options. It is on this basis of requests and problems with which specific types of family are confronted[12] that *post hoc* analysis of policy measures should be undertaken, according to the axiom which says that the impact of action of a social unit on other units can be stated best where impact is generally given by the receiving system – where, in other words, the *resonance principle* holds.

MODEL 2. In line with the autonomy-based uniqueness supposition is the following hypothesis: as more and more women and men want to combine in one way or another a living as *partners, parents and employees*, it is quite probable that measures to improve the conditions to realize this combination, i.e. the compatibility of different role requirements of adult family members, will achieve the expected response. Central conditions relate to the demands of the labour market, the working schemes of parents, the economic position

[11] The results of recent research on the motivation of women concerning paid work and/or care for children show that religious commitments can bring about clear decisions in favour of a family-centred life (see Spieß *et al.*, 1991:93).

[12] De Hoog (1989:146–7) puts forward the thesis that policy has to be based on research and has to be oriented towards the biggest groups of all the different family arrangements and to be specified relatively to these groups.

of family households and day-care arrangements for children (McIntosh, 1983; Kaufmann, 1990).

MODEL 3. From the moment that the erosion of the bourgeois family began, political measures (based on a socialist, social-democratic or Catholic and/or Protestant Christian perspective) that were designed to ensure a minimum standard of living for the 'deviant cases', e.g. women living with one or more children without being married, were constantly being reinterpreted and expanded, or 'normalized', leading to a system of implicit family policy that gradually is coming to grips with those normative changes and gets more neutral, i.e. non-specific characteristics (see Brands-Bottema, 1989).[13]

MODEL 4. The above-mentioned '1990 initiative' will probably accelerate the ongoing increase in the contribution of women to the formal economy in the Netherlands. The demand for paid work is rising and the demand for day care is rising too, leading to a gap that is being filled in with white, grey or black paid work on the one hand, and grey and legal (public or private) day-care arrangements and parent initiatives on the other. It is also leading to more pressure on the political system to expand the capacity of day-care organizations. Moreover, one can suppose that powerful firms may establish more work-related day care in order to attract more specially qualified labour.

9.3. Family Forms in the 1980s

9.3.1. *Timing of Critical Events*

AGE OF WOMEN AT BIRTH OF THE FIRST CHILD. As a result of the processes of fertility reduction and postponement for reasons of educational and occupational careers, the mean age of women at birth of their first child has risen since the early 1970s. At the moment, this mean age is a little over 27 years for marital births, and about one year lower for births out of wedlock. From the 1990 distributions of all births by birth order and age of the mother, we calculated that one-quarter of the first births is realized at age 25.1 of the women. So, in the Netherlands age group 25–29 is the one in which

---

[13] Nevertheless, much still points to the thesis that lone-parenthood is discouraged systematically by the welfare system (Ester and Nauta, 1989; Van Herwaarden *et al.*, 1990) and also by the Christian Party (see Brands-Bottema, 1989). See also Section 9.4.

the critical event 'birth of first child' is currently concentrated. However, it is quite feasible, because of the current tendency of increased fertility (of all birth orders) at higher ages (Bosveld *et al.*, 1991), that in future there will be a shift towards the older extreme of this age group, if not into the next-higher group.

AGE OF WOMEN ENTERING THE 'EMPTY-NEST' PHASE. A greater individual variability, and thus a greater arbitrariness of the central tendency looked for, may be assumed for this critical event. In a preliminary stage of our research we used three different estimation methods and all three resulted in a mean age just over 50. Nevertheless, for several reasons, primarily reasons of between-country comparability,[14] it was decided that the oldest age group involved in our analysis – that in which the experience of entering the 'empty-nest' phase is currently starting for most women – should be 45–49.

9.3.2. *Structural Characteristics of Family Life*

In this section we will present a number of statistics on the structural characteristics of family life in the Netherlands during the 1980s, as much as possible following a standard list of items, and presenting these statistics for the two age groups identified in Section 9.3.1.

MARITAL STATUS DISTRIBUTION. Table 9.2 features the marital status distributions of women aged 25–29 and 45–49 in the Netherlands, on 1 January 1981, 1986 and 1991. More than those for age group 45–49, the trends in age group 25–29 exhibit a substantive continuation of trends that have been visible since the early 1970s, that is, a continuous rise in the proportions never-married and an equally continuous fall in the proportions married (plus separated). This has to do with the well-known trends of marriage postponement and growing incidence of (pre-marital) cohabitation: many of those never-married do in fact have a partner. Experts nowadays agree in their opinion that the post-1986 decline in the proportions divorced in these age groups is first of all due to this steep fall in the numbers married in these age groups, i.e. the numbers 'at risk' of divorce. In fact, the current actual

---

[14] Another important reason has to do with the labour market: since people leave the labour market at a younger age than ever before, it has become almost impossible to re-enter the labour market after a long break and/or at the age of 50 and beyond.

Table 9.2. *Women, aged 25–29 and 45–49, by marital status, the Netherlands, 1981–1991*

Marital status	1981[a]		1986[a]		1991[a]	
	No.	%	No.	%	No.	%
Age 25–29						
Never married	118,032	20.9	192,187	32.1	266,843	41.9
Married (+ separated)	425,991	75.3	379,685	63.5	349,465	54.9
Divorced	20,055	3.5	25,036	4.2	19,665	3.1
Widowed	1,287	0.2	1,073	0.2	781	0.1
Total	565,365		597,981		636,754	
Age 45–49						
Never married	23,238	6.2	20,813	5.2	23,203	5.2
Married (+ separated)	321,388	85.2	330,359	83.2	362,026	81.3
Divorced	18,388	4.9	32,474	8.2	47,032	10.6
Widowed	14,383	3.8	13,473	3.4	13,300	3.0
Total	377,397		397,119		445,561	

[a] 1 January.

Source: NCBS, Annual Statistics on Population Structure by Sex, Age and Marital Status.

number of break-ups of intimate relationships (official divorces, plus separations of cohabitors) is estimated as being higher than ever before.

The marital status distributions of age group 45–49 reflect to a much higher extent the more traditional patterns. Take, for example, age group 45–49 on 1 January 1991. At age 25–29, on 1 January 1971, 82.7 per cent of this cohort were already married, against only 13.9 per cent who were still never-married. They took their fundamental life-course decisions in a period when the so-called 'Golden Age of Marriage' was coming to an end, and this is reflected in a relatively low proportion of never-marrieds. Nevertheless, 10 per cent of this age group was divorced (as compared with only 5 per cent in the 45–49 age group 10 years earlier), reflecting the post-1970 rise in divorce rates and the simultaneous decrease in remarriage rates. For evident reasons, it is only in this oldest age group that the proportion widowed gains some importance.

DISTRIBUTION BY PARTNER ARRANGEMENT. With the Second Demographic Transition developing in the Netherlands, as elsewhere in the modern industrial countries, marital status has lost much of its traditional value as an indicator of living arrangement. Not all married persons live with their legal spouse, and considerable proportions of non-married persons live together with a partner. Table 9.3 provides an overview of the changes in partner

Table 9.3. *Women, aged 25–29 and 30–34, by partner arrangement, the Netherlands, 1982–1988 (%)*

	Living in parental home	No partner at all Alone	No partner at all With children[a]	Cohabiting Not married	Cohabiting Married	Other
Age 25–29						
1982 (N=1,630)	4	10	4	9	72	1
1988 (N=1,523)	7	14	3	16	59	0
Age 30–34						
1982 (N=1,626)	1	6	5	4	83	0
1988 (N=1,427)	2	9	6	7	76	0

[a] One-parent families.

Source: Netherlands Fertility Survey 1982; Netherlands Fertility Survey 1988; INRO/TNO PRIMOS Household Projection Model 1990.

arrangement status that took place during the 1980s in age group 25–29. Because we could not find the equivalent data for age group 45–49, in this case we tried to provide some historical perspective by adding data for age group 30–34. Like in Table 9.2, the column 'cohabiting, married' shows the retreat of the traditional married-couple family between 1982 and 1988. On the other hand, there are clear gains for the 'non-traditional' partner arrangements such as non-married cohabitation and living alone. The rise over time in the proportions living in the parental home reflect the modest rise in the average age at leaving home that occurred in the 1980s. The proportions of females in age groups 25–29 and 30–34 heading a one-parent family have remained rather stable, and roughly correspond with the proportions divorced in Table 9.2.

MARITAL STATUS/PARTNER ARRANGEMENT AND NUMBER OF CHILDREN. Table 9.4 displays percentage distributions of women belonging to the two age groups 25–29 and 45–49 by number of children actually present in the household and by living arrangement, at the beginning and at the end of the 1980s. 'Living alone', 'living as an unmarried couple', 'living as a married couple' and 'others' are the living arrangement categories, the latter one including the female lone parents.

First, looking at the distributions by number of children of all women in the age groups, and comparing between the two age groups, we see both for 1981 and for 1990 age differences that fit the life-cycle model. Women 25–29 years old have much higher proportions in the 'no children' category

Table 9.4. *Women, aged 25–29 and 45–49, by living arrangement and number of children actually living in the household, the Netherlands, 1981–1982 and 1989–1990*

No. of children	Living arrangement				
	Living alone	Unmarried couple	Married couple	Other	Total
1981–2					
Age 25–29					
0	100	87	31	71	45
1	–	8	30	16	24
2	–	3	31	11	24
3 and more	–	2	8	3	6
Age 45–49					
0	100	57	13	24	19
1	–	10	21	28	21
2	–	28	34	23	31
3 and more	–	5	32	25	29
1989–90					
Age 25–29					
0	100	90	39	70	61
1	–	7	30	17	20
2	–	3	24	10	15
3 and more	–	1	7	3	4
Age 45–49					
0	100	73	22	19	29
1	–	18	29	51	29
2	–	10	34	23	30
3 and more	–	–	15	7	12

Sources: 1981–2: Clara H. Mulder, analysis of Housing Demand Survey 1981–2, as part of practical work at the University of Utrecht, under supervision of Prof. Dr. P. Hooimeijer; 1989–90: Housing Demand Survey 1989–90.

and much higher proportions with two and more children, compared with 45–49-year-old women. When compared over time, we observe that childlessness among women 25–29 has increased significantly over the decade, from 45 to 61 per cent, reflecting the ongoing process of delayed childbearing. Among women 45–49 we see a similar increase in the proportion with no children in the household. In this age group, the proportion with no children in the household increases from 19 to 29 per cent, and that with one child from 21 to 29 per cent, whereas the proportion with two children remains stable and that with three and more children decreases from 29 to 12 per cent. We assume that these changes have much more to do with accelerated home-leaving of young people in the 1970s and 1980s than with a significant drop in fertility between the two cohorts.

When looking next at the various living arrangements, we observe that the aforementioned tendencies for all women are reflected in the figures for women living in a married couple. This is no surprise since childbearing is still concentrated in the married status. But even among married 25–29-year-old women, 31 per cent had no children in 1981–2 and 39 per cent in 1989–90. On the other hand, more than half did already have one or two children, and 8 resp. 7 per cent had three or more. Among women 45–49, both at the beginning and at the end of the decade, one in three had two children in their household; but, whereas in 1981–2 another one in three had three or more children, in 1989–90 a similar one in three had one child only in the household. The proportion without co-resident children almost doubled, from 13 to 22 per cent.

That childbearing is still concentrated in the married status is also reflected by the distributions for the other living arrangements. Among cohabiting 25–29-year-old women, the proportion with no children in the household is 87 in 1981–2 and 90 in 1989–90; 8 resp. 7 per cent have one child living in their household, and the proportions with two and more children are still very small. The same holds, although in a slightly less extreme sense, for women in the category 'others', probably because there are more divorced women in this category who have children with them who have remained in their custody. This explanation seems even more valid for the categories 'unmarried couple' and 'others' in age group 45–49, particularly in 1989–90. Women living alone are by definition all in the category without co-resident children.

9.4. Some Aspects of the Family Life Situation

9.4.1. *Issues: Income, Labour Force, Education and Housing*

INCOME. About two-thirds of all Dutch women (and mothers) participate in the labour market with a part-time contract. Precisely because part-time work does not involve so many weekly hours of paid work, it is important to know whether or not there are income differences between one- and two-income households. A representative survey among some 4,000 respondents (NCBS, 1986), in which one- and two-income households were matched according to, e.g., education, age, family phase and source of income, ended up with the following results. On the whole, the position of two-income households is more favourable than that of one-income households. Two-income households can operate on a higher (household) budget and buy more consumer durables. There is more variation in the way they spend their time off; they participate more in social life and go on holidays more often; they have more living space and their medical consumption is lower. When these results are checked and balanced, some differences remain that can not be attributed to age, level of education, position or family phase. Two-income households do have higher incomes, they do go on holidays and to the cinema more often; also, in their own perception, they are more often subjected to noise pollution.

So: greater subjective financial strength, but not so much difference as the investigators expected. We can assume that this reflects the fact that two-income households very often combine a higher income of the man/husband with a lower income of the woman/wife, and double income may often be the result of economic pressure, i.e. the perception that a second income is necessary in order to keep up with one's standard of living. The fact that a family has two breadwinners has to be attributed to the desire to maintain a minimum standard of living of the family, as well as to personal preferences.

According to NCBS data, average disposable annual income of different household types in 1987 varied from Dfl. 33,900 for non-active and Dfl. 37,900 for active non-parent families, to Dfl. 44,500 for non-active married partners with children and Dfl. 48,100 for economically active married partners with children (NCBS, 1991a:269). The average income of one-parent families and of married partners with children is more than twice the minimum income level, according to these figures.[15] But figures for 1981 give a quite different picture, as can be seen in Table 9.5.

However, more revealing than measures of average income are measures of income distribution, differentiated by the family life situation. In Section 9.1 we focused on the question of pluralization versus polarization from the point of view of demographic characteristics of the family life situation. There, we opted for the pluralization perspective. However, when looking at 1989–90 data showing the distributions of household income for a number

[15] See Section 9.2 on families and poverty. We must leave aside here whether these data and the data concerning poverty are based on the same definitions and the same period; therefore, a proper comparison cannot be made. International comparative research (Dirven *et al.*, 1990) shows that the Netherlands takes an average position with respect to the relation of income of married women to that of their working husbands: for the Netherlands, this ratio amounts to 1:1.5.

Table 9.5. *Income data for a number of selected household types, the Netherlands, 1981*

Household type	Average income (Dfl. '000)
Single person who has been married ≥ 65	16
Single-parent family with children > 18	17
Unmarried single	21
Single person who has been married	22
Single-parent family with children < 18	23
Couple without children, woman ≥ 65	24
Couple with children exclusively ≥ 18	31
Couple without children, woman 35-64	33
Couple with children < 18	36
Persons living together with children < 18	38
Living together without children, woman < 35	39
Couple without children, woman < 35	42

Source: M.J.H. Ploegmakers and L.Th. van Leeuwen, *Huishoudtype, positie in het huishouden en inkomen* (Household Type, Household Position and Income), Wageningen, 1987:55, as quoted in De Hoog (1989:139).

of selected family life situations,[16] one gets the idea that, *as soon as the economic variable is attached to the demographic variables, pluralization in the demographic sense dovetails with polarization in the socio-economic dimension of family life situations*. This same idea emerges from similar data on the 1981 situation. Moreover, it is in line with the general message of findings in the international literature. For example, with respect to the position of women in particular, Winchester (1989:70) points to the fact that

the analysis of the feminization of poverty has contributed to an understanding of the causes of socio-economic polarization, and its unequal impact on women and men. . . . On the one hand is the group described . . . as 'new urban women': skilled, professional, independent women who develop successful careers and are financially secure. At the other extreme are dramatically increasing numbers of women below the poverty line, mainly households with no resident adult male, including lone female parents and lone elderly women.

Two-income families, whether cohabiting couples or married-couple families, fare better than one-income families, irrespective of the number of

---

[16] Detailed data are presented in our original Country Report (Kuijsten and Schulze, 1992; see also fn. 2) and in Kuijsten (1992). The data have been taken from a special tabulation made for us by NCBS, and based on the Housing Demand Survey 1989-90.

children they have to care for. But in age group 25–29, for married couples this difference is slightly smaller than for non-married couples. Another striking finding is that this difference between one-income and two-income family life situations seems to be influenced only insignificantly by the number of resident children. So, it seems that the relevant difference is not at the level of household income, but at that of *per capita* income: the number of adults and children who have to share in the spending of the household income.

PARTICIPATION IN THE LABOUR MARKET, EDUCATIONAL LEVEL AND LEVEL OF VOCATIONAL TRAINING. Participation in the labour market in different European countries is far from homogeneous.[17] OECD data[18] with respect to full-time (35 hours per week and more) and part-time (less than 35 hours per week) employment show that the Netherlands has by far the highest proportion of part-time employment (33 per cent). The development of part-time employment in the Netherlands shows that since 1977 the rate of such contracts has doubled. It is supposed that part-time work will become even more important in the near future.

Part-time employment in the Netherlands is primarily part-time work done by women: of the 2.3 million women that had employment in 1989, 62 per cent worked part-time, as against only 16 per cent of all men.[19] *This extreme and gender-specific division between full-time and part-time employment in the Netherlands must be taken into account when looking at the question of compatibility of work and family within the policy framework.*

Female labour-force participation rates in the Netherlands have risen over the past decades. In Table 9.6 we present some cohort-specific information for 1981 (Hartog and Theeuwes, 1985:S240). The striking differences between unmarried and married women with respect to labour-force participation in 1960 were reduced considerably in two decades: obviously, parenthood has become a weakened barrier to participation in the labour market.

In 1987, the overall participation rate of 25–49-year-old women was 56.1 per cent in the Netherlands, 5 percentage points below the EU average (NCBS, 1991a:82). Besides, the age schedule of female labour-force participation is still highly affected by the 'three-phase' model of labour-force

---

[17] For an overview of labour-force participation of women in Europe, see Becker (1989).

[18] NRC-Handelsblad, 2 November 1991.

[19] Part-time work for women is concentrated in farming, work in restaurants and in the cleaning business. This is a major reason why professional segregation of women is stronger in the Netherlands than e.g. in (West) Germany.

Table 9.6. *Labour-force participation of women by age and marital status, the Netherlands, 1960–1979*

Age	Not married			Married		
	1960	1971	1979	1960	1971	1979
25–29	77.0	78.9	77.7	8.1	18.3	34.5
30–34	72.4	70.7	71.4	6.7	15.6	28.2

participation among Dutch married women (for more details see Plantenga, 1992).

The 1980s were characterized by the growing labour-force participation of women irrespective of the age of their youngest child. From 1983 to 1987, labour-force participation of women with a youngest child 0–2 years of age rose from 22 to 31 per cent; among those whose youngest child was 3–5, it rose from 28 to 47 per cent, and among women with a 6–13-year-old youngest child it rose from 38 to 48 per cent (OECD, 1990).[20] This rather crude and global picture is confirmed by more detailed figures for young women (25–34) resulting from the National Fertility Surveys 1982 and 1988. In comparison with Belgium, Denmark, France, Great Britain and Germany, the participation rates are lower and, once again, reflect the relatively low participation rate of women in the Netherlands labour force. Yet, the Dutch data show a similar trend: women who have given birth to at least one child are continuously broadening their participation in the labour market.

The general tendency of growing participation in the labour market by mothers is partially blurred by two important constraints: (i) the fact that the labour market has no constant capacity to absorb the entire female work potential at a given moment, so that there are important discouragement effects, and (ii) the fact that day-care provisions are not co-ordinated with regional labour-market developments. Comparison of data referring to 1982 and 1988 with respect to mothers having children between 0 and 3 years of age confirms that the number of women who decide not to go to work has been reduced for every age group of mothers (from 82 to 73 per cent), that part-time work has risen considerably (from 14 to 22 per cent on average), and that full-time work hardly increased: only from 3 to 5 per cent (NCBS, 1990*b*:100).

The most striking figures in Table 9.7 are those for the 25–29-year-old women who have full-time jobs (30 hours or more): 92 per cent in 1981–2

[20] The numbers presented here are taken from a histogram presentation and thus may be unprecise with respect to the original sources.

Table 9.7. *Women, aged 25–29 and 45–49, by work status and number of children actually living in the household, the Netherlands, 1981–1982 and 1989–1990*

No. of children	Hours worked per week				
	None	< 10	10–29	30+	Total
1981–2					
Age 25–29					
0	19	12	65	92	45
1	35	47	18	4	24
2	37	36	14	3	24
3 and more	10	5	4	1	6
Age 45–49					
0	15	12	18	57	19
1	21	23	23	14	21
2	32	39	33	17	31
3 and more	32	26	26	13	29
1989–90					
Age 25–29					
0		27	66	94	61
1		34	23	4	20
2		31	9	1	15
3 and more		8	2	1	4
Age 45–49					
0		24	29	54	29
1		30	31	25	29
2		32	31	17	30
3 and more		15	10	4	12

Source: see Table 9.4.

and 94 per cent in 1989–90 have no children in the household, another 4 per cent have one child, and 4 resp. 2 per cent only have two or more children. When women do have the responsibility for children, they either work part-time or take up the role of housewife. This holds too for the age group 45–49, although the differences are smaller: 46 per cent of women working full-time in 1989–90 in this age group also have responsibility for co-resident children, against 71 per cent of women working 10–29 hours per week.

Between-country differences in labour-force participation reflect cultural differences (with respect to requested combinations of paid work and family tasks for women *and* for men; see Becker, 1989) that may become smaller over time, i.e. with a stronger European integration. The *'relevance of social norm change' with respect to labour participation of mothers* has been discussed by Romme (1990). Between 1971 and 1986 a representative sample of Dutch people was asked: 'What do you think of a married woman with school-going children who works?' The following answers could be given: (1) recommended, (2) not objectionable, or (3) objectionable. Romme interprets the combined percentages of 'recommended' and 'not objectionable' as an indication of support for the norm regarding female labour. The data (Romme, 1990:92) show that *the normative support for mothers of school-going children going to work has on the whole risen over the period from 57 per cent in 1971 to 68 per cent in 1986.*[21] Moreover, the Dutch population that was born between 1891 and 1960 has experienced a linear trend towards more openness in intergenerational relations in the educational level. Although this trend is stronger for men than for women, in principle both patterns are of the same type (Ganzeboom and De Graaf, 1989*a* and 1989*b*).

HOUSING BY NUMBER OF CHILDREN AND BY FAMILY TYPE; HOUSING ALLOWANCES. Research results with respect to housing needs in the Netherlands (Housing Demand Survey 1985–6, see NCBS, 1987; Housing Demand Survey 1989–90, see NCBS 1991*b*) provide relevant data on some important trends on the housing market with respect to the first half of the 1980s (see NCBS, 1987:24–7).[22]

Rates of ownership with respect to different types of dwelling have risen from 1981 to 1985. For different cohorts there are different trends to be observed: people under the age of 25 do not participate in the generally growing ownership development: most of them still rent a flat. The proportion of home ownership has risen from 22.9 per cent in 1981 to 24.7 per cent in 1985, for all households taken together. In the same period, one-parent families have lost a part of their ownership rate, which declined from 27.8 to 24.5 per cent. The ownership rates for people with a lower income (up to Dfl. 23,000 net per annum) diminished from 24.8 per cent in 1981 to 21.3 per cent in 1985 (when this income bracket was up to Dfl. 25,000 net per year). At the same time, for people with a higher income the home ownership rate has risen: from 46.7 per cent in 1981 (more than Dfl. 26,000

---

[21] Romme (1990) makes use of the data quoted because he wants to construct a projection model that is better than a status quo projection model in forecasting how the participation of women in the labour market will develop. Within that model he makes use of a reference group approach which is operationalized by cohort data. For further evidence see Van der Lippe and Siegers (1990).

[22] The data in this section refer primarily to the 1987 NCBS publication; in table 9.8, the changes that have taken place in the second half of the 1980s are represented by percentage point changes in brackets.

net per year) to 51.3 per cent in 1985 (more than Dfl. 29,000 net per year).

At the overall level, of all one-family households (that is to say, the main inhabitants), 72 per cent live in a flat/house with four or five rooms in the early 1980s, and 73 per cent have such a dwelling at the end of the 1980s (Table 9.8).

The proportion of the income that is paid in rent or mortgage for the flat or the house has risen between 1981 and 1985, but it did so most of all for one-person households (from 16.5 per cent in 1981 to 19.5 per cent in 1985) and one-parent families (from 15.9 per cent in 1981 to 18.6 per cent in 1985). In general, one can say that for people with a lower income the rent takes a bigger part of the household budget than for people with a higher income. With respect to owner-occupiers (of flat or house), one can even observe a reduction of housing costs from 1981 to 1985 (overall, from 12.5 to 12 per cent; for house owners paying a mortgage from 16.6 to 15 per

Table 9.8. *Households, main inhabitants by structure of household and characteristics of the housing, 1987, and changes between 1987 and 1991 (%)*

		One-family households			Multiple-family households
	Total	Married couple	Married couple with children	One parent	
No. of rooms					
2 or less	3 (−1)	7 (−1)	0 (=)	3 (−1)	[a]
3	12 (−1)	20 (−1)	6 (−1)	15 (+1)	[a]
4	44 (=)	45 (−1)	44 (−1)	47 (+3)	30 (+)[b]
5	29 (+1)	20 (+3)	35 (=)	26 (−1)	30 (+)
6 or more	12 (+1)	8 (+1)	16 (=)	9 (−1)	33 (−)
Total					
(abs. x 1,000)	3,700.3	1,192.0	2,141.4	366.9	9.9
Type of housing					
One-fam. house	80 (+2)	73 (+2)	87 (+2)	64 (+2)	78 (+2)
Flat	20	27	13	36	22
Total					
(abs. x 1,000)	3,700.3	1,192.0	2,141.4	366.9	9.9

[a] Undisclosed for privacy reasons.
[b] On behalf of the fact that in 1987 and in 1991 different data were undisclosed, no percentage changes can be given in this column.

Source: NCBS (1987:39) (based on a partly reproduced and adapted table); NCBS (1991*a*:39–40) (based on a partly reproduced and adapted table).

cent). Some 61 per cent of all people who look for a flat or house to buy or rent prefer a one-family house. Among all people who in 1985 were starters on the housing market, 41.9 per cent were interested in one-family housing, as against 48.7 per cent in 1981. The tendency that can be observed is that people who look for one-family housing belong more and more to the category that (try to) move within the housing market after having lived on their own for some time (i.e. outside the family in which they were born).

The relation between housing and household type shows that the one-family house is the typical habitat of the Dutch two-parent family (80 per cent in the early and 87 per cent in the late 1980s); most of the one-parent families live in one-family houses too (64 per cent in 1987). Among two-parent families living in one-family dwellings, 44 per cent live in a habitat with four rooms; one-parent families predominantly live in houses or flats with four rooms (47 per cent in 1987, against 50 in 1991). A very small minority of all two-parent families and some 2 per cent of all one-parent families have a housing situation that is clearly below average. Given the fact that housing provision has to do with age and the residential career (see NCBS, 1987:64), one may suppose that the families that have to cope with a shortage in housing are to a large extent relative newcomers on the housing market and may improve their situation over time. Still, one must conclude that among families with young children in particular, there is a considerable portion that has problems in obtaining sufficient dwelling space within a given time.[23]

Housing is influenced by individual housing allowances (IHA – in Dutch, *individuele huursubsidie*). Everaers (1989) mentions some relevant relationships between housing allowances and household characteristics. First, more people than were expected have made use of individual housing allowances from 1984 on, since a bigger share of households belongs to those with a relatively low income. Second, fewer than average households of those that receive or received an IHA live or lived in one-family houses (about 50 per cent, as against the 80 or 82 per cent average).

---

[23] One must mention here that there are local policy measures concerning housing and there is special attention to housing problems, too. Slot and Minkman (1990:126) report that 22 per cent of the inhabitants of Amsterdam have problems concerning their housing situation – problems that are independent of those concerning individual housing allowances.

9.4.2. *Families and Poverty*

Observers of the Dutch welfare system praise the fact that in the Netherlands a lot has been done to prevent people from falling into extreme poverty (De Waard, 1991; Segalman, 1986). Given this fact, it may seem quite understandable that the theme of 'poverty' is not very often written about in the Netherlands. One can find some information under the heading of households at a minimum income level. Goossens *et al.* (1990) have recently done some research in this field. Their target groups were different types of household, among them families with one and families with two parents. At the end of 1988, 126,000 single-parent families based their living on allowances (Goossens *et al.*, 1990:260); their average income was Dfl. 15,600 per year.

There are 48,000 families among these which are characterized by the fact that the adult who contributes the better part to the household budget is of Dutch nationality. These families constitute 9 per cent of all households that receive allowances; 41 per cent of them have one child, 37 per cent have two and 12 per cent have three children (Goossens *et al.*, 1990:267). The average income per year is Dfl. 24,600; only 7 per cent of these families consider their income sufficient. In 37 per cent of all these families, one of the two parents is doing paid work. Looking at developments between 1983 and 1988, De Hoog and Van Ophem (1990)[24] stress the fact that all households dependent on benefits have lost ground when compared with households that earn a living with paid work. Comparison of different family types shows that nuclear families living on benefits are less well off than one-parent families and other households.

9.4.3. *'Life-Style' Patterns in the 1980s*

As a summary of the discussions above on the demographic and socio-economic characteristics of family life situations of women aged 25–29 and 45–49 in the 1980s, we present in this section the 'top-six' lists of 'life-style' types at the beginning and at the end of the decade. The lists have been constructed by linking Housing Demand Survey data to data from other sources.

We start with women aged 25–29, whose top-six list is given in Table 9.9. Like Table 9.10, it shows the six life-style types with the highest proportional shares in 1981–2 and in 1989–90, plus their gains or losses in percent-

---

[24] The data sets that are used by these authors to compare the economic situation of different kinds of families are not in all respects representative for the Netherlands.

Table 9.9. *Top-six 'life-style' ranking, women 25–29 years, the Netherlands, 1981–1982 and 1989–1990*

1981–2			1989–90		
Rank	%		%	Rank	Diff.
1	23.5	Married, 2+ children, one-income	13.1	4	−10.4
2	19.3	Married, no children, two-income	18.5	1	−0.8
3	16.6	Married, 1 child, one-income	9.2	5	−7.4
4	10.0	Single	16.4	2	+6.4
5	5.5	Cohabiting, no children, two-income	14.6	3	+9.1
6	4.9	Married, 2+ children, two-income	(4.0)	–	−0.9
–	(4.8)	Living with parents	7.3	6	+2.5
	15.4	Other	16.9		

Table 9.10. *Top-six 'life-style' ranking, women 45–49 years, the Netherlands, 1981–1982 and 1989–1990*

1981–2			1989–90		
Rank	%		%	Rank	Diff.
1	36.8	Married, 2+ children, one-income	22.7	1	−4.1
2	15.2	Married, no children, two-income	16.1	2	+0.9
3	12.5	Married, 1 child, one-income	12.3	3	−0.2
4	7.2	Single	(8.0)	–	+0.8
5	5.4	Cohabiting, no children, two-income	9.9	4	+4.5
6	5.1	Married, 2+ children, two-income	8.2	6	+3.1
–	(4.2)	Living with parents	8.7	5	+4.5
	13.6	Other	14.1		

age points over the decade. In terms of the concepts of pluralization and polarization, as explained in Section 9.1.1, we first interpret the slight rise in the proportional share of the category 'other', from 15.4 to 16.9 per cent, as a sign of still ongoing pluralization in this age group in the middle of its family formation period. In 1981–2, the traditional family life-style (married, two or more children, one income) is still the largest category even in this young age group, but at the end of the decade it has already tumbled down to rank 4, with a relative loss of 10 percentage points. At the end of the 1980s, the top position has been taken over by the more modern life-style type of the childless two-income couple (although with a slightly smaller proportional share than it had in 1981–2!), with the equally modern life-style types 'single' and 'childless two-income cohabitors' in ranks 2 and 3. It is these two types that show the biggest gains in proportional shares, with 6.4 and 9.1 percentage points respectively. In terms of the household economic consequences discussed in Section 9.4.1, we consider these findings as support of our polarization interpretation. A final point of interest in Table 9.9 is the 2.5 percentage point rise in the proportion of 25-29-year-old women still (or again) residing in their parents' home, which reflects the rise in the mean age at leaving the parental home as observed in the 1980s.

In contrast, as shown in Table 9.10, age group 45–49 shows a much smaller amount of change over the 1980s in its top-six list. Positions 1–3 have remained the same, although in a relative sense the traditional family type in first place has lost much more in this age group (a percentage point loss of 14.1!). When combined with the smaller gains for the two-income married couple without children, with one child or with two or more children in ranks 5, 4 and 2 resp., we suppose that this significant fall in proportional share of the number-one life-style type has to do equally with the post-1965 overall fertility drop and with more women successfully looking for (part-time) jobs when the children are old enough to take care of themselves. Again, pluralization/polarization seem less pronounced in this age group than in the younger 25–29 age group. But, we must not forget that the most important category at the one extreme of the polarization axis – that of the lone-parenting women – does not feature in these top-six lists of life-style types.

9.5. Compatibility of Family and Employment

9.5.1. *Child-Care Arrangements by Family Type and by Employment of Mother/Father*

Day-care institutions including school-based care in the Netherlands[25] fulfil the following criteria: social and intellectual development of the child and/or pedagogical advice to the parents, provision for a maximum of 12 hours per day for at least two part-days per week, by people who are not the children's parents, and for children up to 12 years of age (Den Hertog, 1989).[26]

Data on women (at first birth in an age lower than 30) with children dif-

---

[25] For a taxonomy of all the different types of day-care organizations in Europe and elsewhere, see OECD (1990:127). For the characteristics of the different Dutch day-care services, see Maassen van den Brink (1991:22).

[26] In the article by Den Hertog one can find the numbers with respect to the capacities of day-care services in The Netherlands in 1988 (Den Hertog, 1989:12). The number of places in regulated child care for different countries can be found in OECD (1990:131). Developments concerning Dutch (and British) corporation activities for improving the compatibility of women's and men's paid work, child-rearing and partnership are presented in Hootsmans (1992).

ferentiated with respect to working situation and day care used around the moment of first birth can be found in Table 9.11. One important result: in 1985–7, only 2 per cent of all mothers made use of a 'crèche' (day-care centre for the entire working day) for their babies and continued work without reduction; another 2 per cent took a cut in working hours and made use of a 'crèche'. There is a tendency for more women to go on working after giving birth to a child (13 per cent in 1979–81, 23 per cent in 1985–7: see also Section 9.4.1).

The data in Table 9.11 show that a majority of women stop working after having given birth to a baby. Regulated child-care arrangements are used only by a minority. Mothers who continue working after the birth of their first child mostly rely on unregistered child care. The demand for child-care services is growing, and, thanks to the stimulation measures being taken by the state (see Section 9.2), one can say that provision is growing too. Still, the situation for mothers and young families who are searching for child-care places is often very difficult (Elle, 1991).

Table 9.11. *Women with children, by work situation and child-care use around the period of delivery of the first child, the Netherlands, February 1988 (%)*[a]

	1979–81	1982–4	1985–7	Total
Did not work at the start of the pregnancy	26	25	29	27
Worked after the start of the pregnancy, and after birth of child stayed working same number of hours or increased that number and arranged child care by means of				
Partner, family, friends	6	8	7	7
Day-care arrangements	1	2	2	2
Started working for fewer hours and arranged child care by means of				
Partner, family, friends	5	8	12	8
Child-care arrangements	1	1	2	2
Stopped working	61	55	46	54
Sample (N = 100%)	481	513	504	1,498

[a] Women under 30 at the time of delivery of the first child.

Source: NCBS (1990*b*:99).

With respect to the way in which the political system is trying to broaden the provision of day care, it is not yet certain whether such measures will be successful on both the demand and the supply side, for several reasons: (i) the demand of the labour market is not in all respects very strong; (ii) working women are engaged mostly in part-time work, and (iii) parental leave (following the special national laws that often are changed in favour of the mothers by special labour contracts) is firstly not compensated by allowances and, secondly, tied to a continuation of work. Furthermore, if the staff of the day-care services are going to be better paid in the future, the costs of places in the various forms of care for children might become unattractive, if not prohibitive, for those earning lower wages.

9.5.2. *Division of Labour in the Household with Special Reference to Child Care*

The division of labour in the household with special reference to child care has not very often been the target of research on the level of the family in the Netherlands. Careful research has been done by Tavecchio *et al.* (1984). They analysed postal questionnaires of 166 married partners with at least two children between the age of 0 and 3.5 years; wives and husbands were asked about the actual and the preferred division of the following family tasks: (i) caring (e.g. making the beds, changing nappies), (ii) doing chores (e.g. fixing a flat bicycle tyre) and (iii) pedagogical activities (e.g. cuddling or punishing the children). Moreover, attention was paid to the structure of activities both on working days and on Sundays.

The actual and the preferred division of family tasks within the whole sample show the same structure, yet there is a tendency towards a more egal-itarian division of labour in the preferred pattern. The lion's share of all the tasks is carried out by the wives.[27] 'Items relating to interaction with the children . . . are considered . . . to be least tied to sex-roles . . .' (Tavecchio *et al.*, 1984:234), and the desirability of sharing household tasks equally is dependent on the socio-economic status of the household. Although only 17 per cent of all women in the sample are working outside the home (3 per cent of them full-time), one can see that the spouses of families where

---

[27] The given method does not allow us to answer the question: 'Does this mean that in this case wives overestimate their own share . . ., or does it mean that husbands overestimate their contribution. . .?' (Tavecchio *et al.*, 1984:235). A more precise assessment of the relative contribution to family tasks requires other research methods, such as the diary method (see Gershuny, 1990).

both adults participate in paid work share the family tasks in a more egalitarian way than 'traditional' spouses do. Nevertheless, 'even in families with employed wives, the emphasis remains upon the wife's fulfilling specific household tasks' (Tavecchio *et al.*, 1984:240). Given the fact that participation of women in paid work has risen on the whole since 1979[28] (the time when the data for the above-summarized research were collected), and taking into account that marriage – in contrast to its alternative cohabitation – seems to be related to a more conservative pattern of partnership of spouses with respect to division of labour (Van der Avort, 1987:237), one can hypothesize that today one would observe a growing tendency towards symmetry of wife and husband and the two parents in a partnership with respect to the division of family tasks.

Looking at the relevant literature, we can only partly check whether or not this hypothesis holds for the 1980s. We can rely on data collected in time-budget research.[29] The data lack information about child care and pedagogical action with respect to young children because the sample excluded households with children up to 12 years. Nevertheless, some relevant information can be extracted:

• More and more people experience biographical patterns that do not coincide with the 'normal' sequence: childhood, general education, vocational education, leaving the parental home, paid work, marriage, partnership and parenthood.

• There is a general trend of augmentation with respect to the different tasks that are fulfilled by adults. Three realms and their overlap are considered: work, household and education. People with combinations of at least two of the mentioned tasks in the age range from 20–50 have increased from 37 per cent in 1975 to 43 per cent in 1985 (Knulst and Van Beek, 1990:117).[30]

• In many households with members of the post-war generations, the gender-specific division of labour has changed. The ideals of the emancipa-

[28] For the post-war time an increasing participation in paid work by women in the Netherlands has been observed by Hartog and Theeuwes (1985).

[29] The Netherlands has a remarkably well-established data set with respect to time-budget research; in 1975, 1980 and 1985 three diary-surveys were held; the results are summed up in Knulst and Van Beek (1990).

[30] The average is expressed in a diagram (Knulst and Van Beek, 1990:116). As the combination of different tasks has been growing in recent years, one may wonder in which regional setting the combination of daily activity patterns is easier or more difficult. Explorative research in this field (Droogleever Fortuijn and Karsten, 1989) produces the hypothesis that task combination can more easily be realized in urban than in suburban areas.

tion movement have not yet been attained, but there is a growing proportion of households in which the two partners have a job and share household tasks as well as the care-taking of family members (Knulst and Van Beek, 1990:112).

• Looked at in the long term, housework is changing from the specialized work of housewives to a general side-activity of adults living on their own. On average, both in 1975 and in 1985 people spent 19 hours a week doing household jobs. The variety of contributions has changed: since 1975 fewer people contribute both very small and very high proportions of their time to household tasks. The group of full-time housewives has reduced and has grown older (Knulst and Van Beek, 1990:115).

• Women aged 20 and older worked 36 hours per week in the home on average in 1975, and 33 in 1985. Men aged 20 and older worked 10 hours in 1975 and 12 hours in 1985. The change is attributed to:
(a) the growing participation of women in work in the formal sector;
(b) a reduction of household tasks with respect to the reduction of family members;
(c) a diminishing readiness to work at home among women and a concomitant increasing willingness to do so among men (Knulst and Van Beek, 1990:115).

However, it is only in the so-called *new households* – where both partners have a job – that a change with respect to the division of labour can be observed: men participate more, and at the same time their partners participate less. The change can be expressed by the following ratios: women/men = 4:1 in 1975 against 3:1 in 1985. *Traditional households* are characterized by the fact that men have contributed more to household tasks (from 1975 to 1985) but their partners did not reduce their amount of time spent in household activities. For traditional households the ratios are: women/men = 6:1 in 1975 and 4.5:1 in 1984.

• Relatively large time budgets, where household duties take up more than 60 hours per week, can be observed in the following groups: (i) two-income families between 20 and 50 years of age, (ii) people with high degrees of formal education, and (iii) *parents of young children* (Knulst and Van Beek, 1990:117).

• It shows that cohort-related information is becoming more important: differences between various kinds of population groups with respect to their time budgets were the same in many cases over the observed 10 years. Where differences could be found, however, the most important inequalities are related to *age classes* (Knulst and Van Beek, 1990:122).

There seems to be a trend of gradual disappearance of those traditional households where the husband or partner/father is the only breadwinner and where the wife or partner/mother specializes in doing the housework and/or child care, and where activities of adult family members are strongly centred around the house.

9.6. Summary and Conclusions

9.6.1. *Summary of Empirical Results*

We summarize our observations and highlight the facts that, in our view, will be relevant for international comparison.

1. When looking at the demographic trends, it is clear that the Netherlands has played its part in what has been labelled the Second Demographic Transition. What's more, in terms of speed of fertility decline, postponement of childbirth and spread of cohabitation before marriage, the Netherlands belongs to the vanguard group of countries in this transition process.

2. The development of family forms after the Second World War is characterized by changes at two different levels: (i) at the cultural level, the bourgeois family type has lost its monopoly position and formerly deviant family forms are now accepted as equal living arrangements; (ii) at the quantitative level, one can see that the distribution of types of living arrangement and/or family form is more varied. In this way, the Second Demographic Transition has certainly contributed to the *growing pluralization of family forms and life-styles* that has been mentioned in Section 9.1.1 and is documented further in Sections 9.3 and 9.4.

3. On the other hand, Dutch women who are part of the paid labour force show a participation rate that is still below the EU average. Of almost all the working women in European countries, Dutch women are the *outstanding part-timers*. For that reason, when demographic indicators are combined with socio-economic indicators, there are some signs of a *growing polarization between life-style types* in the socio-economic dimension of family life situations, but perhaps not so much as may be the case in other countries which show higher rates of female labour-force participation combined with higher proportions of women working full-time.

4. Taking into account that we do not have access to detailed data directly related to housing and family, we must still suppose that the *housing situation* of families is fair and rather homogeneous. One might however hypothesize that newcomers on the housing market – including young families – have some difficulties in finding a flat or a house quickly enough.

5. Dutch women and men have improved their *level of schooling and vocational training* over the last decades, and one can say that human capital has been improving in such a way that gender differences have diminished and basically do not constitute an obstacle to equal access to the labour market.

6. Within families, we attribute a growing responsiveness of male partners to increase their contribution to family and work activities to the fact that women are taking part in paid work. Still, the better part of *household chores* is done by women, and in two-income households the role of the quasi-professional housewife is fading.

7. *Provision of day-care services is relatively meagre* (although one has to take into account the fact that children may enter school at the age of 4). The type of policy that was followed in order to expand regulated day care up to the end of the 1980s can be summarized under the principle of private responsibility for day care. From 1990 onwards a new policy has emerged which incorporates a stronger public responsibility for regulated day care. In other words, the Netherlands has left the 'British solution' and taken its first steps on the way to the 'Swedish solution' of handling day-care demand (for this typology, see OECD, 1990).

8. The combination of a strong demand for work, the desire to bring up children and (at least for the vast majority) to live with a male partner has – given the low provision of day-care services – brought about the *'Dutch solution' for this compatibility problem*: part-time work for women/mothers. The thesis is supported by the fact that, of all women aged 25–29 who are working 30 hours or more per week, 7 per cent in 1981–2 and 6 per cent in 1989–90 only have children.

9. *Parental leave* did not exist – at least not at a national scale – during the 1980s. The introduction of a national law in favour of unpaid parental leave is of *almost purely symbolic effect*: there is no income substitute, and part-time work has to be continued (20 hours a week) after maternal leave in order to qualify. So, one has to suppose that the introduction of this law will have hardly any impact on family life if it is not materially implemented within collective agreements between e.g. firms and trade unions. Otherwise, it must be expected that, for most families trying to combine education or paid work and parenthood, everyday life will continue to be characterized by a series of stressful situations as a result of the relatively large numbers of hours spent in both paid work and household tasks, and the insecurity and organizational problems concerning the use of day-care arrangements.

10. Although on the legal level cohabiting and married couples with children are regarded as almost equal, one can infer that the *combination*

of policy, labour market and orientation of the relevant population is more conservative – and thus, as we suppose, more obstructive to the needs of parents who want to combine parenthood, partnership, household work and paid work – than one might think at first glance.

Summing up the most relevant findings, we may state that, with respect to demographic questions, the economic situation and the level of schooling of parents, the data presented are very informative. With respect to other issues, such as day care, child rearing in 'normal' families, housing and the qualifications that are demanded for the job of adults who are at the same time parents, we are not so well informed.

9.6.2. *Discussion: Possible Policy Impacts on the Distribution of Family Forms, Living Conditions of Different Family Types, and Everyday Life Arrangements*

A triangular relationship between the political system (especially that part concerned with family policy), the family system and the economic system of the Netherlands has to be taken into account when trying to reach conclusions regarding the impact of family policy on family life, both for the present and for the near future.

Concerning the level of legal acceptance of different family forms, a liberal openness can be observed. On the level of the financially most relevant policy measures (taxes, child allowances), different family forms are treated equally, whether the parents are married or not. But, with regard to the position of one-parent families in the welfare system as a whole, one has to admit that they are less well-off than complete families. There are even results that indicate that two-parent families living on benefits are worse off than one-parent families: this may be due to the fact that the orientation of government towards a male-breadwinner household has not yet led to the perception that structural unemployment has its impacts not only on individual persons but also, and especially, on families and must be taken into account on the political agenda.

Measures taken to enable the combination of parenthood, paid work and partnership are basically restricted to pregnancy and maternity leave arrangements, and are still relatively weak with respect to e.g. parental leave and the expansion of regulated day-care services. One may conclude, therefore, that the growing orientation of adults of both sexes towards combining paid work, partnership and parenthood is at least partially frustrated by a lack of supportive political measures. The fact that political measures are lacking in this field (in comparison with other European countries) has to be attributed to characteristics of the political system in the Netherlands, to the existing focus of its welfare system which is work-oriented, and to the fact that the financial power of the political system is to a great extent absorbed by legally defined tasks which might be difficult to change.

But the possible frustration of families whose adult partners both wish to participate in the labour market might be reduced hypothetically by the facts that: (i) Dutch women still have a strong orientation to devote their lives to motherhood after having given birth to a child, and (ii) the quantitative, regional and qualitative demands of the labour market in the Netherlands, i.e. the demand for working women by the economy, are not in tune with the labour offered by women.

Corresponding to our general hypothesis of resonance (see Section 9.2.2), one must assume that a lot of families co-exist with different orientations regarding the priorities of objectives for their life in general and their ideas about the ideal everyday life. With respect to all those who want to combine paid work of both adults, partnership and parenthood, one can suppose that a good deal of them will evaluate their situation positively because their income, or their work organization (with respect to collective contract measures in a special firm) or the regional market of day-care services does allow them to realize such compatibility.

However, among the families whose adult members share the same preferences (the 'would-be combiners' or the 'combiners'), one has to suppose that there are a lot of people who cannot integrate (or not in a smooth manner) their intentions; for those, one can discern two hypothetic groups: (i) those who are well aware of the problems they are facing (insecurity about the reliability of the existing day-care arrangement, financial shortcomings, being forced to make arrangements with relatives, the perception of shortcomings with respect to education) and are trying to improve their situation, and (ii) those who have adapted with some kind of resignation to the problems that arise in their everyday life.

Research designed to analyse the different life situations and to observe the reality that families have to cope with might point to the development of political measures designed to make complex life requests compatible at the level of the family group, as well as at the level of larger collectivities (the firm, the local community and society as a whole).

References

Baanders, A.N., Van Leeuwen, L.Th. and Ploegmakers, M.J.H. (1989), *Nederlandse huishoudens in de periode 1960-1985* (Netherlands Households in the Period 1960-1985), Ministerie van Volkshuisvesting, Ruimtelijke Ordening en Milieubeheer, DGVH, The Hague.

Becker, U. (1989), 'Frauenerwerbstätigkeit: Eine vergleichende Bestandsaufnahme' (Labour-force participation of women: a comparative assessment), *Aus Politik und Zeitgeschichte*, B28/9:22–33.

Beets, G. (1991), 'Population policy in the Netherlands', in G.C.N. Beets *et al.* (eds.), *Population and Family in the Low Countries 1991*, Swets & Zeitlinger, Amsterdam/Lisse: 200–9.

Bosveld, W., Wijsen, C. and Kuijsten, A. (1991), 'The growing importance of fertility at higher ages in the Netherlands', paper prepared for the European Population Conference 1991, organized by EAPS/IUSSP/INED, Paris, 21–25 October 1991, PDOD, Amsterdam (PDOD paper No. 3).

Brands-Bottema, G.W. (1989), 'Het gezinsbeeld in de politiek' (The image of family in the political system), *Gezin*, 1:149–63.

Bronsema, H.J. and Van der Erf, R.F. (eds.) (1992), *Emancipatie en bevolkingsontwikkeling: Hechte partners?* (Emancipation and Population Development: Close Partners?), Nederlandse Vereniging voor Demografie, The Hague.

Buissink, J.D. (1971), 'Regional differences in marital fertility in the Netherlands in the second half of the nineteenth century', *Population Studies*, 25:353–74.

Clerkx, L.E. and Van IJzendoorn, M.H. (1992), 'Child care in a Dutch context: on the history, current status and evaluation of non-marital child care in the Netherlands', in M.E. Lamb, K.J. Sternberg, C.-P. Hwang and A.G. Broberg (eds.), *Child Care in Context: Cross-cultural Perspectives*, Lawrence Erlbaum Associates, Hove, Sussex, London, and Hillsdale, NJ: 55–79.

Corver, C.J.M., Van der Heiden, A.M., De Hoog, C. and Van Leeuwen, L.Th. (1979), *Huishouden, huwelijk en gezin: Een analyse op basis van de gezinssociologische censusmonografieën* (Household, Marriage and the Family: an Analysis on the Basis of Family Sociological Census Monographs), Staatsuitgeverij, The Hague (Monografieën Volkstelling 1971, No. 18).

De Feijter, H. (1991), *Voorlopers bij demografische veranderingen* (Forerunners in Demographic Changes), NIDI, The Hague (NIDI Report No. 22).

De Graaf, P.M. and Ultee, W.C. (1991) 'Arbeidsmarktmobiliteit en partner-effecten: een analyse van arbeidsgeschiedenissen van (echt)paren in Nederland tussen 1980 en 1986' (Labour-market mobility and partner effects), *Tijdschrift voor Arbeidsvraagstukken*, 7:27–42.

De Hoog, C. (1989), 'Het gezin: ontwikkeling en actualiteit' (The family: developments and actual situation), *Gezin*, 1:128–48.

—— and Van Ophem, J.A.C. (1990), 'Gezinnen en armoede' (Families and poverty), *Gezin*, 2:144–56.

Dekker, J.J.H. and Groenendijk, L.F. (1991), 'The Republic of God or the Republic of Children? Childhood and child-rearing after the Reformation: an appraisal of Simon Schama's thesis about the uniqueness of the Dutch case', *Oxford Review of Education*, 17:317–35.

Den Hertog, J.A. (1989), 'Arbeidsdeelname van vrouwen en het tekort aan kinderopvang' (Female labour-force participation and the lack of child-care facilities), *Bevolking en Gezin*, 18:1–22.

De Swaan, A. (1989), *Zorg en de Staat*, Bakker, Amsterdam (English-language version: *In Care of the State: Health Care, Education and Welfare in Europe and the U.S.A. in the Modern Era*, Polity Press, Cambridge).

DeVos, S. and Palloni, A. (1989), 'Formal models and methods for the analysis of kinship and household organization', *Population Index*, 55:174–98.

De Waard, M. (1991), 'De desintegratie van onze morele gemeenschap: Ralf Dahrendorf over het ontstaan van een Europese onderklasse' (The de-integration of our moral society), *NRC-Handelsblad*, 3 August 1991, Zaterdags Bijvoegsel.

Dirven, H.J., Lammers, J. and Ultee, W.C. (1990), 'Werkend en toch economisch afhankelijk?' (Working and still economically dependent?), *Sociale Wetenschappen*, 33:61–93.

Douma, W.H. (1975), *Het gezin tussen verleden en toekomst: Een sociologisch onderzoek in twee verstedelijkende plattelandsgemeenten voor en na de jaren zestig: beschrijving, analyse en beschouwingen* (The Family between Past and Future: A Sociological Investigation in Two Urbanizing Communities before and after the Sixties: Description, Analysis and Reflections), Veemen, Wageningen.

Droogleever Fortuijn, J. and Karsten, L. (1989), 'Daily activity patterns of working parents in the Netherlands', *Area*, 21:365–76.

Dumon, W. (1991), 'Family policy in the EC countries: a general overview', in G.C.N. Beets *et al.* (eds.), *Population and Family in the Low Countries 1991*, Swets & Zeitlinger, Amsterdam/Lisse: 1–16.

Dumon, W.A. and Deneffe, C. (1992), *Gezinswetenschappelijke documentatie 17 (1992)* (Family Sciences Documentation 17 (1992)), GIDS, Leuven.

Elle (1991), *'Er zijn nog 70.000 wachtenden voor u'* (As many as 70,000 people still queue), August.

Emancipatie in arbeidsorganisaties (1991) (Emancipation in Labour Organizations), Dienst Collectieve Arbeidsvoorwaarden, Ministerie van Sociale Zaken en Werkgelegenheid, The Hague.

Engelen, Th.L.M. and Hillebrand, J.H.A. (1986), 'Fertility and nuptiality in the Netherlands, 1850–1960', *Population Studies*, 40:487–503.

Ester, P. and Nauta, A.P.N. (1989) 'Vijftien jaar Sociale en Culturele Rapporten in Nederland' (Fifteen years of reporting on social issues in the Netherlands), *Sociale Wetenschappen*, 32:176–93.

Esveldt, I. and Van Nimwegen, N. (1992), *Naar een kindvriendelijker samenleving?* (Towards a More Child-Friendly Society?), NIDI, The Hague (NIDI Report No. 28).

Everaers, P. (1989), 'Het woningbehoeftenpanel 1988' (The Housing Demand Panel

1988), *Planning: Methodiek en Toepassing*, 35:12–4.

Frinking, G.A.B. (1986), 'De ambivalentie van het bevolkingsbeleid in Nederland' (The ambivalence of population policy in the Netherlands), *Christen Democratische Verkenningen*, 6:121–6.

—— (1990), 'Kiezen voor kinderen: De rol van de overheid ter discussie' (Opting for children: bringing the role of the government up for discussion), *Gezin*, 2:88–94.

—— and Nelissen, J.H.M. (eds.) (1988), *Het kind als keuze: Demografische ontwikkelingen in Nederland* (Children from Choice: Demographic Developments in the Netherlands), SDU-Uitgeverij, The Hague.

Ganzeboom, H.B.G. and De Graaf, P.M. (1989*a*), 'Intergenerationele opleidingsmobiliteit in Nederland van geboortecohorten 1891–1960' (Intergenerational educational mobility in the Netherlands of birth cohorts 1891–1960), *Sociale Wetenschappen*, 32:263–78.

—— and De Graaf, P.M. (1989*b*), 'Veranderingen van onderwijskansen in Nederland tussen 1900 en 1980' (Changes in educational opportunities in the Netherlands between 1900 and 1980), in I. Gadourek and J.L. Peschar (eds.), *De open samenleving? Sociale veranderingen op het terrein van geloof, huwelijk, onderwijs en arbeid in Nederland* (The Open Society? Social Changes in the Field of Religion, Marriage, Education and Work in the Netherlands), Van Loghum Slaterus, Deventer: 58–78.

Gerris, J.R.M. and Van Acker. J. (1990), *Gezin: Aspecten van sociale ondersteuning en intern functioneren* (Family: Aspects of Social Support and Internal Functioning), Swets & Zeitlinger, Amsterdam/Lisse.

Gershuny, J. (1990), 'International comparisons of time budget surveys: methods and opportunities', in R. von Schweitzer *et al.* (eds.), *Zeitbudgeterhebungen: Ziele, Methoden und neue Konzepte* (Time Budget Surveys: Aims, Methods and New Concepts), Metzler-Poeschel, Stuttgart (Schriftenreihe Forum der Bundesstatistik, herausgegeben vom Statistischen Bundesamt, Vol. 13): 23–53.

Goossens, F.A. (1986), *Quality of Attachment in Children of Working and Non-Working Mothers*. Acco, Leuven/Amersfoort.

Goossens, R.C. and De Vos, E.L. (in co-operation with De Hoog, C. and Van Ophem, J.A.C.) (1990), *De huishouding van minima* (Household Management at Minimum Incomes), Landbouwuniversiteit, Vakgroep Huishoudstudies, Wageningen.

Grunell, M. (1985), *Thuis in de jaren vijftig: Vrouwen over de hoeksteen van de samenleving* (At Home in the 1950s: Women about Society's Cornerstone), 2nd edn., University of Amsterdam, Amsterdam.

Haks, D. (1982), *Huwelijk en gezin in Holland in de 17de en de 18de eeuw: Processtukken en moralisten over aspecten van het laat 17de- en 18de-eeuwse gezinsleven* (Marriage and the Family in Holland in the Seventeenth and Eighteenth Centuries: Case Records and Moralists on Aspects of Late Seventeenth- and Eighteenth-Century Family Life), Van Gorcum, Assen.

Halman, L., Huenks, F., De Moor, R. and Zanders, H. (1987), *Traditie, secularisatie en individualisering: Een studie naar de waarden van de Nederlanders in een Europese context* (Tradition, Secularization and Individualization). Tilburg University Press, Tilburg.

Hartog, J. and Theeuwes, J. (1985), 'The emergence of the working wife in Holland', *Journal of Labour Economics*, 3:S235–55.

Havinga, T. (1983), *Huisvrouwen en herverdelen van huishoudelijk werk* (Housewives and the Redistribution of Homemaking Tasks). Trendrapport. Stafafdeling Externe Betrekkingen Ministerie van Sociale Zaken en Werkgelegenheid, The Hague.

Heeren, H.J. (1985), *Bevolkingsgroei en bevolkingsbeleid in Nederland* (Population Growth and Population Policy in the Netherlands), Kobra, Amsterdam.

Hofstee, E.W. (1972), 'Enkele opmerkingen over de ontwikkeling van de vruchtbaarheid in Nederland' (Some observations on the development of marital fertility in the Netherlands), in R.F. Beerling *et al.* (eds.), *Onderzocht en overdacht. Sociologische opstellen voor Prof. Dr. F. van Heek* (Studied and Considered: Sociological Essays for Prof. Dr. F. van Heek), Universitaire Pers Rotterdam, Rotterdam (Boekaflevering *Mens en Maatschappij*, 47): 43–91.

Hoogmoed, R.S. (1989), 'De anti- respectievelijk pronatalistische discussie in Nederland' (The anti- respectively pro-natalist discussion in the Netherlands), *Bevolking en Gezin*, 18:75–93.

Hootsmans, H. (1992), 'Beyond 1992: Dutch and British corporations and the challenge of dual-career couples', in S. Lewis, D.N. Izraeli and H. Hootsmans (eds.), *Dual-Earner Families: International Perspectives*, Sage, London: 185–203.

Hulko, J. (1990), 'Family policy in Western Europe', *Yearbook of Population Research in Finland*, 27:5–27.

Idenburg, Ph.A. *et al.* (eds.) (1983), *De nadagen van de verzorgingsstaat: Kansen en perspectieven voor morgen* (The Aftermath of the Welfare State: Chances and Perspectives for Tomorrow), Meulenhoff, Amsterdam.

Jansweijer, R.M.A. (1987), *Private leefvormen, publieke gevolgen: Naar een overheidsbeleid met betrekking tot individualisering* (Private Life-Styles, Public Consequences: Towards a Government Policy Relating to Individualization), Staatsuitgeverij, The Hague.

Jonker, J.M.L. (1984), *Balans van de gezinssociologie* (Family Sociology on the Balance), SISWO, Amsterdam.

Kapteyn, P. (1980), *Taboe: Ontwikkelingen in macht en moraal, speciaal in Nederland* (Taboo: Trends in Power and Morality, Particularly in the Netherlands), De Arbeiderspers, Amsterdam.

Kaufmann, F.-X. (1990), *Zukunft der Familie: Stabilität, Stabilitätsrisiken und Wandel der familialen Lebensformen sowie ihre gesellschaftlichen und politischen Bedingungen* (The Future of the Family: Stability, Stability Risks and Change of Family Life Forms and Life Phases; Their Social and Political Conditions), Beck, Munich.

Kinderopvang (1984), Reactie op de adviesaanvraag van 26 juli 1984 over het voor-lopig regeringsstandpunt inzake kinderopvang (Day Care: Reaction to the Call for Advice of 26 July 1984 with Respect to an Outline of the Governmental Point of View on Day Care), Emancipatieraad Advies No. 84/19, September 1984, The Hague.

Kloek, E. (1989), *Gezinshistorici over vrouwen: een overzicht van het werk van gezinshistorici en de betekenis daarvan voor de vrouwengeschiedenis* (Family Historians on Women: an Overview of the Work of Family Historians and its Meaning for Women's History), SUA, Amsterdam.

Knulst, W.P. and Van Beek, P. (1990), *Tijd komt met de jaren* (Time Comes with the Years), Sociaal en Cultureel Planbureau, Rijswijk.

Kooy, G.A. (ed.) (1985), *Gezinsgeschiedenis: Vier eeuwen gezin in Nederland* (Family History: Four Centuries of the Family in the Netherlands), Van Gorcum, Assen.

Kronjee, G.J. (1989), 'Gezin, levenscyclus en sociale verandering' (Family, life cycle and social change), *Beleid en Maatschappij*, 26:322–31.

Kuijsten, A.C. (1992), 'Demografische ontwikkelingen' (Demographic develop-ments), *Gezin*, 4:170–85.

—— and Klijzing, E. (1990), 'Domestic histories in the Netherlands: a comparison of generations', in H.A. Becker (ed.), *Life Histories and Generations*, ISOR, Utrecht, Vol. 2: 307–40.

—— and Schulze, H.-J. (1992), 'Changing family structures in the 1980s: the case of the Netherlands'. Country Report prepared for the International Research Pro-ject, "Family Life and Family Policies in Europe", Amsterdam.

Langeveld, H.M. (1985), *Binding in vrijheid: een studie naar toekomstige gezinnen, relaties en hulpverlening* (Tied Down in Freedom: a Study of Future Families, Relationships and Social Aid), Sociaal en Cultureel Planbureau, Rijswijk (Soci-ale en Culturele Studies No. 6).

Leeuw, F.L. (1984), *Overheid en bevolkingsgroei: Een evaluatie van beleidstheorieën* (The State and Population Growth: an Evaluation of Policy Theories), VUGA, The Hague.

Liefbroer, A. (1991), *Kiezen tussen ongehuwd samenwonen en trouwen* (Choosing between Unmarried Cohabitation and Marriage), Centrale Huisdrukkerij Vrije Universiteit, Amsterdam.

Maassen van den Brink, H. (1991), 'Arbeidsdeelname tegen elke prijs?' (Labour-force participation at any cost?), in Singer and Tijdens (1991): 9–27.

Manting, D. (1994), *Dynamics in Marriage and Cohabitation: an Inter-temporal, Life Course Analysis of First Union Formation and Dissolution*, Thesis Publishers, Amsterdam (PDOD Publications Series A: Doctoral Dissertations).

——, Kuijsten, A. and Helleman, J. (1992), 'From youth to adulthood: transitions of female birth cohorts in the Netherlands', in G.C.N. Beets *et al.* (eds.), *Population and Family in the Low Countries 1992: Family and Labour*, Swets & Zeitlinger, Amsterdam/Lisse: 55–76.

McIntosh, C. (1983), *Population Policy in Western Europe: Responses to Low*

Fertility in France, Sweden and West Germany, M.E. Sharpe Inc., New York/ London.

Moors, H. and Koesoebjono, S. (1990), 'Een baan en een gezin' (A job and a family), *Demos*, 7:52–5.

——, Van Leusden, H. and Hogen Esch, I. (1989), *Opvattingen over het bevolkings- vraagstuk en de acceptatie van beleid* (Opinions on the Population Problem and on Policy Acceptance), NIDI, The Hague (NIDI Report No. 7).

Moss, P. (co-ord.) (1990), *Kinderopvang en verzorging in de Europese Gemeen- schap: 1985–1990* (Child Care in the European Community: 1985–1990), Commission of the European Community, Brussels.

NCBS (Netherlands Central Bureau of Statistics) (1986), *Well-being of the Population in the Netherlands 1983: Financial Strength of One- and Two-Income Households*, Staatsuitgeverij, The Hague.

—— (1987), *Woningbehoeftenonderzoek 1985–86: Huisvestingssituatie, woonlasten en verhuizingen, landelijke kerncijfers* (Housing Demand Survey 1985–86: Housing Situation, Amount of Rent, Moves, National Indicators), SDU/Uitgeverij, The Hague.

—— (1990*a*), *Onderzoek Gezinsvorming 1988: Samenwonen, trouwen, geboortenrege- ling, werken en kinderen krijgen* (Netherlands Fertility Survey 1988: Cohabitation, Marriage, Birth Control, Em-ployment and Fertility), SDU/Uitgeverij, The Hague.

—— (1990*b*), *Statistisch Jaarboek 1990* (Statistical Yearbook 1990), SDU/Uitgeverij, The Hague.

—— (1991*a*), *Statistisch Jaarboek 1991* (Statistical Yearbook 1991), SDU/Uitgeverij, The Hague.

—— (1991*b*), *Woningbehoeftenonderzoek 1989–90: Huisvestingssituatie, woonlasten en verhuizingen, landelijke kerncijfers* (Housing Demand Survey 1989–90: Housing Situation, Amount of Rent, Moves, National Indicators), SDU/Uitgeverij, The Hague.

OECD (1990), *Employment Outlook*, Organization for Economic Co-operation and Development, Paris.

Outshoorn, J. (1986), 'The rules of the game: abortion politics in the Netherlands', in: J. Lovenduski and J. Outshoorn (eds.), *The New Politics of Abortion*, Sage, London: 5–26.

Peeters, H., Dresen-Coenders, L. and Brandenbarg, T. (eds.) (1988), *Vijf eeuwen gezinsleven: Liefde, huwelijk en opvoeding in Nederland* (Five Centuries of Family Life: Love, Marriage and Upbringing in the Netherlands), SUN, Nijmegen.

Pelzer, A. (1991), 'Van experiment tot basisvoorziening' (From experiment to primary provision), in Singer and Tijdens (1991): 77–95.

Plantenga, J. (1992), 'Women and work in the Netherlands: some notes about female labour force participation and the nature of the welfare state', in *Acta Demo- graphica 1992*, Physica-Verlag, Heidelberg: 47–56.

Qvortrup, J. (1992), *Family – Youth – Childhood: an Inventory of Important Re- search Institutes and Researchers in the Fields of Family, Youth and Childhood in the EEC Member States – 1992*, Ministry for Social Affairs, Copenhagen.

Relatievormen in Nederland (1989) (Life-Styles in the Netherlands), NIDI, The Hague (NIDI Report No. 8).

Romme, A.G.L. (1990), 'Projecting female labor supply: the relevance of social norm change', *Journal of Economic Psychology*, 11:85–99.

Rood-De Boer, M. (1990), 'Rechtsvragen met betrekking tot ouderschap' (Legal questions with respect to parenthood), *Gezin*, 2:181–8.

Sardon, J.-P. (1991), 'La primo-nuptialité en Europe: éléments pour une typologie' (First marriage in Europe: elements for a typology), paper prepared for the European Population Conference 1991, organized by EAPS/IUSSP/INED, Paris, 21–25 October 1991.

Schellekens, J. (1991), 'Determinants of marriage patterns among farmers and agricultural laborers in two eighteenth-century Dutch villages', *Journal of Family History*, 16:139–55.

Schülein, J.A. (1990), *Die Geburt der Eltern: Über die Entstehung der modernen Elternposition und den Prozeß ihrer Aneignung und Vermittlung* (The Birth of Parents: on the Creation of Modern Parenthood and the Process of its Acquisition and Mediation), Westdeutscher Verlag, Opladen.

Schulze, H.-J. (1985), *Autonomiepotentiale familialer Sozialisation: Personale und Soziale Differenzierung als Grundlage der neuorientierten sozialstrukturellen Sozialisationsforschung* (Autonomy Potentials of Family Socialization), Enke, Stuttgart.

——, Tyrell, H. and Künzler, J. (1989), 'Vom Strukturfunktionalismus zur System-theorie der Familie' (From structural–functional theory to systems theory of the family), in R. Nave-Herz and M. Markefka (eds.), *Handbuch der Familien- und Jugendforschung, I. Familienforschung*, Luchterhand, Neuwied/Frankfurt: 31–43.

Segalman, R. (1986), *The Swiss Way of Welfare: Lessons for the Western World*, Praeger, New York.

Sevenhuysen, S.L. (1987), *De orde van het vaderschap: politieke debatten over ongehuwd moederschap, afstamming en huwelijk in Nederland 1870–1900* (The Order of Fatherhood: Political Debates on Single Motherhood, Descent and Marriage in the Netherlands 1870–1900), Stichting Beheer IISG, Amsterdam.

Singer, E. (1989), *Kinderopvang en de moeder-kindrelatie: pedagogen, psychologen en sociale hervormers over moeders en jonge kinderen* (Child-Care Arrangements and the Mother–Child Relationship), Van Loghum Slaterus, Deventer.

—— and Tijdens, K. (eds.) (1991), *Uit en thuis: Wetenschapsters over kinderopvang in Nederland* (Away and at Home: Women Researchers on Day Care in the Netherlands), Jan van Arkel, Utrecht.

Slot, J. and Minkman, M. (1990), *Gebruikersonderzoek Voorzieningen 1989* (Survey on the Use of Community Services), Bureau of Research and Statistics, Amsterdam.

Spieß, E., Nerdinger, F.W. and Von Rosenstiel, L. (1991), 'Motivation of repro-ductive behaviour and the professional motivation of women', in J.J. Siegers, J. de Jong-Gierveld and E. van Imhoff (eds.), *Female Labour Market Behaviour and Fertility: a Rational-Choice Approach*, Springer, Berlin: 87–100.

Stalpers, J.A. and Tilborghs, D.J. (1981), *Het beklemde gezin* (The Oppressed Family), Rabobank, Tilburg.

Tas, R.F.J. (1992), 'Huwelijksontbindingstafel naar duur van het huwelijk, 1986–1990' (Marriage dissolution table for the Netherlands by duration of marriage, 1986–1990), in NCBS, *Maandstatistiek van de Bevolking* (Monthly Bulletin of Population Statistics), 40(6):31–7.

Tavecchio, L.W.C., Van IJzendoorn, M.H., Goossens, F. and Vergeer, M.M. (1984), 'The division of labor in Dutch families with preschool children', *Journal of Marriage and the Family*, 46:231–42.

Tyrell, H. (1989), 'Ehe und Familie: Institutionalisierung und Deinstitutionalisierung' (Marriage and family: institutionalization and de-institutionalization), in K. Lüscher, F. Schultheis and M. Wehrspaun (eds.), *Die 'postmoderne' Familie: Familiale Strategien und Familienpolitik in einer Übergangszeit* (The 'Post-Modern' Family: Family Strategies and Family Policy in an Era of Transition), Universitätsverlag, Konstanz: 285–312.

Van Dam, M. and Van IJzendoorn, M.H. (1990), *Are Infants of Working Mothers Insecurely Attached?* Centre for Child and Family Studies, Leiden.

Van de Kaa, D.J. (1987), 'Europe's Second Demographic Transition', *Population Bulletin*, 42(1), Population Reference Bureau, Washington, DC.

Van den Akker, P.A.M., and Van der Avort, A.J.P.M. (1986), 'Children after parental divorce: short-term and long-term consequences and conditions for adjustment', in F. Deven and R.L. Cliquet (eds.), *One-Parent Families in Europe: Trends, Experiences, Implications* (Proceedings of the CBGS International Workshop on One-Parent Families, Brussels, 1985), NIDI, The Hague: 83–110.

Van der Avort, A.J.P.M. (1987), *De gulzige vrij-blijvendheid van expliciete relaties* (The Greediness of Modern Explicit Relationships), Tilburg University Press, Tilburg.

Van der Lippe, A.G. and Siegers, J.J. (1990), 'De relatie tussen beroepsdeelname van gehuwde vrouwen en hun houding ten opzichte van beroepsdeelname: een simultane logitanalyse' (The relationship between labour-force participation of married women and their attitude towards labour-force participation: a simultaneous logit analysis), *Sociale Wetenschappen*, 33:94–112.

Van der Woude, A.M. (1972), *Het Noorderkwartier: Een regionaal historisch onderzoek in de demografische en economische geschiedenis van Westelijk Nederland van de late Middeleeuwen tot het begin van de negentiende eeuw* (The Noorderkwartier: a Study in the Demographic and Economic History of Western Parts of the Netherlands from the End of the Middle Ages till the Beginning of the Nineteenth Century), Wageningen (AAG Bijdragen 16, 3 vols.).

Van Heek, F. (1956), 'Roman Catholicism and fertility in the Netherlands: demographic aspects of minority status', *Population Studies*, 10:125–38.

Van Herwaarden, F.G., Pommer, E.J. and Hooijmans, E.M. (1990), *Gecumuleerd beleid* (Cumulated Policy), Sociaal en Cultureel Planbureau, Rijswijk.

Van Imhoff, E. (1990), 'Sterke stijging uitgaven sociale zekerheid verwacht' (An expectation of strongly rising social security costs), *Demos*, 8:57–60.

Van Leeuwen, L.Th. (1990), *Patronen in de individuele levensloop: Een verkennende studie* (Patterns in the Individual Life Course: an Explorative Study), Nederlandse Gezinsraad, The Hague.

Van Nimwegen, N. (1991), 'Population research in the Netherlands during the eighties: an overview', in G.C.N. Beets *et al.* (eds.), *Population and Family in the Low Countries 1991*, Swets & Zeitlinger, Amsterdam/Lisse: 123–31.

Van Stolk, B. and Wouters, C. (1983), *Vrouwen in tweestrijd: Tussen thuis en tehuis; relatieproblemen in de verzorgingsstaat, opgetekend in een crisiscentrum* (Women in Two Minds: Between Home and Women's Shelter), Van Loghum Slaterus, Deventer.

Veenhoven, R. and Van der Wolk, E. (eds.) (1977), *Kiezen voor kinderen?* (To Choose Children?), Intermediair, Amsterdam.

Wallerstein, I. and Smith, J. (1990), 'Households as an institution of the world-economy', in J. Sprey (ed.), *Fashioning Family Theory: New Approaches*, Sage, Newbury Park, Calif.

Weeda, I. (1982), *Ideaalbeelden rond leefvormen: Variatie in denken over huwelijk, gezin en andere leefvormen* (Ideal Concepts Concerning Living Arrangements: Varying Attitudes with Regard to Marriage, Family and Alternative Living Arrangements), Van Loghum Slaterus, Deventer.

—— (1989), 'Waarden en ervaringen ten aanzien van leef- en relatievormen' (Values and experiences with regard to living arrangements), in *Relatievormen* (1989): 110–27.

Winchester, H.P.M. (1989), 'Women and children last: the poverty and marginalization of one-parent families', *Transactions of the Institute of British Geographers*, N.S.15:70–86.

Wijsen, C. (1993), 'Timing the fertility life course: a deliberate choice', paper prepared for the IUSSP XXIInd General Population Conference, Montreal, Canada, 24 August – 1 September 1993, PDOD, Amsterdam, 1993 (PDOD paper No. 20).

Zwier, B. and Mostert, E. (1989), *Kinderopvang: Zorgen voor de generatie van morgen* (Day Care: Care for Tomorrow's Generation), VUGA, The Hague.

10 Sweden: a Case of Solidarity and Equality

TUIJA MEISAARI-POLSA

Statistiska Centralbyrån, Stockholm, Sweden

Social rights in Sweden, including those related to families, are based on two guiding ideas: the idea of solidarity, and that of equality. Therefore, the aim of the complex system of Swedish family policy measures is, firstly, to maintain a reasonable standard of living for all family forms and, secondly, to increase possibilities for both women and men to choose their own way of life and to combine family life and work. This chapter shows that the solidarity- and equality-based social policy in Sweden is at the same time modern and family-friendly. After describing family policy, family forms, family life situation and everyday life of families, the chapter summarizes policy effects on family forms in Sweden. The results demonstrate that, in some respect, Swedish family policy is relevant with respect to demographic trends, but the relationship between family policy and demographic trends is complicated.

10.1. Introduction

The aim of this section is to present general trends in Swedish family structures. Three main questions will be answered: What are the historical characteristics of marriage and the family in Sweden? What main demographic trends can be observed in the 1980s – homogeneity or heterogeneity, pluralization or polarization? On which data is this study based?

10.1.1. *Changing Family Structures: Historical Characteristics*

Cohabitation that more or less resembles marriage but without the legal institution of marriage has existed to a varying degree throughout Swedish history. When Christianity came to Sweden, the church wedding began to replace the pre-Christian Germanic marriage rituals and ceremonies. Despite many laws and regulations replacing one another, this process took more than a half-millennium from the introduction of Christianity into Sweden in the twelfth century (Carlsson, 1972).

In 1686, church marriage became complementary to civil marriage. The civil form of marriage was prohibited in 1743, after the church wedding had become obligatory for a fully valid marriage in 1734. Civil marriage again became permissible in 1908.

In the early twentieth century, a considerable number of couples lived together without being married in some parts of the country. Studies available (e.g., Karlsson, 1951; Trost, 1967*a*, 1967*b*, 1971) establish the existence of long engagements in Sweden. As a consequence, relatively long cohabitation periods prior to weddings were not uncommon.

In the 1930s, many couples who lived in difficult circumstances did not enter a marriage contract but instead cohabited in a so-called 'Stockholm marriage'. Before civil marriages were permitted, many couples entered into so-called common-law marriages (Löfgren, 1972; Matovic, 1984; Persson, 1971; Trost and Lewin, 1978; Wikman, 1937).

In the middle of the eighteenth century, 2 per cent of all children in Sweden were born to unmarried parents. This proportion increased, and by 1900 it was 11 per cent of all children. In the 1930s, almost half of all children in the forestry regions in the northern parts of Sweden were born out of wedlock. Since 1900, there have been some variations in the share of children born to unmarried parents, but throughout the century it mostly hovered around 10–15 per cent. From 1965 onwards, however, the proportion of children born to unmarried parents has shown a sharp upswing, to 47 per cent in 1990. This, by international standards, high proportion can be seen as a function of the high numbers of cohabiting unmarried couples.

The traditional family formation system was comprised of three periods: a period when a couple goes steady, the engagement period, and finally marriage. In this system, the couple did not co-reside until after the wedding. To a large extent, couples co-resided definitively and stayed together 'Till Death did them part'.

In modern Swedish society, it has been possible for couples to live together prior to marriage without any intention to cohabit for a long period of time or for the rest of their lives. It is not necessary for co-resident couples ever to get married. The social acceptance of cohabitation can, therefore, be said to be extensive in modern Swedish society. Co-resident couples can themselves choose to become cohabitants or to get married, because cohabitation is to a large extent equivalent to traditional marriage. Family law has become more and more similar for cohabiting and married couples, even though some differences remain. Consequently, the co-resident status has been pluralized during the last decades, and Sweden has obtained a relatively large group of cohabitors.

There is no polarization of the Swedish family system towards two completely different groups; instead, there is a growing tendency towards one of the poles. In other words, more and more women give birth relatively late in their lives and then have their children in rapid succession.

10.1.2. *Demographic Trends in the 1980s*

The population in Sweden showed continuous growth during the 1980s. The country now has about 8.7 million inhabitants. Population increase was especially rapid in the second half of the decade, owing to a relatively large natural increase and positive net migration. Since the 1930s, when immigration started to exceed emigration, an increasing share of the population has been born abroad. In 1990, 790,000 (9.2 per cent) of Swedish inhabitants, and in 1992, 835,000 (9.6 per cent), were foreign-born, and every seventeenth person living in Sweden has a foreign citizenship (Table 10.1).

The changes in the age structure are characteristic for developed countries, as Sweden has grown older owing to the decreasing proportion of children and the increasing proportion of persons over 65 years. According to the latest projection for 1991–2025, there will be the same number of people over 65 in the year 2000 as in 1990, but with more people in the highest age groups (Lundström *et al.*, 1991).

Crude marriage and divorce rates displayed only slight changes during the 1980s. By Western standards, a lower proportion of Swedish couples get married and a higher proportion get divorced than in most Western countries.

Perhaps the most interesting factor in Sweden, as compared with most other countries, is that women's mean age at first marriage is higher than the mean age of mothers at birth of the first child – and even higher than the mean age of mothers at birth of any child. This is, of course, related to cohabitation. Under these circumstances, the number of children born out of wedlock per 1,000 live births has shown a rapid upward trend. Almost half of Swedish children have parents who are not married but who (very often) live together in a consensual union.

As a consequence of the rising fertility of the late 1980s, all fertility measures show higher values for 1990 than for 1980 and 1985: the crude birth rate (14.5), the total fertility rate (2.13), and the net reproduction rate (1.03). The total fertility rate has been declining since 1990.

Table 10.1. *Summary of demographic trends in Sweden during the 1980s*[a]

	1980	1985	1990
Population			
Population size (in 1,000 inhabitants, 31 Dec.)	8,318	8,358	8,591
Population increase per 1,000 of mean population	1.78	1.85	7.43
Natural increase per 1,000 of mean population	0.63	0.53	3.36
Net migration rate per 1,000 of mean population	1.15	1.33	4.07
Foreign-born persons (%)	7.5	7.8	9.2
Foreign citizens (%)	5.1	4.6	5.6
Age structure			
Population below age 15 (%)	19.4	18.1	18.0
Population between 15 and 44 (%)	41.8	42.8	41.9
Population between 45 and 64 (%)	22.4	21.7	22.3
Population over 65 (%)	16.4	17.4	17.8
Old-age dependency ratio[b]	25.5	27.0	27.7
Marriage and divorce			
Crude marriage rate per 1,000 of mean population	4.5	4.6	4.7
Mean age at first marriage (women)	28.8	30.2	30.2
Crude divorce rate per 1,000 of mean population	2.4	2.4	2.3
Fertility			
Crude birth rate per 1,000 of mean population	11.7	11.8	14.5
Mean age of mother at birth of first child	25.5	26.1	26.3
Mean age at childbirth (any child)	27.8	28.5	28.5
Total fertility rate	1.68	1.73	2.13
Net reproduction rate	0.81	0.83	1.03
Children born to unmarried parents (per 1,000 live births)	397.2	463.5	470.0
Mortality			
Crude death rate per 1,000 of mean population	11.1	11.3	11.1
Infant mortality (per 1,000 live births)	6.9	6.8	6.0
Life expectancy (women, at age 0)	81.9	82.7	83.4
Life expectancy (men, at age 0)	75.9	76.8	77.8

[a] Cohabitation, a very widespread phenomenon in Sweden, is excluded from this table but will be discussed further below. [b] (Population $65+$ / population 15–64) $\times$ 100.

Sources: Folkmängd, Part 3: 1980, 1985 and 1990; *Befolkningsförändringar*, Part 3: 1980, 1985 and 1990.

Swedish life expectancy at birth is high for both sexes, and the crude death rate is relatively low. Infant mortality decreased between 1980 and 1990, even though it was already low at the start of the decade.[1]

---

[1] *Befolkningsstatistik 1992*, Part 3; *Folkmängd*, 1980, 1985 and 1990, Part 3; *Befolkningsförändringar*, 1980, 1985 and 1990, Part 3.

10.1.3. *Description of Data Sources*

Statistics on new and existing marriages in Sweden go back very far, but it was a long time before statistics on the phenomenon of cohabitation were produced. Nevertheless, even before the first Population and Housing Census that could be used for measuring cohabitation (in 1975), some measurement of numbers of cohabitors did exist (Näsholm, 1972a, 1972b). The Population and Housing Censuses have revealed that the proportion of cohabiting couples among all co-resident couples increased between 1975 and 1985 from 12, via 15 (in 1980), to 20 per cent. In 1990, their share was only 19 per cent, owing to the December 1989 marriage boom that was a result of the changes in the law on widows' pensions.

Swedish statistics show that it is most common for marriages to be preceded by a cohabitation. There are relatively large variations in the proportions of cohabiting couples in different parts of the country and in different age groups. It is a widespread but – at least in Sweden – false assumption that cohabitation is a phenomenon that is particularly metropolitan. In 1985, the proportion of cohabiting couples among all co-resident couples in the age range 20–39 years was highest in the western parts of northern Sweden. Age differentials in cohabitation will be discussed below.

The figures based on the Population and Housing Censuses may underestimate the real proportion of cohabitation, owing to the fact that it is difficult to tell exactly when a couple started cohabiting. A man and a woman can even have differing opinions about the moment when they started to live together. Another source showing proportions of cohabitors is the Statistics Sweden Surveys on Living Conditions; they provide annual figures that are a few percentage points higher than those from the Population and Housing Censuses, also produced by Statistics Sweden.

Since detailed specifications of the sources employed in this chapter are presented both in footnotes and at the end in the list of references, only the main types of sources used are mentioned here:

1. some monographs which provide background information;
2. demographic reports concerning family structure and change in Sweden;
3. population statistics, including both register data and statistics based on the Population and Housing Censuses in 1980, 1985, and 1990;
4. different survey data produced by Statistics Sweden; and
5. statistics from other public authorities, mainly from the National Social Insurance Board.

10.2. Family Policy in Sweden

The aim of this section is to review the most important family policy measures and their application. After that, some hypothetical impact models will be discussed in order to improve the understanding of the relationship between family policy and family life in Sweden.

10.2.1. *Family Policy concerning the Relationship of Family and Employment*

In this section, two guiding principles of Swedish family policy – solidarity and equality – are emphasized. The idea of equality is described in more detail, that of solidarity only very briefly. Sweden is a society with a high degree of solidarity. Both principles legitimate universal social rights in the country.

FAMILY-RELATED SOCIAL POLICY AND EQUALITY OF THE SEXES. Since men's, even fathers', right to employment has never been challenged, the Swedish employment-related family policy has to a great extent been a matter of equality of the sexes on the labour market and of women's possibilities to combine family life and work. As fathers' right to family life has also been acknowledged, the gender-specific equality laws have become neutral laws as regards sex. In this connection, the most important component of the Swedish term 'equality' is equality of the sexes. In Sweden, the term means that, irrespective of sex, all individuals in society have equal rights, responsibilities, and opportunities.

Reforms that aim at equality of the sexes began to be enacted in the middle of the nineteenth century, when women's position in society was juridically and economically inferior. In the early twentieth century, Swedish women did not have the same rights as men to inheritance and property, employment and payment for work, and education and political participation. What is more, they had a minority status in their family; before marriage, a woman's father made decisions about her life, and after her wedding her husband did. The struggle for women's equal rights has been long, fragmentary, and mainly successful since women have continued to win rights in an increasing number of areas.

Since the middle of the nineteenth century, the focus of equality at work has moved from opening the closed doors to education and gainful employment to ensuring equality inside the workplace and inside the educational system, from the mainly legal questions of status to legal measures to increase the ability of both men and women to choose their own way of life, and from gender-specific equality laws to neutral laws as regards sex.

MORE THAN 100 YEARS OF REFORMS. In the field of family, the most important reform was to remove the minority status of women: firstly, among unmarried women over 25 years old in 1858, and later also among those who were married (the new Marriage Code in 1921). The next step was to declare both parents as a child's legal guardians in 1950.

Other family-related legal measures are: (i) family planning measures such as legalization of contraception, abortion, and sterilization, and sex education curricula; (ii) support in terms of child allowances and the maternity/parental insurance system; (iii) separate income tax assessments for wives and husbands (which means that, for the first time, not only a husband but also his wife were acknowledged as breadwinners in the family); (iv) the right to a six-hour working day for parents of small children; and (v) a ban on dismissing employees because of pregnancy, childbirth, or marriage.

Over the past 150 years, different schools and occupations have been opened to women. Nowadays all of them are open for women, and since 1983 even military service. The Equal Opportunities Act of 1980 prohibited discrimination on the grounds of sex and proposed active measures for implementation. The controlling agency within this field is the so-called Equal Opportunities Ombudsman. The new Equality Opportunities Act, which is adapted to the legislation in the European Union, came into effect on 1 January 1992. Among other things, it made it obligatory for all workplaces with more than ten employees to have an equality plan, and for all employers to make it easier for employees to take up their right to parental leave.

By Nordic standards, women in Sweden got the right to vote and take office relatively late (1919). In Finland, for example, this occurred in 1906.

FRAGMENTARY EQUALITY LEGISLATION. Today, separate laws deal with different topics in the field. For example, laws on equality include the Equal Opportunities Acts of 1980 and 1992, which are labour laws against gender discrimination in working life. Regulations regarding equality in the Swedish educational system have also been discussed, but the Swedish legislative assembly has not yet acted in this direction.

Other Nordic countries also have passed sex equality laws: Iceland in 1976, Denmark in 1976 and 1978, Norway in 1979, and Finland in 1987. In contrast to Sweden, both Finland and Norway have legislation covering, with certain exceptions, all fields of society.

REMAINING INEQUALITIES. The reforms mentioned above have made Swedish society more equal, but Sweden has not yet managed to attain its goal of an equal society. This is manifested in the following facts: Sweden has the most sex-segregated labour market in the entire Western world; relatively few women hold decision-making positions; gender-specific differences in payment for work still exist; and women perform more unpaid work than men.

FAMILY-RELATED SOCIAL SECURITY SYSTEM. The Swedish social insurance system includes several family-related benefits, of which the most important ones are pregnancy cash benefits, parents' cash benefits connected with childbirth, temporary parents' cash benefits, child allowances, and maintenance advances.

Furthermore, there are also some benefits connected with special groups of children (care allowances for ill or disabled children under 16 years who require special care for at least six months, allowances for children adopted by only one person). Even in the pension insurance system, there are some family components: the child supplement and the child pension. Another relevant cash benefit is the municipal housing allowances.

Finally, family planning, sterilization, and abortion counselling are free of charge, if provided by a medical practitioner who is affiliated with the insurance scheme.

PARENTAL INSURANCE. Parental insurance comprises three cash benefits: pregnancy benefits and the above-mentioned two types of parents' cash benefits. They are paid to expectant mothers and parents, respectively.

When an expectant mother is unable to continue her normal work tasks during the final two months of pregnancy, she can be shifted to lighter work or she can be given pregnancy cash benefits for a maximum of fifty days. Pregnancy cash benefits have been paid out to an increasing number of women – almost 34,000 insured women in 1991 (Table 10.2).

Related to childbirth, the parent is entitled to a maximum of 450 cash-benefit days at home per child. The parents can decide how to divide the time. This type of parents' cash benefit is payable any time before the child has reached the age of 8 years or has completed her/his first grade of compulsory school. For 360 days the benefit is on a level with 90 per cent of the sickness cash benefit but not under the guaranteed level, and for the remaining 90 days the amount is on the guaranteed level (SEK 60 per day).[2] The benefit

---

[2] SEK 60 equals US$7.60.

Table 10.2. *Pregnancy cash benefit, Sweden, 1981–1991*

	No. of persons ('000)	Average no. of benefit days
1981	8.1	36
1982	8.1	37
1983	10.0	38
1984	13.0	39
1985	16.9	39
1986	21.5	38
1987	24.6	38
1988	28.9	38
1989	32.6	39
1990	35.6	39
1991	33.5	38

Source: National Social Insurance Board (1993).

Table 10.3. *Persons receiving parent's cash benefit, Sweden, 1986–1991*[a]

	No. of days for which benefits are received ('000)	Of whom: mothers (%)
1986	371	77.0
1987	421	75.5
1988	344	76.9
.. ..		
1989	359	75.4
1990	399	73.9
1991	437	73.5

[a] The dotted line in the table indicates when changes were made in the rules.

Source: National Social Insurance Board (1993).

days are mainly drawn by mothers, and 84 per cent of the benefit days are drawn before the child has reached the age of 2 (Table 10.3).

The temporary parents' cash benefits consist of three benefits: the '10-day benefit' ('daddy days'), parents' cash benefits for temporary child care, and 'contact days'. The '10-day benefit' entitles the father of a newborn child to a special compensation in connection with childbirth. In 1991, it was used by 85 per cent of the fathers (104,800) of children born in this year.

Table 10.4. *Parent's cash benefit for temporary child care, Sweden, 1981–1991*[a]

	Persons receiving benefit		Benefit days		Children for whom benefit is paid	
	Number ('000)	Of whom: women (%)	Number ('000)	Of whom: women (%)	Number ('000)	% of children 0–12 years
1981	537	58.2	3,223	64.2	511	41.4
1982	546	59.1	3,236	65.6	528	39.9
1983	573	59.3	3,610	66.3	554	42.4
1984	568	60.3	3,689	66.3	545	42.3
.. ..						
1985	620	59.8	4,156	66.9	603	47.2
.. ..						
1986	642	59.4	4,223	65.6	628	48.6
1987	673	58.9	4,572	64.8	658	52.2
.. ..						
1988	737	58.7	5,661	65.2	715	56.1
.. ..						
1989	725	59.1	5,238	65.5	705	54.2
.. ..						
1990	762	58.8	5,731	65.5	744	55.9
1991	743	59.0	5,524	65.9	733	53.7

[a] The dotted lines in the table indicate when changes were made in the rules.

Source: National Social Insurance Board (1993).

A parent can also stay at home to care for a child under 12 years of age (16 in certain cases) for 60 days per year per child (parents together). The benefit can be paid for an additional 60 days per year per child when the child is ill. The number of insured persons who have drawn such benefits has increased from 537,000 to 762,000 during the 1980s, that is, by more than 40 per cent (Table 10.4). Two-thirds of the benefit days have been drawn by mothers. The average number of benefit days varies for the different age groups but it is, in general, eight days (for children 0-12 years).

The two-day benefit per year for 'contact days' is drawn by the parents of children between 4 and 12 years of age in connection with visits to the child's day nursery, after-school centre, or school. The contact days were paid for 29 per cent of children in this age group (254,400 children), 56 per cent of these being for children aged 8–12 years.

ALLOWANCES. A child under the age of 16 receives a basic child allowance, provided that s/he lives in Sweden. Between 1.6 and 1.7 million children aged 0–15 have received this child allowance each year during the 1980s.

Families with three or more children are also entitled to receive a large-family supplement. In addition, extended child allowances can be obtained for children aged 16 years and over if they are still in compulsory school. The annual amount of the basic child allowance has tripled from 1980 to 1991, that is, from SEK 3,000 to SEK 9,000 (Tables 10.5 and 10.6).

If the parent who does not have custody of the child pays a low or no maintenance allowance to the person who has care of the child, a maintenance advance can be awarded. A maintenance advance is payable until the child reaches the age of 18 or until the age of 20 if the child is still in school (not above higher secondary school). In December 1990, the number of children receiving the maintenance advance was about 273,000. The proportion of children aged 0–17 years receiving a maintenance advance was around 15 per cent during the 1980s. The government has proposed changes in the maintenance advance scheme. Another topic that has been discussed lately

Table 10.5. *Size of child allowance, Sweden, 1992*

Type of benefit	Annual amount (SEK)
Maintenance advance, extended maintenance advance for students and a special allowance for adopted children	13,480
Child allowance and additional allowance:	
1 child	9,000
2 children	18,000
3 children	31,500
4 children	49,500
5 children	72,000
For additional children	22,500

Source: National Social Insurance Board (1993).

Table 10.6. *Changes in size of the basic child allowance since October 1980, Sweden*

Period	Annual amount (SEK)
October 1980–December 1982	3,000
January 1983–December 1984	3,300
January 1985–December 1986	4,800
January 1987–December 1989	5,820
January 1990–December 1990	6,720
January 1991–December 1991	9,000

Source: National Social Insurance Board (1993).

Table 10.7. *Child allowance, Sweden, 1981–1991*

Children aged 0–15, in December ('000)		Payments (SEK)		
		Total	of which:	
			Extended child allowance[a]	Additional child allowance
1981	1,709	5,171	.	.
1982	1,678	5,204	.	123
1983	1,648	5,786	.	302
1984	1,629	5,741	.	350
1985	1,622	8,287	.	509
1986	1,618	8,284	9	519
1987	1,614	10,099	81	653
1988	1,620	10,316	82	806
1989	1,634	10,416	81	934
1990	1,655	12,305	94	1,143
1991	1,675	16,390	126	1,268

[a] Before July 1986, the benefit was administered by the Central Study Assistance Committee.

Source: National Social Insurance Board (1993).

is a care allowance for a parent who stays at home in order to take care of his/her children.

When the child is adopted by only one person, an allowance similar to the maintenance advance is payable for the child. The number of children receiving this type of allowance has been between 550 and 600 since 1985.

Parents with a disabled or ill child that needs special supervision or care for at least six months are entitled to a child care allowance. A rising number of care allowances was paid during the 1980s, from 11,000 in 1981 to 16,000 in 1991. Since 1992, lone parents are entitled to a relatively small annual allowance.

FAMILY COMPONENTS OF THE PENSION SYSTEM. The child pension is payable to a child under 18 (in some cases until the child is 20) whose mother and/or father is dead. Because of changes in the pension system in 1989, by which widows' pensions were abolished, there are two schemes depending on when the parent(s) died, that is, before or after the end of 1989. Child pension is paid not only under the basic pension scheme but also under the supplementary pension scheme if the deceased was entitled to a supplementary pension. The number of child pensions, in terms of both basic pension and supplementary pension, decreased from the beginning of the 1980s to the end of the decade. In the former case, the number dropped from 40,000 to 29,000 during the period 1981–9 (in 1991 it was up to 30,000) and, in the latter case, from 43,000 to 30,000 during the period 1981–91.

Since January 1990, child supplements are payable only to children who qualified for child supplements in December 1989. Prior to that, every child under 16 with a parent older than 65 years receiving an old-age pension or with a parent receiving a disability pension was entitled to a child supplement. The annual number of child supplements fluctuated between 21,000 and 27,000 during the 1980s (20,000 in 1991).

In sum, families make use of the policy measures mentioned above. Furthermore, although there is equal access to family-specific measures, women utilize these measures to a greater extent than men.

10.2.2. *Hypothetical Impact Models: Family Forms, Life Situation, and Everyday Life*

Several factors can be mentioned as possible determinants for the Swedish family forms, e.g. in terms of the number of family members and the legal status of the co-resident couples. The most important determinants may be classified into four main categories; demographic factors, family-related policies, economic situation, and attitudes/norms in society.

To a varying degree, different demographic developments influence each other. On the one hand, the role of mortality for the total fertility rate (TFR) has been reduced since the turn of the century, and infant mortality is at a low level. On the other hand, mortality is, of course, of utmost importance for the number of older singles in Sweden.

We may disregard the effects of migration on family structures, that is, differences between ethnic groups, since only two of the thirteen largest immigrant groups have a much higher TFR than women born in Sweden, and the co-residence status (single, cohabitor, and married person) of those immigrant groups is only slightly different from that of Swedes (Meisaari-Polsa, 1991).

The other two demographic factors, mainly fertility but also to some extent nuptiality, do have an effect on family forms. Firstly, the tendency to get married is of consequence for the legal status of the co-resident couples. Secondly, at least until the mid-1960s, there was also a strong relationship between nuptiality and fertility in Sweden, owing to the fact that until then most births occurred within marriage. Nowadays, half of the children are born to unmarried mothers, so that marriages are less useful as a factor for explaining fertility than before or than in many other countries.

Finally, the higher fertility is, the more children there are in the families. If cohort fertility is relatively stable, as in Sweden, then the fluctuations in the period fertility rate depend to a great extent on the redistribution of childbearing over the life span, that is, on variations in timing and spacing. These fertility changes are related to developments with regard to different demographic factors mentioned above and different legal, economic, and other circumstances produced, among other things, by public policy. These developments stimulate decisions of postponement or advancement. Nevertheless, there is no simple relationship between demographic changes and public policy.

The purpose of post-war public policy has not been to raise fertility to a high level, but to raise it to a level at which Swedish couples want to have it. Non-pro-natalist public policies can, nevertheless, have pro-natalist effects when they facilitate the combination of family and work. Swedish public policy continues to reduce obstacles to women's labour-force participation, and to minimize parents' costs related to children.[3] This affords women a greater chance to combine motherhood and labour-force participation and to have as many children as couples see fit.

Therefore, Swedish public policies can to a certain degree have an indirect impact on reproductive behaviour of Swedish women, (i) by changing their conditions that (ii) change their preferences for number of children, timing of childbearing, and spacing of births. Since the number of children is relatively stable, public policies may have influenced the number of children only by holding it at the level of two. On the other hand, in the cases of timing and spacing of births, some evidence of the influence of policies can be presented here.

Coale (1973) revised classical demographic transition theory by claiming three necessary conditions for the fertility transition from high to low rates: (i) couples have to feel that they gain by controlling their fertility; (ii) fertility control is acceptable in their society; and (iii) means of fertility control are available. These conditions are also necessary for maintaining fertility at a desired level, because the central aim of modern Swedish public policy is that all children should be wanted.

As regards determinants of the development of family forms, the major issue that has been raised for discussion is the following: Why did fertility in Sweden rise in the late 1980s, and even more quickly than in many other

---

[3] For economic aspects of the Swedish family policy, see Söderstrom and Meisaari-Polsa (1995).

Western European countries? All Swedish demographers who have studied this question regard the recent increase in fertility as temporary (e.g. Martinelle, 1990; Hoem, 1990 and 1992). Fertility increase is the result of several simultaneous developments. The increase of the late 1980s is due especially to (i) the catching-up of postponed births during the 1970s, and (ii) the shortening of birth intervals, that is, earlier births of second and third children.

Changes in attitudes, e.g. as regards gender equality and the two-child norm, have contributed to fertility development during this century. Some major shifts in marriages, cohabitation, divorces, and separations are also due to public policy and the legal framework. Finally, life situation and everyday life of Swedish families are determined both by most of the factors mentioned above, including social policy, and by the life stage of the family.

10.3. Family Forms in the 1980s

The question of Swedish family forms in the 1980s will be addressed first, by determining the timing of critical events, and then, by describing Swedish family forms and their changes.

10.3.1. *Timing of Critical Events*

Since the mid-1960s, average age at first marriage has increased from under 24 to almost 28 years for women, and from over 26 to over 30 years for men (*Befolkningsförändringar*, 1990, Part 3). As a consequence of a rising trend starting in the mid-1970s, mean age of women at childbirth was relatively high in 1991: the mean age at birth of the first child was 26.5, at that of the second 28.9, and at that of the third child 31.5 (Table 10.8). It has primarily been women born in the late 1940s and in the early 1950s who postponed childbirth (*Befolkningsstatistik* 1991, Part 4; Meisaari-Polsa and Söderström, 1995).

10.3.2. *Family Forms and their Changes*

This section will focus on the Swedish family structure at different stages of the family life cycle. The focus will be not only on marital status but also on cohabitation, that is, on whether the couple is living together in a consensual union, i.e. without a marriage licence. The purpose of this section

Table 10.8. *Mean age of mother at birth of the first, second, and third child, Sweden, 1975–1991*

| | Mean age of mother at birth of | | |
	First child	Second child	Third child
1975	24.5	27.4	30.0
1976	24.8	27.6	30.3
1977	24.9	27.7	30.5
1978	25.1	27.9	30.6
1979	25.3	28.1	30.8
1980	25.5	28.3	31.0
1981	25.6	28.4	31.1
1982	25.7	28.6	31.3
1983	25.9	28.6	31.4
1984	26.0	28.7	31.5
1985	26.1	28.8	31.5
1986	26.1	28.9	31.5
1987	26.2	28.9	31.6
1988	26.2	28.9	31.6
1989	26.2	28.9	31.6
1990	26.3	28.8	31.5
1991	26.5	28.9	31.5

Source: Befolkningsstatistik 1991, Part 4.

is to place the family forms of the 1980s in a broader perspective than is the case in the more specialized subsequent sections that deal with family size, lone parents, and so on.

Table 10.9 shows that the difference between the family structure in 1985 and in 1990 is relatively small. Families that consist of a couple living in a consensual union tend to be young and childless. From the age of 30 onwards, most couples are married and have children. Middle-aged married women are, for obvious reasons, in the middle of their family lives and have the most children of all age groups. When the women are over 45, the families have become much smaller, so that almost half of the families in that age group have no children living at home.

When studying the relative numbers of individuals, one gets a somewhat different but generally unchanged picture for the period 1985–90. The three largest groups are those in the household position 'child'[4], childless married persons who live with their partners (mostly older persons), and 'others'.

---

[4] Children 0-15 years old.

Table 10.9: *Families by woman's age^a and number of children, Sweden, 1985 and 1990 (%)*

No. of children	Age group											
	1985						1990					
	20–24	25–29	30–34	35–39	40–44	45–49	20–24	25–29	30–34	35–39	40–44	45–49
Cohabiting, married												
0	7	8	5	5	16	44	8	9	6	5	16	44
1	8	14	12	14	26	26	9	14	11	12	24	25
2	4	18	32	35	26	10	5	18	30	33	25	10
3+	1	6	14	16	8	2	1	6	17	19	10	2
Cohabiting, not married												
0	55	21	7	4	5	6	52	21	7	4	5	7
1	14	13	7	5	3	2	14	12	6	4	3	2
2	3	8	8	5	2	1	3	7	7	5	2	0
3+	0	1	2	1	0	0	0	1	2	2	0	0
Lone parents^b												
1	7	7	8	9	9	7	7	8	7	8	10	8
2	1	3	4	5	4	2	1	3	5	6	4	2
3+	0	1	1	1	1	0	0	1	2	2	1	0
Total	100	100	100	100	100	100	100	100	100	100	100	100

^a When lone father, by father's age.
^b Including married parents not living with their partner.

Sources: Folk- och bostadsräkningen 1985 and 1990.

The latter group includes singles living alone, married but not co-residing persons, and persons in various types of institution.

MARITAL AND COHABITATIONAL CHANGES. From the beginning of the 1930s to the mid-1960s, first marriages have followed the same pattern as period fertility. The relationship between new marriages and fertility became weaker in the mid-1960s. Since the 1930s, there have been three peaks in the number of first marriages: in the early 1940s, in the mid-1960s, and in 1989. The 1989 peak was caused by a new pension law under which the widows' pension was abolished. There are, however, transitional regulations which entitle older women still to get their widows' pension. Surprisingly, not only older women who could gain this right by marrying their partners but younger women as well got married to a considerably greater extent than usual (Meisaari-Polsa *et al.*, 1990; *Befolkningsförändringar* 1990, Part 3).

The peak in the number of divorces in the 1970s was related to a new divorce law in 1974, which made it easier to get divorced if the couple did not have children. The drop in marriages since the mid-1960s does not mean that family formation has not been intensive. On the contrary, levels of family formation were a little higher in 1985 than in the mid-1960s. Owing to the 1989 peak in the number of marriages, the 1990 numbers of recorded unions are below the 1985 values. New consensual unions dominate among newly formed families in all age groups. The 1980 peak numbers of new cohabiting couples can be observed at ages 20–29 and those of newly married couples at ages 25–34, that is, about five years later. As a result of the 1989 marriage peak, the 1990 pattern is different, since the youngest age groups dominate among newly formed families, which shows that such changes are possible even over short periods (Meisaari-Polsa *et al.*, 1990; *Familjeförändringar kring 1980 och 1985*; *Familjeförändringar kring 1990*).

Separations and divorces were most frequent among young couples, especially among cohabiting couples, both in 1986 and in 1991. Every ninth co-resident couple in which the woman was 20–24 years old separated or got divorced in 1991. Cohabiting couples, who are often relatively young, are therefore not as stable as married couples. It is always easier to move apart if the couple has not legalized its relationship (Meisaari-Polsa *et al.*, 1990; *Familjeförändringar kring 1990*).

The risk of family dissolution in terms of divorces is highest after three years of marriage. In other words, instead of the usual 'seven-year crisis' in marriages, in Sweden there is a 'three-year crisis'. Irrespective of marriage duration, the tendency to divorce has increased since 1955 (Meisaari-Polsa *et al.*, 1990).

The absolute numbers of Swedish formations and dissolutions of unions in the 1980s are summarized in Figure 10.1. The most important feature is that, in total numbers, more union formations and dissolutions occurred in 1990 than in 1980. In addition, most newly formed couples are cohabiting couples. Finally, union dissolutions among younger couples are most often a result of couples moving apart, whereas among the older ones they are more often caused by death.

To sum up the results in this section, the Swedish family is not 'dead', as Popenoe (1988) stated. It is alive and well – but partly in a different form than before (cohabitation without benefit of marriage licence). There is also considerable dynamics not only in terms of union dissolution, but also in terms of union formation.

FERTILITY TRENDS, EXTRA-MARITAL FERTILITY, AND CHILDLESSNESS. Since the beginning of the twentieth century, between 85,000 and 140,000 live births have been registered each year in Sweden. The lowest numbers of

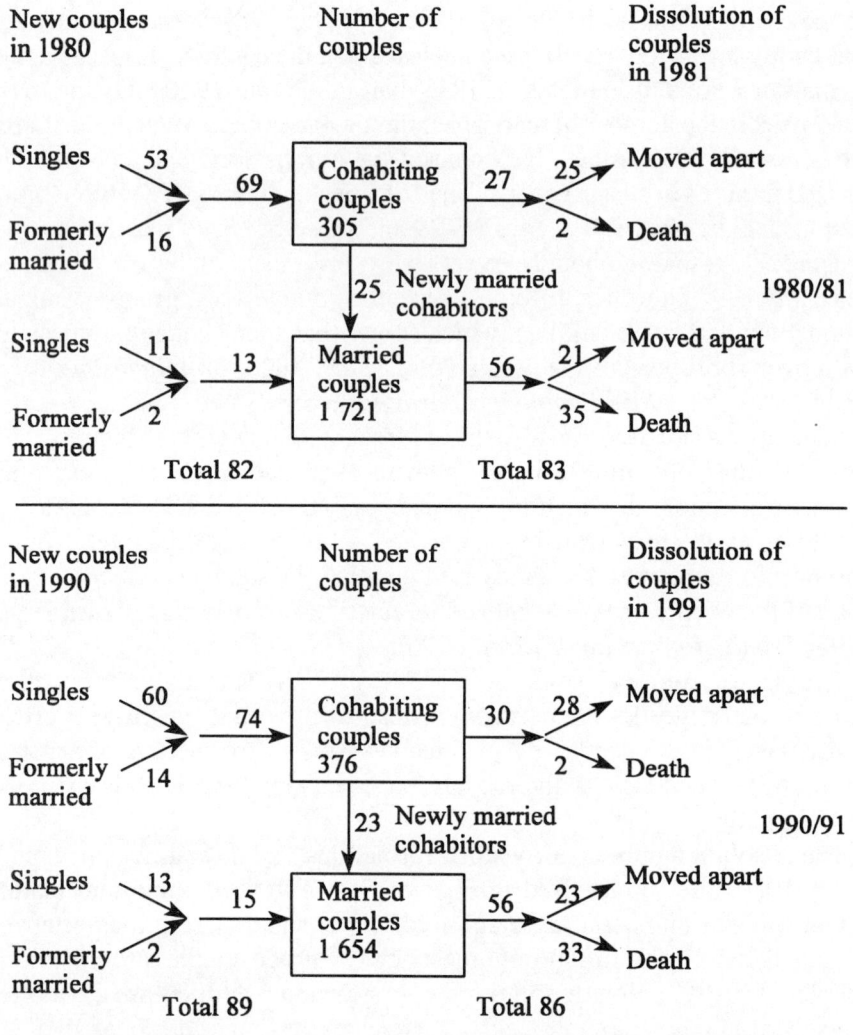

Sources: Meisaari-Polsa *et al.* (1990); *Familjeförändringar kring 1990.*

Figure 10.1. Formation and dissolution of Swedish families around 1980 and 1990 ('000)

live births were observed during the Depression of the 1930s and around 1980; in the early 1980s the numbers rose again (Meisaari-Polsa and Söderström, 1995).

After a dramatic drop in fertility from the beginning of this century, total fertility rates have hovered around two children. Since then, peak TFR figures have come in cycles of about twenty years: in the immediate post-war periods of the 1920s and the mid-1940s, about twenty years after the Second World War, and, finally, the latest peak in 1990 (TFR 2.13). Monthly figures for 1990 show a break in the upward trend at the end of that year, and TFR was 2.09 in 1992. The fact that period fertility rates hovered around two children does not, however, mean that Swedish couples made decisions to have more children during those peak periods. Rather, the fluctuations are a direct consequence of changes in the timing of childbirths, either forward or backward. For example, women born in the late 1930s and in the early 1940s had their children relatively early in their lives. Despite times of increasing and decreasing period fertility, cohort completed numbers of children have remained around two children per woman. In other words, the so-called two-child norm has remained widespread in Sweden (Meisaari-Polsa and Söderström, 1995; *Befolkningsstatistik* 1992, Part 4).

Basic to the Swedish equal opportunities policy is the belief that women as well as men ought to be able to support themselves. Accordingly, both genders need to have education and gainful employment. Therefore, it is very important for a woman to obtain education and labour-market connections before bringing children into the world. This means that the proportion of childless women is higher among the younger generations who have postponed having children. Data from the Fertility Register show that younger cohorts have lower levels of cumulative fertility at all ages.

The right to abortion was introduced, in principle, in 1975. By the mid-1960s, it had already become easier to terminate a pregnancy on demand. This means that a more liberal interpretation of existing laws was a more important factor in explaining the increasing number of performed abortions than the enactment of the new law. Legal abortions can also be measured in terms of relative numbers, that is, per 1,000 live births: there were about 338 in 1983 and 284 in 1992. In 1976, a new law was enacted which increased the number of sterilizations that could be performed primarily for birth control purposes (*Befolkningsstatistik* 1992, Part 4).

As the practice of cohabitation became successively more frequent in the 1960s and onwards, the proportion of illegitimate children followed the same pattern. Only one child in ten was born out of wedlock in 1955, compared with one in two in 1992 (*Befolkningsstatistik* 1992, Part 4).

Children have been born at shorter intervals since the enactment of the so-called '15-month rule' in 1974, which eventually became a '30-month rule' in 1986. If the interval between two births was less than the above-mentioned number of months, the parent receiving parental leave got the same income compensation during parental leave for the second child as during the first parental leave. This is especially advantageous for women who worked full-time before the birth of their first child but only part-time between the first and the second birth. Another determinant of the trend in TFR during the 1980s was birth postponement during the 1970s. A shortening of birth intervals was registered among women of all ages, and the catching-up during the 1980s of births postponed during the 1970s occurred among older cohorts (Martinelle *et al.*, 1992; Hoem, 1992; Meisaari-Polsa and Söderström, 1995; Lundström *et al.*, 1991; Martinelle, 1990).

FAMILY SIZE. The number of private households without children increased in absolute and relative numbers during the ten-year period 1975–85, from 66 to 71 per cent. Consequently, the proportion of households with children decreased successively.

It is obvious that the number of children depends not only on the age of the woman, but also on the family form; marriage, cohabitation, or living without a partner. Children 0–17 years of age living at home are most common in families where the parents are married. These couples more often also have three or more children. Cohabiting couples are more prone to be childless or to have fewer children than married couples, but they do have children to a greater extent than do women without partners. Among all family forms, the share of families with children living at home is highest among the middle-aged (35–39 years) (*Folk- och bostadsräkningen*, 1975, 1980, 1985 and 1990).

PARTNERSHIP ARRANGEMENTS. These are correlated with the number of children in the family. In other words, if the woman lives with her child(ren) then she is most often married or cohabiting. This applies to all age groups. The pattern of family size among co-residing women is entirely different from that among women without a partner in a family. Firstly, among non-co-residing women aged 20–49, the most common number of children living at home is zero. Secondly, the number of children of married or cohabiting women varies to a greater degree with age of the woman. Therefore, the number of children in these types of families is age-specific and differs according to the life cycle of the woman. The most common family size at the age of 20–24 is no children. As the woman gets older, the number of co-resident children first increases and then decreases. Finally, at age 45–49, couples without children living at home become a majority among the families (*Folk- och bostadsräkningen*, 1985 and 1990).

LONE-PARENT FAMILIES AND ONE-PERSON HOUSEHOLDS. The number of lone-parent families increased by 4 per cent during the period 1985–90. Except for the oldest groups, lone parents tend to be mothers. The proportion of mothers has undergone only slight changes during the period in question; only in the age group under 20 has it increased, and above 54 years it has decreased.

Between 20 and 49 years, the proportion of lone-parent families is relatively low, at 15–20 per cent of all families with children. The high proportions of lone-parent families in the ages up to 19 and over 49 follow different patterns. In the former case, the parent is a single person, and not formerly married. In the latter case, the parent is most often living without a partner owing to divorce or death.

The most interesting change over the course of time is that the proportion of lone-parent families among all families with children has shown an increasing trend in all ages above 24, especially in the oldest age groups (Figure 10.2) (*Folk- och bostadsräkningen*, 1985 and 1990).

Throughout the 1980s, one-person households have totalled more than one million. The proportional changes during the five-year periods from

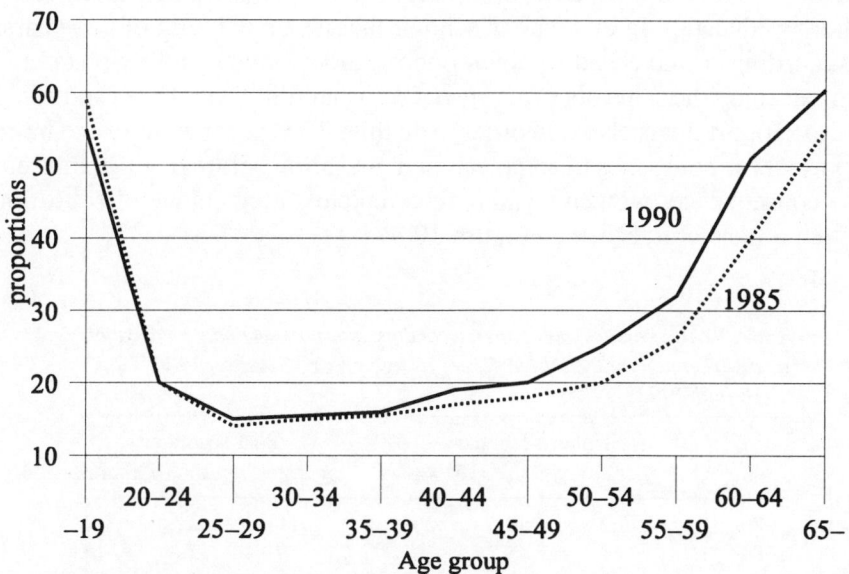

Source: Folk- och bostadsräkningen, 1985 and 1990.

Figure 10.2. Proportions of lone-parent families among families with children, by age group of lone parent, Sweden, 1985 and 1990

the mid-1970s have been remarkable; in 1975–80 and 1980–5 there was a 15 per cent increase, and in 1985–90 a 14 per cent increase (*Folk- och bostadsräkningen*, 1975, 1980, 1985 and 1990).

10.4. Aspects of the Family Life Situation

This section gives an overview of some crucial aspects of the family life situation. How are family life situations made up, and how is education, participation in paid work, housing, and income combined at the family level?

10.4.1. *Education, Labour-Force Participation, and Housing*

EDUCATION. The level of education among both women and men rose during the 1980s; the proportions of both upper-secondary and post-secondary education have increased in all age groups, except that of post-secondary education in age group 20–24 (Table 10.10 and Figure 10.3). The most marked difference between the genders concerns upper-secondary education: according to Labour Market Survey data, in comparison with men, women have chosen a shorter education in this type of school, that is, a maximum of two years.

According to the Swedish equal opportunities policy, both women and men can enjoy the same opportunities of being gainfully employed and being able to support themselves. In order to do this, it has become more and more important for both sexes to complete their education before having children. As a consequence, women wishing to complete a long course of education postpone their childbearing (Figure 10.4).

Table 10.10. *Persons with upper-secondary and post-secondary education as a percentage of the labour force, by age group, Sweden, 1980, 1984, 1988 and 1992*

	Upper-secondary			Post-secondary		
	20–24	25–44	45–64	20–24	25–44	45–64
1980	62	40	26	11	22	12
1984	69	45	29	9	26	14
1988	73	50	35	12	28	19
1992	76	53	35	12	29	22

Source: Labour Market Surveys.

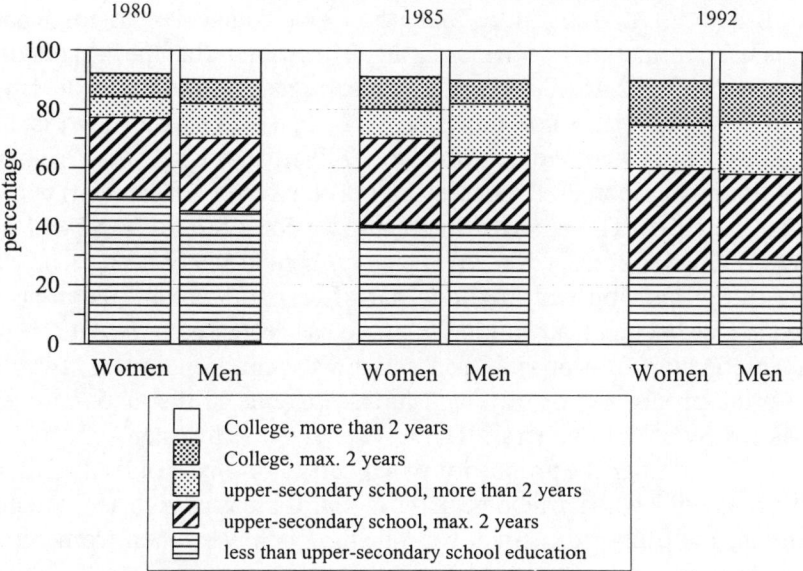

Source: Labour Market Surveys.

Figure 10.3. Level of education among 20–64-year-olds, Sweden, 1980, 1985 and 1992

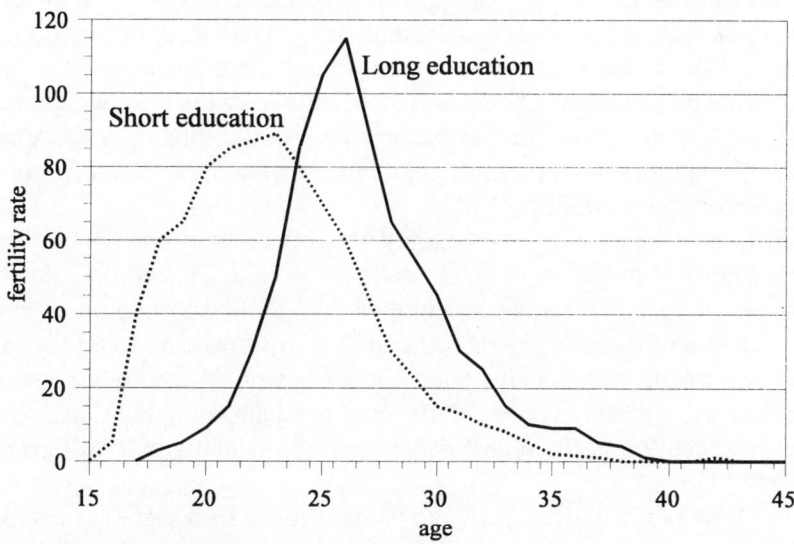

Source: Martinelle (1990).

Figure 10.4. Fertility rates for first children, by age and educational level, Swedish women born in 1940 (rates per 1,000 women)

LABOUR-FORCE PARTICIPATION. Since the 1960s, female labour-force participation has continuously been increasing. The result is that the vast majority (84 per cent) of the 2,465,000 Swedish women aged 20–64 were in the labour force in 1992. This does not, however, mean that every woman works full-time. The proportion of women who work full-time or long part-time hours (20–34 hours) has increased, but only half of all women (48 per cent) worked full-time in 1992. The changes in the proportion of 20–64-year-old men (2,539,000) with different degrees of employment have not been great, even though the proportion working long part-time hours among them has increased somewhat and that working full-time has decreased in recent decades.

The interesting question is: if the families have children, especially young ones, is the proportion of male and female parents in the labour force as high as for Swedes in general? The answer is 'yes' for men, but 'no' for women. Even though the proportion of women 25–44 years old with children under the age of 7 who participate in the labour force is as high as for women in general, the proportion employed full-time is lower when women have young children.

If we compare shares of labour-force participation in the different age groups, there are noticeable changes even among men over time. Female participation rates in ages 16–24 began to drop around 1980 and then showed a tendency to rise again. The same is true for men aged 16–19. In the early 1990s, rates among 16–24-year-olds, both women and men, declined again. Another type of trend can be observed among men aged 55–64, whose labour-force participation has decreased steadily over the past two decades. Finally, as lengthy education has become more and more common among women, female labour-force participation rates have increased in all age groups except the youngest.

When there are children in the family, the proportion of men in the labour force is higher than that of women in all age groups. This could mean that it is more difficult for women in families with children to combine child-rearing and gainful employment, although the difference between the sexes is relatively small, except in the youngest generation. Nevertheless, women and men without children are gainfully employed almost to the same extent. The only exception is the oldest generations, in which gender differences are much bigger.

In 1992, 84 per cent of women and 88 per cent of men were in the labour force; 4 per cent of women, by international standards a very low figure, and 0.1 per cent of men in age category 20–64 cited housework as their main activity. Among those in the labour force, persons absent from their work are included. The share of absent women is higher than the corresponding share for men, especially when the family has pre-school children; e.g., 51 per cent of women with children under 3 were absent, compared with 14 per cent of men in similar circumstances (Table 10.11). Figure 10.5 shows the reasons for absence from work in 1992. When looking at the entire age group 20–64 and also only at those with children under 7, one observes the biggest gender difference in the importance of care for children (inclusive parental leave) as a reason for absence from work.

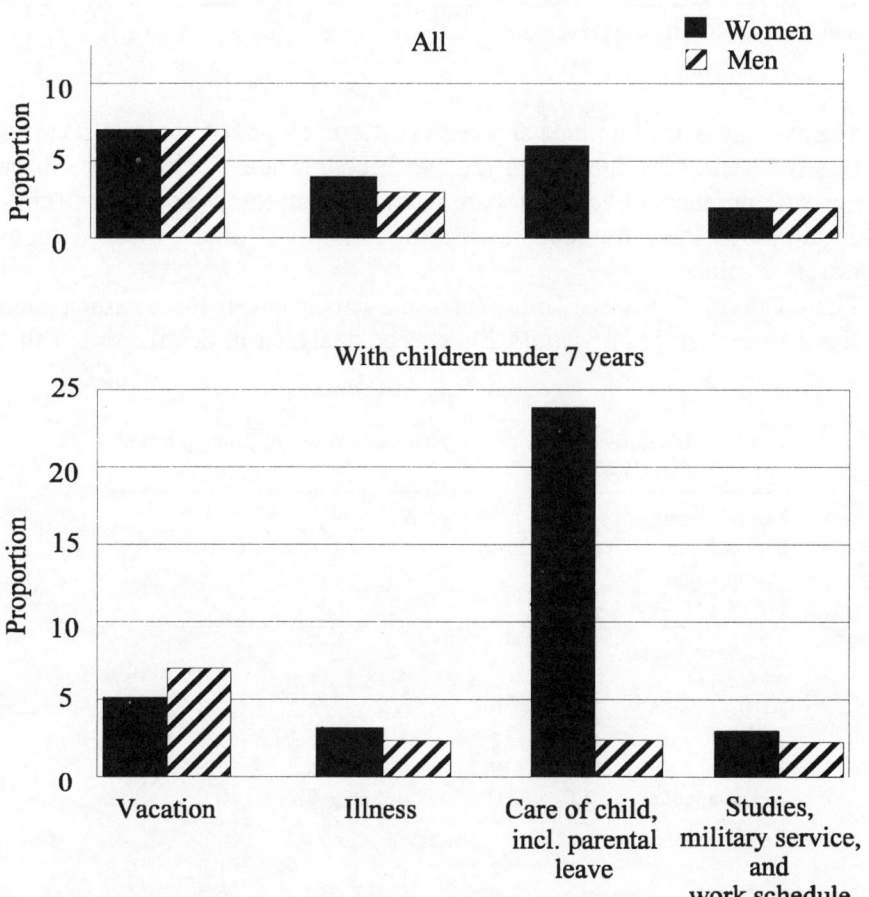

Source: Labour Market Surveys.

Figure 10.5. Reasons for absence from work, Sweden, 1992: proportions absent during the entire week, among employed persons 20–64 years

Table 10.11. *Gainfully employed women and men with children under 17 years, Sweden, 1992 (%)*

Age of youngest child	Proportion of gainfully employed who were							
	At work		of which:				Absent	
			1–34 hours		35+ hours			
	Women	Men	Women	Men	Women	Men	Women	Men
Under 3	77	89	47	5	53	95	51	14
3–6	86	93	59	4	41	96	16	11
7–10	89	94	51	4	49	96	14	10
11–16	91	93	41	4	59	96	14	10

Source: Labour Market Surveys.

The average working time per week in different types of household varies between 32 and 43 hours. Men register higher values. In addition, there are greater numbers of hours of work when the households do not have children, although the difference between households with and those without children is minor.

The relationship between family form and female labour-force participation at the different stages of family life can be analysed in detail using Table

Table 10.12. *Labour-force participation of women by family form and age, Sweden, 1990 (%)*

Family form/ labour-force participation (hours per week)	Age group					
	20–24	25–29	30–34	35–39	40–44	45–49
Childless singles						
0	15.2	5.4	2.3	1.8	2.0	2.7
1–19	2.3	0.9	0.3	0.2	0.3	0.4
20–34	4.8	2.2	1.3	1.0	1.3	2.1
35+	28.4	17.7	9.9	6.5	7.5	10.7
Not available	2.0	0.6	0.2	0.2	0.2	0.2
Lone parents						
0	1.7	2.2	2.2	1.9	1.4	0.8
1–19	0.2	0.3	0.4	0.4	0.3	0.2
20–34	0.7	1.9	2.8	3.0	2.4	1.4
35+	1.3	2.6	4.1	5.9	5.8	3.7
Not available	0.3	0.3	0.2	0.2	0.2	0.1

(table is continued)

Table 10.12. *(cont.)*

Family form/ labour-force participation (hours per week)	Age group					
	20–24	25–29	30–34	35–39	40–44	45–49
Childless cohabitors						
0	3.5	1.7	0.5	0.4	0.5	0.7
1–19	0.7	0.4	0.1	0.1	0.1	0.1
20–34	2.7	1.4	0.6	0.5	0.8	1.0
35+	16.3	11.4	4.4	2.4	2.8	3.4
Not available	0.5	0.1	0.0	0.0	0.0	0.0
Cohabiting parents						
0	3.1	4.5	3.0	1.6	0.6	0.3
1–19	0.5	1.0	0.8	0.4	0.2	0.1
20–34	1.6	4.3	4.8	3.4	1.8	0.7
35+	2.5	4.5	4.4	3.9	2.6	1.2
Not available	0.3	0.4	0.2	0.1	0.0	0.0
Married co-residents, childless						
0	0.8	0.9	0.6	0.6	1.6	4.0
1–19	0.1	0.2	0.1	0.1	0.4	1.3
20–34	0.4	0.6	0.6	0.7	3.6	10.9
35+	2.1	4.5	3.3	2.9	8.4	20.6
Not available	0.1	0.1	0.1	0.1	0.2	0.4
Married co-residents, 1 child						
0	1.7	2.9	2.1	1.5	2.2	2.1
1–19	0.3	0.6	0.5	0.4	0.8	0.9
20–34	0.9	2.9	3.2	3.7	7.6	7.3
35+	1.2	3.6	3.7	5.3	11.1	10.6
Not available	0.2	0.2	0.2	0.2	0.3	0.2
Married co-residents, 2+ children						
0	1.4	6.1	9.4	7.6	3.8	1.3
1–19	0.2	1.5	3.0	2.9	1.7	0.6
20–34	0.5	5.8	17.1	21.3	12.9	3.8
35+	0.5	4.0	10.8	16.2	12.3	4.3
Not available	0.1	0.5	0.7	0.6	0.4	0.1
Married, not co-resident (all)	0.9	1.8	2.1	2.0	1.9	1.8
Total	100	100	100	100	100	100

Source: Folk- och bostadsräkningen, 1990.

10.12. The table has been simplified by aggregating the smallest group of families, which consists of married couples who do not live together.

In the youngest generation of women presented here, the 20–24-year-olds, the most common combination of family characteristics is that of non-married childless couples, co-resident or non-co-resident, working either full-time (45 per cent) or not at all (19 per cent). Those who are outside the labour force are mainly students (and perhaps younger persons who have not yet managed to get a job). Since Swedish women start childbearing relatively late in their lives, the youngest group of women could, therefore, both study and work full-time (35 or more hours per week). At the next higher age (25–29 years), the proportion of women in different categories in terms of family form and degree of labour-market connection varies more than among the youngest group, since more women marry and have children. Nevertheless, the largest group is still that of non-married women who work full-time regardless of whether or not they are co-residing (17.7 per cent).

There is a break in the development between age groups 25–29 and 30–34. The proportion of childless non-married non-co-resident women who work full-time is lower, whereas the share of married co-resident women is higher than among the younger women. At the same time, the above-mentioned married women differ greatly with respect to their labour-market participation. Working long part-time (20–34 hours per week) is the most frequent pattern, followed by no labour-market connection at all, and only after that comes working full-time. This pattern is even more dominant in the next age group, the 35–39-year-olds. The middle-aged family pattern is a married couple with two children living at home. Nevertheless, middle-aged women have different preferences with regard to gainful employment.

The children of the oldest age groups of women have already left home in order to live somewhere else. Therefore, the proportion of childless married women who work long part-time or full-time is particularly higher than in the younger groups. The pattern of the older middle-aged, on the other hand, begins to resemble the circumstances of the older women (Labour Market Surveys; *Folk- och bostadsräkningen*, 1990).

HOUSING. On the basis of the Population and Housing Census, it is possible to compare standards of living in terms of dwelling standard and tenure status in different types of private household. The most important question for us is whether households with children have better, worse, or equivalent housing standards as other groups in Sweden.

Families with children tend to prefer to buy detached or terrace houses, probably in order to have more play space for their children. Almost two in three families with children own their own house, which is much more than in any other group of private households (Table 10.13). This does not,

Table 10.13. *Household types by dwelling standards and tenure status, Sweden, 1990 (%)*

Type of household	No. of rooms[a] per occupant	% of house-holds with spacious dwellings	Tenure status				
			Ownership dwellings	Tenant-owning[b]	Lease	Others	Total
With children	1.4[c]	21	61	9	28	2	100
Reference member							
16-24 years of age	2.2	15	7	16	64	13	100
25-44 years of age	1.7	24	40	14	41	5	100
45-64 years of age	2.1	47	55	12	30	3	100
65+ years of age	2.6[d]	41	34	18	43	5	100
At least one foreign-born person 16+ years old	1.7	28	33	14	47	6	100
All households	2.0	35	41	15	40	4	100

[a] Including kitchen. [b] Tenant-owning in a housing co-operative. [c] 1985. [d] 65–79 years of age.

Source: Folk- och bostadsräkningen, 1985 and 1990.

however, mean that families with children have more rooms per occupant than other households: they have only 1.4 rooms, including the kitchen, per family member, and a mere 22 per cent of these families have spacious dwellings (more than one room per occupant, excluding the kitchen and one other room). Only youths not living with their parents have a lower proportion of spacious dwellings.

In sum, Swedish families with children may have more outdoor play space for their children, but they have less indoor space for each member of the household. The relatively small indoor space is probably connected with the life cycle of these families. The parents in families with children have not yet reached the top of their careers. Therefore, they cannot always afford to buy larger houses. Moreover, it is quite common that smaller children share bedrooms. Even when the family has more rooms per occupant in earlier family phases, the number of rooms per occupant successively decreases after one or more children have arrived (*Folk- och bostadsräkningen*, 1985 and 1990).

10.4.2. *Family, Income and Poverty*

The economic situation of Swedish families will here be described, with the indicators disposable income and proportion of the population under the poverty level. 'Disposable income' in this context means the sum of all incomes and positive transfers to families (such as allowances) minus final taxes. Note that single non-gainfully employed men and women can manage economically, e.g. by means of family allowances, social assistance, and study grants/loans.

In general, a gainfully employed couple has a larger disposable income than a family with a single employed adult, whose income, on the other hand, is larger than that of non-employed persons (Table 10.14). It is only among couples that childless families have a higher income than one-child families. Otherwise, the rule is that the more children a family has, the higher the income it earns is and the more money it receives in transfers. Nevertheless, this does not mean that every member of a larger family has more money at his/her disposal. According to the Income Distribution Survey, another measure, disposable income per 'consumer unit', indicates that disposable income decreases with the number of family members.

Table 10.14. *Disposable income for various family types, age 20–64, Sweden, 1988*

Family type	Mean income (SEK '000)		
	0 gainfully employed	1 gainfully employed	2 gainfully employed
Co-resident			
0 children	112.4	137.3	178.8
1 child	90.7	136.5	185.7
2 children	..	144.2	196.8
3 children	..	155.7	201.3
1 child or more	104.7	148.0	193.4
Single women			
0 children	54.5	77.1	–
1 child	82.4	105.6	–
2 children	91.2	128.5	–
1 child or more	91.4	116.1	–
Single men			
0 children	48.6	84.2	–
1 child	..	130.9	–
2 children	..	..	–
1 child or more	..	131.4	–

Source: Income Distribution Survey.

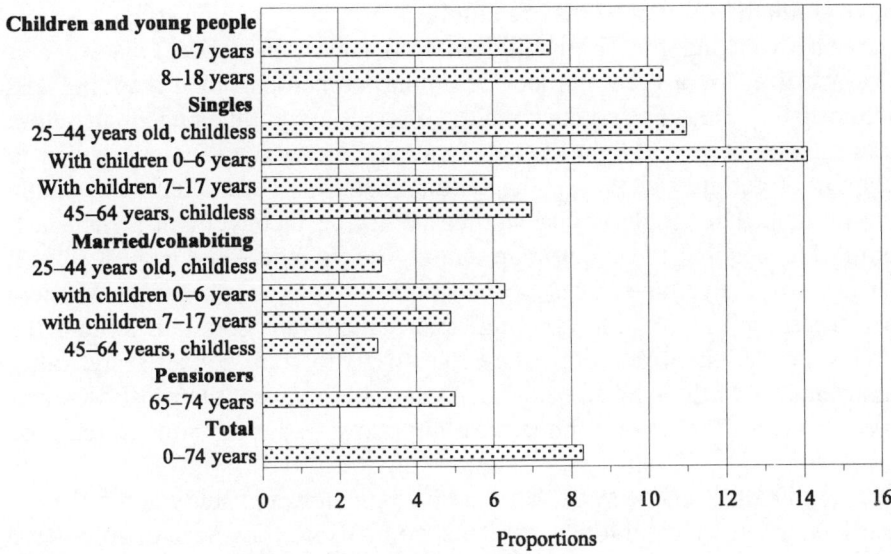

Source: Landgren Möller (1989).

Figure 10.6. Proportions of population living below the poverty line in different groups, Sweden, 1985

Compared with other population groups, lone parents with children 0–6 years seem to be less well-off: every seventh lone parent with small children lives below the poverty line; that is, the quotient of the disposable income and the living costs is under 1. Even in two-parent families, most families below this poverty line have pre-school children. Note that more than 10 per cent of childless singles in the ages 25–44 years are 'poor'; that is, they have a low but reasonable standard of living. The risk of being poor is, there-fore, highest if the family consists of a lone adult and is in an early phase of its life cycle (Landgren Möller, 1989).

10.4.3. *'Life-style' Patterns in the 1980s*

Life-styles vary over different stages of a person's life cycle. A person's life can be divided roughly into three stages with some general character-istics, even though some men and women never experience family life and therefore never live through the second of these stages.

(i) EARLY-ADULT LIFE-STYLE, BEFORE THE FIRST CHILD. The younger women have gradually prolonged the pre-childbearing period by investing in education and working life first; children come later, if at all. This stage is characterized by a great number of young women and men studying and working full-time. The young couples co-reside at a younger age than before and the age of sexual debut has decreased. Since young women began to cohabit or get married earlier than young men, there are much more single young men than single young women. Working inconvenient ('unsocial') hours has become more common among the youngest age groups. Of all age groups, the youngest ones are most prone to divorce or separate. Musical activities such as playing, singing, and dancing are common among the youngest adults; in addition, they like to go to rock concerts and other amusements in their leisure hours. Among both sexes, the most common spare-time activity in this and in the other two stages is listening to records.

(ii) THE FAMILY LIFE-STYLE. This style dominates, and study and full-time work decrease, in the middle stage of a woman's life. Swedish couples have their children, on average two of them, in this stage (women with less education earlier than those with a longer educational career). Nevertheless, modern Swedish women use only a small fraction of their fertile period for childbearing. Almost all women, and especially those with more education, work or study right up to the birth of the first child, after which they quit work and/or study for a shorter or longer period. The proportion of women who stay at home in order to do household work and care for their children increases at the beginning of this stage and decreases at the end of it. Most women have gainful employment between their first and second child, and at increasing rates also between their second and third child. Mothers tend to work in the home for a longer period after their second child than after their first-born.

Gradually, the total employment rate increases at the end of this stage, mainly because of the increasing number of women who work part-time. Women with higher educational qualifications and those with a white-collar background are gainfully employed to a greater degree than those with less education and a blue-collar background. The proportion of men who study or have gainful employment tends to be relatively constant over the life stages. This is true even when they have young children. For women, having children causes another division of labour within their households. If we add up housework and gainful employment, the amounts of women's and men's work are the same, but women have more housework. The distribution of the total number of working hours per week therefore differs between men and women. While men have much more leisure time during weekends, women's leisure hours are more evenly distributed over the week. Outdoor activities increase with age of both women and men. In this life stage one can observe that the older the couple is, the lower the tendency to divorce or separate is.

(iii) LATE-ADULT LIFE-STYLE. Women return to full-time or part-time work after the period of child-rearing. In age category 50 and over, couples and single women dominate, because of men's shorter length of life. Women generally engage in mass media and cultural activities more than men, and the oldest women are the most interested in attending cultural events (Bernhardt, 1983; Nordström, 1993; Nordenstam, 1984; Arvidsson *et al.*, 1982; Rydenstam, 1988; Johansson, 1990; Labour Market Surveys).

10.5. Everyday Life of Families

How do parents and children get along in their everyday lives regarding child-care arrangements and division of labour within the household?

10.5.1. *Child-Care Arrangements*

CHILD-CARE FACILITIES.[5] The modern Swedish child-care system has its origin in the crèches of the nineteenth century and in kindergartens developed around the turn of the century. While the crèches took care of the children of non-married mothers as a form of charity, the aim of the kindergartens, which were provided for a fee, was to stimulate the development of children of the more affluent families.

Alva Myrdal wanted to combine the best sides of the two systems in her so-called large nurseries (*storbarnkammare*), preferably free of charge as in the case of crèches and with special pedagogics as in kindergartens. This proposal resembles today's day-care system for pre-school children.

As more and more women began to participate in the labour market in the 1960s, expansion of the child-care system became an absolute necessity and its extension has continued since then. In general, the Swedish system of pre-school and after-school activities has expanded over the last twenty

---

[5] Sources used for this section are the Survey of Child Care Needs, the Survey of Living Conditions, and *Förskolor* 31-12-1992 (Statistiska meddelanden S 10 SM 9301).

years. The aims of child care are defined by government and Parliament, whereas the supervisory authority has been the National Board of Health and Welfare. The Social Services Act regulates the provision of day care and gives the municipal authorities the responsibility for municipal child care.

The Swedish Parliament decided in 1985 that day-care services would be made available to all children aged 1½–6 needing them by 1991, and that existing services would be improved. The goal has not been reached, but the number of day-care places has increased. The shortage of day-care places has a negative effect on the policy aim of equality; it not only affects women's labour-force participation, but also lessens the possibility for working-class families to get a day-care place.

Another decision made by the Swedish Parliament will have a negative effect on future child-care demand in the country, namely, the decision in 1991 about flexible compulsory school attendance. This means that, if the parents consider their child to be sufficiently mature to start school at the age of 6 and they want this, the child must be allowed to begin his/her school career one year earlier than usual and so finish one year earlier too.

Swedish child care includes pre-school and schoolchildren up to 12 years old. The most common form of non-municipal child care is a private child-minder. In 1992, the organized forms of non-municipal child care comprised 1,116 private and co-operative day-care centres and after-school centres, mostly parental co-operatives (779). It is, therefore, a relatively less often used alternative to municipal child care.

There are about 14,000 municipal pre-school and after-school centres in operation. The most popular form of municipal child care is day-care centres (more than 7,300 in operation) which are open all day for children up to 6 years old. Day-care centres have a pedagogic programme and trained staff. Family day care means that child-minders employed by the municipalities take care of children in their own homes. These child-minders, who care for children aged from a few months to 12 years, are most common in more thinly populated areas.

The term 'family day care' formally also includes so-called 'three-family systems' where two or three families employ a common child-minder for a total of three or four children. The child-minder cares for the children in one of the homes. Parents of infection-susceptible children in particular have chosen this kind of child-care service.

All children who have not been registered in the child-care system have a right to group activities in an open pre-school or in a part-time pre-school ('play school'); 1,500 open pre-schools are intended for children 0–6 years old. The first open pre-school started as an experiment in 1972. In the open pre-schools, the carers are pre-school teachers together with parents or child-minders. These schools have different opening hours. If they are open at least three days a week, public subsidies can be obtained. The charge-free part-time pre-schools are open three hours a day, mainly for children aged 5–6 years old who are not registered in day-care centres. This 'play school' conducts educational activities.

Activities for children aged 7–12 have also been planned for out-of-school hours and during school holidays in after-school centres. There are 3,100 such centres and 2,000 centres providing both day care and after-school activities. Since 1988, after-school centres have adopted a pedagogic programme.

Municipal child care is not only universal (covering all children) but takes into consideration children with special needs as well: sick or disabled children, children whose home language is other than Swedish, and children whose parents have inconvenient or irregular working hours.[6]

DEMAND AND USE OF CHILD-CARE FACILITIES. In 1991, there were almost 794,000 children under the age of 7, compared with 765,000 the year before. In 1990, 48 per cent of the children had a place in the municipal child-care system. In the 1980s, two types of child care for children 0–6 years old had grown more common: namely, parental care (44 per cent in 1990) and municipal child care (48 per cent in 1990). At the same time, private child care was used to a small and decreasing degree, from 24 to 8 per cent of cases (Table 10.15). Of the children who were cared for only by their parents, 22 per cent had a parent who was at home on parental leave. It was the parents themselves who most often took care of infants.

The biggest difference between the child-care situation for older children (7–12 years old) in 1980 and 1990 is that the proportion of children looked after by municipal child care has increased at the expense of the proportion of children cared for by a parent only. The result of this change is shown

---

[6] Home child-minders employed by municipalities look after and nurse sick children in the children's homes when the children cannot stay in the day-care centres, in after-school centres, or in family day care. There are not so many home child-minders throughout the country and their number is decreasing. According to the law, the municipalities are obliged to give disabled children priority to pre-school and after-school centres. Both in multilingual and in homogeneous Swedish-speaking pre-school groups, children with home languages other than Swedish can receive special instruction in their home language. Home language means that one or both parents has/have another language than Swedish and that the family uses that other language in its everyday life. In some cases, parents have inconvenient or irregular working hours, e.g., parents working in shifts, early in the morning or at night. For these families, some night-care centres, special family day-care centres, after-school centres, and child-minders are available.

in Table 10.16: in 1990, almost the same proportion of children 7–12 years old were cared for by a parent only as had a place in municipal child care; 37 per cent of 7–12-year-olds took care of themselves.

Figure 10.7 illustrates the demand for municipal child care for pre-school children up to 1992. According to the parliamentary resolution of 1985, all children who need a day-care place should have one. That goal has not been reached, but the number of children without municipal child care has been reduced.

Figures 10.8 and 10.9 show the trends in the numbers of children registered in different types of municipal child care during 1970–91: the number of children in day-care centres is on an upswing; those in family day care are decreasing now after a period of increase; and those in part-time pre-schools peaked in 1978 after which they started to drop again.

On 31 December 1992, the day-care centres provided care for 316,000 pre-school children, and the part-time pre-schools for 61,000 children. Moreover, after-school centres cared for 127,000 children aged 7–12. In total, 135,000 children 0–12 years old were registered in municipal family day care. The figures should be compared with the numbers of children in private pre-schools and in private-home day care, 20,000 and 100,000 children, respectively. In 1987, municipal child care at inconvenient working hours was provided for 5,605 children, mainly in the form of family day care (4,907).

Table 10.15. *Care for 1–6-year-olds, Sweden, 1980 and 1990 (%)*

Forms of care	1980	1990
Parent/guardian at home	40	44
Private care	24	8
Municipal care	36	48

Source: Survey of Child Care Needs.

Table 10.16. *Care for 7–12-year-olds, Sweden, 1980 and 1990 (%)*

Forms of care	1980	1990
Cares for itself	28	37
Parent only	49	27
Private care	11	8
Municipal care	12	28

Source: Survey of Living Conditions.

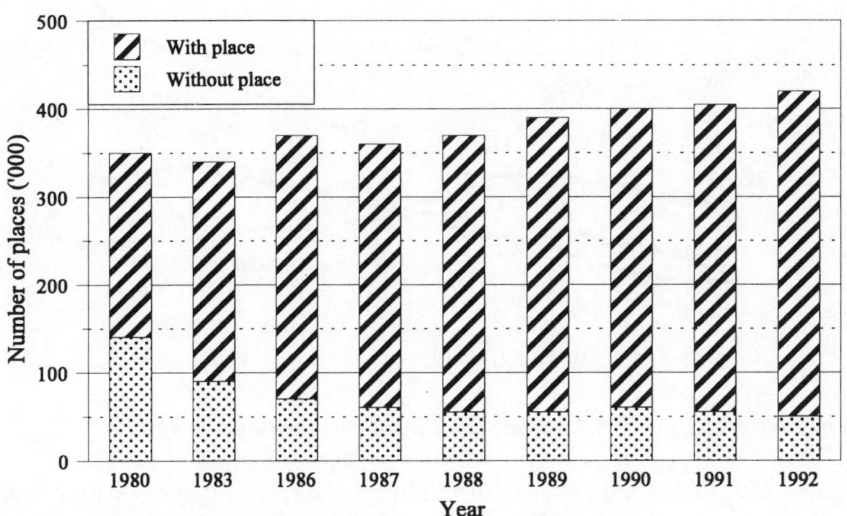

Source: Survey of Child Care Needs.

Figure 10.7. Demand for municipal child-care places for pre-school children, Sweden, 1992 ('000)

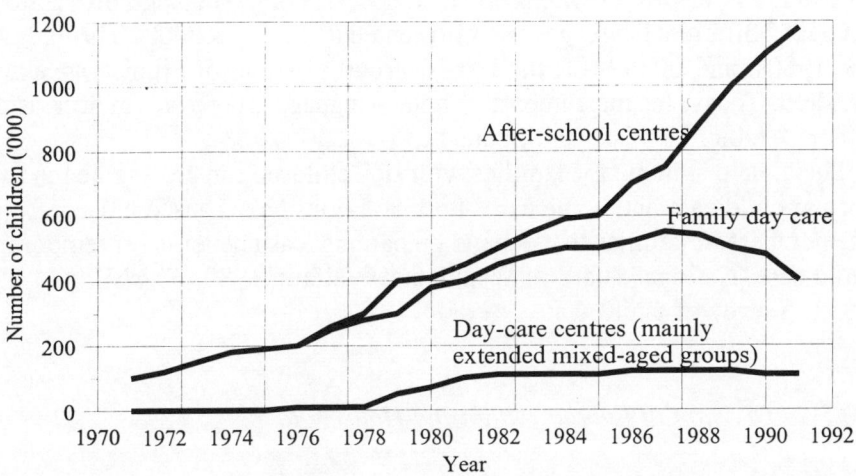

Source: Förskolor, fritidshem och familjedaghem, various years.

Figure 10.8. Registered numbers of children 0–6 years old in day-care centres, family day care, and part-time pre-schools, Sweden, 1970–1991

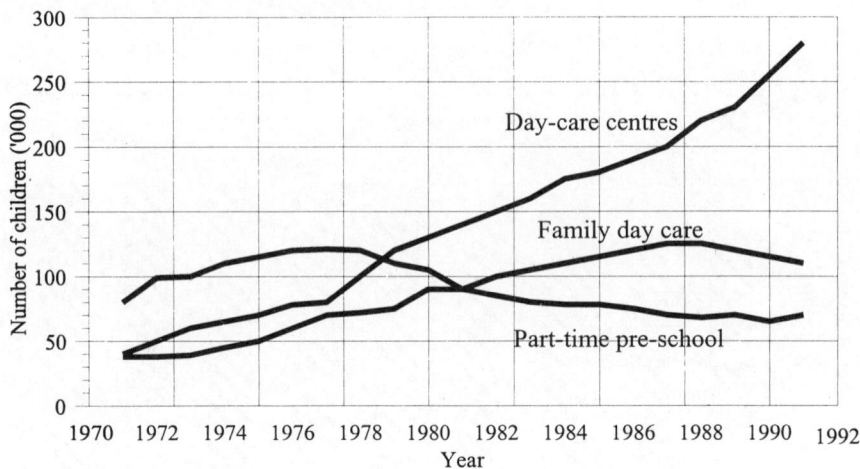

Source: Förskolor, fritidshem och familjedaghem, various years.

Figure 10.9. Registered numbers of children 7–12 years old in day-care centres, family day care, and after-school centres, Sweden, 1970–1991

The number of children with a home language other than Swedish who are registered in municipal child care was about 38,000 pre-school children in 1992, 31 per cent of whom obtained special home-language instruction. About 50 different languages are represented in the pre-schools. Throughout the 1980s, and in 1990–1, the largest group was that of Finnish-speaking children. Today, the most important home-language groups are (in decreasing order) Arabic, Finnish, and Spanish.

Social help at home for families with sick children can be obtained in two forms: child care and home care. Both activities have caused a decrease in the numbers of families that depend on parents' cash benefits for temporary child care (National Board of Wealth and Welfare, 1989; *Förskolor* 31-12-1992; Survey of Child Care Needs).

10.5.2. *Division of Labour within the Household*

One of the goals of the Swedish equal opportunities policy is to attain a fairer gender distribution with regard to paid and unpaid work. The Statistiska Centralbyrån has carried out a pilot study on time use in 1984–5. A full-scale time-budget survey, which is the result of Governmental Bill 1987/8:105, has not yet been completed. The results provided in this section, therefore, are from the pilot study.

All activities in the household that take place within a specified time period have been registered. The distribution of time both over the week as a whole and during the weekdays has been studied, but only the former will be discussed here. Activities have been classified into five large groups: free time, personal needs, study, housework, and gainful employment. Note that some of the groups in the pilot study are too small to be mentioned in the text and in the graph.

Unpaid work constitutes an important part of the productive activities in any society. Nevertheless, it has most often been omitted from the national accounts and statistics. The Swedish Time Use Survey shows that total work hours during a week, that is, comprising both paid work and unpaid housework, are almost equal for men and women.

Not surprisingly, the genders allocate their time differently between these two activities. In comparison with that of women, a larger part of men's work is paid work. As for unpaid work, the opposite is true. Note that even greater differences were registered among the different age groups, irrespective of sex. The highest work burden is found among middle-aged women and men.

Co-resident fathers of younger children and co-resident mothers (regardless of age of the children) have the smallest amount of free time and time for personal needs (Figure 10.10). The proportion of men with gainful employment does not change much according to family cycle, whereas it does for women; about 70 per cent of mothers of older children work outside the home, but only about 40 per cent of mothers of younger children do.

The total number of working hours, i.e. gainful employment plus housework, is about the same for both sexes. Naturally, it is easier for both men and women to work more when they have no children living at home than when they have young children to care for. While women are more prone to use their right to parental leave, the difference between these two groups of women is greater than that between the same groups among men.

In the same study, the respondents were asked whether they perceived a lack of time during weekdays. Table 10.17 shows the distribution of responses by married/cohabiting parents with children. The majority did experience a lack of time. The activities curtailed by lack of time were mainly housework and recreation. As for women, the lack of time for work in the home was the more common answer, and for men lack of time for recreation. Having children, especially younger ones, implies that the parents do not have enough time for everything they want to do (Rydenstam, 1988).

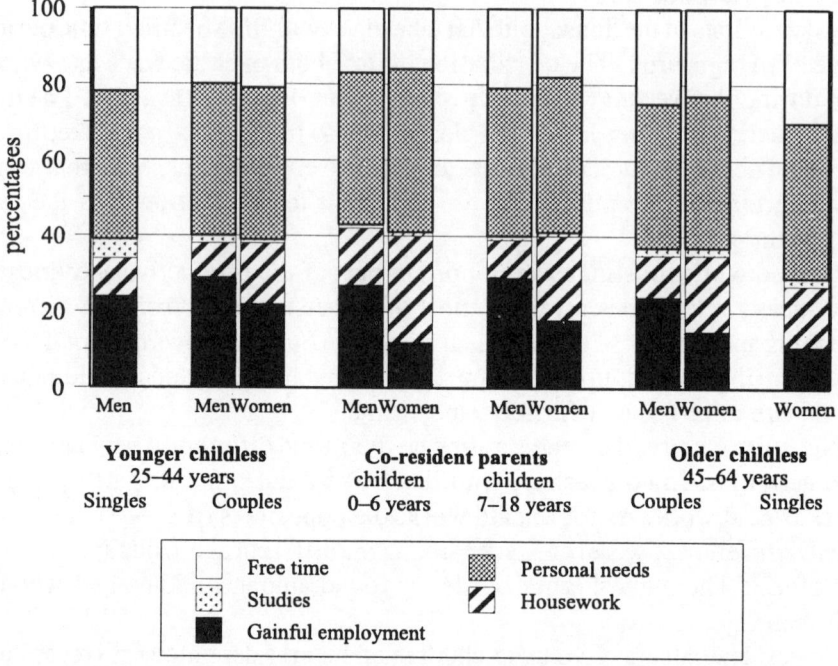

Note: 'Childless' means that the person in question does not have any child living at home.

Source: Rydenstam (1988).

Figure 10.10. Mean time during a whole week for activities, by sex and family cycle, Sweden (%)

10.6. Summary and Conclusions

The Swedish custom of cohabitation has a relatively long history, especially in certain parts of the country. Yet, Sweden has no statistics on cohabitation prior to the early 1970s which could be compared with the marriage statistics based on parish registers that started in the mid-eighteenth century. Despite regional variations, marriage has been the most accepted family form throughout this century. Since the mid-1960s, cohabitation has become more widespread. At the same time, living alone and lone parenthood have become more prevalent throughout the country. When couples have children, they very often follow the so-called 'two-child norm'. Period fertility has hovered around two children, but cohort completed fertility at the end of women's

Table 10.17. *Perceived lack of time on weekdays and activities cur-tailed because of lack of time, married/cohabiting parents with chil-dren, Sweden (%)*

	Women, age of child		Men, age of child	
	0–6	7–18	0–6	7–18
No lack of time	24	27	25	32
Lack of time	76	73	75	68
of which, for:				
Work	..	1	..	1
Work in home	34	23	22	17
Education	8	14	7	3
Recreation	35	33	39	47
Other	..	3	7	..

Source: Rydenstam (1988).

fertile period has remained about two.

Some impacts of family policy on family formation and dissolution, and on the (everyday) life of families, can be mentioned. The purpose of Swedish family policy is not primarily to increase the number of children per family, but to make it easier for parents to have the number of children that suits them. The idea is to facilitate the combination of family life and gainful employment, e.g. by social policy measures and equality policy. In this connection, the interesting question concerns the relationship between family-related policies and family life.

Marriage legislation seems to have at least a twofold effect on family life in Sweden. Firstly, cohabitation has been put on an almost equal footing with marriage, which makes it easier to cohabit. Consequently, the proportion of cohabiting couples has increased since the mid-1960s. Secondly, family dynamics in the form of divorces first increased and then stabilized at a relatively high level after the new divorce law in 1974. Even though there is also a high tendency to co-reside, the share of adults living without partners, but with or without children, has increased.

According to Swedish tax laws, spouses are taxed separately; that is, both sexes are perceived as breadwinners in the family. Therefore, it is economically more advantageous for Swedish women to have jobs than would be the case in a system of joint taxation. This being so, a high and increasing share of women are gainfully employed.

Pension regulations too have had an impact on family forms, as can be observed in the 1989 marriage boom. That year, the rules for widows' pensions were changed and it became necessary for older women to marry in order to receive a widow's pension according to the interim regulations. Younger age groups of women lost this right completely.

Public social policy has resulted in compensation for losses connected with having and rearing children. In addition, labour-market regulations allow six-hour working days for parents of young children and prohibit dismissal arising from pregnancy, childbirth, or marriage. These and other measures have made it easier to combine family and work. The goal of municipal child care for all children who need it is also a step in that direction. Therefore, Sweden has come closer to its goals of equality policy, first and foremost equal opportunities for both sexes.

In consequence of the idea of equal educational and career opportunities, women are giving birth relatively late in their lives, often after they have obtained education and a labour-market connection. That is, the timing of births has changed. The spacing of births has changed too, but not the average completed number of children per woman.

As shown above, the upswing in period fertility during the 1980s was at least in part a result of the so-called '30-month rule' which made it economically advantageous to give birth to one's next child within two and a half years of the former one. Nevertheless, completed family size has remained very close to the level of two children per woman.

Why has the completed family size not increased now that the Swedish government has made it economically possible to have children and to work at the same time? Public benefits and other measures may have had an effect by making it possible for couples to choose the number of children they prefer, often two. In that case, the Swedish equality and social policies have succeeded in reaching one of their goals. In this sense, the solidarity and equality-based social policy in Sweden is at the same time modern, family-friendly, and, in some respects, relevant with respect to demographic developments.

References

Arvidsson, A. *et al.* (1982), *Kvinnor och barn: Intervjuer med kvinnor om familj och arbete* (Women and Children: Interviews with Women about Family and Work), Statistiska Centralbyrån, Stockholm (Information i prognosfrågor 1982:4).

Bernhardt, E. (1983), *Arbete och barn: Kvinnors sysselsättning i de barnafödande åldrarna* (Work and Children: Employment Patterns among Women in the Childbearing Ages), Statistiska Centralbyrån, Stockholm (Information i prognosfrågor 1983:4).

Carlsson, L. (1972), *Jag giver Dig min dotter* (I Give You my Daughter), Part II,

Nordiska, Stockholm.

Coale, A.J. (1973), 'The demographic transition reconsidered', in IUSSP, *International Population Conference Liège 1973*, Vol. I, IUSSP, Liège: 53–72.

Hoem, J.M. (1990), *Remarkable Recent Fertility Developments in Sweden: an Interpretation*, Department of Demography (Stockholm Research Reports in Demography 61), Stockholm.

—— (1992), *Public Policy as the Fuel of Fertility: Effects of a Policy Reform on the Pace of Childbearing in Sweden in the 1980s*, Department of Demography (Stockholm Research Reports in Demography 69), Stockholm.

Johansson, L. (1990), *Män och barn: Svenska mäns familjebildning och barnplaner. Resultat från en enkätundersökning* (Men and Children: Family Formation among Swedish Men and their Plans for Children), Statistiska Centralbyrån, Stockholm (Demografiska rapporter 1990:2).

Karlsson, G. (1951), *Adaptability and Communication in Marriage*, University of Uppsala, Uppsala.

Landgren Möller, E. (1989), *Barns levnadsvillkor* (Children's Living Conditions), Statistiska Centralbyrån, Stockholm (Levnadsförhållanden 62).

Löfgren, O. (1972), 'Familj och hushåll: släkt och äktenskap' (Family and household: kindred and marriage), in M. Hellspong and O. Löfgren, *Land och stad* (Countryside and Town), Liberläromedel, Lund: 227–84.

Lundström, H., Martinelle, S. and Qvist, J. (1991), *Sveriges framtida befolkning: Prognos för åren 1991–2025* (The Future Population of Sweden: Projections for the Years 1991–2025), Statistiska Centralbyrån, Stockholm (Demografiska rapporter 1991:1).

Martinelle, S. (1990), *The Timing of First Birth: Analysis and Prediction of Swedish Birth Rates*, Bakgrundsmaterial från Demografiska Funktionen 1990:1 (Background Material from Demographic Section), Statistiska Centralbyrån, Stockholm.

——, Qvist, J. and Hoem, J. (1992), *Fruktsamhet ur livsperspektiv* (Fertility in a Life Perspective), Statistiska Centralbyrån, Stockholm (Demografiska rapporter 1992:1).

Matovic, R.M. (1984), *Stockholms äktenskap: Familjebildning och partnerval i Stockholm 1850–1890* (Stockholm Marriage: Family Formation and Partner Choice in Stockholm 1850–1890), Liberförlag, Stockholm.

Meisaari-Polsa, T. (1991), 'Familj och barnafödande' (Family and nativity), in *Tema invandrare: Levnadsförhållanden* (Focus on Immigrants: Living Conditions), Statistiska Centralbyrån, Stockholm (Report no. 69): 44–54.

—— and Söderström, L. (1995), 'Recent Swedish fertility changes in perspective', in C. Lundh (ed.), *Demography, Economy and Welfare: Scandinavian Population Studies, Vol. 10*, Lund University Press, Lund (Lund Studies in Economic History 1): 11–27.

——, Nilsson, Å., Sellerfors, H. and Tryggveson, R. (1990), *Familjebildning och familjeupplösning under 1980-talet* (Family Formation and Family Dissolution

346 *Tuija Meisaari-Polsa*

in the 1980s), Statistiska Centralbyrån, Stockholm (Demografiska rapporter 1990:1).

Näsholm, A. (1972*a*), 'Sammanboende gifta och sammanboende ogifta' (Married and unmarried co-residing couples), in *Familj och Aktenskap* (Family and Marriage), SOU 1972, Vol. 41, Stockholm: 355–71.

—— (1972*b*), 'Riksförsäkringsverkets föräldraundersökning' (Parent Study of the National Social Insurance Board), in *Familj och Aktenskap* (Family and Marriage), SOU 1972, Vol. 41, Stockholm: 372–6.

National Board of Wealth and Welfare (1989), *Barnomsorgen och de obekväma barnen* (Child Care and Inconvenient Children), SoS Report 1989:29.

National Social Insurance Board (1993), *Social Insurance Statistics: Facts 1992*, NSIB, Stockholm.

Nordenstam, U. (1984), *Ha barn: men hur många? Kvinnors syn på barn, familj och arbete* (Children: But How Many? Interviews with Women about Children, Family and Work), Statistiska Centralbyrån, Stockholm (Information i Prognosfrågor 1984:4).

Nordström, G. (1993), *Fritid 1976–1991* (Leisure Time 1976–1991), Statistiska Centralbyrån, Stockholm (Levnadsförhållanden 85).

Persson, L. (1971), *Samvetsäktenskap eller civiläktenskap* (Cohabitation or Civil Marriage), Acta Regiae Societatis Scientiarum et Litterarum Gothoburgensis, Humanoria, No. 7, Göteborg.

Popenoe, D. (1988), *Disturbing the Nest: Family Change and Decline in Modern Societies*, Aldine de Gruyter, New York.

Rydenstam, K. (1988), *Så använder vi tiden* (How We Use our Time), Statistiska Centralbyrån, Stockholm (Levnadsförhållanden 59).

Söderström, L. and Meisaari-Polsa, T. (1995), 'Swedish family policy: economic aspects', in C. Lundh (ed.), *Demography, Economy and Welfare: Scandinavian Population Studies, Vol. 10*, Lund University Press, Lund (Lund Studies in Economic History 1): 178–99.

Trost, J. (1967*a*), 'Some data on mate-selection: complementarity', *Journal of Marriage and the Family*, 29:730–8.

—— (1967*b*), 'Some data on mate-selection: homogamy and perceived homogamy', *Journal of Marriage and the Family*, 29:739–55.

—— (1971), *A Marriage Panel: Methods and Distribution of Frequencies*, Research Reports from the Department of Sociology, Uppsala University, Special Series: Family Research, FF 16.

—— and Lewin, B. (1978), *Att sambo och gifta sig: Fakta och föreställningar* (Cohabit and Get Married: Facts and Conceptions), SOU 1978, Vol. 55, Stockholm.

Wikman, K.R.V. (1937), 'Die Einleitung der Ehe: Eine vergleichende ethnosoziologische Untersuchung über die Vorstufe der Ehe in den Sitten des schwedischen Volkstums' (The introduction to marriage: a comparative ethno-sociological study on the preliminary stage of marriage in the popular morals of the Swedes), *Acta*

Academiae Aboensis, Humaniora XI, 1, Akademi, Åbo.

Statistiska Centralbyrån, Stockholm, statistical reports:

Befolkningsförändringar (Population Changes), Part 3: 1980, 1985, and 1990.
Befolkningsstatistik (Population Statistics), Part 3 and 4: 1991 and 1992.
Familjeförändringar kring 1980 och 1985 (Family Formation and Dissolution around 1980 and 1985), Statistiska meddelanden Be 15 SM 9201.
Familjeförändringar kring 1990 (Family Formation and Dissolution around 1990), Statistiska meddelanden Be 15 SM 9301.
Folkmängd (Population), Part 3: 1980, 1985, and 1990.
Folk- och bostadsräkningen (Population and Housing Census), 1975, 1980, 1985, and 1990.
Förskolor, fritidshem och familjedaghem (Pre-schools, After-school Centres, and Day Care in Private Homes), Statistiska meddelanden (Statistical Reports), selected years.

Statistiska Centralbyrån, Stockholm, other sources:

Fertility Register
Income Distribution Surveys
Survey of Child Care Needs
Labour Market Surveys
Surveys of Living Conditions

11 Switzerland: the Family Neglected by the State

BEAT FUX

Sociological Institute, University of Zürich, Switzerland

This chapter summarizes family change, family life and family policy in Switzerland during the 1980s, based on various data sets. As in other European countries, traditional living arrangements retain their importance, especially during the early family-formation phase. The increase of new life forms (pluralization) seems a phenomenon that occurs most of all in earlier stages (e.g. unmarried cohabitation) or in later biographical phases (e.g. lone-parent families). Furthermore, there is little evidence for changes in the intrafamilial division of labour between spouses. However, low extra-marital fertility, a comparatively late first marriage age of men and women, a rapid increase of voluntary childlessness and a rather high rate of part-time employed women are peculiarities of the Swiss case. Some of these trends might be influenced by certain deficiencies in family-related policies that clearly favour marital life forms. In this respect, I try to formulate some tentative impact hypotheses.

11.1. Introduction

Switzerland is known for its almost total abstinence in matters of family-related policies. Schultheis (1992) called the current situation – with slight exaggeration – an 'embryonic family policy'. Important reasons for this omission may be found in the specific Swiss federalism and the division of the Swiss state into three or four rather segregated language regions. This structure tends to create different systems of values and attitudes, as well as differences in the distribution of various living arrangements or heterogeneous family-policy arrangements. Not least because of these circumstances, there is a certain lack of representative data sources. I shall therefore refer to data and results of various studies, adopting something like a 'patchwork' technique, to reconstruct the main trends and processes concerning family formation and family life in Switzerland. Since such a methodology seems quite risky, I start this report by trying to highlight the most important demographic trends based on registration and census data. This strategy enables the validation of the analyses following afterwards. In a second step I shall sketch the most relevant theoretical and empirical literature. After that, I shall describe the data sets used for the analytical part of this chapter.

Four issues will be raised in the subsequent sections. First, in Section 11.2, I shall outline the most important changes and modifications of family-related policies in Switzerland during the last decade. In order to find some policy-impact models, it is necessary to retrace the pathways of recent Swiss activities. Special emphasis will be put on those policies that are bound to ease the combination of family and employment for women. Yet, the political activities will be dealt with in a broader sense too, including for example family laws, marital property rights and social insurance laws. The changes within the family during the 1980s, discussed in Section 11.3, form the main part of this contribution. That section describes the distribution of different living arrangements or family and household forms. Since on a national level adequate data are not available, the dynamics of family formation in Switzerland during the 1980s have hardly been analysed yet. New data sets such as Microcensus 1988 reduce this backlog somewhat.

According to the framework of the study, the dynamics within two critical phases in the life course will be considered: the *early family formation phase* and the *early post-parental phase*. Economic aspects of the family life situation, more specifically the income distribution, the risk of poverty for different family types and the housing situation, are the main topics of Section 11.4. Everyday life of families and the division of labour within the household will be discussed in Section 11.5, which also examines different child-care arrangements. The chapter concludes with a summary of the main results.

11.1.1. *Demographic and Family-Related Trends in the 1980s*

The demographic and family-related trends in Switzerland during the 1980s were much less dramatic or drastic than during the preceding two decades. Nevertheless, it seems necessary to give a brief sketch of the major demographic developments so as to gain insight into the processes affecting family formation and family life. Table 11.1 summarizes the major changes.

Table 11.1. *Summary table of demographic trends in Switzerland during the 1980s*

	1980	1985	1990
Population			
Population size ('000 inhabitants)[a]	6,304	6,456	6,674
Population increase (%)	0.50	0.45	1.15
Natural increase (%)	0.23	0.23	0.30
Net migration rate	0.27	0.21	0.85
Foreigners (%)	14.8	14.9	16.7
Asylum-seekers (*N*)	1,882 [b]	9,703	35,836
Age structure			
Population below age 15 (%)	20.0	17.5	17.0
Population between 15 and 44 (%)	44.5	45.8	45.3
Population between 45 and 64 (%)	21.8	22.5	23.1
Population over 65 (%)	13.8	14.2	14.6
Dependency ratio (%)[c]	20.8	20.7	21.3
Marriage and Divorce			
Crude marriage rate (CMR)	5.7	6.0	6.9
Total first marriage rate (women below age 50)	0.66	0.66	0.75
First marriage age (women)	25.2	26.1	27.0
Crude divorce rate (CDR)	1.7	1.8	2.0
Total divorce rate (TDR)	0.27	0.30	0.33
Fertility			
Age at birth of first child	26.4	27.0	27.6
Age at birth of any child	27.9	28.3	29.0
Crude birth rate (per 1,000 inhabitants, CBR)	11.7	11.5	12.5
Total fertility rate (TFR)	1.55	1.52	1.59
Net reproduction rate (NRR)	0.74	0.72	0.76
Extra-marital fertility	4.7	5.6	6.1
Parity progression ratio (first birth)[d]	0.90 [e]	0.84	0.82 [f]
Cohort-spec. estimations for childless families (%)	10.0 [g]	–	18.0 [h]
Mortality			
Crude death rate	9.4	9.2	9.5
Infant mortality	9.1	6.9	6.8
Life expectancy (men, at age 0)	72.4 [i]	–	74.0 [j]
Life expectancy (women, at age 0)	79.1 [i]	–	80.8 [j]

[a] Population at 1 January. [b] 1979. [c] 65+ / 15–64 X 100.
[d] Period-specific probability of a first birth (parity progression ratio).
[e] 1981. [f] 1988.
[g] Birth cohorts 1936–49. [h] Birth cohorts 1951–5.
[i] 1978–83. [j] 1989–90.

Sources: FSO, *Statistisches Jahrbuch der Schweiz* and *Bevölkerungsbewegung in der Schweiz*, various years; Council of Europe, *Recent Demographic Developments in Europe*, various years; Hoffmann-Nowotny and Fux (1991); *Neue Zürcher Zeitung* (1991); Höpflinger (1991*a* and 1991*b*).

POPULATION GROWTH. After a period with rather low growth rates, the permanently resident population is again increasing. From 1983 onwards, annual growth rates level with the average rates for 1950–60 or 1960–70 (e.g., 1.1 per cent or 76,700 persons in 1990, compared with 0.6 per cent or 37,700 in 1981). This can be explained by migration processes rather than by natural increase. In 1990, natural increase contributed only 9.4 per cent to the annual growth rate. On the other hand, we observe that, apart from 1982, the level of *net* inward migration has risen continuously, showing a total of 57,100 in 1990 (in 1981: 23,700). Therefore, the percentage of foreigners in Switzerland – traditionally one of the highest in Europe – increased markedly. In addition to the number of permanently resident foreigners, those of seasonal workers and asylum-seekers also increased sharply in the second half of the 1980s. The population gains of the final five years of the decade influenced the marital and fertility behaviour patterns and family formation less than they did the age structure of the Swiss population.

AGE DISTRIBUTION. Outstanding changes of the age structure during the 1980s are related to (i) very low proportions of children (together with Denmark, Germany and Austria), (ii) progressive levels of ageing, (iii) low birth rates and (iv) a highly positive net migration. The last trend mainly affects the population of working age. The old-age dependency ratio[1] rose, particularly in the second half of the 1980s. While these basic demographic trends influence the family-related processes more indirectly, the changes in marital and divorce behaviour patterns seem to relate much more closely to the phenomena highlighted in this chapter.

MARRIAGE. Similar to what happened in most European countries, in Switzerland the number of marriages per 1,000 inhabitants (the crude marriage rate, CMR) also sharply declined from the end of the 1960s and early 1970s. A break in this trend took place during the 1980s, however. Even if this development may have been influenced by the age structure of the population or the proportion of remarriages (Gilliand, 1991:14), we can observe that total first marriage rates (TFMR) also slightly increased in recent years. Despite the changes in values and behavioural norms (e.g. postponement of first marriages or refusal to marry), there are signs of a reverse trend in the second half of the 1980s, and not only in Switzerland (Council of Europe, 1991:14ff.). Comparable to the Scandinavian experiences, the increase of these marriage indicators was accompanied by rising birth rates.

[1] The number of people aged 65 and over, related to the number of people aged 15–64.

Such fluctuations can be interpreted correctly only if we consider that, in this country too, consensual unions are beginning to receive moral and legal recognition. Conservatively defined census data show that in 1990 8 per cent of all family households were consensual unions. According to our survey 'Population and Welfare', 39 per cent of all respondents below age 65 have a positive, 46 per cent a neutral and only 15 per cent a negative attitude towards unmarried cohabitation. With a side-glance at possible impact models, we have to remember that changes in legal provisions about marriage, marital property rights or social insurance laws may have period effects on marital behaviour (Findl, 1990).

Statistically not independent from the development of marriage rates, the age at first marriage rose constantly during the 1980s. With an average age at first marriage of 27.0 years (women), Switzerland ranks highest after Sweden and Denmark. Even considering that the sequence of individual decisions – to marry first and after that give birth to a child – has been inverted (Lüscher and Engstler, 1991:48ff.; Fux, 1994), we can observe a close relationship between the first marriage age and the age at birth of the first child. During the last decade the age at first birth has risen by 1.2 years in Switzerland. At present, a woman has her first child when she is 27.6 years old. Using this indicator as well as the mother's average age at birth of all children of all birth orders (in 1990: 29 years) as an operationalization, we can say that the early family formation phase extends over the second half of the twenties. Reflecting the fact that average age at first birth is remarkably higher than for example in Germany (during the 1980s: 0.8 year higher on average), I decided to select women between 26 and 30 for the analyses below of the first critical stage in the family biography.

FERTILITY. Since the middle of the 1960s, crude birth rates have been declining. However, during the second half of the 1980s this trend slackened or even reversed. We can observe that crude birth rates (which are influenced by the age structure) as well as total fertility rates and net reproduction rates show an upward movement. Lowest total fertility rates and net reproduction rates are to be found between 1985 and 1987. *Cohort-specific indicators* provide a different picture: average completed fertility or the lifetime births per woman for female generations born 1940–60[2] (Table 11.2) show a continuous birth decline. We can assume that fundamental changes in individual values and norms are apt to influence future trends in reproductive behaviour.

---

[2] Values for 1946 and onwards are completed by estimates based on the age-specific fertility rates of the year of observation.

Table 11.2. *Average completed fertility (lifetime births per woman) for generations born 1940–1960, Switzerland, 1985*

Year of birth	Av. completed fertility	Year of birth	Av. completed fertility
1940	2.09	1950	1.78
1941	2.05	1951	1.74
1942	2.00	1952	1.71
1943	1.94	1953	1.70
1944	1.89	1954	1.67
1945	1.85	1955	1.65
1946	1.86	1956	1.62
1947	1.82	1957	1.59
1948	1.81	1958	1.57
1949	1.80	1959	1.57
		1960	1.56

Source: Council of Europe, *Recent Demographic Developments in Europe*, Council of Europe, Strasbourg, 1991:42.

CHILDLESSNESS. This hypothesis receives further support from a glance at the development of permanent childlessness. Both period-specific parity progression ratios for first births (the probability of giving birth to a first child) and cohort-specific estimates for permanent childlessness increase. With Germany, Great Britain, and the Netherlands, Switzerland seems to belong to the group of countries where the trend towards childlessness during the 1980s was strongest. Various factors correlate with this fact, e.g. comparably low extra-marital fertility, high first marriage ages, the postponement of family formation, but also the prolongation of the average education and formation phase, the increase in female labour-force participation and the rise of new living arrangements (Höpflinger, 1991*b*:300ff.; Prioux, 1993).

LIFE EXPECTANCY. Although mortality indicators are of minor importance for our purposes, it should be mentioned that the life expectancy of the Swiss population (especially that of women) is the highest in Europe.

This short summary of the major demographic trends may serve as a guide for the in-depth analyses below. Since the survey data sources are not satisfactory in all aspects, we need this background information for the validation of our findings.

11.1.2. An Outline of Recently Published Theoretical and Empirical Literature

In this section the empirical and theoretical literature concerning the topics of interest will be summarized. A brief survey is given of recent publications that have influenced the scientific discussion in Switzerland. For a more complete overview of the state of family-related research in Switzerland, I recommend Fleiner-Gerster *et al.* (1991), which contains an extensive bibliography.

Apart from a well-known publication by Wilhelm Bickel (1947), the field of demographic theory has been neglected in recent years. The same impression is gained after summarizing the topic of actual trends of the household composition. In addition to an older report on the state of the family (Bundesamt für Sozialversicherungen, 1978), there is literature compiling the situation of the family from an all-embracing perspective (Schnyder, 1982; Kellerhals *et al.*, 1984; Kellerhals and Coenen-Huther, 1990; Gilliand, 1984 and 1990; Hoffmann-Nowotny, 1987; Hoffmann-Nowotny *et al.*, 1984, and 1992; Höpflinger, 1986 and 1987; Fleiner-Gerster *et al.*, 1991; Fux, 1994).

Whereas in research in the French-speaking part of Switzerland issues such as solidarity, types of interaction within the family and policy-related questions were predominant, changing family forms or living arrangements were examined in scientific research mainly in the German-speaking part of the country. Since the late 1970s, especially at the Sociological Institute of the University of Zürich, various surveys have been carried out (Fux, 1994; Hoffmann-Nowotny *et al.*, 1984 and 1992). Currently, this subject is being continued by the Institute's participation in the Population Policy Acceptance project (PPA).

The main topics of the surveys conducted at the Universities of Geneva and Lausanne were marriage patterns and interactions among family members (Kellerhals *et al.*, 1982; Kellerhals, 1987). Contributions to the study of reproductive behaviour were carried out at the University of Konstanz (Lüscher and Engstler, 1991). Economists at the University of Fribourg have published a study in which the budgets of different family types were analysed (Deiss *et al.*, 1988).

Women at work and gender roles have been topics of several surveys or secondary analyses (Borkowsky and Streckeisen, 1982 and 1989; Borkowsky *et al.*, 1985; Held and Murray, 1984; Mordasini, 1985; Streckeisen, 1989; Hungerbühler, 1989; Fragnière and Mermoud, 1989; Höpflinger *et al.*, 1991). The OECD-standardized Swiss labour-force surveys at the Federal Statistical Office provide new information and new insights into the working behaviour of the whole population.

Even if the investigation and evaluation of processes in the field of social, population and family policy are 'stepchildren' of the social sciences in Switzerland, there is comprehensive literature reviewing the different ideological positions and the empirical evidence in this country (Wagner, 1985; Gilliand, 1988; Fragnière and Christen, 1988; Möckli, 1988). One single publication discusses the present situation in Switzerland (Kommission 'Bevölkerungspolitik', 1985). Literature with an even much wider scope deals with the old-age pension system and its consequences on living arrangements and the social security of elderly people.

Various studies have been carried out on the history of the social insurance system in Switzerland (Binswanger, 1986; Lalive d'Epinay *et al.*, 1983; Lalive d'Epinay, 1991). A survey at the beginning of the 1980s concerning the financial situation of the elderly population (Schweizer, 1984) inspired the scientific research related to the risks and differentials of poverty (Gilliand, 1983; Freiburghaus and Zimmermann, 1984) on a regional level (Marazzi, 1987; Mäder *et al.*, 1991), as well as macrosociological or economic analyses on a national level (Buhmann *et al.*, 1989; Frey and Leu, 1988).

Research on family policy in a narrower sense has been undertaken by both jurists and social scientists (Koller, 1984; Grossenbacher, 1987). The long-term evolution of Swiss family policy was also dealt with in our comparative survey (Hoffmann-Nowotny *et al.*, 1992; Fux, 1994). Special topics in the field of family-related policies, e.g. the use of child-care arrangements, have also been studied. Of special interest in this context is a national research programme concerning changes in living arrangements and some interdependencies with the social security system. First reports are actually in print.

11.1.3. *Data Sources Used for the In-Depth Analyses*

For the analyses in this chapter I consulted various publications and data sources from the Federal Statistical Office. In addition to such secondary sources, I reanalysed six survey data sets. Since each of them has different sample universes, it may be helpful to illustrate their design. Table 11.3 summarizes the main variables covered, their characteristics and their spatial references. The reports in which the results have been published are also mentioned.

On this (data) basis, it seems possible to outline new results of family-related processes covering most of the aspects emphasized in the project

Table 11.3. *Description of data sets used in the analyses*

Survey [Reference] (Publications)	Sample size and units	Spatial reference
Determinants of birth decline [Hoffmann-Nowotny 1980] (Hoffmann-Nowotny *et al.*, 1984)	•632 married couples (married cohorts from 1970 on)	•German- and French-speaking parts of Switzerland
Female working biographies and professional careers [Streckeisen 1981] (Borkowsky *et al.*, 1985; Streckeisen, 1989)	•1200 non-single female persons (age 25–62)	•German- and French-speaking parts of Switzerland
Family formation among younger females [Höpflinger 1986] (Höpflinger and Erny-Schneuwly, 1989)	•587 women (age 22–29)	•Agglomeration of Zürich
Family forms and family policy in the North-western part of Switzerland [Fux 1986] (Hoffmann-Nowotny *et al.*, 1992)	•607 married women (marriage cohorts from 1970 on)	•North-western part of Switzerland
Micro-census 1988: Leisure time and culture [Micro-census 1988] (FSO, 1990)	•26,269 households •67,717 persons	•1% sample of Swiss population
Labour-force survey [SAKE 1991] (FSO, 1991)	•24,000 households	•all parts of Switzerland

'Family Life and Family Policies in Europe'. Nevertheless, it is important to stress that only the two last-mentioned data sets in Table 11.3 are fully representative for the entire Swiss population.

Table 11.3 *(cont.)*

Characteristics of the survey	Main variables
•cross-sectional •face-to-face •representative random sample	•social background •values and norms •familial biography •division of labour
•retrospective life histories •face-to-face •representative random sample •slight biases	•social background •life-histories (on education, formation, profession and family) •division of labour •use of child-care arrangements
•cross-sectional •face-to-face •representative random sample •slight biases	•social background •experiences with different living forms •values and norms •division of labour
•cross-sectional •face-to-face •representative random sample	•family forms and sizes •life-histories (family formation and work) •values and norms •evaluation and use of family policy arrangements •division of labour •use of child-care arrangements
•cross-sectional •face-to-face and mailing interviews •representative random sample	•household structures •family forms •background variables •housing situation •values and norms
•cross-sectional •telephone-interviews •representative random sample	•background variables •formation, profession •labour-force participation •housing

11.2. Family Policy in Switzerland

Recent developments in family-related policies in Switzerland are understandable only against the background of the Swiss political system, i.e. the *liberal tradition*, the country-specific *federalism* and the form of *direct democracy*. Each influences the ideological positions behind the discourse on specific family policy matters, as well as the heterogeneity of the cantonal family policy systems. Any attempt to formulate hypothetical impact models has to reflect the most important cultural cleavages between cantons. Even if the code of civil law, the social insurance scheme and social policy issues lie within the competence of the Confederacy, the actual features of family policy arrangements (child and family allowances) are quite different between the 26 cantons owing to their autonomy to enact the law. Other topics of relevance to family life are exclusively matters of these subnational units (e.g. policies about schooling and formation (subsidiaries), housing and fiscal policy or parenthood education). The very strong position of the cantons produces divergences with respect to structure and development of family policy arrangements.

The most important cleavages influencing the standard of cantonal family policy arrangements may be found between the language regions (German-*v*. French- and Italian-speaking areas) and between the opponents in the cultural struggles of the last century (rural and Catholic cantons *v*. urban and liberal cantons – Fux, 1994). Despite these heterogeneous features of family-related policies in the cantons, there are parallel developments as well. After a short summary of the history of Swiss family policy, I will focus on the most important trends during the past decade.

11.2.1. The Historical Background of Family-Related Policies in Switzerland

Similar to the experiences in other countries, there exists in Switzerland a so-called family policy *'avant la lettre'*. Early forms of family-related policies can be found from the late seventeenth century. These arrangements, based mainly on either the ideology of charity (social Catholicism) or on the idea of patronage (e.g. housing policies sponsored by entrepreneurs), were partly influenced by similar developments in France (Le Play).

A *first cycle* of governmental family policy appears during the last quarter of the nineteenth century. Then, the discussions concerning the implementation of the code of civil law (*Zivilgesetzbuch*) began. In marriage law, on the one hand, the traditional form of patriarchal family was upheld. On the other hand, most of the marriage bans were eliminated. The code of civil law was adopted in 1876; the marriage law was modernized in 1909. During this period, family-related policies were achieved by means of the rights of inheritance or by the implementation of progressive taxes so as to reduce imbalances between families and single persons. Also, the legislation of compulsory schooling and the implementation of a comparatively modern law concerning legal protection for pregnant mothers and for children (*Fabrik-gesetz*, 1877, revised 1899) bear some relevance. Within this first cycle we also find important discussions with respect to a general social insurance scheme. Despite these discourses, adoption of an old-age pension law did not take place before the middle of this century (1948).

The experience of the fertility decline and the economic crisis of the late 1920s initiated a *second cycle* of family-related policy around 1930–1945. The economic protection of the family (*Familienschutz*) was then the focal point of political efforts. The debates led to the establishment of a so-called 'family article' (Art. 34quinquies) in the Federal Constitution. Even today, this paragraph remains the only substantial product of family-related policies in Switzerland. As a result of this article, federal government is entitled to introduce statutory family allowances on a national level, to support efforts in the field of housing policy and to establish a maternity insurance. It is only with respect to the maternity insurance, however, that federal government has an explicit mandate to expound a national law. As to family allowances, it must be mentioned that corresponding laws lie at cantonal level. Between 1945, when the family article was accepted by the Swiss population, and 1965, all cantons established family allowance laws. They differ largely because in the French-speaking part of the country parity-specific payments are mainly the rule (Figure 11.1); generally, the allowances are much higher in these parts of the country too. The payment of allowances is organized by cantonal, communal or even private offices (*Familienausgleichskassen*). So, except for financial provisions for agricultural workers and small peasants, the federal government has not used its legal competence, even when several attempts were made to harmonize cantonal laws. The situation concerning maternity insurance is confusing. Although several political advances were made to establish maternity insurance, so far no satisfactory legal solution has been found. During the 1980s, legislation for such an insurance was rejected twice by the Swiss population.

11.2.2. *Focal Points of the Swiss Family Policy during the 1980s*

A *third cycle* of activities in the field of family-related policies began in the late 1970s and the corresponding discussions are still going on. On the basis of the experience of the second demographic transition (birth decline, increasing divorce, pluralization of living arrangements) and the fact that new cultural orientations had arisen since the late 1960s, the representatives of

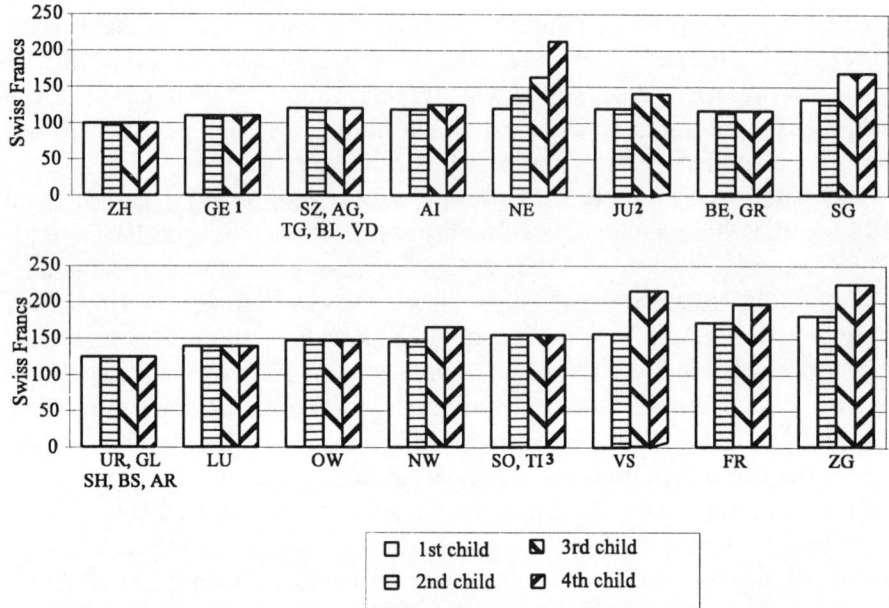

Notes: [1] For children more than 10 years old: CHF 135; [2] CHF 142 for families with 3 and more children; [3] SO rounded from CHF 155, TI from CHF 161.

Figure 11.1. Family allowances in Swiss cantons, 1991

different ideological positions tried to find new answers. Here I shall try to describe first the strategies of the most important political forces, then the main results of the recent discussions in the field of family policy; finally, I shall formulate some hypothetical impact models.

A first trend may be qualified as an ideological encapsulation of the right-wing conservatives, who were trying to resist the pluralization of family forms and the loss of traditional norms. During the 1980s they fought with little success against the liberalization of abortion (an initiative was defeated by plebiscite in 1985) and against a modernization of the family and marital property law. (A small majority of the Swiss population adopted the revised law in 1984.) On the other hand, they supported attempts to assist families either by means of financial subsidies (fiscal policy) or on an organizational level.

Family policy was traditionally a focal point of interest in moderate conservative parties (e.g. the CVP, Christian Popular Party). Trying to resume their power base throughout the 1980s, they began to *search for new con-*

cepts. On different political levels, they lobbied for family issues. Further, they supported the implementation of an 'equal rights' article in the Federal Constitution (Art. 4, adopted by plebiscite in 1981) and attempts for the legislation of a maternity insurance (although two proposals were finally rejected by plebiscite in 1984 and 1987), as well as the modernization of the adoption law (in force since 1973), the children's law (in force since 1978) and the family and marital property law (in force since 1986). Consensus ruled between the Conservatives, the Social Democrats and the liberal parties, that all these revisions plus the revision of the divorce law should lead to the replacement of a legal situation that clearly favoured traditional male-dominated family forms with one favouring a family form based on equality and partnership between man and woman. The moderate conservatives were also successful in fiscal policy – in 1988 new tax relief measures for families were adopted by the federal parliament. In 1990 these measures were extended.

Even if family-related policies in Switzerland seem the domain of Christian and conservative parties, we should not forget the activities of the left (Social Democrats) and liberal parties. Within social democracy there are generally two leading ideas: first, the continuing consolidation of the Swiss social security system, and secondly, the attempt to minimize discrimination against women. Therefore, it is not surprising that left-wing activities focused on the tenth revision of the old-age pension scheme, which should improve the extent of pensions and reform the legal situation of (married) women. In addition, they were equally active in housing policy. Owing to the fact that, after the adoption of women's suffrage in 1971, the Social Democrat party was rejuvenated by a well-educated female generation, it also became active in the traditional branches of family policy. Therefore, by seizing the initiative the Social Democrats finally tried to introduce the overdue maternity insurance, which was later rejected by the population. They were more successful in their attempt to insert the 'equal rights article' (Art. 4) into the Constitution. In this question, and in many of the above-mentioned ones, the Social Democratic party collaborated with those in the middle of the political spectrum. While the adoption of the equal rights article led to many modifications of lower-ranking laws (e.g. cantonal law), the elimination of paragraphs discriminating against women progressed only slowly, a fact that was criticized especially by the women's movement, which in the late 1970s and early 1980s was another important political force.

In the field of family policy, the role of the various liberal parties, which in Switzerland are more or less right-wing oriented, is of minor importance. Although there is without any doubt a consensus with other parties about the continuing modernization of laws in various fields (civil law, family law, equal rights, liberalization of the abortion law, etc.), they opposed any attempt to consolidate the Swiss system of social security. For example, regarding maternity insurance, their argument that this insurance would incur increasing costs or would have negative effects on the labour market was rather successful.

Before formulating some hypothetical impact models of family-related policies, I shall very briefly summarize the contents of the most important family policy measures (allowances, fiscal policy and family and marital property law), and the present situation concerning maternity insurance.

ALLOWANCE SCHEMES. As illustrated in Figure 11.1, there exist very heterogeneous allowance schemes at cantonal levels. The extent of family allowances in 1991 ranges from CHF 100 to CHF 224 per month per child, depending on the place of residence, and in several cantons also depending on the number of children. Thirteen cantons provide monthly educational allowances, which replace the child allowances; the amount ranges from CHF 135 to CHF 288. Again, the amount of these benefits differs in several cantons according to birth order. In 11 cantons non-recurring birth allowances of between CHF 500 and CHF 1200 are provided. The age limits for payments, too, differ widely between the cantons, according to a child's income or its potential capability of earning its living (15–25 years). Although the allowances are generally higher in the French-speaking parts of Switzerland, the perception of the allowance scheme is worse. In a survey by UNIVOX (SGPS, 1991), 39 per cent of the population in the western part of Switzerland judged Swiss family policy as 'bad' to 'very bad', in comparison with 26 per cent in the German-speaking population. While the proportion of the Swiss-French population judging the cantonal family policies as 'good' to 'very good' was 13 per cent, the corresponding proportion among the Swiss-German population was 18 per cent.

FISCAL POLICY. In the field of fiscal policy, procedures to reduce imbalances between families and single persons are just as heterogeneous as are family allowances. In all cantons, taxes are based on the total income of the family. Depending on the place of residence, families obtain different tax rebates. These reductions refer to the marital status, the number of children and the labour-force participation of a married woman. The calculation procedures provide either different tax scales for families and single persons or fixed tax rebates or tax reductions, depending on the total family income. It is almost impossible to compare and to quantify these cantonal tax systems.

It can only be pointed out that these rebates are connected with the marital status of a family and that the total amount of all tax reductions is again higher in the western parts of Switzerland.

MATERNITY INSURANCE. Concerning maternity insurance, it must be admitted that there is no general arrangement. Private health insurance companies generally consider maternity as an illness! Only the costs of pregnancy controls and of births (hospital costs) are subsidized by the government. There is neither obligatory maternity leave nor maternity benefit. As a result of the maternity protection laws, women are not allowed to work for eight weeks before and after confinement. Generally, it is the rule that employed women do get paid during this period, but this benefit is based on collective or private contracts. The introduction of efficient maternity protection (*Mutterschaftsinitiative*) was attempted in 1984. This initiative aimed at the takeover of the entire costs of maternity by federal government, the establishment of parental leave and a legal protection against the dismissal of pregnant women. The initiative was rejected by a substantial majority of the population. Another attempt to introduce maternity insurance within the framework of the federal health insurance law (*Bundesgesetz über die Krankenversicherung*) was also defeated by plebiscite in 1987. Therefore, at present there remains a prohibition against pregnant women working, but no maternity benefits whatsoever.

11.2.3. *Impact Hypotheses Concerning the Swiss Situation in the Field of Family Policy*

If we summarize the family policy situation with regard to the position of the family in Switzerland, we have to emphasize that only very weak arrangements and more or less unsystematic measures exist. Most of these are explicitly addressed to *marital* living arrangements. This situation might influence the fact that alternative living arrangements diffused relatively late in Switzerland in comparison with neighbouring countries. It also might have effects on the structuring of female biographies (e.g., late marriage ages; low extra-marital birth rates; low female employment rates). In order to distinguish between the various possible effects of the Swiss family policy, I will try to formulate several impact hypotheses.

1. On aggregate levels (cantons, countries) I assume that the capacity to influence the number of children by means of family policy is very weak. In other words, there is no causal correlation and no direct impact between

the family policy arrangement and the fertility quantum.

2. But this first hypothesis does not exclude the possibility of indirect effects. So I postulate *interdependencies* between the standard of cantonal family policies and (the tempo and quantum of) fertility. The extent of family policy arrangements can be interpreted as an expression of divergent political cultures. While we can observe on the one hand a *familist* tradition, or a family-oriented political climate (especially in the French-speaking parts of Switzerland), that corresponds with relatively high fertility rates and with the comparatively late beginning of similar demographic processes such as the decline of second births in the middle of the 1960s, on the other hand we also find a liberal and *individualistic* political climate corresponding with low birth rates and an early beginning of the second demographic transition (Fux, 1994:337–51).

3. People perceive the present state of family-related policies as insufficient. Only 27 per cent of all respondents (Population and Welfare) evaluate the current family policy as 'good' or 'very good'. The implementation of a parental leave scheme, lower income taxes and better housing conditions are the measures that are demanded most frequently (Fux *et al.*, 1993:177ff.). This negative evaluation of family-related policies might influence individual behaviour; for example, the comparatively high first marriage age and high mother's age at birth of her first child and the relatively low extra-marital birth rates can partly be explained by lacks in corresponding benefits.

4. Furthermore, the *marriage-orientedness* of the Swiss family policy has side-effects on family formation processes. Linking the right to family policy benefits (e.g. fiscal policy) exclusively to the married status of a couple leads to a polarization. Either couples decide to marry in order to reduce a lot of constraints in everyday life, or they refuse to marry and probably remain permanently childless. The observation of rapidly increasing proportions of permanently childless women during the 1980s strengthens this hypothesis.

5. The legally induced tie between the right to family policy benefits and the married status of a couple enforces *individual solutions* concerning the combination of work and family among women as well as *self-organization* of the intrafamilial division of labour. To compensate for the lacking public child-care facilities, Swiss women are obliged to renounce employment more often than women in other countries. This form of politically promoted indirect expulsion of women from the labour market corresponds with the above-mentioned polarization of living arrangements as well as with the fact that new living arrangements spread relatively late and less widely in comparison with neighbouring countries.

6. The time lag of this prohibitive structural situation in comparison with

the legal situation that is in force (the revised family law favoured the ideal of partnership, the modernization of the marital property law and better alimonies in case of divorce) probably accelerated the increasing *divorce rates* during the second half of the 1980s. It also may have stimulated individual *decisions to marry* during the same period.

7. Because of competing values within the field of family-related policies (equal rights between men and women, individualization, emancipation of women on the one hand, and the favouring of marital family arrangements on the other), new living arrangements such as *cohabitation* with or without children and *lone-parent families* are much less frequently observed in Switzerland than in other countries.

8. People living in such new family arrangements consequently experience more constraints in their *everyday life*. Their housing situation is more often worse than that of married couples, and they are at risk of poverty much more frequently.

11.3. Family Forms in the 1980s

11.3.1. *Marital Behaviour*

Concerning family formation and marital behaviour, we have already noted the increasing number of first marriages since 1985 after a rapid decrease during the 1960s and the early 1970s and a stabilization during the first half of the 1980s (Table 11.1). Concerning remarriages (total remarriage rates for women: 1961: 61; 1970: 60; 1975: 48; 1980: 47; 1984: 49), a similar development can be observed. The average interval between divorce and remarriage rose from 5.1 years in 1961 to 6.5 years in 1984. Even if this development seems an effect of the fact that the 'baby-boom generation' reached marriageable age, we should keep in mind that the increase coincides with the revision of the family and marital property laws. Possibly these legal modifications influenced marital behaviour, in the sense that certain obstacles were removed that had kept people from marrying.

A second trend is the *postponement* of marriage and births until later biographical phases. All *divorce indicators* were rapidly growing during the same period. Regarding the age schedule, too, we observe some temporal variation in marital behaviour. Up to age 41, the proportion of unmarried people was higher in 1988 than in 1980. The proportion of married people, by consequence, was lower for all ages up to 50. The proportion of younger divorcees (up to age 35) dropped during the 1980s. Therefore, the exploding divorce rates were caused by the older age groups.

The most important trends to be deduced from the above are as follows. First, among younger men and women, marriage has become less favoured. This refusal to marry as well as the postponement of marriage have to be contrasted with an increasing proportion of cohabiting people (cf. below). Secondly, concerning the early family formation phase, the increase in divorce seems less important. On this basis, the distribution of marital statuses in the early family formation phase and the early post-parental phase are quite evident (Table 11.4). In age group 26–30 the proportion of divorced people decreased (in 1988, it was half that of 1980) owing to the timing of marriages. The proportion widowed was stable during the 1980s but not important in this age group. The share of unmarried men and women rose drastically and the proportion of married people decreased inversely by nearly a third. In the early post-parental phase the share of divorcees nearly doubled. All other statuses remained fairly stable during the 1980s.

Table 11.4 includes cross-sectional data only. These sources do not allow us to describe the life-course dynamics of marital statuses. Nevertheless, I assume that the selection of the early family formation phase as reference group and the fading out of familial biographies probably led to an underestimation of the effective variation of living forms. Both during the antecedent phase (between leaving the parental home and the formation of one's own family) and later (cf. divorce trends) there is undoubtedly a process of pluralization to be observed (Höpflinger and Erni-Schneuwly, 1989:37ff.).

Table 11.4. *Marital statuses within selected age groups of women in various Swiss data sets (%)*

Data set	Unmarried	Married	Divorced	Widowed	N
Age group 26–30					
Census 1980	27.2	68.3	4.2	0.3	236,956
Registration 1988[a]	42.3	54.9	2.6	0.2	264,000
Micro-census 1988	38.8	58.8	2.1	0.3	2,644
Census 1990	37.1	59.4	3.2	0.3	289,953
Age group 46–50					
Census 1980	9.5	79.6	6.4	4.5	195,039
Registration 1988	8.8	77.4	10.6	3.1	220,100
Micro-census 1988	7.1	82.0	7.5	3.4	2,127
Census 1990	8.7	76.3	11.3	3.5	227,012

For comments, see Höpflinger 1986: the sample universe covers only younger (first age group) respondents.

[a] Registration 1988: age group 25–29.

I generally assume a *funnel-shaped* contraction in the variety of living arrangements towards the early family formation phase. Later in the life course, the differentiation of living arrangements will recommence. The main contributor to this renewed variety of living arrangements after the early family formation phase is certainly the divorce factor.

11.3.2. *Fertility Trends, Extra-marital Fertility and Childlessness*

FERTILITY TRENDS. Considering fertility development, an overall perspective reveals a process that is quite similar to that observed in marital behaviour. As in most European countries, birth decline began in Switzerland in the late 1960s. Both period and cohort indicators drastically sank. This trend slackened or even reversed into an upward movement during the second half of the 1980s (Table 11.1). The main cause for this increase can again be found in the changing age structure of the Swiss population. Besides this rather general finding, there exist some substantial trends.

EXTRA-MARITAL FERTILITY. Although extra-marital fertility is traditionally low in Switzerland, both period-specific and cohort-specific rates of extra-marital childbearing rose continuously during the last decade. Nevertheless, with only 6.1 per cent births out of wedlock in 1990, Switzerland ranks among the European countries with the lowest illegitimacy ratios.

CHILDLESSNESS. Childlessness, on the other hand, is noted as a significant trend. The proportion of permanently childless women is drastically increasing. Cohort-specific estimations show that the proportion of childless families nearly doubled during the past decade (Table 11.1).

Both facts – the low but increasing illegitimacy ratio and the increasing proportion of childlessness – lead us to assume that any deviation from a marriage-based living arrangement is negatively sanctioned by society, an attitude that is supported by the legal and the family policy system in Switzerland. Under these circumstances, permanent childlessness seems to serve as a niche that younger cohorts in particular choose more frequently. The marriage-oriented Swiss legal system (cf. fiscal policy) more or less offers women two alternatives: either refuse parenthood, or legitimize an extra-marital procreation or birth. With Lüscher and Engstler (1991:48ff.), I assume that in recent times the sequence of two basic decisions has changed. While older cohorts first decided to marry and then to give birth to a child (children), among younger couples the decision to marry is dependent on or motivated by procreation.

11.3.3. *Family Size*

Even if total fertility rates and net reproduction rates tend to increase slightly, we have to bear in mind that the causes of reproductive behaviour have changed. This might be illustrated by contrasting period and cohort data.

Initially, fertility decline was caused more or less by the decreasing number of women having more than two children. Up to birth cohort 1932, the proportion of such larger families was fairly stable. The drop in the number of large families was the predominant factor of that first stage in fertility decline (Figure 11.2). From about cohort 1945, this proportion tends to stabilize, and declines in period fertility rates also slackened. Despite this trend break with regard to period indicators, the drop in completed fertility is still ongoing (Table 11.2). These controversial trends may be explained as an effect of the growing proportion of childless women. In other words, childlessness seems the major factor within a second stage in the birth decline.

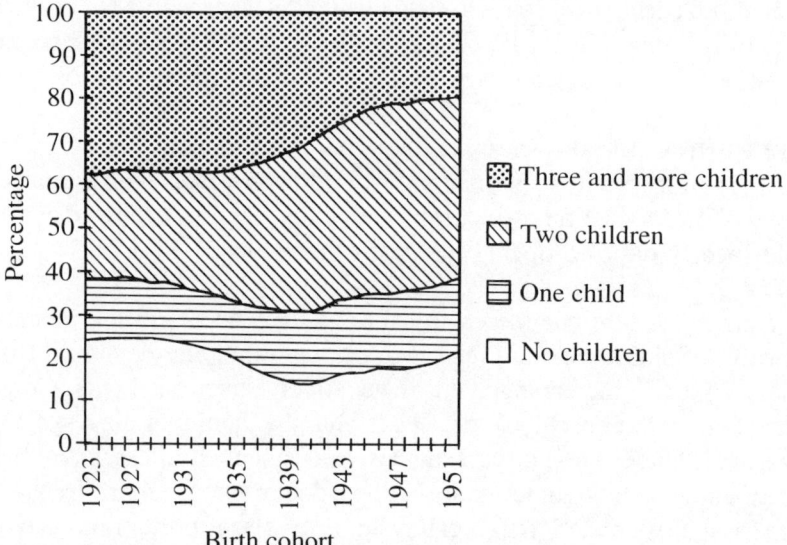

Source: Council of Europe (1990:110).

Figure 11.2. Family size distribution of female birth cohorts, Switzerland, 1923–1951

Table 11.5. *Number of children within selected age groups of women in various Swiss data sets (%)*

Data set	No. of children							
	Age group 26–30				Age group 46–50			
	0	1	2	3+	0	1	2	3+
Census 1980[a]	28.4	30.4	33.2	7.9	21.1	29.2	29.8	19.9
(*N*) ('000)	(89.2)	(95.3)	(103.9)	(25.0)	(68.7)	(94.9)	(96.9)	(64.5)
Streckeisen 1981	25.0	29.6	35.5	9.9	7.9	13.9	30.9	47.3
(*N*)	(38)	(45)	(54)	(15)	(13)	(23)	(51)	(78)
Fux 1986[b]	19.3	35.3	36.0	9.3	31.6	15.8	26.3	26.3
(*N*)	(29)	(53)	(54)	(14)	(6)	(3)	(5)	(5)
Micro-census 1988	48.5	21.5	23.2	6.9	30.4	24.6	30.4	14.6
(*N*)	(1,103)	(489)	(527)	(157)	(634)	(512)	(634)	(305)

[a] Households: head of the household at age 25–34 and 45–54, children below age 25 (cf. FSO and Blanc, 1985).
[b] Married women only.

Concerning those critical phases in familial biographies, we get more detailed information by comparing the number of children in various surveys (Table 11.5). Even if the sample universes are not completely comparable, three trends can be observed. First, we find a *concentration* towards smaller families; secondly, there is a trend to *postpone births*; thirdly, there is an increasing and comparatively high number of females tending to *remain childless*. The highest share of childless women was found in urban areas. Because of the sample definitions, our 1986 survey (Hoffmann-Nowotny *et al.*, 1992) probably underestimates the proportion of childless families. Almost the same feature might be documented within the older age group.

The change towards two-child families may also be illustrated by comparing selected birth cohorts. Among the cohorts 1936–40, 10 per cent of women have no children, 20 per cent have one child, 37 per cent have two children and 33 per cent have three or more children. Women born in 1951–55 clearly favour two children: 18 per cent have no children, 21 per cent have one child, 42 per cent have two children, and 19 per cent have three or more children (Höpflinger, 1991*a*:306).

When breaking down the average number of children by marital status (Table 11.6), we find a close connection between childbearing and marriage. Up to the present, among cohabiting couples fertility is comparatively low. Even in urban contexts (Höpflinger, 1986) unmarried women tend not to have any children. The number of divorcees with children also remained comparably small, although it is increasing. More than every second divorced woman remains childless; within the older age group, the share of female divorcees without children is slightly higher still. Unfortunately, there are no corresponding registration or census data.

Concerning the early post-parental phase, there is a rather similar situation. Never-married men and women are predominantly childless and live by preference in one-person households. More than two out of three divorcees are childless; however, the ratio of divorcees with dependent children is growing. Within both age groups the segment of widowed persons is small.

Table 11.6. *Number of children by marital status and age group of women, Switzerland, 1981–1988 (%)*

No. of children	Never-married	Married	Divorced	Widowed	N
Data set: Höpflinger 1986					
Age group 26–30					
0	100	36	25	0	212
1	0	28	34	0	54
2	0	33	33	0	64
3 or more	0	3	8	0	7
N	215	56	66	0	337
Data set: Micro-census 1988					
Age group 26–30					
0	96	27	57	(50)	1,084
1	4	30	17	(17)	487
2	0	33	26	(33)	517
3 or more	0	10	0	0	153
N	681	1,508	46	(6)	2,241
Data set: Streckeisen 1981					
Age group 46–50					
0	–	7	(11)	(20)	13
1	–	13	(33)	(0)	23
2	–	30	(44)	(40)	51
3 or more	–	50	(11)	(40)	78
N		150	10	(5)	165
Data set: Micro-census 1988					
Age group 46–50					
0	93	23	52	49	628
1	4	26	27	22	512
2	2	34	18	21	633
3 or more	2	17	3	9	304
N	128	1,736	145	68	2,077

Table 11.7. *Partner arrangement by number of children: women, Switzerland, 1988*

No. of children	Partner in household		No partner in household	
	N	*%*	*N*	*%*
Age group 26–30				
0	747	39	356	93
1	473	25	16	4
2	527	27	9	2
3 or more	157	8	0	0
N	1,895	(100)	381	(100)
%	83.3		16.7	
Age group 46–50				
0	443	25	191	66
1	461	26	51	18
2	594	33	40	14
3 or more	297	17	8	3
N	1,795	(100.1)	290	(100)
%	86.1		13.9	

Data set: Micro-census 1988

11.3.4. *Partner Arrangements*

The close connection between marriage and procreation also influences the partner arrangements. In 1988, more than 80 per cent of women were living in a common household with a partner (married or unmarried). Most of the partnerless arrangements are one-person households and households without children. Among the older age group, the share of partnerless arrangements is higher because of the increasing number of divorced and widowed persons. Table 11.7 shows that partnerless households with children in relation to all partnerless households amount to 6 per cent only in the younger age group, but form 34 per cent among women in their early post-parental phase.

Households with only one partner are a heterogeneous category, containing one-person households as well as lone-parent families, separated but not legally divorced partnerships and people who are living apart together. The total of all these living arrangements, however, is rather small, even among those in the younger age group.

11.3.5. *One-Parent Families*

The structure of partner arrangements leads one to assume that one-parent families are not favoured in Switzerland. In relation to all private households, the share of one-parent families has increased only slightly since 1960 (1960: 4.1 per cent; 1970: 4.0 per cent; 1980: 4.4 per cent); in relation to all families with children, it is around 10 per cent. Therefore, Switzerland ranks with France, Spain and Ireland among those European countries with the lowest shares of lone-parent families. If we break down this living arrangement by age of the parent, we can distinguish two main types of lone-parent family (Figure 11.3). We find two peaks: one for persons below age 20, and another for persons between about 33 and 43. Most in the younger group are never-married mothers. This seems to be a phenomenon that is traditionally – with negative connotations – called a '*ledige Mutter*'. Among the older one-parent families, the share of divorcees is much higher. Therefore, we can assume that the increase in this living arrangement is more or less an effect of increasing divorce rates and decreasing remarriage rates. Again, we can observe that neither in the early family formation phase nor in the early post-parental phase are one-parent families a relevant feature. Among all lone-parent families, the proportions of those with dependent children (below age 12) and those with older children are 40 and 60 per cent, respectively.

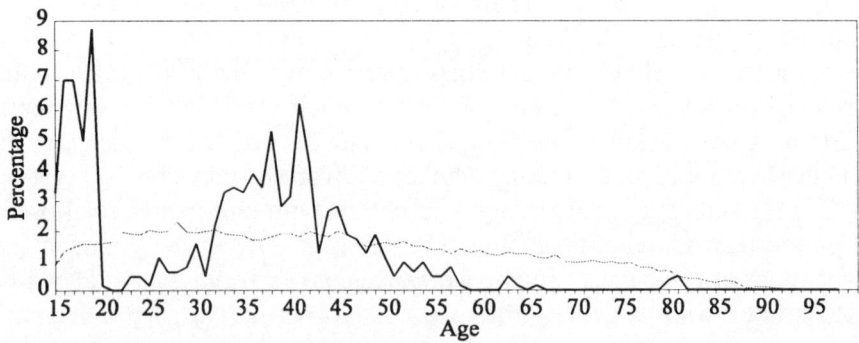

Note: Bold line: age distribution of heads of one-parent families; thin line: age distribution of the entire population.

Source: Fux (1992:26).

Figure 11.3. Lone-parent families by age of head, Switzerland, 1988 (Micro-census)

11.3.6. *One-Person Households*

One-person households represent another important category of partnerless households. The proportion of one-person households in relation to all households increased from 14 per cent in 1960 to 20 per cent in 1970, 29 per cent in 1980 and 32.4 per cent in 1990. The absolute number of one-person households rose in all major age groups and among all marital statuses. The highest rates of increase can be observed in the category of younger men and women (below age 35) and among older women (above age 55). Within younger sub-populations most persons living alone are never-married people, while among the older age groups divorcees and particularly widowed females are the most important contributors to these increased rates. This shows that one-person households refer to a very heterogeneous group of living arrangements.

A closer look at the age groups that are of most interest to us reveals in more detail that the share of women living alone at age 25–34 in relation to all women of the same age group nearly doubled in each recent decade. While in 1960 3.1 per cent were living in a one-person household, we note 5.9 per cent in 1970, 11.3 per cent in 1980 and 14.9 per cent in 1990. In the early post-parental phase there was also an increasing, though far less dramatic, trend: in 1960 the proportion of 46–50 year old women living in a one-person household was 5.8 per cent; in 1970 it was 7.5 per cent, in 1980 it had climbed to 9.7 per cent, and in 1990 it was 10.6 per cent (Censuses 1960–1990).

11.3.7. *Cohabitation*

Owing to modifications in the categorization of family types, the Federal Statistical Office offers hardly any comparable data on the number or the development of cohabitational arrangements. According to census data from 1980, the proportions of females in consensual unions in each age group are 8.8 (20–24), 5.6 (25–29), 3.0 (30–34), 2.1 (35–39), 1.4 (40–49), 0.9 (50–59), and 0.4 per cent (60+).

However, survey data suggest that since 1980 the percentage of men and women who are currently living in a consensual union or have experienced cohabitation has risen remarkably. Even if this living arrangement seems to be just a transitory one for most of the respondents, it is undoubtedly of growing importance. A small survey carried out in 1985 in the German-speaking part of Switzerland (Hoffmann-Nowotny and Fux, 1991:85) reveals

Table 11.8*a*. *Typology of living arrangements, age group 26–30 (Census: 25–34), Switzerland, 1980–1991*

Living arrangement	N	%	Rank	Comments
Data set: Census 1980 (households)				
Age group 25–34				
One-person household	128,434	27	1	
Living with parents,				
relatives or non-relatives	3,396	1	8	
Cohabitation	20,425	4	6	narrow definition
Lone parent	13,933	3	7	
Childless family	73,057	15	4	
Family with 1 child	78,988	17	3	
Family with 2 children	92,443	19	2	
Family with 3+ children	21,253	5	5	
Sum of private households	476,043	91		
Data set: Höpflinger 1986				
Age group 26–30				
One-person household	75	22	1	never-married 73 (21.7%)
Living with parents,				
relatives or non-relatives	35	11	6	with parents 5 (1.5%);
				with other persons 24 (7.1%)
Cohabitation	39	12	5	
Lone parent	7	2	7	
Childless family	65	19	2	
Family with 1 child	49	15	4	
Family with 2 children	59	18	3	
Family with 3+ children	6	2	8	
Sum	335	101		
Data set: Micro-census 1988				
Age group 26–30				
One-person household	669	31	1	unmarried 634 (29.0%);
				divorced 22 (1.0%)
Living with parents,				
relatives or non-relatives	147	7	6	with other persons 114 (5.2%)
Cohabitation	438	20	2	without children 402 (18.4%);
				probably overestimated
Lone parent	33	2	8	
Childless family	333	15	3	
Family with 1 child	307	14	4	
Family with 2 children	212	10	5	
Family with 3+ children	48	2	7	
Sum	2,187	101		

(table is continued)

Table 11.8*a*. *(Cont.)*

Living arrangement	N	%	Rank	Comments
Data set: SAKE 1991 (Projection: *N* in 1,000 households)				
Age group 26–30				
One-person household	43	17	3	
Living with parents	1	0	9	
Cohabitation	18	7	7	
Lone parent	7	3	8	
Childless family	38	15	4	
Family with 1 child	53	21	1	
Family with 2 children	51	20	2	
Family with 3+ children	22	9	5	
Other arrangements	21	8	6	
Sum	253	100		

9 per cent female cohabitants among women in their early family formation phase. Another survey (Höpflinger, 1986) reveals a share of 12 per cent of cohabitants among 26–30-year-old women in 1986, and the 1988 Microcensus gives a share of 20 per cent (Table 11.8). Because of different definitions of the term 'cohabitation', the last figure might be an overestimation. In the early post-parental phase, consensual unions are of marginal importance.

Although these data are not sufficiently reliable, I would point out that cohabitation has become more and more socially accepted. At least during the intermediate phase (between leaving the parental home and the formation of an own family), quite a few men and women do cohabit. Finally, in comparison with other European countries, above all the Scandinavian ones, Switzerland ranks in a middle position.

Tables 11.8 and 11.9 give more detailed information on the distributions by household type. Three trends are evident:

1. Up to the present, *marital union* with or without children remains the predominant living arrangement for women aged 25–30.

2. However, the increasing percentage of *one-person households* and *consensual unions* is now challenging the dominance of traditional family types (married couples with children).

3. The share of the *extended families* (e.g. households with at least three generations, couples living with relatives or with other persons) has dropped sharply during the past decades.

Table 11.8*b. Typology of living arrangements, age group 46–50 (Census: 45–54), Switzerland, 1980–1991*

Living arrangement	N	%	Rank	Comments
Data set: Census 1980 (households)				
Age group 45–54				
One-person household	37,151	9	5	
Living with parents,				
relatives or non-relatives	8,445	2	7	
Cohabitation	4,367	1	8	narrow definition
Lone parent	25,318	6	6	
Childless family	65,053	16	3	
Family with 1 child	73,685	18	2	
Family with 2 children	82,936	20	1	
Family with 3+ children	54,011	13	4	
Sum of private households	416,336	85		
Data set: Micro-census 1988				
Age group 46–50				
One-person household	156	8	5	not married 80 (3.2%); divorced 51 (2.0%)
Living with parents,	102	5	6	with parents 58 (2.3%);
relatives or non-relatives				with relatives 15 (0.6%); with other persons 32 (1.3%)
Cohabitation	80	4	8	unmarried 18 (0.7%); divorced 32 (1.3%); widowed 30 (1.2%)
Lone parent	92	4	7	
Childless family	381	18	3	
Family with 1 child	433	21	2	
Family with 2 children	573	27	1	
Family with 3+ children	278	13	4	
Sum	2,516	100		
Data set: SAKE 1991 (Projection: *N* in 1,000 households)				
Age group 46–50				
One-person household	23	13	4	
Living with parents	0	0	9	
Cohabitation	4	2	8	
Lone parent	7	4	7	
Childless family	41	23	1	
Family with 1 child	35	20	2	
Family with 2 children	30	17	3	
Family with 3+ children	14	8	6	
Other arrangements	21	12	5	
Sum	175	99		

Table 11.9. *Development of family households, Switzerland, 1960–1990 (all ages)*

	1960	1970	1980	1990
Family households total ('000)	1,243	1,527	1,632	1,828
(% of all households)	78.0	74.0	66.4	64.3
Persons living in family households				
(% of the entire population)	85.7	84.8	81.9	80.1
Family household by arrangement (%)				
(Married) couple with no children in the household	24.2	28.5	34.3	39.9
(Married) couple, no children, with other persons	6.6	4.0	1.7	1.5
Head of household, no children, with relatives	1.1	0.7	0.6	0.4
(Married) couple with children	45.5	51.5	51.8	47.6
(Married) couple with children and other persons	14.7	8.4	4.0	2.7
Head of household with children	5.3	5.3	6.6	7.2
Head of household with children and other persons	2.6	1.6	1.0	0.8

Note: Since 1980 non-marital cohabitations are added to family households but subtenants are excluded.

Data basis: Censuses 1960–1990.

Source: Sommer and Höpflinger (1989:26); Census 1990.

11.4. Special Aspects of the Family Life Situation

11.4.1. *Women at Work*

During the last few decades, the women in Switzerland, as in the rest of Europe, have become better integrated into the educational system and the labour market. Nevertheless, for Swiss women the combination of occupation and family seems more conflictive than for women in other countries. The tradition of political liberalism and the corresponding lack of family policy arrangements in the field of economic integration (no parental leave, few child-care facilities, etc.) forces women to find individual solutions to combining family and employment and reducing personal conflicts.

The expansion of the educational system and the longer duration of education are important factors responsible for the above-mentioned postponement of family formation. This can be documented by comparing the number of children according to educational status of women across the 1980s. In the younger age group it is women of higher educational statuses who more often remain childless; women whose education ends after compulsory schooling do not show a similar variation in the timing or number of children. With regard to the beginning of the post-parental phase, Figure 11.4 reflects the general drop in family size. In this age group there exist minor differences only according to educational status of women. Inclusion of women aged 30–35 shows these results to remain stable. But we have to remember that the Streckeisen data set excludes single persons, who are frequently childless.

LABOUR-FORCE PARTICIPATION. When we now look at the situation of women at work, we observe that the labour-force participation ratios for all Swiss women have increased continuously, though with higher rates of increase

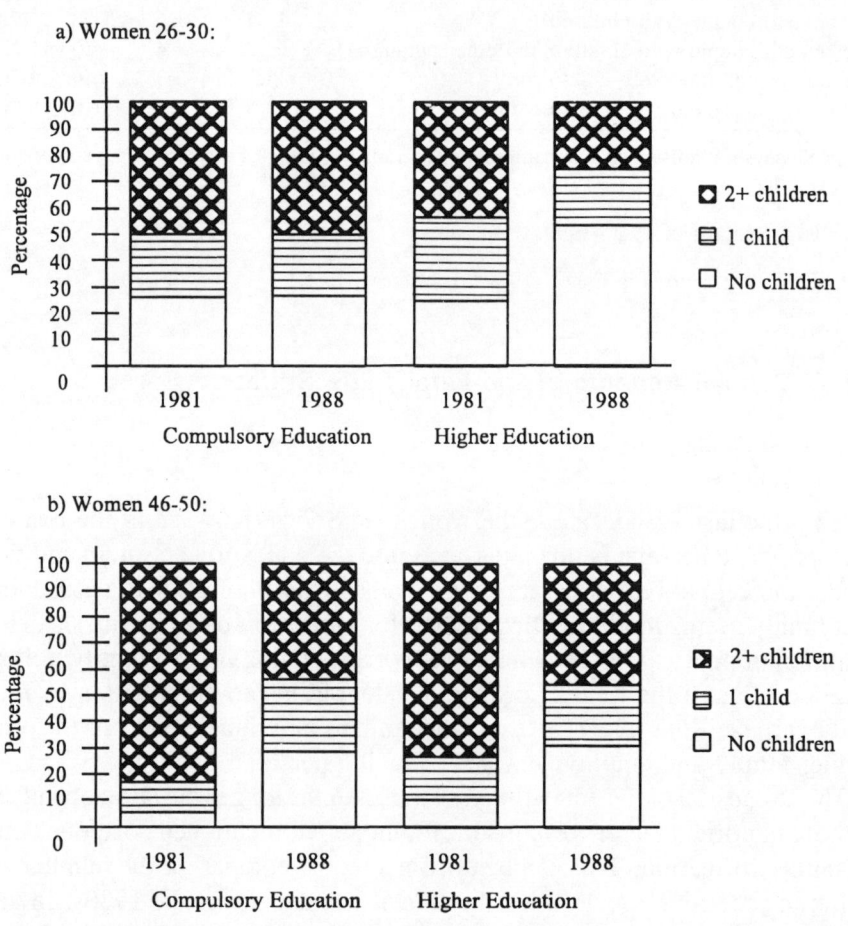

Data base: Streckeisen 1981; and Micro-census 1988.

Figure 11.4. Number of children by educational status in selected age groups, Switzerland, 1981 and 1988

in the 1950s and again in the late 1980s (1950: 39 per cent; 1960: 51 per cent; 1970: 52 per cent; 1975–80: 51 per cent; 1986–7: 54 per cent; and 1991: 54.8 per cent – Höpflinger *et al.*, 1991:87; FSO, 1991:10). Therefore, regarding the share of married women out of all employed women, Switzerland ranks in a middle position in Europe. In Sweden, Germany and France, for example, women are more often integrated into the labour market. On the other hand, the Netherlands and the southern European countries have lower participation rates.

By comparing the age distribution of employed women in 1960 and 1980, two trends should be mentioned. Women in younger age groups (20–50) are well integrated in the labour market system. Among elderly female persons, however, we observe the opposite trend. The share of women above age 60 has remarkably decreased since 1960, probably resulting from the comparatively late legislation of the old-age pension scheme in Switzerland (1948).

If we consider the degree to which women are gainfully employed in this country, we can see that part-time jobs are favoured by Swiss women. Part-time employment is more widespread than in many other European countries; only in the Scandinavian countries, the Netherlands and Great Britain is the percentage higher. In 1986–7 every third (33 per cent) and in 1991 more than every second working woman (52.6 per cent) in Switzerland was a part-time employee. The relation between full-time and part-time employment shows an age-specific variation too. The share of full-time employed women decreases drastically at the beginning of the family-formation phase: in 1991, full-time employed women made up 77.7 per cent of all employed women among those aged 15–24, 45.1 per cent among women aged 25–39, 37.8 per cent among 40–54-year-old women, 36.4 per cent among women aged 55–64, and 24.7 per cent among women aged 65 and over (FSO, 1991:5). Compared with women, Swiss men have almost without exception a full-time occupation. (For the same age categories, the comparable proportions for men were 87.1, 94.1, 95.0, 91.6 and 35.7 per cent, respectively: FSO, 1991:5.) In a cross-period perspective, only marginal variations in the male patterns of labour-force participation can be observed.

Female employment varies with the presence of children and with the type of living arrangement. In all age groups, the proportions gainfully employed among women with children are much lower than among those without children. While 'men with children' (above age 25) are usually full-time employed, the share of full-time employees is lower among 'childless men' owing to several factors (education, unemployment, invalidity, etc.) (Figure 11.5). The definition of 'children' (below age 15 only) causes empty cells

with children under 15

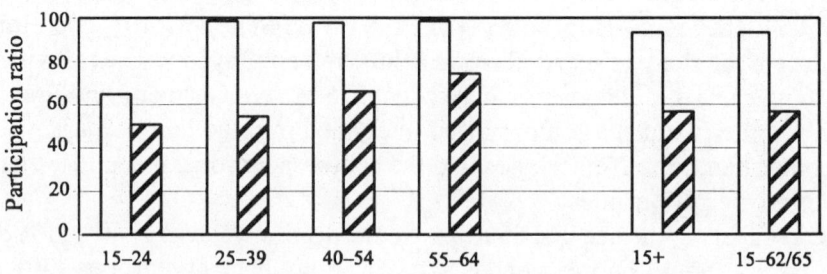

without children under 15

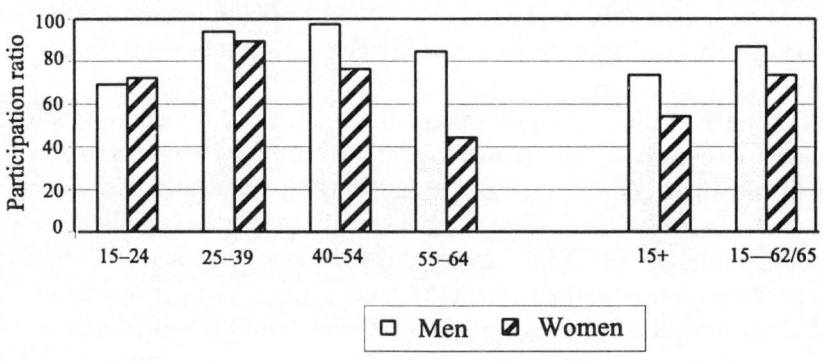

☐ Men ☒ Women

Note: 15+: all persons above age 15; 15–62/65: all persons between 15 and the age of retirement.
Source: FSO (1991:4).

Figure 11.5. Labour-force participation ratios by age, sex and family type, Switzerland, 1991

for the higher age groups of men and women.

The 1980 census data allow us to break down female activity ratios by marital status and number of children (Table 11.10). Married women with children in particular are absent from the labour market: only one in six married women with one child and one in ten women with two or more children are full-time employed. This general structure applies to the other marital statuses as well, but the restrictions on employment are much lower. The fact that divorced women with at least two children show the highest proportion of full-time employment points to certain constraints in the Swiss system of social security. Because in most of the Swiss cantons alimony laws were not established before the 1980s, and because divorced women often lose a regular income after separation from their husbands, they are forced to take up employment. Differences in age distribution between the marital status categories probably also influence these differentials.

As analyses of more recent survey data (Micro-census 1988) show, the patterns in female labour-force participation did not change substantially through the 1980s. Up to the present, women seem to be prevented from rejoining the labour-market system as soon as they give birth to a child. More detailed information can be found in Table 11.11.

Table 11.10. *Labour-force participation of mothers, Switzerland, 1980*

Extent of employment	Activity ratios of mothers in households with children below age 18 (%)		
	No. of children		
	1	2	3+
Married			
Full-time	15	10	10
Part-time	22	20	18
Total	37	30	30
Cohabiting			
Full-time	40	30	22
Part-time	26	30	21
Total	66	60	43
Separated			
Full-time	39	28	18
Part-time	31	35	33
Total	70	63	51
Divorced			
Full-time	60	41	27
Part-time	29	41	41
Total	89	82	68
Widowed			
Full-time	22	15	12
Part-time	29	29	23
Total	51	44	35

Data basis: Census 1980.

Source: Lüscher (1985).

Table 11.11. *Female labour-force participation, selected age groups, Switzerland, 1988 (%)*

Living arrangement	Extent of employment							
	Age group 26–30				Age group 46–50			
	0%	<50%	>50%	100%	0%	<50%	>50%	100%
Single	2.3	1.0	1.6	17.4	1.0	–	–	6.3
Cohabiting, partner employed 100%	–	–	2.5	15.2	–	–	–	–
Married, partner employed 100%								
0 children	7.3	–	4.0	12.0	13.1	1.1	3.2	5.1
1 child	11.4	–	0.9	1.4	14.8	1.6	2.3	3.6
2+ children	9.0	–	–	0.9	19.5	1.6	1.4	4.6
Divorced, childless	–	–	–	–	–	–	–	2.8
Divorced, 1 child	–	–	–	–	–	–	–	1.5
Other arrangements	13.2				16.5			
Total (N)	100 (1373)				100 (1275)			

Data set: Micro-census 1988.

OCCUPATIONAL SEGREGATION. A rather inharmonious situation exists for women also with regard to occupational segregation, which is worse in Switzerland than in other countries. In relation to the overall number of female employees, those in senior management posts are proportionally un-

Table 11.12. *Household income by family type, Switzerland, 1975–1986 (1986=100)*

	All house-holds	One-person house-hold	Lone-parent families[a]	Child-less couple	Couple with children		
					1	2	3
Coefficient of equivalence	–	*0.73*	*1.37[b]*	*1.00*	*1.24*	*1.43*	*1.60*
Male's income	85.2	90.8	79.3	75.6	86.4	87.8	87.4
Female's income	6.0	0.1	0.3	16.0	5.2	3.9	3.2
Children's income	0.4	0.0	0.5	0.0	0.5	0.4	0.7
Total work income	91.6	90.9	80.1	91.6	92.1	92.1	91.3
Other resources	8.4	9.1	19.9	8.4	7.9	7.9	8.7
Total income (%)	100	100	100	100	100	100	100
Total income (CHF)	71,335	52,375	52,375	77,989	70,081	72,156	78,068
Income–expenses	7.7	9.9	4.5	13.0	6.3	5.6	7.0

[a] With one child.
[b] Lone-parent families in urban contexts.

Sources: Deiss (1991:266); Deiss *et al.* (1988:55 and 60).

derrepresented in the labour market. In administration/management and production, they are strongly underrepresented. Where a segregation index of value 1.0 indicates an equal representation of women in a specific sector, we find values of 0.2 for management jobs and 0.4 for production jobs. Women are overrepresented in the traditional female sectors: clerical staff (segregation index 1.4), sales (1.5), and services (1.8) (Höpflinger *et al.*, 1991:59). In an international comparison, only Luxemburg shows an even higher gender segregation. Traditional gender norms and political corporatism are the most important factors explaining this segregation (Charles, 1987). These gender-specific patterns in the labour-market integration also lead to comparatively low wages for female employees in those sectors where women are overrepresented. Another effect is that the share of hidden or clandestine unemployment is highest among younger married women (FSO, 1991:7).

11.4.2 *Income Situation and Housing*

Recently the income situation of Swiss families has been analysed (Deiss *et al.*, 1988; Deiss, 1991). Deiss and his colleagues based their study on equivalence scales, the so-called 'coefficient of equivalence' being a measure that allows them to express the costs of children, indicating deviations from the average income of a childless couple. The birth of a first child reduces the household income by one-quarter, the second birth by one-fifth and the third child by one-sixth. Table 11.12 summarizes the major results, namely the coefficients of equivalence and the income situation of various types of family. Unfortunately, the authors did not break down the family types by age of respondent. However, their findings show that financial burdens rise with the number of children. Not only family size, but also the age of the children is important. Thus, in one-child families the coefficient of equivalence increases from 1.24 to 1.33 if the child is older than 16. A mother's labour-force participation triples the coefficient for the first child if she earns more than 10 per cent of the total household income, owing to the costs of child-care arrangements. The costs of children are generally higher in urban areas and in the German-speaking regions. The presence of children makes it more difficult for families to become owners of a house or flat. In terms of absolute household income, the conditions for lone-parent families are, not surprisingly, the worst.

The income situation and the cost of children influence the housing conditions of Swiss families. Generally we can say that private ownership of a house or flat is comparatively rare in Switzerland. According to 1980 census data, as few as only 30 per cent of all households own the dwelling in which they are living. By international comparison, this rate is very low. Apart from younger people, the unemployed and foreigners, it is younger families, one-parent families and families with three and more children in particular that belong to the high-risk groups on the housing market. These groups are significantly overrepresented in the tenant category, they change their place of dwelling more frequently and the standard of their accommodation is the lowest. In these living arrangements, the amount paid for rent in relation to the total household income is higher than in any other group. Also, the household density (number of persons per room) is much higher. One-parent families, divorcees, and young and large families are not only disadvantaged on the housing market, they also experience poverty more frequently.

11.4.3. *Family Types and their Poverty Risks*

Worldwide, Switzerland belongs to the group of countries with the highest income per capita. Nevertheless, several studies carried out in recent years have pointed to the fact that the proportion of people near or even below the relative poverty line is quite high and has been increasing since about 1975. According to the indicators chosen, between 150,000 and 550,000 persons are living in an economically problematic situation. Related to the entire population, the share of people who currently experience poverty ranges between 2.7 and 9.3 per cent. The risk of poverty is lowest among married couples and households with two earning persons. By contrast, divorced women with dependent children in particular, as well as one-parent families and retired people, are overrepresented among the poor. As in most other countries, in Switzerland a U-shaped relationship between age and poverty can be observed, with lowest poverty risks at ages 40–59 (Buhmann, 1988; Frey and Leu, 1988).

11.5. Everyday Life of Families

11.5.1. *Division of Labour within the Household*

As far as survey data on the intrafamilial division of labour can show, traditional patterns in the organization of everyday life within different family

Table 11.13. *Organization of everyday life, Switzerland, 1981 and 1986 (survey data)*

| | Division of everyday work (%) | | | | | | | |
| | Age group 26–30 | | | | Age group 46–50 | | | |
	Mostly he	Both	Mostly she	(N)	Mostly he	Both	Mostly she	(N)
Data set: Streckeisen 1981								
Cleaning	1.4	13.3	85.3	(143)	0.0	6.3	93.7	(158)
Washing	0	4.8	95.2	(145)	0.0	0.6	99.4	(158)
Tidying up	2.8	24.1	73.1	(145)	0.6	8.0	91.4	(163)
Washing the dishes	2.1	32.8	64.1	(145)	1.2	23.9	74.8	(155)
Repairs	66.7	19.6	13.8	(138)	64.1	16.9	19.0	(142)
Ironing/patching	0.0	0.7	99.3	(143)	0.0	0.0	100	(158)
Shopping (small)	2.8	22.0	75.2	(141)	5.3	10.9	75.8	(151)
Shopping (big)	3.4	65.5	31.0	(145)	7.4	43.8	48.8	(162)
Cooking	1.4	27.8	70.8	(144)	1.9	12.4	85.7	(161)
Gardening	21.6	42.0	36.6	(88)	22.5	35.0	42.5	(120)
Child care	2	84.5	13.6	(110)	4.6	63.8	31.5	(130)

| | Age group 26–30 (Married couples) | | | | Age group 46–50 (Cohabiting couples) | | | |
	Often he	Both	Seldom he	(N)	Often he	Both	Seldom he	(N)
Data set: Höpflinger 1986								
Cleaning	41.6	8.3	50.0	(180)	50.0	28.3	21.7	(46)
Washing	25.5	3.9	70.6	(180)	21.7	28.3	50.0	(46)
Tidying up	16.1	1.1	82.8	(180)	0	69.6	30.4	(46)
Washing the dishes	46.7	18.9	34.4	(180)	39.2	45.7	15.2	(46)
Shopping	57.5	27.9	12.3	(179)	43.5	43.5	13.0	(46)
Cooking	47.7	18.3	33.9	(171)	41.3	30.4	28.3	(46)

arrangements are quite stable (Table 11.13). Unequal gender roles and norms influence the patterns of the division of labour in everyday life. Even in urban areas and in 'new' living arrangements, men tend to refuse to participate in tasks for which, by tradition, women are responsible. Chores such as tidying up the dwelling or washing are usually done by women. Cohabiting people, most of them childless, show a slight trend towards a more equal distribution of tasks. But not later than after the birth of a child, the so-called 'Pascha-syndrom' – the father shirking out of his responsibilities for doing household chores – (Höpflinger, in Hoffmann-Nowotny *et al.*, 1984:195) seems to recommence.

It must be supposed, however, that this stable pattern of intrafamilial division of labour also reflects certain deficiencies in the social policy system.

The demand for child-care facilities is high but their corresponding availability is low. We therefore have to assume that many respondents are obliged to practise these household labour patterns not voluntarily. We also should keep in mind the findings concerning the costs of a (first) child, as well as the unequal wages for men and women in the Swiss economic system.

11.5.2. *Availability and Use of Child-Care Facilities*

Over the country as a whole, about 430 crèches with approximately 15,000 places were counted in 1987–8. Therefore, only 6 per cent of all children below age 4 were able to have a place in a day-care facility (ILO, 1988). Most of these are run by private organizations, though frequently they are subsidized by the municipalities. Only 18.5 per cent are communal crèches, so it is not astonishing that day-care facilities are often quite expensive. Depending on the parent's income and local arrangements, daily costs range between CHF 3 and CHF 30.

Estimates were published by Pro Juventute, mentioning an absolute number of 22,000 extra-familial child-care places (crèches, kindergartens, daily minder, etc.) for employed women or lone-parent families. We also have to point out that Switzerland has not yet established a public day-care system. On the other hand, demand for such facilities has been estimated as 250,000 places at the minimum. This situation undoubtedly puts women at a disadvantage and influences their exit from the labour market after the birth of the first child (Table 11.14).

11.6. Evaluation of Findings

The integration of women into the educational and labour-market systems continued during the 1980s. These processes are probably the most important factors signalling the emergence of a new biographical phase: that between leaving the parental home and formation of an own family. During this phase, an increasing variety of living arrangements can be found. Survey data concerning this stage of life show a wide variety of living arrangements and life-styles, as well as substantial dynamics within individual biographies. Young people try out various living arrangements as long as they have no children. This pluralization of life forms in a pre-marital phase is an important contributor to the delays in family formation and childbearing.

Table 11.14. *Demand by married women for additional facilities from the government, by age of the children, Switzerland*

Additional facilities demanded	Age of child			
	<4	4–7	8–15	16–20
Child allowances	69	56	41	25
Family allowances	51	39	29	20
Maternity allowances	63	8	3	1
Crèches	31	29	4	0
Playing fields	20	59	24	1
Kindergartens	3	38	1	0
School facilities	1	6	41	20
Subsidies	1	5	43	43
Leisure-time facilities	3	14	46	49
Grants (*Stipendien*)	1	1	6	70
Facilities are sufficient	9	0	9	8

Data set: Fux 1987.

Source: Fux (1992).

Our cross-sectional analyses for women aged 26–30 (when most women give birth to a first child) illustrate a *funnel-shaped* reduction in the variety of living arrangements with the beginning of the early family-formation phase. On the one hand, we observe that the share of traditional living arrangements has remained quite stable up to the present. The traditional pattern of a marriage-based family with children seems as dominant as in former times. However, a fundamental change in the structure of individual decisions has to be mentioned. Whereas in the past couples first decided to marry and then to become parents, currently the decision to marry normally succeeds the decision to have a child.

This change corresponds with the observation of increasing numbers of cohabiting people and a drastic rise in the proportion of permanently childless women. Furthermore, there is a decreasing trend in the prevalence of extended families and a rise in the proportion of individuals who live alone. We also find a fall in the average number of children per family. The funnel-shaped concentration towards marital living arrangements during the early family-formation phase probably can be explained, at least in part, by the legal and family policy provisions that clearly favour marriage-based forms of partnership.

On the level of individual behaviour, the formation of a marital union and the birth of a first child coincide with the fact that traditional role patterns and norms still predominate. Most Swiss women leave full-time employment at this stage. This form of reorientation towards traditional patterns in the division of labour seems to be supported by the labour-market situation, which shows comparatively high gender segregation, few part-time jobs for women and low wages for them. The deficiencies in the family policy system (few extra-familial child-care arrangements, no parental leave, etc.) and a fiscal policy that favours marital life forms are other important factors.

The presence of a child also changes the intrafamilial division of labour. While the wife carries out the traditional female tasks (cleaning, ironing, washing, etc.) as well as looking after the baby, the husband participates in household chores only slightly more frequently than before. On the other hand, it is the husband who is normally responsible for small repairs and partly for keeping the garden. This so-called 'Pascha-syndrom' was seen to recede slightly among cohabiting couples.

At the end of the early family-formation phase, the pluralization of living arrangements recommences. The most important factors are the increasing numbers of divorced people and the decreasing probability of reconstituting a new family. Therefore, we can see that new living arrangements such as lone-parent families are overrepresented in the later phases of the family cycle.

Lone-parent families and divorced people, but also younger families and couples with a large number of children, are at a significant disadvantage on the housing market. They also belong to the high-risk groups concerning the threat of poverty. As economic studies show, the birth of a first child is quite expensive. Thereafter, net disposable income per household member decreases substantially with each additional child. Again, lone parents are among the groups that experience the highest constraints.

It must be concluded that the stability of family-formation processes, particularly in early stages in the life cycle, is influenced by deficiencies and arrears in the Swiss family policy system.

References

Bickel, W. (1947), *Bevölkerungsgeschichte der Schweiz seit dem Ausgang des Mittelalters* (A History of the Swiss Population from the End of the Middle Ages), Büchergilde Gutenberg, Zürich.

Binswanger, P. (1986), *Geschichte der AHV* (A History of the AHV (Swiss State Pension Scheme)), Pro Senectute Verlag, Zürich.

Blanc, O. (1985), 'Les ménages en Suisse' (Households in Switzerland), *Population*, 40:657–74.

Borkowsky, A. and Streckeisen, U. (1982), 'Wiedereinstieg von Frauen in den

Beruf' (Reintegration of women into professional life), *Schweizerische Zeitschrift für Soziologie*, 8:279–310.

—— and Streckeisen, U. (1989), *Arbeitsbiographien von Frauen* (Work Biographies of Women), Rüegger Verlag, Grüsch.

——, Kästli, E., Ley, K. and Streckeisen, U. (1985), *Zwei Welten – ein Leben* (Two Worlds – One Life), Unionsverlag, Zürich.

Buhmann, B. (1988), *Wohlstand und Armut in der Schweiz* (Prosperity and Poverty in Switzerland), Rüegger Verlag, Grüsch.

——, Enderle, G., Jäggi, C. and Mächler, T. (1989), *Armut in der reichen Schweiz: Eine verdrängte Wirklichkeit* (Poverty in Rich Switzerland: a Repressed Reality), Orell Füssli Verlag, Zürich.

Bundesamt für Sozialversicherungen (1978), *Bericht über die Lage der Familie in der Schweiz* (Report on the Situation of Families in Switzerland), Bern.

Charles, M. (1987), 'Geschlechtsspezifische Arbeitsmarktsegregation in der Schweiz' (Gender-specific segregation in the Swiss labour market), *Schweizerische Zeitschrift für Soziologie*, 13:1–27.

Council of Europe (1990), *Cohort Fertility in Member States of the Council of Europe*, Council of Europe, Strasbourg.

—— (various years), *Recent Demographic Developments in Europe*, Council of Europe, Strasbourg.

Deiss, J. (1991), 'Budgets familiaux et compensation des charges' (Family budgets and compensation of charges), in Fleiner-Gerster *et al.* (1991:261–92).

——, Guillaume, M.-L. and Lüthy, A. (1988), *Kinderkosten in der Schweiz* (Cost of Children in Switzerland), Universitätsverlag Freiburg Schweiz, Freiburg.

Findl, P. (1990), 'Kohortendaten zu Wiederheirat und Legitimierung in Österreich seit 1984' (Cohort-data on remarriage and acknowledgement in Austria from 1984), Deutsch-österreichisch-schweizerisches Demographentreffen Innsbruck 1990 (mimeo).

Fleiner-Gerster, Th., Gilliand, P. and Lüscher, K. (eds.) (1991), *Familien in der Schweiz* (Families in Switzerland), Universitätsverlag Freiburg Schweiz, Freiburg.

Fragnière, J.-P. and Christen, G. (1988), *Securité sociale en Suisse* (Social Security in Switzerland), Éditions Réalités Sociales, Lausanne.

—— and Mermoud, P. (1989), *Le temps des bénévoles* (The Time of Voluntary Work), Cahiers du CFPS, Sion.

Freiburghaus, D. and Zimmermann, W. (1984), *Wirtschaftliche Lage der Rentner* (The Economic Situation of Old Age Pensioners), Haupt, Bern.

Frey, R.L. and Leu R.E. (eds.) (1988), *Sozialstaat unter der Lupe: Wohlstandsverteilung und Wohlstandsumverteilung in der Schweiz* (The Welfare State Scrutinized: the Distribution and Redistribution of Prosperity in Switzerland), Helbing und Lichtenhahn, Basel.

FSO (Federal Statistical Office) (various years), *Bevölkerungsbewegung in der Schweiz* (Demographic Trends in Switzerland), Bern.

—— (various years), *Statistisches Jahrbuch der Schweiz* (Statistical Yearbook of Switzerland), Bern/Zürich.

—— (1990), *Freizeit und Kultur: Mikrozensus 1988, Grunddaten* (Leisure Time and Culture: Micro-census 1988, Basic Data), FSO, Bern.

—— (1991), *SAKE 1991* (Swiss Labour Force Survey 1991), FSO, Bern.

Fux, B. (1992), 'Einelternfamilien im Spannungsfeld zwischen Individualisierung und personaler Überlastung' (Monoparental families in the clinch between individualization and personal strain)', *Sozialarbeit*, 92:21–9.

—— (1994), *Der familienpolitische Diskurs: Eine theoretische und empirische Untersuchung über das Zusammenwirken und den Wandel von Familienpolitik, Fertilität und Familie* (The Discourse on Family Policies: a Theoretical and Empirical Investigation on Interrelations and Changes in Family Policies, Fertility and Families), Duncker & Humblot, Berlin.

——, Bösch, A. and Gisler, P. (1993), 'Bevölkerung und Wohlfahrt: Schlussbericht Phase 1' (Population and welfare: final report on Phase 1 of the project), Zürich (manuscript).

Gilliand, P. (1983), *Rentiers AVS: Une autre image de la Suisse* (State Pensioners: Another View of Switzerland), Éditions Réalités Sociales, Lausanne.

—— (ed.) (1984), *Famille en rupture, pensions alimentaires et politique sociale* (Families in Dissolution, Alimony and Family Policies), Éditions Réalités Sociales, Lausanne.

—— (1988), *Politique sociale en Suisse* (Social Policy in Switzerland), Éditions Réalités Sociales, Lausanne.

—— (1990), *Pauvreté et sécurité sociale* (Poverty and Social Security), Éditions Réalités Sociales, Lausanne.

—— (1991), 'Population et structures familiales en Suisse' (Population and family structures in Switzerland), in Fleiner-Gerster *et al.* (1991:3–30).

Grossenbacher, S. (1987), *Familienpolitik und Frauenfrage in der Schweiz* (Family Policies and the Question of Women's Rights in Switzerland), Rüegger Verlag, Grüsch.

Held, Th. and Murray, B. (1984), 'Collective images of gender', *Schweizerische Zeitschrift für Soziologie*, 10:723–82.

Hoffmann-Nowotny, H.-J. (1987), 'The future of the family', in *European Population Conference 1987: Plenaries*, IUSSP and Central Statistical Office of Finland, Helsinki: 113–200.

—— and Fux, B. (1991), 'Present demographic trends in Europe', in Council of Europe, *Seminar on Present Demographic Trends and Lifestyles in Europe (18–20 September, 1990)*, Council of Europe, Strasbourg: 31–98.

——, Höpflinger, F., Kühne, F., Ryffel, C. and Erni, D. (1984), *Planspiel Familie: Familie, Kinderwunsch und Familienplanung in der Schweiz* (Planning Game Family: Family, Desire for Children and Family Planning in Switzerland), Rüegger Verlag, Diessenhofen.

——, Höhn, Ch. and Fux, B. (eds.) (1992), *Kinderzahl und Familienpolitik im*

Drei-Länder-Vergleich (Number of Children and Family Policies: a Comparison of Three Countries), Boldt-Verlag, Boppard am Rhein.

Höpflinger, F. (1986), *Bevölkerungswandel in der Schweiz* (Demographic Change in Switzerland), Rüegger Verlag, Grüsch.

—— (1987), *Wandel der Familienbildung in Westeuropa* (Changes in Family Formation in Western Europe), Campus Verlag, Frankfurt/New York.

—— (1991*a*), 'The future of household and family structures in Europe', in Council of Europe, *Seminar on Present Demographic Trends and Lifestyles in Europe (18–20 September 1990)*, Council of Europe, Strasbourg: 291–338.

—— (1991*b*), 'Neue Kinderlosigkeit: Demographische Trends und gesellschaftliche Spekulationen' (New childlessness: demographic trends and societal speculations), in G. Buttler, H.-J. Hoffmann-Nowotny and G. Schmitt-Rink (eds.), *Acta Demographica*, Physica-Verlag, Heidelberg: 81–100.

—— and Erni-Schneuwly, D. (eds.) (1989), *Weichenstellungen: Lebensformen im Wandel und Lebenslage junger Frauen* (Course Setting: Life-Styles in Transition and the Situation of Young Women), Haupt, Bern.

——, Charles, M. and Debrunner, A. (1991), *Familienleben und Berufsarbeit: Zum Wechselverhältnis zweier Lebensbereiche* (Family Life and Employment: the Interrelations between two Areas of Life), Seismo Verlag, Zürich.

Hungerbühler, R. (1989), *Unsichtbar – Unschätzbar: Haus- und Familienarbeit am Beispiel der Schweiz* (Invisible – Inestimable: Household and Family Work, Switzerland as an Example), Rüegger Verlag, Grüsch.

ILO (1988), 'Work and family: the child care challenge', *Conditions of Work Digest*.

Kellerhals, J. (1987), 'Les types d'interaction dans la famille' (Types of interaction in the family), *Année Sociologique*, 37:153–79.

—— and Coenen-Huther, J. (1990), 'Familles suisses d'aujourd'hui: évolution récente et diversité' (Swiss families today: recent evolution and diversity), *Cahiers Médico-Sociaux*, 34:7–31.

—— *et al.* (1982), *Mariages au quotidien, inégalités sociales, tensions culturelles et organisation familiale* (Marriage in Everyday Life, Social Inequality, Cultural Tensions and Family Organization), Favre, Lausanne.

—— *et al.* (1984), *Microsociologie de la famille* (Microsociology of the Family), PUF, Coll. "Que sais-je?", Paris.

Koller, R.A. (1984) *Die kantonalen Familienzulagengesetze: Ein systematischer Vergleich der Gesetze in den Kantonen AG, BS, BE, GE, LU, SG, SH, UR, VS und ZH* (Cantonal Family Allowances: a Systematic Comparison of the Laws in Ten Cantons), Eigenverlag, Zürich.

Kommission 'Bevölkerungspolitik' (ed.) (1985), *Sterben die Schweizer aus? Die Bevölkerung der Schweiz: Probleme, Perspektiven, Politik* (Are the Swiss Dying Out? The Population of Switzerland: Problems, Prospects, Policies), Haupt, Bern.

Lalive d'Epinay, C. (1991), *Viellir, ou la vie à inventer* (Getting Old, or to Give

New Sense to Life), L'Harmattan, Paris.

—— *et al.* (1983), *Vieillesses: Situations, itinéraires et modes de vie des personnes âgées aujourd'hui* (Old Age: Situations, Life Courses and Life-Styles of Today's Elderly People), Georgi, Saint-Saphorin, Lausanne.

Lüscher, K. (1985), 'Frauen zwischen Familie und Erwerb: Streiflichter auf die schweizerische Volkszählung 1980' (Women between family and employment), *Neue Zürcher Zeitung*, 185:17.

—— and Engstler, H. (1991), *Formen der Familiengründung in der Schweiz: Eine Analyse amtlicher Daten über die Geborenen 1979–1987* (Types of Family Formation in Switzerland: an Analysis of Official Data concerning Persons Born 1979–1987), FSO, Bern.

Mäder, U., Biedermann, F., Fischer, B. and Schmassmann, H. (1991), *Armut im Kanton Basel-Stadt* (Poverty in the Canton Basel-Stadt), Social Strategies Publishers Co-operative Society, Basel.

Marazzi, C. (1987), *La povertà in Ticino* (Poverty in the Canton of Tessin), Dipartemento Opere Sociali, Bellinzona.

Möckli, S. (1988), *Der Schweizerische Sozialstaat: Sozialgeschichte, Sozialphilosophie, Sozialpolitik* (The Swiss Welfare State: Social History, Social Philosophy, Social Policy), Haupt, Bern.

Mordasini, B. (1985), *Das Erwerbsverhalten in der Schweiz: eine empirische Analyse* (Occupational Behaviour in Switzerland: an Empirical Analysis), Eigenverlag, Basel.

Neue Zürcher Zeitung (1991), 'Die Bevölkerungsentwicklung – erneut ein brisantes Thema: Wieder beschleunigtes Wachstum seit Mitte der achziger Jahre' (Population development – again an explosive topic: accelerated growth from the middle of the 1980s), 297(21/22 December 1991):17ff.

Prioux, F. (1993), 'L'infécondité en Europe' (Infertility in Europe), in A. Blum and J.-L. Rallu (eds.), *European Population. II: Demographic Dynamics*, Éditions John Libbey Eurotext, Montrouge: 231–51.

Schnyder, B. (ed.) (1982), *Familie: Herausforderung der Zukunft; La famille: un défi face à l'avenir* (The Family: a Challenge to the Future), Proceedings Symposium at the University of Freiburg, Switzerland, 26-28 November 1981, Universitätsverlag Freiburg Schweiz, Freiburg.

Schultheis, F. (1992), 'Familienpolitik in Grenzen: Aspekte eines interkulturellen Vergleichs sozialpolitischer Leistungen für Familien im Drei-Länder-Eck' (Family policies within boundaries: aspects of an inter-cultural comparison of social welfare in the 'Three-Countries-Triangle' (Switzerland, Germany, France)), in Hoffmann-Nowotny *et al.* (1992:42–63).

Schweizer, W. (1984), *Die wirtschaftliche Lage der Rentner in der Schweiz* (The Economic Situation of Old Age Pensioners in Switzerland), Haupt, Bern/Stuttgart.

SGPS (Schweizerische Gesellschaft für Praktische Sozialforschung) (ed.) (1991), *UNIVOX 1991: Basisdaten für Öffentlichkeitsarbeit, Informationspolitik, Sozialpolitik* (UNIVOX 1991: Basic Data for Public Services, Information Policies,

Social Policies), Adliswil, Bern.

Sommer, J. and Höpflinger, F. (1989), *Wandel der Lebensformen und soziale Sicherheit: Forschungslücken und Wissensstand* (Changing Life Forms and Social Security: Gaps in Research and State-of-the-Art), Rüegger Verlag, Grüsch.

Streckeisen, U. (1989), *Arbeitsräume von Frauen – Zwischenräume der Gesellschaft: zur Problematik biographischer Übergänge* (Working Areas of Women – Gaps in Society: The Problems of Biographic Transitions), Eigenverlag, Bern.

Wagner, A. (1985), *Wohlfahrtsstaat Schweiz: Eine problem-orientierte Einführung in die Sozialpolitik* (Welfare State Switzerland: a Problem-Oriented Introduction to Social Policy), Haupt, Bern.

12 Ten Countries in Europe: an Overview

ANTON KUIJSTEN and KLAUS PETER STROHMEIER

University of Amsterdam, Amsterdam, the Netherlands and Ruhr-Universität, Bochum, Germany

12.1. Demographic Trends in the 1980s

As we mentioned in our introductory chapter, aggregate demographic figures such as birth rates or marriage and divorce rates are only very superficial indicators of changes in the structures of family life. Nevertheless, they are important as indications of convergences or divergences in a significant aspect of the societal context in which structures of family life are embedded: changing between-country differentials in prevalence of demographic events contribute to changing between-country variation in familial and household structures.

How homogeneous were the demographic contexts of the ten countries compared in this volume during the 1980s? Each chapter has provided an avalanche of figures on the demographic trends during the decade, and we would like to begin this concluding chapter by summarizing them. To that end, we have collected five sets of data, for 1980, 1985 and 1990, that are reproduced in Tables 12.1–12.5.

12.1.1. *Population*

The countries differed significantly in population size. Four big countries, with over 50 million inhabitants each (the Federal Republic of Germany, Italy, the United Kingdom and France), contrast with four others having fewer than 10 million inhabitants each (Sweden, Switzerland, Denmark and Ireland), with the former German Democratic Republic (16 million) and the Netherlands (14 million) in between (Table 12.1). Decennial population growth did not correlate with population size. The smallest country, Ireland, had the highest decennial population growth (9.05 per cent), but Switzerland (5.87 per cent), the Netherlands (5.69 per cent) and France (5.30 per cent) show relatively high growth rates as well. The populations of the three other large countries (the Federal Republic of Germany, Italy and the United Kingdom) increased by a little bit more than 2 per cent, that of Sweden by 2.7 per cent. The smallest decennial population growth could be observed in Denmark (0.25 per cent). The former German Democratic Republic is the only country that shows a population decline between 1980 and 1990 (-1.83 per cent).

These growth differentials have been only moderately stable over the decade. The annual rates of population increase in Table 12.1 show that in 1980 it was Ireland, the Netherlands, France and Switzerland that had the highest population increase (over 5 per 1,000). In 1985, the rate of increase in Ireland had tumbled down to a mere 0.9 per 1,000, but the highest rates were still observed in the Netherlands, France and Switzerland, although in the Netherlands the rate was only slightly over 5 per 1,000. In 1990 it was the Federal Republic of Germany that led the list (16.7 per 1,000), followed by Switzerland (11.5 per 1,000), the Netherlands (7.9 per 1,000), Sweden (7.5 per 1,000) and France (5.6 per 1,000). At that time, population decline in the former German Democratic Republic, having been zero in 1980 and -1 per 1,000 in 1985, had deepened to -24.7 per 1,000! A striking feature of the figures in Table 12.1 is that all relatively fast-growers experienced some check in growth in the middle of the decade, whereas in the four countries with the lowest positive rates of increase in 1980 (Sweden, Italy, the United Kingdom and Denmark) population increase was higher in 1985 than in 1980, and higher again in 1990 than in 1985.

The countries that lead the list with respect to total population increase also do so with respect to natural increase, with the exception of Sweden in 1990. In fact, there is a weak correlation between rate of overall growth and rate of natural increase, suggesting that the latter is the main determinant of the former. That does hold for some of the ten countries, but certainly not for all. Three rather special cases catch the eye. The first one is Ireland: it has the highest overall decennial population increase, it heads the list in 1980 with respect to annual population increase, and it has the highest rate of natural increase of all in 1980, 1985 and 1990. But at the same time, Ireland is low on the list with respect to net migration rate, particularly in 1985, when it experienced net migration *losses* even, instead of gains. The second exception, the Federal Republic of Germany, provides an almost perfect mirror image: its overall decennial population increase is one of the lowest, but it headed the list in 1990 with respect to annual population increase, not because of its rate of natural increase, which was almost zero, but because of its net positive migration rate, which was the highest of all! The third exception is the former German Democratic Republic: a kind of

Table 12.1. *Summary table of demographic trends during the 1980s: population*

	1980	1985	1990
Denmark			
Population size ('000)[a]	5,122	5,111	5,135
Population increase (%)	0.04	0.10	0.22
Natural increase (%)	0.11	0.02	0.19
Net migration rate	0.01	0.19	0.17
Foreigners (%)	–	2.1 [b]	–
Asylum-seekers ('000)	0.2	9	5
France			
Population size ('000)[a]	53,731	55,157	56,577
Population increase (%)	0.55	0.46	0.56
Natural increase (%)	0.47	0.39	0.42
Net migration rate	0.08	0.07	0.14
Foreigners (%)	6.8 [c]	6.8	6.3
Asylum-seekers ('000)	19	29	55
Federal Republic of Germany			
Population size ('000)[a]	61,439	61,049	62,679
Population increase (%)	0.36	−0.05	1.67
Natural increase (%)	−0.15	−0.19	0.02
Net migration rate	0.51	0.15	1.65
Foreigners (%)	–	7.2	7.7
Asylum-seekers ('000)	108	74	193
German Democratic Republic			
Population size ('000)[a]	16,740	16,671	16,434
Population increase (%)	0.00	−0.10	−2.47
Natural increase (%)	0.04	0.07	−0.18
Net migration rate	−0.05	−0.11	−2.29
Foreigners (%)	–	–	1.2
Asylum-seekers ('000)	–	–	–
Great Britain/UK			
Population size ('000)[a]	56,285	56,596	57,459
Population increase (%)	0.04	0.27	0.33
Natural increase (%)	0.16	0.14	0.27
Net migration rate	−0.12	0.13	0.06
Foreigners (%)	3.1 [d]	–	3.1
Asylum-seekers ('000)	10	6	30
Ireland			
Population size ('000)[a]	3,215	3,537	3,506
Population increase (%)	1.18	0.09	0.37
Natural increase (%)	1.20	0.82	0.62
Net migration rate	−0.02	−0.74	−0.25
Foreigners (%)	6.7 [e]	–	–
Asylum-seekers ('000)[h]	–	–	0.06

Table 12.1. *(continued)*

	1980	1985	1990
Italy			
Population size ('000)[a]	56,388	57,080	57,576
Population increase (%)	0.16	0.21	0.29
Natural increase (%)	0.15	0.05	0.06
Net migration rate	0.01	0.16	0.23
Foreigners (%)	0.5	–	0.8
Asylum-seekers ('000)[i]	2	5	3
Netherlands			
Population size ('000 inhabitants)[a]	14,091	14,454	14,893
Population increase (%)	0.83	0.52	0.79
Natural increase (%)	0.48	0.38	0.46
Net migration rate	0.36	0.14	0.33
Foreigners (%)	3.8 [f]	–	4.3
Asylum-seekers ('000)	1	6	21
Sweden			
Population size ('000)[a]	8,303	8,343	8,527
Population increase (%)	0.18	0.19	0.75
Natural increase (%)	0.06	0.05	0.34
Net migration rate	0.11	0.13	0.41
Foreigners (%)	–	8.7 [g]	5.3
Asylum-seekers ('000)	–	15	29
Switzerland			
Population size ('000)[a]	6,304	6,456	6,674
Population increase (%)	0.50	0.45	1.15
Natural increase (%)	0.23	0.23	0.30
Net migration rate	0.27	0.21	0.85
Foreigners (%)	14.8	14.9	16.7
Asylum-seekers ('000)	3	10	36

[a] Population at 1 January.
[b] 1984. [c] 1982.
[d] 1981, including population of NCWP-ethnic origin.
[e] 1981, people born outside the Republic of Ireland.
[f] 1981; 5.4 when including population from SAM-ethnic origin.
[g] 1984; 8.7 when including foreign-born population.
[h] Covering help organizations.
[i] UNCHR, OECD and UN for refugees; not very reliable according to R.F. van der Erf (personal communication).

Sources: all country reports in this volume; Council of Europe (various years); Mammey (1987:86); Coleman (1994:298); Kuijsten (1994:23); R.F. van der Erf (personal communication).

deep low on the demographic weather map of the 1980s, with low to negative overall population growth, low to negative rates of natural increase and, above all at the end of the decade when the Berlin Wall began to crumble, relatively high net outmigration.

The countries with high net immigration rates are supposedly those that also feature high proportions of foreigners in their population. Generally speaking, this is indeed the case, as is suggested by the proportions of foreigners in countries such as Switzerland (16.7 per cent in 1990), the Federal Republic of Germany (7.7 per cent), Sweden (5.3 per cent) and the Netherlands (4.3 per cent). But caution is needed since generalization is risky: in the field of migrants, stocks are inert and flows are volatile. Moreover, international migration and migrants, more than any other demographic phenomenon, suffer from inconsistencies when it comes to definitions and classifications, hence the data are not always strictly comparable. What is beyond any doubt, however, despite data deficiencies here as well, is that the Federal Republic of Germany is by far the largest receiver of asylum applicants (almost 200,000 in 1990), followed by France (55,000), Switzerland (36,000), the United Kingdom (30,000) and Sweden (29,000). Apart from Ireland, Italy is lowest on both proportion of foreigners and number of asylum-seekers, but probably not that low when undocumented immigration and residence are taken into account.

12.1.2. *Age Structure*

There are relatively large between-country differences in age structure. As shown in Table 12.2, in 1980 proportions of country populations aged 0–14 varied between 18.5 (the Federal Republic of Germany) and 30.6 (Ireland), and in 1990 these proportions were 15.1 resp. 27.3 in the same countries. So, neither country changed its position as number 1 resp. 10 on the list, and neither changed the range between the highest and the lowest value (slightly over 12 percentage points). In between these highest and lowest values, there were many position changes over the 1980s for other countries, since, with the exception of the former German Democratic Republic, all countries experienced a decline in the proportion of their population under age 15, albeit some much more than others. Differences in tempo and timing of fertility declines in the past 25 years explain these differential reductions in the proportions under 15 years of age. The reductions were most substantial in Italy (about 22 per cent, decline in proportion from 22.3 to 17.3 per cent), the Federal Republic of Germany (over 18 per cent, decline in proportion from 18.5 to 15.1 per cent), and the Netherlands (also over 18 per cent, decline in proportion from 22.4 to 18.3 per cent). Thus, whereas in 1980 the two German states, Sweden and Switzerland were the four countries with the lowest proportions of population under 15, in 1990 it was the Federal Republic of Germany, Switzerland, Denmark and Italy. And, whereas in 1980 it was Ireland, the Netherlands, Italy and France that had the highest proportions under 15, in 1990 it was Ireland, France, the former German Democratic Republic and the United Kingdom. Quite outlying in this set of ten countries is Ireland, of course: the proportion of its population under age 15, 30.6 per cent in 1980 and 27.3 in 1990, contrasts with lows of 22.4 per cent in 1980 (the Netherlands) and 20.3 per cent in 1990 (France). Ongoing extremely high fertility till the mid-1980s (see Table 12.4) and continued net emigration, particularly among the young adult population, explain Ireland's outlier position in this respect.

On the whole, the reverse of the story on between-country differences in proportions of young people in the population holds for that on differences in proportions of aged people, i.e. 65 and over. In this case, Ireland and the Netherlands show the lowest proportions over the whole decade, and it is Sweden rather than the Federal Republic of Germany that features the highest level of ageing. Moreover, the gap between the highest and the lowest proportion widens between 1980 and 1985 from 5.6 to 7.3 per cent, before narrowing again to 6.4 per cent in 1990. The greatest change in rank order position is that of the former German Democratic Republic, from eighth place in 1980 to third place in 1990. In fact, the GDR and, to a much lesser extent, the Federal Republic are the two countries that have experienced a decline in their level of ageing over the 1980s. That of France was the same in 1980 and 1990, and all other countries witnessed an increasing ageing level, most of all the Netherlands and Sweden. It should be noted that these changes in proportions of the aged are caused not only by fertility falls in the recent past, as was mentioned with respect to the changing proportions under 15, but also by other irregularities in the age structure with causes that go back much further.

This holds even more with respect to old-age dependency ratios, which relate the size of age category 65 + to that of another age category, in this case (Table 12.2) 15–64. Irregularities in the age structure stemming from the past now can influence both nominator and denominator in such ways that, although long-term trends can be fairly robust, short-term fluctuations can be quite erratic. The latter is precisely what happened in the ten countries over the 1980s. In two of them, the Netherlands and Denmark, the old-age dependency ratio increased both from 1980 to 1985 and from 1985 to 1990.

Table 12.2. *Summary table of demographic trends during the 1980s: age structure (%)*

	1980	1985	1990
Denmark			
Population below age 15	20.8	18.7	17.2
Population between 15 and 24	15.0	15.4	15.0
Population between 25 and 65	49.8	51.0	52.2
Population over 65	14.4	14.9	15.6
Dependency ratio[a]	22.2	22.4	23.2
France			
Population below age 15	22.3	21.2	20.3
Population between 15 and 24	15.8	15.5	15.0
Population between 25 and 65	47.9	50.3	50.7
Population over 65	14.0	13.0	14.0
Dependency ratio	22.0	19.8	21.3
Federal Republic of Germany[b]			
Population below age 15	18.5	15.3	15.1
Population between 15 and 20	10.0	10.1	7.3
Population between 21 and 64	55.8	60.0	62.3
Population over 65	15.7	14.7	15.3
Dependency ratio	23.9	21.0	22.0
German Democratic Republic			
Population below age 15	19.5	19.2	19.5 [c]
Population between 15 and 24	16.4	15.7	13.4 [c]
Population between 25 and 65	48.3	51.5	53.7 [c]
Population over 65	15.7	13.6	13.3 [c]
Dependency ratio	24.3	20.2	19.8 [c]
Great Britain/UK			
Population below age 15	20.9	19.3	19.0
Population between 15 and 24	15.5	16.4	14.8
Population between 25 and 65	48.5	49.2	50.5
Population over 65	15.1	15.1	15.7
Dependency ratio	23.6	23.0	24.0
Ireland			
Population below age 15	30.6	29.7	27.3
Population between 15 and 24	17.4	17.5	17.1
Population between 25 and 65	41.3	42.2	44.2
Population over 65	10.7	10.6	11.4
Dependency ratio	18.2	17.8	18.6
Italy			
Population below age 15	22.3	19.5	17.3
Population between 15 and 24	15.3	16.4	16.3
Population between 25 and 65	49.3	51.4	52.3
Population over 65	13.1	12.7	14.1
Dependency ratio	20.3	18.7	20.6

Table 12.2. *(continued)*

	1980	1985	1990
Netherlands			
Population below age 15	22.4	19.4	18.3
Population between 15 and 24	17.4	17.3	16.4
Population between 25 and 65	48.7	51.2	52.6
Population over 65	11.5	12.1	12.7
Dependency ratio	17.4	17.7	18.4
Sweden			
Population below age 15	19.6	17.5	17.8
Population between 15 and 24	13.5	13.9	13.8
Population between 25 and 65	50.6	50.7	50.6
Population over 65	16.3	17.9	17.8
Dependency ratio	25.4	27.7	27.6
Switzerland			
Population below age 15	19.7	16.9	16.6
Population between 15 and 24	15.3	15.5	13.7
Population between 25 and 65	51.2	53.0	54.7
Population over 65	13.8	14.6	15.0
Dependency ratio[c]	20.8	21.3	21.9

[a] 65+ / 15-64 X 100.
[b] Be aware of different age categories.
[c] 1989.

Sources: all country reports in this volume; Council of Europe (various years); *Statistisches Jahrbuch für die Bundesrepublik Deutschland* (various years); Statistisches Bundesamt (1993); United Nations (1993).

In three countries (France and the two Germanies) it decreased in both periods. Three other countries (Ireland, Italy and the United Kingdom) witnessed a decrease between 1980 and 1985 and an increase between 1985 and 1990, with the opposite occurring in Sweden. The latter country held the position of the highest dependency ratio over the entire decade, and the Netherlands and Ireland consistently held the positions of the lowest ratio. No further systematic patterns and trends can be discerned.

12.1.3. *Marriage and Divorce*

Comparison of the indicators with respect to marriage and divorce (Table 12.3) to some extent reveals tendencies of convergence between the ten countries studied. With respect to the crude marriage rate (CMR), i.e. the

Table 12.3. *Summary table of demographic trends during the 1980s: marriage and divorce*

	1980	1985	1990
Denmark			
Crude marriage rate (CMR)	5.2	5.7	6.1
Total first marriage rate (women below age 50)	0.53	0.57	0.60
First marriage age (women)	24.8	26.3	27.6
Crude divorce rate (CDR)	2.7	2.8	2.7
Total divorce rate (TDR)	0.40	0.46	0.44
France			
Crude marriage rate (CMR)	6.2	4.9	5.1
Total first marriage rate (women below age 50)	0.71	0.54	0.56
First marriage age (women)	23.0	24.3	25.7
Crude divorce rate (CDR)	1.5	1.9	1.9
Total divorce rate (TDR)	0.22	0.30	0.29
Federal Republic of Germany			
Crude marriage rate (CMR)	5.9	6.0	6.5
Total first marriage rate (women below age 50)	0.66	0.59	0.64
First marriage age (women)	23.4	24.6	25.9
Crude divorce rate (CDR)	1.6	2.1	1.9
Total divorce rate (TDR)	0.23	0.30	0.29
German Democratic Republic			
Crude marriage rate (CMR)	8.0	7.9	6.3
Total first marriage rate (women below age 50)	0.81	0.74	0.60
First marriage age (women)	21.3	22.2	23.7
Crude divorce rate (CDR)	2.7	3.1	2.0
Total divorce rate (TDR)	0.32	0.38	0.22
Great Britain/UK			
Crude marriage rate (CMR)	7.4	6.9	6.5
Total first marriage rate (women below age 50)	0.77	0.67	0.62
First marriage age (women)	23.0	23.8	25.2
Crude divorce rate (CDR)	2.8	3.1	2.9
Total divorce rate (TDR)	0.38	0.42	0.41
Ireland			
Crude marriage rate (CMR)	6.4	5.3	5.0
Total first marriage rate (women below age 50)	0.83	0.68	0.69
First marriage age (women)	24.1	25.0	25.9
Crude divorce rate (CDR)	n.a.	n.a.	n.a.
Total divorce rate (TDR)	n.a.	n.a.	n.a.
Italy			
Crude marriage rate (CMR)	5.7	5.2	5.4
Total first marriage rate (women below age 50)	0.77	0.66	0.66
First marriage age (women)	24.1	24.5	25.6
Crude divorce rate (CDR)	0.2	0.3	0.5
Total divorce rate (TDR)	0.03	0.04	0.08

Table 12.3. *(continued)*

	1980	1985	1990
Netherlands			
Crude marriage rate (CMR)	6.4	5.7	6.4
Total first marriage rate (women below age 50)	0.68	0.57	0.65
First marriage age (women)	23.1	24.4	25.9
Crude divorce rate (CDR)	1.8	2.3	1.9
Total divorce rate (TDR)	0.25	0.35	0.28
Sweden			
Crude marriage rate (CMR)	4.5	4.6	4.7
Total first marriage rate (women below age 50)	0.53	0.53	0.56
First marriage age (women)	26.4	27.5	27.6
Crude divorce rate (CDR)	2.4	2.4	2.3
Total divorce rate (TDR)	0.42	0.45	0.44
Switzerland			
Crude marriage rate (CMR)	5.7	6.0	6.9
Total first marriage rate (women below age 50)	0.66	0.66	0.75
First marriage age (women)	25.2	26.1	27.0
Crude divorce rate (CDR)	1.7	1.8	2.0
Total divorce rate (TDR)	0.27	0.30	0.33

Sources: all country reports in this volume; Council of Europe (various years).

annual number of marriages per 1,000 of the average population, between-country variation dropped from 3.5 in 1980 to 2.2 in 1990. Sweden has had the lowest rate over the whole decade, but the red lantern that was held by the former German Democratic Republic in 1980 and 1985 had been taken over by Switzerland in 1990. In four countries (Sweden, Denmark, Switzerland and the Federal Republic of Germany) CMR in 1990 was higher than in 1980, in the Netherlands the 1990 value was the same as that in 1980, and in the five other countries the 1990 value was lower than that for 1980. The peculiar thing in this tendency towards convergence is that it was caused by two contrasting developments: increases in CMR in those countries that had the lowest values in 1980, and simultaneous decreases in countries with high values in 1980. This is quite different from the kind of expectation that would have been derived from the 'second demographic transition' frame of reference: the 'laggards' in the process do indeed seem to catch up their backlogs, but at the same time the 'forerunners' already seem to be over the hill and have started their way back.

Something similar is shown by the total first marriage rates for females. TFMR can be interpreted as the ultimate fraction at age 50 that will have experienced a first marriage under condition of age-specific first marriage rates as observed in a calendar year. Between-country variation dropped from 0.30 in 1980 to 0.19 in 1990. It is Sweden again that showed the lowest values during the whole decade, although France (in sixth place in 1980!) shows the same low value as Sweden in 1990 (0.56). Ireland had the highest value in 1980 (0.83), but the number 10 position was taken over by the former German Democratic Republic in 1985 (0.74) and by Switzerland in 1990 (0.75). Again, we see increases in TFMR over the decade in countries that had low values in 1980 (Sweden, Denmark and Switzerland) and the greatest decreases in countries that had the highest TFMRs in 1980, particularly the former German Democratic Republic, France, the United Kingdom and Ireland.

Mean age of women at first marriage has increased in all ten countries, in most cases in the second half of the decade more than in the first half. There was a tendency for increases to be greater in countries with lower values in 1980. The former German Democratic Republic was the clear outlier, its mean age at first marriage consistently being some one and a half years below that of the second on the list, the United Kingdom. Denmark, Switzerland and Sweden had the highest mean ages at marriage over the whole decade (generally speaking, above 25 in 1980, above 26 in 1985 and above 27 in 1990). Again, between-country variation in mean age at first marriage declined from 5.1 years in 1980 to 3.9 years in 1990. The amount of increase in mean first marriage age varied from 1.2 years in Sweden and 1.5 in Italy, to 2.7 years in France and 2.8 in the Netherlands and Denmark.

Crude divorce rates (annual number of divorces per 1,000 of average population) were typically highest in the mid-1980s and then stabilized or fell thereafter. Leaving out Ireland, where divorce is officially not allowed, Italy is the outlier with exceptionally low crude divorce rates, followed by France, the Federal Republic of Germany, the Netherlands and Switzerland (around 1.9 in 1990). The Scandinavian countries and the United Kingdom have the highest levels, which have also remained quite stable over the decade (around 2.8). In 1980 they were accompanied by the former German Democratic Republic, but at the end of the 1980s the crude divorce rate there had dropped to the level of the middle group.

A similar impression can be obtained from comparing period total divorce rates: on the whole higher in 1985 than in 1980 or 1990, highest in the Scandinavian countries and in the United Kingdom, nil in Ireland and still exceptionally low in Italy, plus a slight decrease in between-country variation over the 1980s.

12.1.4. *Fertility*

Similar slight decreases in between-country variation can be observed in some fertility indicators (Table 12.4), but definitely not in all. The first one mentioned, average mother's age at birth of the first child, is an exception to that rule, its between-country variation rising from 4.1 years in 1980 to 5.3 in 1990. The major reason seems to be differential intensity of first-birth postponement, from no change (22.3 years over the whole decade) in the country with the lowest mean age at first birth (the former German Democratic Republic) to continued increase in the Netherlands and Switzerland, which in 1980 already showed the highest mean age at first birth (27.6 years in 1990 in both countries). Everywhere except in the GDR there was an

Table 12.4. *Summary table of demographic trends during the 1980s: fertility*

	1980	1985	1990
Denmark			
Age at birth of first child	24.6	25.5	26.4
Age at birth of any child	26.9	27.7	28.3
Crude birth rate (per 1,000 inhabitants, CBR)	11.2	10.5	12.3
Total fertility rate (TFR)	1.55	1.45	1.67
Net reproduction rate (NRR)	0.74	0.70	0.80
Extra-marital fertility	33.2	43.0	46.4
Period parity progression ratio (first birth)	0.72	0.66	0.77
Cohort-specific estimations for childless families (%)	–	8.3 [b]	10.7 [c]
France			
Age at birth of first child	24.9	25.9	27.0
Age at birth of any child	26.8	27.5	28.3
Crude birth rate (per 1,000 inhabitants, CBR)	14.9	13.9	13.5
Total fertility rate (TFR)	1.95	1.81	1.78
Net reproduction rate (NRR)	0.93	0.87	0.85
Extra-marital fertility	11.4	19.6	30.1
Period parity progression ratio (first birth)	0.82	0.76	0.77 [d]
Cohort-specific estimations for childless families (%)	8.8 [a]	7.4 [b]	8.0 [ce]
Federal Republic of Germany			
Age at birth of first child	25.2	26.2	26.9
Age at birth of any child	27.0	27.7	28.4
Crude birth rate (per 1,000 inhabitants, CBR)	10.1	9.6	11.5
Total fertility rate (TFR)	1.45	1.28	1.48
Net reproduction rate (NRR)	0.68	0.60	0.69
Extra-marital fertility	7.6	9.4	10.5
Period parity progression ratio (first birth)	0.69	0.58	0.64
Cohort-specific estimations for childless families (%)	10.8 [a]	13.2 [b]	15.2 [c]

Table 12.4. *(continued)*

	1980	1985	1990
German Democratic Republic			
Age at birth of first child	22.3	22.3	22.3 [f]
Age at birth of any child	24.5	24.8	25.4 [f]
Crude birth rate (per 1,000 inhabitants, CBR)	14.6	13.7	12.0 [f]
Total fertility rate (TFR)	1.94	1.73	1.57 [f]
Net reproduction rate (NRR)	0.93	0.83	0.75 [f]
Extra-marital fertility	22.8	33.8	33.6 [f]
Period parity progression ratio (first birth)	1.01	0.83	0.78
Cohort-specific estimations for childless families (%)	11.4 [a]	8.6 [b]	7.4 [cg]
Great Britain/UK			
Age at birth of first child	24.4	24.8	25.5
Age at birth of any child	26.7	27.0	27.5
Crude birth rate (per 1,000 inhabitants, CBR)	13.4	13.3	13.9
Total fertility rate (TFR)	1.89	1.80	1.84
Net reproduction rate (NRR)	0.91	0.86	0.89
Extra-marital fertility	11.5	18.9	27.9
Period parity progression ratio (first birth)	0.76	0.70	0.75
Cohort-specific estimations for childless families (%)	10.9 [a]	10.0 [b]	14.2 [c]
Ireland			
Age at birth of first child	24.9	25.6	25.8
Age at birth of any child	28.8	29.3	29.6
Crude birth rate (per 1,000 inhabitants, CBR)	21.8	17.6	14.7
Total fertility rate (TFR)	3.23	2.50	2.19
Net reproduction rate (NRR)	1.52	1.19	1.06
Extra-marital fertility	5.0	8.5	14.5
Period parity progression ratio (first birth)	0.86	0.66	0.71
Cohort-specific estimations for childless families (%)	–	–	17.6 [h]
Italy			
Age at birth of first child	25.1	25.9	26.9
Age at birth of any child	27.5	28.1	28.9
Crude birth rate (per 1,000 inhabitants, CBR)	11.3	10.1	9.8
Total fertility rate (TFR)	1.69	1.41	1.29
Net reproduction rate (NRR)	0.78	0.68	0.63
Extra-marital fertility	4.3	5.4	6.3
Period parity progression ratio (first birth)	0.77	0.65	0.63
Cohort-specific estimations for childless families (%)	13.1 [a]	10.4 [b]	11.4 [c]

Table 12.4. *(continued)*

	1980	1985	1990
Netherlands			
Age at birth of first child	25.6	26.5	27.6
Age at birth of any child	27.5	28.2	29.2
Crude birth rate (per 1,000 inhabitants, CBR)	12.8	12.3	13.2
Total fertility rate (TFR)	1.60	1.51	1.62
Net reproduction rate (NRR)	0.77	0.74	0.78
Extra-marital fertility	4.1	8.3	11.4
Period parity progression ratio (first birth)	0.68	0.65	0.72
Cohort-specific estimations for childless families (%)	12.5 [a]	12.6 [b]	15.3 [c]
Sweden			
Age at birth of first child	25.5	26.1	26.3
Age at birth of any child	27.8	28.5	28.5
Crude birth rate (per 1,000 inhabitants, CBR)	11.7	11.8	14.5
Total fertility rate (TFR)	1.68	1.73	2.14
Net reproduction rate (NRR)	0.81	0.83	1.03
Extra-marital fertility	39.7	46.4	47.0
Period parity progression ratio (first birth)	0.72	0.71	0.90
Cohort-specific estimations for childless families (%)	13.4 [a]	12.6 [b]	13.4 [c]
Switzerland			
Age at birth of first child	26.4	27.0	27.6
Age at birth of any child	27.9	28.3	29.0
Crude birth rate (per 1,000 inhabitants, CBR)	11.7	11.5	12.5
Total fertility rate (TFR)	1.55	1.52	1.59
Net reproduction rate (NRR)	0.74	0.72	0.76
Extra-marital fertility	4.7	5.6	6.1
Period parity progression ratio (first birth)	0.90 [i]	0.84	0.82 [j]
Cohort-specific estimations for childless families (%)	10.0 [k]	–	18.0 [l]

[a] Birth cohort 1940, estimated at age 40.
[b] Birth cohort 1945, estimated at age 40.
[c] Birth cohort 1950, estimated at age 40.
[d] 1989. [e] At age 39. [f] 1989. [g] At age 38.
[h] Birth cohort 1956, estimated at age 36.
[i] 1981. [j] 1988.
[k] Birth cohorts 1936–49.
[l] Birth cohorts 1951–5.

Sources: all country reports in this volume; Council of Europe (various years); Statistisches Bundesamt (1993); W. Bosveld (personal communication).

increase in mean age at birth of the first child. The largest increases could be observed in France (+2.1 years) and the Netherlands (+2.0 years), the smallest in Sweden, which for that reason rose from eighth place on the list in 1980 to fourth place in 1990. In fact, it is the former German Democratic Republic that is the clear outlier, its mean age at first birth being 2.1 years below that of the second on the list (the United Kingdom) in 1980 and 3.2 years lower even in 1990.

With respect to mean age at birth of all children, again the former German Democratic Republic shows the lowest values, some two years below those of the second country on the list (again the United Kingdom), although this indicator shows a similar increase over the decade in the GDR as it also does for the other nine countries. But in another respect, the picture is quite different from that for mean age at first birth: the rank ordering of the countries. This clearly has to do with between-country differences in completed fertility, as is demonstrated by its most extreme manifestation, the Irish case. Ireland, which had the third-lowest mean age at birth of the first child in 1980 and the second-lowest in 1990, at the same time had the highest mean age of the mother at birth of all children, over the whole decade (28.8 years in 1980, 29.6 in 1990). The Netherlands, being the country that showed the biggest increase in mean age at birth of all children (+ 1.7 years), climbed to ninth place in the rank order. Between-country variation remained quite substantial over the decade and decreased only slightly (4.3 years in 1980, 4.2 in 1990).

A comparison of the data on mean age at first birth with those on mean age at first marriage in Table 12.3, both for 1990, leads to conclusions that may seem quite odd. On both indicators, the former German Democratic Republic and the United Kingdom have the lowest scores. But, whereas in the United Kingdom mean age at birth of the first child is 0.3 year higher than mean age at first marriage, in the former GDR it is as much as 1.4 years lower! Similarly, but at the other end of the scale, Denmark and Sweden, with the highest age at first marriage, have mean ages at birth of the first child that are 1.2 resp. 1.3 years lower. The solution to this apparent anomaly is, of course, the combination of widely spread unmarried cohabitation and the societal acceptance of childbearing among both cohabitants and women living alone. It definitely is no coincidence that the three countries in which mean age at birth of the first child is more than one year lower than mean age at first marriage are at the same time the three countries with the highest levels of extra-marital fertility.

Admittedly, levels of extra-marital fertility are measured relatively crudely and in a basically inadequate way in Table 12.4, simply as proportions of births out of wedlock among all births. But, in part just because of that caveat, illegitimacy proportions are nowadays the most discriminating demographic indicators in Europe, both at the national and at the regional level

(Decroly, 1992:262) and this is clearly reflected in our data set too. Grossly speaking, they range from 4 to 6 per cent over the decade in Italy and Switzerland to more than 30 per cent in 1980 and over 40 per cent in 1990 in the Scandinavian countries, and their between-country variation increased from 35.6 per cent in 1980 to 40.9 per cent in 1990! In each of the ten countries illegitimacy ratios grew; it grew the least in some of the countries that had the lowest levels in 1980 (+1.4 per cent in Switzerland, +2.0 per cent in Italy), but the most in countries that held intermediate positions in 1980 (+18.7 per cent in France, +16.4 per cent in the United Kingdom), rather than in the countries that already had high levels of illegitimacy in 1980.

Whereas a clear divergence between the ten countries under study could thus be observed in their illegitimacy levels, at first sight a quite impressive convergence occurred with respect to crude birth rates, total fertility rates and net reproduction rates. A closer look at the data, however, reveals that it is only the dramatic drop in these indicators in Ireland that explains most of the observed drops in between-country variation. With respect to the crude birth rates, the difference between the lowest (that for the FRG in 1980, and for Italy in 1990) and the highest (that for Ireland in both years) more than halved from 11.7, per 1,000 in 1980 to 4.9 per 1,000 in 1990. Leaving Ireland out, however, so that it was France that had the highest value in 1980 and Sweden in 1990, between-country variation becomes only 4.8 per 1,000 in 1980, and 4.7 in 1990. The latter figure points to the eye-catching fact that in 1990 crude birth rates in Ireland and Sweden were almost the same, whereas in 1980 the Irish crude birth rate was almost double the Swedish one. In fact, over the 1980s it was Sweden where the crude birth rate rose most (+2.8 per 1,000), and Ireland where it fell most sharply (−7.1 per 1,000). But other remarkable changes happened as well. Italy, third on the list with 11.3 births per 1,000 of population in 1980, had the lowest birth rate in 1990: 9.8 per 1,000. Next to Ireland, the biggest natality decrease could be observed in the former GDR, with a drop of 2.6 per 1,000 from 14.6 in 1980 to 12.0 in 1990, and, as has now become clear, this process has accelerated still more dramatically in the early 1990s.

Not being confounded by age-structure differences, as crude birth rates are, period total fertility rates show more clearly what in fact has happened: a strange mixture of both convergence and divergence. Convergence, yes, in the sense that from 1980 to 1990 total fertility increased in the five countries that had the lowest levels in 1980 (insignificantly in the Netherlands, the Federal Republic of Germany and Switzerland, by 0.12 in Denmark and by as much as 0.46 in Sweden) and decreased in the other five countries that had the highest levels in 1980 (insignificantly in the United

Kingdom, by 0.17 in France, 0.37 in the former GDR, 0.40 in Italy and as much as 1.04 in Ireland). As a result, and including the Irish case, between-country variation actually halved, from 1.78 in 1980 to 0.90 in 1990. However, once the special case of Ireland is excluded, between-country variation *increased*, from 0.50 in 1980 to 0.85 in 1990, and almost the entire rank order has been turned topsy-turvy. The FRG, with the lowest TFR in 1980 and 1985, is in second place in 1990, after Italy which was in sixth place in 1980. Number 3 in 1990, the former GDR, was number 8 in 1980. And countries such as Sweden and the United Kingdom, with intermediate rankings in 1980, were in ninth resp. eighth places in 1990. The between-country mortality differences that exist (see below) do not have so strong an impact that the picture emerging from the NRR values differs from that emerging from the TFR values, hence we will pay no further attention to them.

Looking at period parity progression ratios for first births, one observes a small increase in the Netherlands and in Denmark, and a more substantial increase in Sweden, which has the highest value of all countries in 1990. In the other seven countries a decline can be observed, most profoundly in Ireland (-0.15) and the former GDR (-0.23). Between-country variation dropped slightly, from 0.33 in 1980 to 0.27 in 1990. Unfortunately, with respect to the cohort-specific estimations for childless families, we could not collect the information for all ten countries. As far as birth cohort 1950 is concerned, we observe in 1990, at age 40 of the women involved, levels of childlessness that vary from 7.4 per cent in the former GDR and 8.0 per cent in France, to 17.6 per cent in Ireland and 18.0 in Switzerland.

12.1.5. *Mortality*

For this last group of demographic indicators (Table 12.5), a similar mix of trends of convergence with trends of divergence can be observed. Convergence seems to be there most clearly in the case of infant mortality. Between-country variation plummeted from 7.7 to 2.6 per 1,000 live births. In all countries the infant mortality rate declined, but in almost perfect rank order it dropped more, the higher the 1980 level was. The effect of that was, again, a lot of change in the rank-order list. Sweden over the whole decade had the lowest infant mortality rate, and Italy had the highest, but in between large position shifts occurred: Denmark tumbled down from second place to seventh, for example, at the same time as the Federal Republic of Germany climbed from ninth place to third.

Crude death rates too converged between 1980 and 1990, between-country variation declining from 6.1 in 1980 to 3.9 per 1,000 of population in 1990, but the pattern behind this convergence is quite confusing, if only because age-structure differences also play their confounding role. Among the five countries with the lowest crude death rates in 1980, two saw their death rate modestly increase (the Netherlands and Switzerland) and three experienced a further decrease (Italy −0.5, France −0.8 and Ireland −0.9 per 1,000). On the other hand, among the five other countries with the higher crude death rates in 1980, there were three that witnessed increases (Sweden +0.1, the FRG +0.3 and Denmark +1.0 per 1,000) whereas the two with the highest 1980 levels experienced a decline: −0.6 per 1,000 in the United Kingdom and −1.7 per 1,000 in the former GDR. Since, as will be demonstrated below, life expectancy in the 1980s improved everywhere and therefore one would be inclined to point to differences in age structure as an explanatory factor for this peculiar situation, it is all the more surprising that there is nevertheless a high correlation between crude death rate and the proportion of the aged (Table 12.2), except for the former GDR, which had a crude death rate in 1990 that was much too high given its age structure.

No wonder, then, that we observe that it was indeed the former GDR that had the lowest life expectancy at birth over the whole 1980s, both for males and for females. At the other end, the Netherlands, Sweden and Switzerland showed the highest life expectancies, except for females for the Netherlands in 1990, whose increase in life expectancy in the second half of the decade lagged behind that of some other countries. But, contrary to what could be observed in crude birth rates and infant mortality rates, in the case of life expectancy at birth of both sexes one sees a slight divergence, between-country variation growing from 4.1 to 4.9 years for males and from 4.6 to 5.0 years for males. As mentioned, and again for both sexes, life expectancy at birth increased everywhere between 1980 and 1990, the gains varying from 0.8 year in Denmark and 0.9 in Ireland to 2.5 years in France and 2.9 in Italy for males, and for females between 0.4 year in Denmark and 0.7 in the Netherlands to 2.5 in France and 2.6 in Italy.

12.2. The Pluralization of Family Life Forms

In considerable contrast to the more generalizing assumptions of 'transitions' and 'trends' prevailing in demography, the approach followed in this book reveals that there are fundamental differences in household and family structures and in the patterns of the organization of everyday life between the

Table 12.5. *Summary table of demographic trends during the 1980s: mortality*

	1980	1985	1990
Denmark			
Crude death rate	10.9	11.4	11.9
Infant mortality	8.4	7.9	7.5
Life expectancy (men, at age 0)	71.2	71.6	72.0 [ac]
Life expectancy (women, at age 0)	77.3	77.5	77.7 [ac]
France			
Crude death rate	10.2	10.0	9.4
Infant mortality	10.0	8.3	7.3
Life expectancy (men, at age 0)	70.2	71.3	72.7
Life expectancy (women, at age 0)	78.4	79.4	80.9
Federal Republic of Germany			
Crude death rate	11.6	11.5	11.9
Infant mortality	12.6	8.9	7.0
Life expectancy (men, at age 0)	69.9	70.8 [d]	72.2 [be]
Life expectancy (women, at age 0)	76.6	77.5	78.7 [b]
German Democratic Republic			
Crude death rate	14.2	13.5	12.5
Infant mortality	12.1	9.6	7.3
Life expectancy (men, at age 0)	68.7	69.5	70.0 [ac]
Life expectancy (women, at age 0)	74.6	75.4	76.2 [ac]
Great Britain/UK			
Crude death rate	11.7	11.8	11.1
Infant mortality	12.1	9.3	7.9
Life expectancy (men, at age 0)	70.8	71.4 [d]	72.7 [c]
Life expectancy (women, at age 0)	76.9	77.2 [d]	78.3 [g]
Ireland			
Crude death rate	9.8	9.4	8.9
Infant mortality	11.1	8.8	8.2
Life expectancy (men, at age 0)	70.1 [bf]	–	71.0 [bc]
Life expectancy (women, at age 0)	75.6 [bf]	–	76.7 [bc]
Italy			
Crude death rate	9.8	9.6	9.3
Infant mortality	14.6	10.5	8.6
Life expectancy (men, at age 0)	70.6	–	73.5 [c]
Life expectancy (women, at age 0)	77.4	–	80.0 [c]
Netherlands			
Crude death rate	8.1	8.5	8.6
Infant mortality	8.6	8.0	7.1
Life expectancy (men, at age 0)	72.4	73.1	73.7 [a]
Life expectancy (women, at age 0)	79.2	79.7	79.9 [a]

Table 12.5. *(continued)*

	1980	1985	1990
Sweden			
Crude death rate	11.0	11.3	11.1
Infant mortality	6.9	6.8	6.0
Life expectancy (men, at age 0)	72.8	73.8	74.9 [g]
Life expectancy (women, at age 0)	78.8	79.7	80.5 [g]
Switzerland			
Crude death rate	9.4	9.2	9.5
Infant mortality	9.1	6.9	6.8
Life expectancy (men, at age 0)	72.4	73.1 [h]	74.3 [ai]
Life expectancy (women, at age 0)	79.1	79.7 [h]	81.2 [ai]

[a] Value for period of 2 years.
[b] Value for period of 3 years.
[c] 1989. [d] 1983. [e] 1988. [f] 1980–2.
[g] 1991. [h] 1984. [i] 1991–2.

Sources: all country reports in this volume; Council of Europe (various years); Van de Kaa (1994).

ten European countries. Behind superficial demo-statistical similarities of countries, for example with respect to fertility indicators, there may be basic differentiations as to the forms of private life. Ireland and Sweden are the two, in the sample of countries studied, that exhibit the highest total fertility rates, both above 2 in the late 1980s; the other end of the scale is marked by Italy and West Germany with extremely low fertility. With regard to the structure of the forms of private life, however, Italy and Ireland belong to the same category, and Italy and West Germany are different extremes. There are general tendencies of change all over Europe, but stronger than these is the existing cross-national variation, which would be misunderstood if it were to be interpreted as an indication of change. Sweden and the other Nordic countries, regarded by Van de Kaa and many others as the 'forerunners' in the second demographic transition, plainly do not exhibit the demographic future of the other countries in Europe.

In contrast to demography, family sociology has always shown a stronger interest in qualitative trends of 'family change'. Our comparative analyses of critical life phases show here that contemporary perspectives on family change, claiming that there is an overall trend of de-traditionalization and a pluralization of family life, overlook the fact that family change today is mainly confined to the younger generations of women in the early parental or pre-parental phase of life. Only here do we see a really substantial pluralization of the forms of private life in general and, under favourable economic and political circumstances, of the family as well. In a way, there is pluralization everywhere, but at the same time it looks different everywhere (Kuijsten *et al.*, 1994). The older age group, in contrast, is characterized by quite a high degree of stability of the traditional forms of married life, though with smaller families and with a moderate increase of female labour-force participation. Structural change in that age group rather seems to be the cumulative effect of shifts within the traditional framework, such as reduced fertility and differences in the timing of when the children leave the parental home. Visible effects of a postponement of the time of leaving the parental home have been observed in Italy and Ireland. In all other cases, there is the opposing trend of the family nest getting empty earlier.

In the age group of the early parental phase there is a considerable decrease in the proportion of married young women everywhere. At the beginning of the 1980s, the share of married women in that younger age group was between two-thirds and three-quarters everywhere; at the end of the decade it was less than one-half in the Federal Republic and the GDR and a mere one-quarter of the young women in Sweden. In all countries there is a common tendency to postpone the start of a family; at the end of the 1980s, in most countries about half of the young women were still without children. Since we have analysed and compared only cross-sectional data (though from different years), we cannot say much about an eventual increase in permanent childlessness. Cohort analyses of fertility in the respective countries show that, in most of them, the trend is rather towards the postponement of the first birth than of increasing voluntary childlessness. However, there are structural variations: whereas in the Federal Republic of Germany the proportion of childless women has been growing, with those women who do have children predominantly having more than one, in Italy – with an almost identical total fertility – a continuous reduction of family size towards the married couple with only one child can be observed (see Chapter 8 above).

With regard to family size, the most marked changes in the number of children throughout the 1980s could be observed in the Netherlands and in Switzerland. In most of the countries studied, proportions of married women with two and more children decreased, with proportions of childless married couples at the same time increasing (as, for example, in Italy) or at least remaining constant (as in Switzerland or the Netherlands, where the childless married couple has become a relatively frequent living arrangement in the young cohort of women). The (old) Federal Republic of Germany has been an exception to this overall trend. On the one hand, the share of married couples with children has reduced from over 50 to less than 40 per cent, which would be in line with the trend; on the other hand, however, the childless married couple has also lost importance. Among the married women with children, there is a shift away from the family type with one child towards the one with two or more children in the late 1980s. Family development in the (former) Federal Republic of Germany is not so much characterized by a reduction of family size as by a remarkable disappearance of the family with children from the lives of young adults and by an increasing linkage of marriage to first parenthood (in those cases where it still happens).

In those countries for which we have comparable information on both the beginnning and the end of the 1980s, the traditional family composed of a married couple and one child (as in Italy or West Germany) or even two or more children (as in Switzerland and the Netherlands) at the beginning of the decade was still the life form in which a relative majority of the young women lived, although there had already been a decline in the number of children compared with the 1960s and 1970s. The predominant internal structure of these families was the traditional breadwinner–homemaker model with a working father and a housewife mother. The picture at the end of the 1980s, however, was completely different and much more differentiated. In most countries the so-called 'new household types' had gained importance and had become the most frequent private living arrangements of the younger cohort of women. This phenomenon is particularly visible in Sweden, but in Switzerland too, and in the Federal Republic of Germany in the 1980s, the 'single' (with a share ranging from 22 to 29 per cent) has taken over the top position from the married couple with a child in the list of life forms of young women. There has even been an increase of the numbers of women living as singles in the Netherlands, although their proportion is considerably lower than in the other countries; the top position there is held by the married couple with two jobs and no child, which denotes prevalence of traditional modes of household formation.

With fertility decline more or less having come to an end everywhere in the 1970s, perhaps the most remarkable change in the structure of private life in the 1980s has been the rapid increase in non-marital cohabitation, a process that Van de Kaa has so nicely phrased as the shift 'from the Golden Age of Marriage to the dawn of cohabitation'. However, despite an increase of cohabitation everywhere, there are still enormous differences from a comparative perspective. In West Germany 'living apart together' with a partner is as frequent as sharing a common household without being married. This is much in contrast to Denmark and, particularly, Sweden, where more women in age group 25–29 live in consensual cohabitation without marriage than in marriage. Where there is cohabitation at this young age it is usually without children, again with the exception of the Nordic countries – in Sweden unmarried couples with children are almost as frequent as married parents with offspring.

With respect to cohabitation and the 'new' household forms in general, Italy and Ireland are the exceptions to the overall trends. Everywhere else, not only cohabitation but also the proportion of lone mothers has considerably grown. Together with the increase of unmarried parenthood, this shows a progressive disentanglement of parenthood and marriage, though in varying degrees, which appears to have gone particularly far in Sweden. On the other hand, our data for the (old) Federal Republic of Germany and Switzerland, as well as for Ireland and Italy, depict an unbroken stability of the linkage, normative and factual, between marriage and parenthood.

In many instances Italy and Ireland present the 'traditional' exceptions to the 'modern' transitory trends in the reorganization of young adults' private lives in Europe. This, no doubt, has to do with cultural differentiations. Neither of these countries has experienced any remarkable increase in cohabitation in the 1980s. As to the structural patterns of relations between men and women, they still are in the 'Golden Age of Marriage'. In both countries there are no noticeable and socially accepted non-family or pre-family forms of life outside the family of descent and beween it and a young woman's own new family. Apparently there are only two alternatives: a young woman either lives with her mother (the life span spent in the parental home is increasing!), or she assumes the status of a married woman and a mother herself. While in Italy this step regularly tends to result in a one-child family, in Ireland it will still end with larger numbers of children. New household types in these countries are practically non-existent.

The example of Ireland and Italy shows quite clearly how misleading classifications in terms of demographic variables alone can be. The two countries are far apart from each other in terms of total fertility rates but are very similar in terms of the forms of life-style. On the other hand, these two are the only ones that we could really conceive of as the one (Italy) being further ahead in a line of development than the other (Ireland). But, then, this developmental line in our special case would not be a 'second demographic transition', which Italy may already have completed and Ireland not yet really entered, as Van de Kaa (1987) has assumed. Rather, it is merely transition number one: the first demographic transition in Europe was the overall reduction of fertility *within* marriage, having reached replacement fertility almost everywhere in the 1960s. Italy has simply continued this first transition after that decade (when the Northern and Western European nations entered the second transition), with fertility of a predominantly married population declining now below replacement level, and with the absence of 'alternative' forms of life of both the family and the non-family type, like lone parenthood, cohabitation or single living.

Everywhere else there is an increasing representation of the childless forms of life in the non-family sector of society and a trend of reducing family size in the family sector. The increasing numbers of young women living in the new household types have (the two exceptions excluded) everywhere led to a growing variation of the forms of private life (though in different degrees). These, however, must not be mistaken as overall pluralizations of family life (as falsely assumed by the theory of the second transition) or as indications of a 'modernization' of the family. The latter would imply that there are successful, socially accepted and politically recognized combinations, both simultaneously and sequentially, of family life and the occupational careers of men and women. Only in Denmark, Sweden and France, however, have we found solid indications of such success. The other extreme is the (old) Federal Republic of Germany. Here we have found an increasingly polarized structure made up of a growing proportion of young women living in 'alternative' non-family households and a shrinking proportion of women with children living in predominantly traditional forms of family life. The option to have a child, and, in particular, to have a second one, here is one element of a simultaneous set of decisions, the other element being leaving the labour market (see also Strohmeier, 1985). Klijzing (1989) has also shown this for the Netherlands, using biographic longitudinal data.

Other data from the Netherlands analysed in this project make it quite clear that such polarization in the forms of life is paralleled by corresponding socio-economic polarizations in the material life situation, with an enormous and still growing economic burden on traditional families (see Chapter 9). Our data show that families with children, in contrast to the forms of life in the non-family sectors of European societies, are economically disadvantaged and underprivileged everywhere. And everywhere, lone mothers are the worst off of all.

The degree of relative disadvantage of the family in comparison to the non-family sector, however, differs considerably between countries. It can be said that, although in terms of comparison of household and family income our secondary analyses of existing data (collected for other purposes than income comparisons) contain some inevitable weaknesses and shortcomings, the economic constraints imposed on family life are less in France and in the two Scandinavian countries than in the other countries studied. This, of course, has to do both with the larger proportions of families with working mothers in these countries and, consequently, two incomes, and with the level of income transfers made to the families, particularly in the case of lone mothers. The heavier economic burden on the family in the other seven countries can be seen to be the result of both deficient regulations and infrastructure, hindering the compatibility of gainful employment and family obligations among young mothers, and insufficient direct and economic support given to the family (Kuijsten *et al.*, 1994).

Between the countries studied, we see clear differences in the supply and organization of day-care facilities which today, given the value that young women everywhere attach to having a job as well as children, are an essential resource for the organization of everyday life in families in accordance with the options of the individual actors. The data show a surprising correspondence between the representation of family forms with working mothers and the national supply of day-care facilities. The former is not so much merely an effect of the latter, as the result of individual couples' adaptation to the constraints and resources existing at the respective national levels.

In the former German Democratic Republic, almost all children will have been in public day care; and in Scandinavia and France also there is a relatively close net, with good coverage of day-care institutions corresponding to the high proportions of working mothers there. In the other countries, on the contrary, there are considerable holes in the net, i.e. with insufficient supply of day-care facilities increasing the stress of families with working mothers and the economic burden of those with (involuntary) housewife–mothers. In these countries the proportions of working mothers with young children are considerably lower. International comparison shows also that in countries with poor day-care supply the representation of the traditional breadwinner–homemaker family is relatively high, with only smaller proportions of 'modern' family arrangements. It also seems that deficits in the political support of the family, and of working mothers in particular, are partly compensated by informal social networks. A very important day-care institution for the young children of working mothers under conditions of rather limited political support is the grandmother.

An additional constraint imposed on working mothers everywhere results from the fact that housework more or less always remains their obligation. Our analyses point to the fact that, despite an increasing participation of mothers in the labour market, there is no new internal pattern of a more egalitarian division of labour between women and their male partners. By the end of the 1980s, more men than in the 1970s seem to have accepted at least some of the obligations stemming from fatherhood; however, they still leave the bulk of the housework to their wives.

Regarding the future of the family in Europe, its dramatic drop as an attractive and desirable biographic option in the younger generations seems to be the predominant problem demanding political solution. A European family policy should not only be directed at the family as a whole, considering, for example, the bad economic status of the family; it should also explicitly be a policy in favour of women, respecting their widespread 'modern' biographic orientation towards a life with both a family and a job as successfully compatible elements of everyday life. Kaufmann (1990:120) has pointed to this as the 'decisive aspect' of a modern European policy in support of the family.

12.3. The Comparative Studies

Comparison of the national structures of private life and, in particular, of family life in Europe may, at the first glance, lead to a surprising puzzle in which even neighbouring countries show extreme diversity – for example, Ireland and the United Kingdom, or the former two Germanies – compared with each other and compared with their neighbours. It was the intention of this book to demonstrate that, at second glance, such a wide diversity can be understood as the joint expression of both variation and change. Since the mid-1960s, there has been a transition in the modes of private life towards more individualization and greater modernity. On the other hand, we have seen that one must be careful not to overestimate the impact of individualization and of the 'pluralizations' in life that go with the so-called 'second demographic transition' (see above). To quote a Swedish colleague when preparing a suggestion for a chapter in our forthcoming second volume, "Why are the Scandinavians always the forerunners?" is too simple a question, and the Irish or the Italians will probably never arrive where the Swedes or the Danes are today. It is true that, in demographic terms, we are all moving in the same direction in Europe; but, in terms of the active social forces and the social processes going on, it appears that most of us are running in different fields.

As a result of the research presented in this volume, it can be said that there are distinct national socio-cultural traditions actually framing an overall trend of increasing modernity and individualization in Europe, and that these traditions do remain visible behind all the transitions that we can actually observe. The objective of this first volume was mainly a stock-taking of these recent changes and of the actual variation of family life in Europe, on the basis of comparable empirical evidence. These empirical results will be systematically categorized, compared and evaluated in Volume II.

Our 'country reporters', in addition, have formulated hypotheses concerning the impacts of family and social policies upon family life and family development in Europe. These 'impact models' are generally based on the assumption of rational actors, equipped with bounded rationality, organizing their lives in a decision-making environment which to a great extent is shaped by the opportunities and constraints of the respective 'policy profiles'.

It was not intended in this volume to theorize, or to make a systematic comparison of the data presented in the individual country reports beyond the level of rather cautious generalizations and interpretations (which we did finally attempt in the preceding sections of this chapter). Consequently, it is left to a subsequent volume to pursue a few central theoretical arguments, and to discuss some comparative aspects of our findings in a more systematic way than could be done in this volume.

We will conclude with a brief outline of the central issues to be further elaborated in Volume II of this book.

Discipline-specific theories in the social sciences tend to build their own specific models of man. Outside economics, the theoretical 'homunculus' of 'rational-actor theory' seems to be intensively debated, and it is particularly controversial in sociology. In our international working group consisting of economists, sociologists and demographers, however, the rational actor turned out to be the only commonly acceptable and practically appropriate model of man to be used to explain the impact of family policies and of other contextual factors upon the micro-behaviour of individuals and families. Demographic structure and the population process as national or Continental macro-phenomena, then, can be modelled as the generally unplanned outcomes of the purposive though unco-ordinated actions of individuals and couples. This is the way in which private and personal actions and decisions gain public and political relevance.

However, although rational-actor theory does provide a framework for analysing such macro–micro dependencies, it leaves important questions unanswered and, sometimes, does not even ask them. Policies affect the rational (i.e. understandable) biographic decisions of individual actors or couples. How do policies affect everyday life actions and typical life situations of individual persons and families? This is the question for the decision-making environment and for everyday life patterns under different policy conditions.

The individual contributions from the European countries presented in this first volume demonstrate that there is indeed a significant correlation of the national distributions of the different forms of private life with the contextual properties and the policy profiles of the countries studied here. These correlations, however, remain basically unexplained.

One part of an explanation that is to be elaborated in the forthcoming second volume is that, empirically, national policies operate in a selective way; i.e., they constitute differential support and constraints for different forms of private life and family life. Each of the different national policy profiles introduced in this volume assumes a certain type of family as normal or regular, which is generally more supported or, to be realistic, less disadvantaged than other types. To young couples and to prospective parents, this implicit image of the 'normal' family serves as an orientation (positive or negative) of biographic decisions and family development. The question of differential political support and of the implicit and explicit national images of the 'normal' family will be dealt with in several contributions in the next volume.

Another question is how, in a comparative perspective, such differential support or discouragement comes into effect. One of the most critical issues, as we have seen, is the combination and compatibility of gainful employment and family tasks, as well as the division of labour among men and women. The management of everyday life is the mechanism that transmits the social and political restrictions and resources of the family environment into family structure. The processes addressed here are as yet underresearched.

An important aspect of the external resources of both working and nonworking parents, and of mothers in particular, is their informal social network, comprised mainly of members of the extended family. Informal social relationships and ties perform functional equivalents to social policy services. In countries with poorer social services, for example in the field of day care or care for the elderly, the informal family network still seems to be tight and support is substantial. The relationships between formal and informal family support need further examination. In this respect; particular emphasis in Volume II will be put on comparative analyses of the situations of children and of the elderly in Europe.

In the phase of historical and cultural change that we dealt with in this volume, there has been not only a fundamental change of the family environment, but also a basic shift in the individual life perspectives of both women and men. The current individualization debate, however, will only superficially illuminate that shift as it focuses upon the individual actor. From recent research in the sociology of marriage and the family, we can learn that there have also been consequential changes at the systemic level of partner relations and parent–child relations. It is hypothesized that there is an increasing dissociation of parenthood and partnership. Satisfactory partner relations tend to be regarded more and more as having their own value irrespective of parenthood, which, working as an internal constraint on family life, would finally put the family at risk. There are clear indications that such an assumption can explain a good deal of the polarizations in private lives that, in the most extreme mode, we have described for Germany. It will have to be determined how well the hypothesis fits elsewhere. And the general question will be addressed of which were the factors that, internally and externally, have been driving family change over the past decades.

In that respect, the role and the relevance of policies have to be re-examined as well. What is needed is not only a systematic overview of the existing variety of family-related policies in Europe, and of the modes in which they operate and come into effect, but also a perspective on the future. What are the principles of family policies in Europe, and what could be the guiding principles of a European family policy? How should such a European family policy be implemented, to make sure that it adequately considers the impressive variety in the forms of life that we observe all over Europe, and that it supports the family, at the same time respecting its autonomy and increasing the biographic options available to women? On the basis of the research documented in this volume, there should be no doubt that only policies that increase the 'degrees of freedom' available to women will have a positive effect on the future of the family in Europe.

References

Coleman, D. (1994), 'The world on the move? International migration in 1992', in *European Population Conference, 23–26 March 1993, Proceedings*, Volume 1, United Nations and Council of Europe, New York, Geneva and Strasbourg: 281–367.

Council of Europe (various years), *Recent Demographic Developments in Europe*, Council of Europe, Strasbourg.

Decroly, J.-M. (1992), 'Les naissances hors mariage en Europe' (Births out of wedlock in Europe), *Espaces, Populations, Sociétés*, 2:259–64.

Kaufmann, F.-X. (1990), *Zukunft der Familie: Stabilität, Stabilitätsrisiken und Wandel der familialen Lebensformen sowie ihre gesellschaftlichen und politischen Bedingungen* (The Future of the Family: Stability, Risks to Stability, Changes in Family Forms and their Social and Political Conditions), Verlag C.H. Beck, Munich; 2nd rev. edn as *Zukunft der Familie im vereinten Deutschland. Gesellschaftliche und politische Bedingungen* (The Future of the Family in Reunited Germany: Social and Political Conditions), Verlag C.H. Beck, Munich, 1995.

Klijzing, E. (1989), 'Beruf und/oder Kinder? Erste Ergebnisse einer Retrospektiv-befragung in den Niederlanden' (A job and/or children? First results of a retrospective survey in the Netherlands), in A. Herlth und K.P. Strohmeier (eds.), *Lebenslauf und Familienentwicklung* (Life Course and Family Development). Opladen, Leske & Budrich, 1989 (Biographie und Gesellschaft, Band 7): 147–64.

Kuijsten, A. (1994), 'International migration in Europe: patterns and implications for receiving countries', in M. Macura and D. Coleman (eds.), *International Migration: Regional Processes and Responses*, United Nations, New York and Geneva (Economic Studies No. 7): 21–39.

——, Strohmeier, K.P. and Schulze, H.-J. (1994), 'Social policy and forms of family life in Europe', *International Social Security Review*, 47(3/4):11–30.

Mammey, U. (1987), 'Problem areas with high in-migration and high immigrant stocks', in Council of Europe, *Proceedings of the Seminar on Demographic Problem Areas in Europe*, Council of Europe, Strasbourg: 83–123.

Statistisches Bundesamt (1993), *Bevölkerungsstatistische Übersichten 1946 bis 1989*, Heft 3, *Sonderreihe mit Beiträgen für das Gebiet der ehemaligen DDR* (Population Statistics Overview 1946 till 1989, Volume 3, Special Issue with Contributions from the Area of the Former GDR), Statistisches Bundesamt, Wiesbaden.

Strohmeier, K.P. (1985), *Familienentwicklung in Nordrhein-Westfalen: Generatives Verhalten im sozialen und regionalen Kontext* (Family Development in North Rhine–Westphalia: Reproductive Behaviour in its Social and Regional Context), Schriftenreihe des Ministerpräsidenten des Landes NRW, No. 47, Düsseldorf.

United Nations (1993), *World Population Prospects: the 1992 Revision*, United Nations, New York.

Van de Kaa, D.J. (1987), 'Europe's Second Demographic Transition', *Population Bulletin*, 41, 1, Population Reference Bureau, Washington DC.

—— (1994), 'The second demographic transition revisited: theories and expectations', in G.C.N. Beets *et al.* (eds.), *Population and Family in the Low Countries 1993: Late Fertility and Other Current Issues*, Swets & Zeitlinger, Amsterdam/ Lisse: 81–126.